The Meaning *of* "Make Disciples"

in the Broader Context *of the* Gospel *of* Matthew

The Meaning of "Make Disciples"
in the Broader Context *of the* Gospel *of* Matthew

A New Approach to Understanding
Discipleship in the First Gospel

Lindsay D. Arthur

Foreword by David R. Bauer

WIPF & STOCK · Eugene, Oregon

THE MEANING OF "MAKE DISCIPLES" IN THE BROADER CONTEXT
OF THE GOSPEL OF MATTHEW
A New Approach to Understanding Discipleship in the First Gospel

Copyright © 2022 Lindsay D. Arthur. All rights reserved. Except for brief quotations in critical publications or reviews, no part of this book may be reproduced in any manner without prior written permission from the publisher. Write: Permissions, Wipf and Stock Publishers, 199 W. 8th Ave., Suite 3, Eugene, OR 97401.

Wipf & Stock
An Imprint of Wipf and Stock Publishers
199 W. 8th Ave., Suite 3
Eugene, OR 97401

www.wipfandstock.com

PAPERBACK ISBN: 978-1-6667-3526-0
HARDCOVER ISBN: 978-1-6667-9216-4
EBOOK ISBN: 978-1-6667-9217-1

MAY 2, 2022 11:32 AM

All Scripture quotations, unless otherwise indicated, are taken from the New American Standard Bible® (NASB®), copyright © 1960, 1971, 1977, 1995 by The Lockman Foundation. Used by permission. All rights reserved. www.lockman.org.

Scripture quotations marked NA28 are taken from Nestle-Aland, *Novum Testamentum Graece*, 28th revised edition, edited by Barbara and Kurt Aland, Johannes Karavidopoulos, Carlo M. Martini, and Bruce M. Metzger in cooperation with the Institute for New Testament Textual Research, Münster/Westphalia, © 2012 Deutsche Bibelgesellschaft, Stuttgart. Used by permission.

I am dedicating this work to: (i) my Wilmore, KY family (Anthony and Adina Headley, Arvid and Judy Metcalf, and Lucia and her late husband, Roy Grammel); (ii) my beloved wife (Margaret) and adorable daughter (Naomi), both of whom have sustained and inspired me throughout this journey; and to (iii) the Lord, Jesus Christ, the master teacher, master leader, and master disciple-maker.

Contents

Foreword by DAVID R. BAUER | ix

Abbreviations | xi

1 INTRODUCTION | 1

2 SURVEY OF LITERATURE | 21

3 INDUCTIVE STUDY OF MATTHEW 28:16–20 | 72

4 INDUCTIVE STUDY OF OTHER MATTHEAN PASSAGES | 112

5 MATTHEAN DISCIPLESHIP IN THE NEW TESTAMENT CANON | 153

6 CONCLUSION AND IMPLICATIONS | 203

Appendix | 211

Bibliography | 213

Index | 227

Foreword

STUDENTS OF MATTHEW'S GOSPEL generally agree that the Missionary Commissioning (28:16–20) functions as the climax to the book. Yet, in spite of this acknowledgement, scholars have given relatively little attention to this passage. And, in fact, they have attended even less to the specific ways that individual passages within the gospel inform the Missionary Commissioning and, conversely, how the Commissioning illumines passages throughout Matthew's Gospel. The value of this study by Lindsay Arthur is that he directly addresses this unfortunate lacuna.

Dr. Arthur correctly observes that most scholars are satisfied to discern the meaning of the key phrase "make disciples" in Matthew 20:19 by considering primarily, if not exclusively, the role of the immediately following phrases, "baptizing them in the name of the Father, Son, and Holy Spirit, teaching them to observe all that I have commanded you." Dr. Arthur acknowledges that these phrases, and particularly the participles "baptizing" and "teaching," are critically important for the interpretation of "make disciples;" and he helpfully explores their significance in depth, and in the process contributes new insights into their meaning and role. But he insists—and this is the real contribution of his study—that the interpretation of "make disciples" must go far beyond what we can discern through these immediately succeeding participial phrases. If this passage does, in fact, form the climax to the book, elements throughout the gospel must participate in any full, robust construal of this command to make disciples. In the process of exploring how the broader context of Matthew's Gospel illumines the Missionary Commissioning, Dr. Arthur's study provides fresh insight into the meaning of passages throughout the gospel and the gospel in the large.

But, although he recognizes that the narrative world of Matthew's Gospel provides the most significant evidence for the meaning of the

Missionary Commissioning, Dr. Arthur is not satisfied to limit himself to the Gospel of Matthew. He concludes his study by relating the themes of the Missionary Commissioning to the same and similar motifs throughout the New Testament, noting how these treatments from other writers of the New Testament illumine Matthew 28:18–20 and how Matthew's Missionary Commissioning fits into these themes as they are presented in the New Testament in the large. This work thus makes a contribution to a New Testament theology of discipleship and of mission. Moreover, insofar as Dr. Arthur employs inductive biblical study, which includes attention to historical background and setting, and links it with insights from narrative criticism, his work has significance also for hermeneutics and exegetical method.

In short, then, this study is informative on a number of levels and instructive in several critical ways. Speaking personally, it was a privilege and a joy to serve as Lindsay Arthur's doctoral supervisor and thus to direct him in the writing of the dissertation that forms the foundation of this book. And I count it as an honor to be able to commend this volume to the academic public, and more specifically to those involved in biblical scholarship.

DAVID R. BAUER
Ralph Waldo Beeson Professor of Inductive Biblical Studies
Asbury Theological Seminary

Abbreviations

In addition to the following, all abbreviations are taken from *The SBL Handbook of Style* (2nd ed; Atlanta: Society of Biblical Literature, 2014).

ACCS	Ancient Christian Commentary on Scripture
AB	Anchor Bible
ABD	*Anchor Bible Dictionary*
ANF	*Ante-Nicene Fathers*
AsTJ	*Asbury Theological Journal*
BBR	*Bulletin for Biblical Research*
BEB	*Baker Encyclopedia of the Bible*
BECNT	Baker Exegetical Commentary on the New Testament
BDAG	Bauer, Walter, Frederick W. Danker, William F. Arndt, and F. Wilbur Gingrich, *Greek-English Lexicon of the New Testament and Other Early Christian Literature*, 3rd ed.
BSac	*Bibliotheca Sacra*
BTB	*Biblical Theology Bulletin*
CBQ	*Catholic Biblical Quarterly*
CBTEL	*Cyclopædia of Biblical, Theological, and Ecclesiastical Literature*
ChrCent	*Christian Century*
ChrTod	*Christianity Today*
CrBC	Cornerstone Biblical Commentary
CurTM	*Currents in Theology and Mission*
DJG	*Dictionary of Jesus and the Gospels*
DNTB	*Dictionary of New Testament Background*

DLNT	*Dictionary of the Later New Testament and Its Developments*
DThT	*Dictionary of Theological Terms*
EDB	*Eerdmans Dictionary of the Bible*
FC	Fathers of the Church
HBD	*HarperCollins Bible Dictionary*
HTA	Historisch-Theologische Auslegung Neues Testament
HThKNT	Herders Theologischer Kommentar zum Neuen Testament
HvTSt	*Hervormde teologiese studies*
IBS	Inductive Bible Study
ICC	International Critical Commentary
Int	*Interpretation*
ISBE	*International Standard Bible Encyclopedia*
IRM	*International Review of Mission*
JAAR	*Journal of the American Academy of Religion*
JACL	*Journal of Applied Christian Leadership*
JETS	*Journal of the Evangelical Theological Society*
JBL	*Journal of Biblical Literature*
JR	*Journal of Religion*
JSNT	*Journal for the Study of the New Testament*
JSNTSup	Journal for the Study of the New Testament Supplement Series
JSOT	*Journal for the Study of the Old Testament*
JWH	*Journal of World History*
LCL	Loeb Classical Library
L&N	Louw, Johannes P., and Eugene A. Nida, eds., *Greek-English Lexicon of the New Testament: Based on Semantic Domains*, 2nd ed.
LTQ	*Lexington Theological Quarterly*
MSJ	*The Master's Seminary Journal*
MSR	Major Structural Relationship
NA^{28}	*Novum Testamentum Graece*, Nestle-Aland, 28th ed.
NAC	New American Commentary
NASB	New American Standard Bible
NBD^3	*New Bible Dictionary*, 3rd ed.
Neot	*Neotestamentica*

NICNT	New International Commentary on the New Testament
NovT	Novum Testamentum
NPNF¹	Nicene and Post-Nicene Fathers, Series 1
NPNF²	Nicene and Post-Nicene Fathers, Series 2
NTS	New Testament Studies
Presb	Presbyterion
QR	Quarterly Review
RB	Revue biblique
ResQ	Restoration Quarterly
RevExp	Review and Expositor
TDNT	Theological Dictionary of the New Testament
Them	Themelios
TJ	Trinity Journal
TynBul	Tyndale Bulletin
WBC	Word Biblical Commentary
WesBC	Wesleyan Bible Commentary
WesTJ	Wesleyan Theological Journal
WW	Word and World
ZNW	Zeitschrift für die neutestamentliche Wissenschaft und die Kunde der älteren Kirche

1

INTRODUCTION

THIS CHAPTER: (i) INTRODUCES the primary biblical text to be examined; (ii) states the underlying research problem and purpose of the intended study; (iii) discusses the theoretical foundations of the methods that I propose to apply towards solving the stated problem; (iv) outlines a methodology and structural design of this investigation; and (v) clarifies three major assumptions upon which my proposed research is based.

Primary Biblical Text of Research

The Greek text (with English translation) that forms the basis of my research reads:

> Οἱ δὲ ἕνδεκα μαθηταὶ ἐπορεύθησαν εἰς τὴν Γαλιλαίαν εἰς τὸ ὄρος οὗ ἐτάξατο αὐτοῖς ὁ Ἰησοῦς, καὶ ἰδόντες αὐτὸν προσεκύνησαν, οἱ δὲ ἐδίστασαν. καὶ προσελθὼν ὁ Ἰησοῦς ἐλάλησεν αὐτοῖς λέγων· ἐδόθη μοι πᾶσα ἐξουσία ἐν οὐρανῷ καὶ ἐπὶ [τῆς] γῆς. πορευθέντες οὖν μαθητεύσατε πάντα τὰ ἔθνη, βαπτίζοντες αὐτοὺς εἰς τὸ ὄνομα τοῦ πατρὸς καὶ τοῦ υἱοῦ καὶ τοῦ ἁγίου πνεύματος, διδάσκοντες αὐτοὺς τηρεῖν πάντα ὅσα ἐνετειλάμην ὑμῖν· καὶ ἰδοὺ ἐγὼ μεθ' ὑμῶν εἰμι πάσας τὰς ἡμέρας ἕως τῆς συντελείας τοῦ αἰῶνος. (Matt 28:16–20 NA28)

> But the eleven disciples proceeded to Galilee, to the mountain which Jesus had designated. When they saw him, they worshiped *him*; but some were doubtful. And Jesus came up and spoke to them, saying, "All authority has been given to me in heaven and on earth. "Go therefore and make disciples of all the

nations, baptizing them in the name of the Father and the Son and the Holy Spirit, teaching them to observe all that I commanded you; and lo, I am with you always, even to the end of the age" (Matt 28:16–20 NASB)[1]

Biblical scholars have traditionally focused their interpretation of μαθητεύσατε ("make disciples," 28:19a) on its three adjacent participles: (i) πορευθέντες, "go(ing)"; (ii) βαπτίζοντες, "baptizing"; and (iii) διδάσκοντες, "teaching." This treatment suggests that μαθητεύσατε is to be understood primarily or solely in terms of the meanings that are supplied by its dependent participles. In other words, the whole is equal only to the sum of its parts.

This book seeks to support the claim that scholarly interpretations of μαθητεύσατε have been too narrow, especially when considered against the full scope of Matthew's Gospel. The evangelist relates a story that comprises far more content that may impact the meaning of μαθητεύσατε than the definitions supplied by these three syntactically subordinate participles that adjoin μαθητεύσατε at the very end of the account. The *author, text,* and *reader* of Matthew's narrative collaborate to inform the full meaning of μαθητεύσατε.[2]

Research Problem and Purpose

Scholars have, up to the present, looked primarily to the attendant participles of μαθητεύσατε for its meaning and have not developed and consistently upheld a line of argument that looks to the entire Gospel of Matthew for a fuller grasp of the term. By this, I am not suggesting that the participles are irrelevant for determining the overall meaning of μαθητεύσατε. Rather, I am contending that *the participles should not be viewed as the only source of meaning for this imperative.* Some scholars agree with my contention in this matter and have alluded to possible broader, Gospel-wide implications of μαθητεύσατε. However, they eventually either leave important matters unaddressed in their treatment—e.g.,

---

1. Henceforth, I will utilize the NASB for the English translation of all biblical references unless noted otherwise.

2. Throughout this book, I use the term "author" to refer to the implied author and "reader" to refer to the implied reader. I will provide definitions for these terms in this introductory chapter. When referring to any other kind of author or reader, I will qualify those terms with the appropriate adjectives (e.g., "historical," "real," "ideal," "intended," etc.).

a comprehensive examination of the textual evidence in 28:16–20 that supports a Gospel-wide search for the meaning of the imperative—or, having hinted at a broader meaning of the term, they withdraw to safer waters by emphasizing the dominance of one of the participles, usually "teaching," to best explain the meaning of μαθητεύσατε. The current situation demands that I examine whether the Matthean Jesus seeks to establish a framework in 28:16–20 that points to a fuller meaning of μαθητεύσατε that resides in the broader context of the Gospel. I propose therefore to argue that Matthew intends that the reader should draw the full meaning of μαθητεύσατε from the entire Gospel and should not limit the significance of the term to the sense that is supplied by one or more of its adjacent participles. For greater clarity, I will argue that the meaning of the term is to be understood within the context of the reader's interaction with every component of the Matthean story.[3]

Research Methodology, Structural Design, and Assumptions

In this study, I will utilize formal analyses that are based on empirical principles of observation (including inductive reading methods and narrative criticism) and that are designed to identify and examine the key narrative elements of the Gospel of Matthew that the Matthean Commission invokes in order to provide a fuller understanding of the meaning of μαθητεύσατε. Along the way, I will examine any evidence provided by the historical background of the text, including: (i) information about the writing itself, or (ii) information about persons or settings mentioned or alluded to in the writing that the writer assumes the reader knows.[4] Within narrative criticism, the narrative world is not hermetically sealed from the real world; indeed, the narrative assumes knowledge of the external world. Matthew's Gospel, like other ancient documents, is not timeless. Therefore, I must bring relevant background information into a broad narrative-critical framework so that I refrain from discussing the biblical text as though it can exist on its own.[5]

---

3. I will investigate shortly the various components that comprise a story, all of which are vitally important in conveying the author's intended message to the reader.

4. Bauer and Traina, *Inductive Bible Study*, 215–16.

5. See Robbins, "Social-Scientific Criticism," 276–77 on the merger between the literary and social-scientific approaches.

Theoretical Foundations of the Inductive Bible Study Method

The inductive Bible study (IBS) method of examining Scripture has been championed with differing degrees of sophistication by various scholars and practitioners. This method gives priority to the scriptural text over against literature about the text. The seminal work of David R. Bauer and Robert A. Traina is perhaps the most authoritative hermeneutical explanation and illustration of IBS that has been written to date.[6] This text serves as my primary discussion partner and guide on IBS matters throughout this book.

A sequel to Traina's *Methodical Bible Study*, Bauer and Traina's work seeks to offer its readers a specific, orderly process for interacting directly with particular biblical texts.[7] It introduces IBS: (i) in the broader sense as "a commitment to move from the evidence of the text and the realities that surround the text to possible conclusions (or inferences) regarding the meaning of the text," and (ii) in the narrower sense as a movement in the history of hermeneutics that originates with the work of William Rainey Harper and Wilbert Webster White.[8] From this movement emerged various emphases, including:[9] (i) the *final form of the text* that exists today (i.e., canonical Scripture), which allows biblical interpreters to focus on analyzing the text that they have rather than allowing the interpretive process to concentrate on the historical unknowns about the text;[10] (ii) the *form of the text*, attending to literary structure and how that informs the meaning of the text; (iii) the *study of biblical books*—the basic literary units of the Bible's final form—which challenges the

---

6. Bauer and Traina, *Inductive Bible Study*.

7. Bauer and Traina, Inductive Bible Study, xiii; see Traina, Methodical Bible Study.

8. Harper was founding president of the University of Chicago, and White established the Biblical Seminary of New York. They were concerned with the almost exclusive focus being paid to higher critical issues that seemed to render Bible study a lifeless exercise that had no clear significance for Christian faith and ministry (Bauer and Traina, *Inductive Bible Study*, 1–2).

9. Bauer and Traina, *Inductive Bible Study*, 2–6.

10. Thomas, "Historical Criticism," 39–52 notes that the church has at different periods viewed the historical accuracy of the Commission differently, and that "radical historical criticism questions the basic historicity of the Commission, Jesus' claim of all power, his command to go to all nations and baptize, and his use of the trinitarian name in connection with baptism." Thomas concludes, however, that the church is better served by dispensing with historical criticism in studying and responding to the Great Commission and to the Synoptic Gospels as a whole. He opines that these works are "historically accurate and deserve to be recognized and preached in that light."

tendency to limit the context of Scripture to a few verses and to engage in a disjointed reading of the text;[11] (iv) a *broad methodological process* that works alongside other exegetical approaches—e.g., form, redaction and narrative criticism; (v) a *dynamic interrelation* between the steps of the IBS process that makes adjustments along the way; and (vi) the development of a *holistic and integrative process* that incorporates all legitimate evidence, deals with the text at various levels, and addresses a range of hermeneutical concerns—i.e., observation and interrogation, interpretation, appropriation and proclamation, and correlation of smaller passages into an overall biblical theology.[12] Bauer and Traina conclude that:

> [IBS] is essentially a comprehensive, holistic study of the Bible that takes into account every aspect of the existence of the biblical text and that is intentional in allowing the Bible in its final canonical shape to speak to us on its own terms, thus leading to accurate, original, compelling, and profound interpretation and contemporary appropriation.[13]

In spite of what seems like a comprehensive and conclusive definition of IBS, the two scholars propose an overall approach to Bible study that is tentative and open-ended.[14] They present their discussion as a working hypothesis and note the overwhelming importance of: (i) the *principle of probability* over absolute certainty, which recognizes that textual evidence may be ambiguous, conflicting, or limited; and (ii) the *principle of reality*, which acknowledges that "pure and absolute induction does not exist," given that everyone brings presuppositions to the text.[15]

Bauer and Traina's approach to IBS pays special attention to the structural analysis of biblical books and passages and the interpretation of individual passages in light of their function within the book as a whole. They believe that authors are deliberate in presenting their material. Therefore, an alert reader may decipher an author's intended meaning by observing and scrutinizing the structural design of the relevant book or passage. For this reason, the scholars emphasize the

---

11. See Bauer and Traina, *Inductive Bible Study*, 63–65 for a discussion of "Compositional Book Study."

12. For a discussion of "Comprehensive and Integrated Study," see Bauer and Traina, *Inductive Bible Study*, 53–56.

13. Bauer and Traina, *Inductive Bible Study*, 6.

14. Bauer and Traina, *Inductive Bible Study*, 6.

15. Bauer and Traina, *Inductive Bible Study*, 26–27.

identification and analysis of: (i) the main units and subunits of the text, looking at major shifts of emphasis within the book;[16] and (ii) the major structural relationships (MSRs)—the "organizational systems" around which various thoughts and themes throughout the book are arranged.[17] The identification of MSRs is, however, not an end in itself. This step must be augmented by asking appropriate questions that seek to bridge the gap between observing and interpreting the text.[18] I propose to utilize Bauer and Traina's IBS system as the cornerstone of my examination of Matthew's text and I expect to discuss other relevant aspects of their methodology as it becomes necessary.

Theoretical Foundations of the Narrative-Critical Method

David Rhoads first used the term "narrative criticism" in his 1982 article "Narrative Criticism and the Gospel of Mark."[19] Rhoads observed that biblical scholars had long practiced literary criticism, which encompassed many approaches to a text. He noted, however, that they had only recently begun to examine the Gospel narratives, including the story world of the narrative and the rhetorical techniques used to tell the story. Rhoads called this kind of examination "the literary study of narrative," or narrative criticism, which includes "plot, conflict, character, setting, event, narrator, point of view, standards of judgment, the implied author, ideal reader, style and rhetorical techniques."[20]

Mark Allan Powell is one of several important contributors to narrative criticism of the New Testament. He comments that narrative critics speak of the *implied author* and the *implied reader*, whose identities are presupposed by the narrative itself. The correct determination of these

---

16. Bauer and Traina, *Inductive Bible Study*, 88.

17. See Bauer and Traina, *Inductive Bible Study*, 94–122 for detailed explanations of the meanings of the MSRs and the implications of their use.

18. For more on the three types—definitive/explanatory, rational, and implicational—of broad questions to ask, see Bauer and Traina, *Inductive Bible Study*, 126–34.

19. Rhoads, "Narrative Criticism," 411–34.

20. Rhoads, "Narrative Criticism," 411–12; see also Aune, *Westminster Dictionary*, 315 who defines narrative criticism as "a type of formalist literary criticism which typically approaches the biblical text as a unified whole (i.e., as a closed, internally consistent story world) . . . while usually bracketing out historical and theological issues"; and Resseguie, *Narrative Criticism*, 18–21 for other perspectives on narrative criticism.

personalities provides a basis for discussing what the author intends and what the reader knows without seeking to unravel the precise identities of the historical author and readers of the text. Powell explains that the reader of a narrative reconstructs the identity of its implied author because the story itself provides a sense of the author's values and worldview. This makes it possible to understand even works that are anonymous because every narrative has an implied author that seeks to convey meaning to its implied readers.[21] The goal of narrative criticism is to read the text from the point of view of the implied reader.[22] Jack D. Kingsbury describes this personality, in the context of the Gospel of Matthew, as follows:

> The term "implied reader" denotes no flesh-and-blood person of any century. Instead, it refers to an imaginary person who is to be envisaged, in perusing Matthew's story, as responding to the text at every point with whatever emotion, understanding, or knowledge the text ideally calls for. Or to put it differently, the implied reader is that imaginary person in whom the intention of the text is to be thought of as always reaching its fulfillment.[23]

Although the implied reader is a hypothetical concept that may be unattainable, it remains a worthy goal that helps to establish criteria for interpretation.[24] Powell and other NT narrative critics provide useful discussion about the major components of narrative criticism: story and discourse,[25] events,[26] characters,[27] and settings.[28] I hope to draw upon

---

21. Powell, *Narrative Criticism*, 5–6; see Booth, *Rhetoric of Fiction*, 71–76, 151–52, 200, 211–21, 395–96, who first developed and explored the concept of the "implied author."

22. Powell, *Narrative Criticism*, 20.

23. Kingsbury, *Matthew as Story*, 38.

24. Powell, *Narrative Criticism*, 21.

25. See Powell, *Narrative Criticism*, 23–34; Chatman, *Story and Discourse*, 43; Resseguie, *Narrative Criticism*, 67–68, 127, 167–92; Uspensky, *Poetics of Composition*; Lanser, *Narrative Act*; Culpepper, *Anatomy of the Fourth Gospel*, 181, 184; and Bauer, *Structure of Matthew's Gospel*, 19–20.

26. Powell, *Narrative Criticism*, 35–50.

27. See Powell, *Narrative Criticism*, 51–67; Perrine and Arp, *Story and Structure*, 67; Resseguie, *Narrative Criticism*, 121–65; and Booth, *Rhetoric of Fiction*, 158.

28. See Powell, *Narrative Criticism*, 69–83; Abrams and Harpham, *Glossary of Literary Terms*, 363; Resseguie, *Narrative Criticism*, 87–114; Rhoads and Michie, *Mark as Story*, 63; Chatman, *Reading Narrative Fiction*, 141; and Bal, *Narratology*, 136–137, 220, 221–22; Bland, "Endangering the Reader's Neck," 313–31.

these scholars' work and employ these components in varying degrees in this study.

Methodology and Structural Design

I propose to take the following approach to arrive at a fuller understanding of the meaning of μαθητεύσατε (28:19a) against the backdrop of the theoretical foundations of IBS and narrative criticism. This study will be undertaken in five broad movements. First, I will undertake a survey of literature that extends from the early centuries of the Common Era until the twenty-first century, focusing on the writers' use of the Matthean Commission (28:16–20) and, more specifically, on their interpretation of μαθητεύσατε.

Second, I will conduct an inductive study of Matthew 28:16–20 (the *primary text*) in order to identify and interpret the author's narrative clues that are intended to guide the reader's understanding of the meaning of μαθητεύσατε and to detect any of its possible links to the broader context of Matthew's Gospel. This step will include an assessment of the structural design of the passage and its key narrative elements relating to events, characters, settings, and rhetoric. The overriding question to be asked at this point is: *What aspects of the primary text, if any, exhibit significant links to the broader context of Matthew's Gospel and might therefore guide the reader to consider these connections when interpreting* μαθητεύσατε? Powell provides a useful list of additional questions that I will expand upon and employ at this stage of the investigation.[29] Some significant features of the passage that will be considered in this phase are events, characters, settings, discourse (including point of view, symbolism, irony, and narrative patterns), and the roles of the implied author and reader. Interrogating the primary text in this manner will help to identify which passages from the main body of Matthew must be examined to determine their contribution to the reader's interpretation of the Matthean Commission and its imperative, μαθητεύσατε.

Third, using the previously outlined inductive method, I will examine relevant passages from Matthew 1:1—28:15 (the *broader text*) to determine how they might help the reader to interpret the meaning of μαθητεύσατε. Passages to be selected from the broader text will comprise key terms or themes featured in the primary text that may unlock

---

29. Powell, *Narrative Criticism*, 103–5.

the meaning of μαθητεύσατε for the implied reader. Cognates with and synonyms for such key terms or themes will also deserve attention at this stage of the analysis. Passages from the broader text that could be of interest to my research at this stage will include episodes in which the Matthean Jesus calls, instructs, provides explanations to, commissions, or socializes with his disciples and the crowds. Occasions during which the narrator and other characters provide important information that might illuminate the meaning of μαθητεύσατε must also be considered.

Fourth, I will attempt to set Matthew's understanding of discipleship within a NT canonical context. Once again, my approach to discerning which NT texts will deserve examination must be highly selective. Therefore, I will emphasize the major points of continuity or discontinuity in the broader NT canon vis-à-vis Matthean discipleship.

Finally, based on the inferences drawn from my analysis, I will return to my primary text and make summary judgments about the meaning of μαθητεύσατε. These conclusions will address what the author intends the reader to deduce about discipleship from the broader context of Matthew. I will conclude my work by identifying and discussing the implications of my research findings for subsequent studies that may be required on this topic.

Major Research Assumptions

Before proceeding further, I would like to clarify my assumptions regarding three important matters that may influence the outcome of this research: the identity of Matthew's implied author, the identity of Matthew's implied reader, and the redactional relationships between the Synoptic Gospels.

Matthew's Implied Author

Bauer and Traina advocate that biblical interpretation should be guided by an appeal to the intention of the author that can be inferred from the text itself—a reference to the implied author. They believe this approach is more realistic and reliable in biblical interpretation for the purpose of deciphering authorial intention because of the lack of direct access to historical or flesh-and-blood authors. This is a text-centered approach that finds meaning that is embedded in the text and avoids linking correct biblical observation, interpretation, and application to one's ability to reconstruct the life or consciousness of the historical author.[30]

Scholars have made various observations about the identity of the implied author of Matthew that inform my own perspective on the matter: (i) first, the author and narrator in literature are generally to be distinguished because the latter may "prove to be limited or untrustworthy as a guide to the story . . . [and] be at odds with the values and norms of the [former]";[31] however, these two personalities in Matthew are virtually identical because they espouse the same system of values throughout the text;[32] (ii) the author ("he"[33]) is an intrusive figure that sometimes addresses an audience that exists outside the story world of the Gospel (e.g., 24:15; 27:8; 28:15);[34] (iii) he periodically interrupts the flow of the narrative with OT fulfillment quotations to comment on the story's characters and events (e.g., 1:23; 2:15; 27:9); he conveys a sense of reliability because of the OT's perception as an authoritative source that expresses God's evaluative point of view (1:22; 2:15; 15:4; 22:31);[35] (iv) by assuming the role of an omniscient third-person narrator, the author is perceived by the reader as an objective observer who knows everything about everyone (e.g., 1:19; 4:1–11; 8:3, 10; 9:2, 3, 21, 36; 12:14; 14:14; 16:7; 17:23; 19:3; 20:34; 21:25; 26:8, 10, 38; 27:18), which produces an illusion of pure reference;[36] by sharing his omniscience with the reader, the

---

30. Bauer and Traina, *Inductive Bible Study*, 42–49.

31. Howell, *Matthew's Inclusive Story*, 164; see also Kingsbury, *Matthew as Story*, 31; and Chatman, *Story and Discourse*, 226–28, 233–37.

32. Howell, *Matthew's Inclusive Story*, 165; see also Kingsbury, *Matthew as Story*, 31.

33. I may at times refer to the (implied) author of Matthew by the masculine pronoun "he" in order to avoid the clumsiness of repeatedly having to refer to this literary entity as "he or she"; in actuality, the (implied) author is the "creating person who is implied by the totality of a given work when it is offered to the world" (Booth, *Critical Understanding*, 269); therefore, my use of the masculine pronoun is not intended to make a judgment regarding the gender of Matthew's historical author.

34. Howell, *Matthew's Inclusive Story*, 166; Kingsbury, *Matthew as Story*, 31, 33, 35 notes that by bursting the bounds Matthew's story world in this manner, the author places himself in the story, temporally, between the resurrection (28:1–15) and the Parousia, "and is situated in the time of the messianic woes and the church's mission to the nations (24:8, 14–15)"; see also Anderson, *Matthew's Narrative Web*, 55–56.

35. Howell, *Matthew's Inclusive Story*, 166–67; see also Kingsbury, *Matthew as Story*, 35; and "Figure of Jesus," 3–36, esp. 6.

36. Howell, *Matthew's Inclusive Story*, 167, 175–76; for more on the "omniscient third-party narrator," see Abrams and Harpham, *Glossary of Literary Terms*, 301–3;

latter learns of matters that are not readily available to the story's characters, including Jesus' fulfillment of OT prophecy and the meaning of key words and phrases (e.g., 1:23; 27:33; 27:46);[37] (v) his choice of pronouns (e.g., "their/your synagogues" 4:23; 9:35; 10:17; 12:9; 13:54; 23:34) might reflect particular points of view about the subject matter at hand;[38] (vi) he reports the same event using different types of speech (i.e., direct vs. indirect) that may influence the reader's perception of the discourse (e.g., 16:21 vs. 17:22ff.; 20:18ff.);[39] (vii) he ends large sections of Jesus' teaching with concluding formulas (7:28; 11:1; 13:53; 19:1; 26:1) that lead to the perception of the existence of five large discourses in Matthew;[40] (viii) he accompanies the Matthean Jesus' character throughout the narrative (3:13–27:56; 28:9–10, 16–20) with few exceptions only (14:3–12; 26:58, 69–75)—these two personalities are so spatially intertwined that, even prior to Jesus' baptism and following his death, the author follows minor characters solely for the purpose providing information about Jesus;[41] (ix) he uses the historical present (λέγει, λέγουσιν, φησίν), extended speeches by Jesus, and the introduction of direct discourse with the present participle (λέγων, λέγοντες) to eliminate temporal distance between the narrator and the story's characters;[42] this repeated temporal alignment results in Jesus' speech being addressed to the reader as well as to the designated audience in the story;[43] (x) he paces the narrative, especially in major

and Kingsbury, *Matthew as Story*, 36–37.

37. Howell, *Matthew's Inclusive Story*, 178–79.

38. Howell, *Matthew's Inclusive Story*, 168–69; Matthew's inclusion of only two passages in which "synagogue" appears with no possessive pronoun (6:2, 5; 23:6) is noteworthy—in both cases, Jesus is involved in direct discourse with the disciples and crowds; otherwise, Jesus uses "their" or "your" and the narrator always uses "their" (Anderson, *Matthew's Narrative Web*, 59).

39. Howell, *Matthew's Inclusive Story*, 169.

40. Howell, *Matthew's Inclusive Story*, 169.

41. Howell, *Matthew's Inclusive Story*, 170–71; see also Kingsbury, *Matthew as Story*, 35–36; and Anderson, *Matthew's Narrative Web*, 66–69.

42. This permits the reader to experience the action of the narrative at the same time as the story's characters. Of the eighty uses of the historical present in Matthew, λέγει is repeated forty-six times, λέγουσιν is repeated fourteen times, and φησίν is repeated once (possibly twice, 13:29; 14:8); λέγων is used forty-nine times, and λέγοντες is repeated forty-seven times (Anderson, *Matthew's Narrative Web*, 62–66).

43. Howell, *Matthew's Inclusive Story*, 172–74; see also Anderson, "Matthew: Gender and Reading," 3–27, esp. 24–26; Combrink, "Structure of Matthew," 61–90, esp. 88; and Kingsbury, *Matthew as Story*, 36. Anderson, *Matthew's Narrative Web*, 61–62 notes that, with rare exception (possibly only 22:23–27), only the narrator and Jesus

discourses, in a way that equates story time and discourse time; when this happens, the narrative is presented as scene rather than "summary" and tends to remain in the foreground of the reader's mind;[44] (xi) he shows partiality by drawing the reader's interest and sympathy towards certain characters (e.g., Jesus; 1:23; 3:17; 4:1–11; 17:5; 26:39, 42), and away from others (e.g., the Jewish leaders; 26:59; 27:18; 28:11–15);[45] (xii) the narrator's commentary reliably reflects the author's norms throughout the Gospel;[46] (xiii) his commentary places the narrative into proper context for the reader;[47] (xiv) he uses generalization commentary mostly in the form of OT fulfillment quotations for the purpose of establishing the reliability and authority of the narrator and the Matthean Jesus;[48] (xv) his use of OT quotations reveals that he considers the events surrounding Jesus' life to be the fulfillment of OT messianic expectations and they tell the reader how to correctly read the narrative;[49] (xvi) his ideological point of

---

ever narrate and therefore have need to use the historical present in the Gospel, which in itself is important because telling a story creates the opportunity to persuade an audience to adopt a particular point of view.

44. Howell, *Matthew's Inclusive Story*, 174–75; at the very end of Matthew's Gospel the narrator, Jesus, the disciples, and the reader are all in the same temporal position—i.e., the period between the resurrection and the Parousia (Anderson, *Matthew's Narrative Web*, 63, 68).

45. Howell, *Matthew's Inclusive Story*, 177.

46. Howell, *Matthew's Inclusive Story*, 178; see also Kingsbury, *Matthew as Story*, 31.

47. Howell, *Matthew's Inclusive Story*, 179–85; see also Chambers, "Commentary in Literary Texts," 323–37, esp. 328. Chatman, *Story and Discourse*, 228 identifies three kinds of commentary that are used in literary texts, all of which are present in Matthew's Gospel: "interpretation" explains the essence of a story element (e.g., 1:23; 27:33; 27:46); "judgment" expresses both negative (e.g., 7:29b; 9:36b; 13:58; 20:24; 21:15b, 18a; 26:8, 59; 27:18; 28:17b) and positive (e.g., 1:19; 7:29a; 9:8; 14:33; 17:6; 27:55–56, 61; 28:7–9) moral opinions; and "generalization" refers outward from the fictional to the real world, either to universal truths (e.g., proverbial sayings) or actual historical facts (e.g., 10:2–4; 28:15–17) for the purpose of making the narrative more plausible. Howell, *Matthew's Inclusive Story*, 187 notes that other examples of commentary include superscription (1:1) and genealogy (1:2–16).

48. Howell, *Matthew's Inclusive Story*, 185–86. This use of commentary highlights almost every aspect of the Matthean Jesus' life and ministry: birth (1:23; 2:6, 15, 18, 23); entry into Galilee (4:15–16); healings (8:17); compassion and gentleness (12:18–21); teaching in parables (13:35); entry into Jerusalem (21:5); passion and death (26:56; 27:9–10).

49. Howell, *Matthew's Inclusive Story*, 187; all OT formula quotations are spoken by the author/narrator himself and because OT Scripture is recognized in Matthew to be the word of God (1:22; 2:15; 15:4; 22:31–32), the author becomes an exponent of

INTRODUCTION   13

view is based on the criterion of whether Jesus and his message are accepted or rejected, and by this standard the story's characters and events are judged;⁵⁰ (xvii) he aligns his point of view with that of the Matthean Jesus on multiple levels;⁵¹ and (xviii) he utilizes the names that the story's

---

God's evaluative point of view in assessing the significance of the life of Jesus (Kingsbury, *Matthew as Story*, 35).

50. Howell, *Matthew's Inclusive Story*, 189. Kingsbury, *Matthew as Story*, 34 remarks that "the evaluative point of view that the author has chosen to make normative is that belonging to God . . . [therefore,] the evaluative point of view that Matthew ascribes to himself as narrator or to any given character is to be adjudged true or false depending upon whether it aligns itself with, or contravenes, the evaluative point of view of God."

51. Howell, *Matthew's Inclusive Story*, 190-93. Howell makes reference to certain "planes of point of view" (see Uspensky, *Poetics of Composition*, 6; and Anderson, *Matthew's Narrative Web*, 55-74, who draws upon Uspensky's work to provide an instructive study of "point of view" in Matthew) to explain how the author of Matthew accomplishes this alignment: (i) *spatially*, the narrator's point of view follows Jesus and the reader is present even when Jesus is alone (e.g., 4:1-11; 14:23; 26:39-41); (ii) *temporally*, the narrator's point of view is synchronized with Jesus, on whom the focus is always directed; (iii) *psychologically*, the narrator presents the inside view of Jesus with more depth and sympathy than other characters (e.g., 8:10; 9:36; 13:58; 14:14; 20:34; 26:37); he presents Jesus' awareness of others' private conversations and thoughts (9:3, 21; 12:15; 16:7-8; 22:18; 26:10) and his accurate prediction of future events of his own lifetime (17:22-23; 20:17-19; 26:2, 21-24, 31-35) and of the reader (21:43; 22:2-14; 24:2), all of which enhances Jesus' reliability in the eyes of the reader; and (iv) *phraseologically*, the narrator interprets Jesus' words for the reader (16:12; 17:13; 21:45) and brings his own ideas into parallel with the Matthean Jesus' language and concepts (e.g., use of δίκαιος/δικαιοσύνη by the narrator, 1:19) and by Jesus (3:15; 5:6, 10, 20, 45; 6:33; 9:13; 10:41; 13:17, 43, 49; 21:32; 23:35; 25:37, 46); the narrator's description of Jesus' and his disciples' "missions" (4:23-25; 9:35-37; 10:1) vis-à-vis Jesus' description thereof (10:7-8); the narrator's description of the Jewish authorities and institutions (4:13; 7:29; 9:35-36; 12:9; 13:54; 22:18) vis-à-vis Jesus' portrayal of them (9:4; 10:17; 12:34; 15:2-9; chapter 23); the narrator's view that Jesus' life and death fulfills OT prophecy (1:22; 2:15, 17, 23; 4:14; 8:17; 12:17; 13:35; 21:4; 27:9) vis-à-vis Jesus' view of the same (5:17; 26:54, 26). Additionally, both the narrator's and Jesus' frequent appeals to Scripture as an adjudicator of truth signals that their points of view are ideologically aligned (Anderson, *Matthew's Narrative Web*, 59-61). Howell, *Matthew's Inclusive Story*, 193-98 uses Matthew 13 to further explain how the evangelist merges the ideological points of view of the narrator and Jesus by allowing the former to utilize the voice of the latter to tell stories and engage in conversation with multiple audiences, simultaneously (e.g., the discourse begins and ends with the usual commentary by the narrator [13:1-3a, 53], while Jesus himself [a narrated character] narrates the parable of the Sower [13:3b-9]). Howell explains that Jesus' practice of speaking in parables (13:11-17) answers not only the disciples' question (13:10), but also offers commentary to the reader about what has preceded. Jesus' interpretation of the parable (13:18-23) and the narrator's initially ambiguous use of αὐτοῖς (13:24,

characters use (sometimes in irony) in referring to Jesus to integrate their evaluative points of view into the plot.[52]

In summary, the (implied) author may be described as an undramatized (i.e., not a character in the story), third-person, omniscient personality who tells the story from an ideological point of view that seeks to persuade the reader to accept and obey Jesus and his message. He achieves this goal by: (i) providing information about Jesus' identity and his significance; (ii) supplying information to the reader that is otherwise unavailable to the story's characters; (iii) portraying Jesus' character favorably through commentary, superscription and genealogy, OT fulfillment quotations, and the arrangement of events and characters' responses; (iv) praising the character traits of those who accept Jesus and obey God's will and censuring those who reject the same; and (v) aligning his ideological point of view with that of the character of Jesus.[53]

Matthew's Implied Reader

Accompanying the notion of the implied author is the implied reader, who is inferred from the text and who is created by the implied author. This hypothetical reader "serves to locate the kinds of expectations the

---

31, 33—later explained in v. 34) also engages the reader. Jesus' question (13:51a) is directed to the disciples on the story level and also to the reader on the narrative level; see also Phillips, "History and Text," 111–38, esp. 119–32.

52. Howell, *Matthew's Inclusive Story*, 201 argues that because the author supplies a genealogy and several OT fulfillment quotations regarding Jesus, the reader knows his identity—as "the Messiah," "the Son of David," "the son of Abraham" (1:1), "God with us" (1:22), "my Son" (2:15), "a Nazarene" (2:23), "my Servant," "my Beloved" (12:17), and "your King" (21:5)—and is therefore able to evaluate the other characters in the story by the names they apply to him: "King of the Jews" by the wise men (2:2), Pilate (27:11), and the cohort of Roman soldiers (27:29, 37); "King of Israel" by the chief priests, scribes and elders (27:42); "Son of God" by Satan (4:3, 6), demons (8:29), the high priest (26:63), passersby at his crucifixion (27:40), the chief priests, scribes and elders (27:43), and the centurion and guards by his cross (27:54); "the Son of the living God" by Peter (16:16); "the Christ" by Peter (16:16) and the high priest (26:63); "glutton," "drunkard," "friend of tax collectors and sinners" (11:9), "Beelzebul" or "demon-possessed" (10:25; cf. 12:24, 27), "law breaker" (12:1–2) and "blasphemer" (9:3; 26:65) by the religious authorities. See also Uspensky, *Poetics of Composition*, 25–32 for a discussion of "Naming as a Problem of Point of View in Literature"; Malina and Neyrey, *Calling Jesus Names*, 35–38; Petersen, "Point of View," 97–121, esp. 111; and Senior, *Passion of Jesus*, on irony in Matthew's passion story (at various places throughout the text).

53. Howell, *Matthew's Inclusive Story*, 202.

text places on readers for the understanding of the text, the kinds of background knowledge, linguistic understanding, and so forth, that the text assumes the reader has and will bring to bear in the construal of the text's meaning."[54] In fact, one could argue that by reconstructing the theoretical responses of this imagined reader, I may be in a position to identify some of the possible effects the biblical narrative might have had on the actual reader.[55]

While I am unable to identify from the narrative alone the historical reader for whom Matthew wrote, I can, however, observe certain qualities about the Gospel's implied reader: (i) this reader knows more than any character group in the narrative and is ultimately called by the author to align *his*[56] ideological point of view with that of Jesus and the narrator;[57] (ii) because the narrator in Matthew is a reliable spokesperson for the author, the distance between the reader and the narratee is to be regarded as negligible also;[58] (iii) the reader can be detected through the author's direct commentary that presupposes some of their competencies;[59] (iv)

---

54. Bauer and Traina, *Inductive Bible Study*, 46; for more about the "implied reader," see Iser, *Implied Reader*, (at various places throughout the text); also Iser, *Act of Reading*, 33-34, who describes this reader as a "sort of fictional inhabitant of the text" that "embodies all the predispositions necessary for a literary work to exercise its effect"; Perry, "Literary Dynamics," 43, for whom the implied reader is "a 'maximal' concretization of the text that can be justified from the text itself while taking into account the norms (social, linguistic, literary, etc.) relevant for its period and the possible intentions of the author"; and Vanhoozer, "Reader in New Testament Interpretation," 259-88.

55. Howell, *Matthew's Inclusive Story*, 42; see also Rhoads and Michie, *Mark as Story*, 137.

56. Bauer, *Gospel of the Son of God*, 33 n. 21 notes that "the portrait of the reader ('implied reader') of the Gospel of Matthew is a male (note, e.g., the masculine participle at Mt 24:15)"; it is for this reason that I use the masculine pronoun throughout my work to refer to the implied reader or "the reader."

57. Howell, *Matthew's Inclusive Story*, 208, 216-17. Anderson, "Matthew: Gender and Reading," 23-24 remarks that since the norms and values of the author are vested in the narrator and Jesus, then "discipleship" that is viewed from this perspective is not to be defined in terms of membership of a specific narrative character group but as the norms and values the author wishes the reader to adopt.

58. Howell, *Matthew's Inclusive Story*, 209; Abrams and Harpham, *Glossary of Literary Terms*, 234 defines the narratee as "the explicit or implied person or audience to whom the narrator addresses the narrative"; for Kingsbury, *Matthew as Story*, 38, the narratee is "whoever it is to whom the narrator (the 'voice' that tells the story) is to be construed as addressing his many remarks"; in Matthew's case, "the narratee proves to be but a stand-in for the implied reader."

59. The author's direct commentary: (i) places the reader in the same spatiotemporal

Jesus frequently addresses the reader together with the characters of the story;[60] (v) some of the story's minor characters interrogate the reader (e.g., 8:27, 29; 12:23; 13:54-56), who possesses a superior knowledge by virtue of following the author's commentary throughout the Gospel;[61] (vi) the author's use of impersonal, indefinite or inclusive pronouns and expressions (e.g., "whoever," "many," "all") in Jesus' teaching makes the reader visible and extends the invitation and demands of discipleship beyond the story's characters;[62] (vii) the Matthean Jesus' major teaching discourses generally conclude by addressing "whoever" would be

position as the author (e.g., the author's references to "let the reader understand" [24:15] and "to this day" [27:8; 28:15]; i.e., that period of time between the resurrection and the Parousia); (ii) establishes a trust relationship between the author and the reader, resulting from the sharing of knowledge [e.g., about Jesus' identity and the significance of his mission (1:1, 2-17, 22-23; 2:15, 17-18, 23); explanatory glosses of words or phrases (27:33, 46); and cultural explanations (22:23; 27:15), all of which assumes that either the reader needs such explanations to be linguistically and culturally competent or to be able to interpret the text correctly]; (iii) increases the reader's dependency on the narrator to correctly interpret the text (e.g., explanations provided by OT fulfillment quotations, or about the authority of Jesus' teaching [7:29], or about the disciples' understanding of Jesus' teaching [16:12; 17:13], or the Jewish leaders' understanding of Jesus' parables [21:45], or about the deceit of the Jewish leaders who rejected Jesus [16:1; 19:3; 26:59-64; 27:18]); (iv) is unavailable to characters in the story; and (v) results in the disciples' experiences being shared directly with the reader (Howell, *Matthew's Inclusive Story*, 212-15).

60. Howell, *Matthew's Inclusive Story*, 218-20; the Matthean Jesus addresses the reader by: (i) referring to extratextual institutions, experiences and events that exist beyond Matthew's narrative world (e.g., promises of Jesus' omnipresence [18:19-20]; teaching that presupposes the existence of a future church community [18:15-20], or false prophets and Messiahs [7:15-20; 24:5, 11, 24], or hardship and persecution [5:11-12; 10:17-20; 23:34; 24:9], or the proclamation of the gospel to the entire world [26:13], or the destruction of Jerusalem [22:7; 23:37-39]); and by (ii) asking rhetorical questions that demand answers from the story's characters and also from the reader in order to maintain audience contact (e.g., 5:13, 46-47; 6:25-31; 7:3-4, 9-12, 16; 9:15; 10:29; 12:26, 27, 29, 34; 16:26; 18:12; 23:17, 19; 26:54) (see also Kennedy, *New Testament Interpretation*, 29, 57).

61. Howell, *Matthew's Inclusive Story*, 220-21.

62. Howell, *Matthew's Inclusive Story*, 221-23; these expressions typically include "whoever" statements (ὅς [often with ἄν or ἐάν], πᾶς, ὅστις [often with ἄν or ἐάν], οὐδείς, τίς, and the substantival participle) (e.g., 5:19, 21, 22, 28, 32, 39, 41; 6:24; 7:8, 21, 24, 26; 9:12, 10:22, 32-33, 37-38, 40-41, 42; 11:6, 11, 15, 27-28; 12:30, 32, 50; 13:9, 12, 43, 52; 16:24, 25; 18:4-6; 19:9, 11-12, 29; 20:26-27; 23:12; 24:13, 36; 25:29; 26:52), and "many" and "all" statements (e.g., 8:11; 11:28; 19:30; 20:28; 22:14; 25:32; 26:28; 28:19), including numerous occurrences of πᾶς with participles or pronouns that assign a generic meaning thereto. See also Malbon, "Disciples/Crowds/Whoever," 124-26; and Prince, "Study of the Narratee," 13.

a disciple, thus bringing the reader in focus;[63] (viii) in the concluding scene of the Gospel (28:16–20), the narrator, the disciples, and the reader are situated in the same temporal zone (i.e., between the resurrection and the Parousia);[64] therefore, Jesus' command (28:19a) and his promise (28:20b) together speak to an audience that is beyond the disciples' story characters[65]; (ix) the disciples as a character group, together with other

63. Howell, *Matthew's Inclusive Story*, 223–25 observes that: (i) the Sermon on the Mount concludes by describing the final judgment of people (7:21–23), suggesting the post-Easter development of the church, and with a parable that comprises "whoever" statements regarding hearing and obeying Jesus' words (7:24–27) (see Patte, *Matthew*, 63, 153–54; also Martin, "The Church in Matthew," 41–56, esp. 43, who argues that "we have access to the church of Matthew largely through the discourses"); (ii) the latter half of the mission discourse deals with discipleship in more general terms and includes a number of "whoever" statements that point to the reader (10:32–33, 37–38, 40–41, 42); (iii) in the parable discourse of Matthew 13, as previously noted, the author utilizes the voice of Jesus to simultaneously converse with multiple audiences; he concludes with a question (13:51a) that is directed to the disciples on the story level and to the reader on the narrative level and also with a "whoever" statement (13:52) that brings the reader into focus; (iv) the community or ecclesiastical discourse includes "whoever" statements (18:4–6), a promise of Jesus' ongoing presence in the community (18:20), and a concluding general warning about unforgiveness (18:35) that speak to an audience that is beyond Jesus' earthly ministry (see Scott, "King's Accounting," 429–42, esp. 429–31, for a discussion of the parable as an allegory that warns of God's dealings with "everyone" who does not forgive); and (v) the eschatological discourse incorporates sayings and parables (about "preparedness" for the End [24:32–25:46] and judgment of "all the nations" [25:31–46]) that relate to the period between the resurrection and the Parousia, which both the disciples and the reader share (see Patte, *Matthew*, 348 for a discussion of the reader's relationship with Matthew's eschatological discourse).

64. Kingsbury, *Matthew as Story*, 38–39 notes that this position is also revealed by various other passages (24:15; 27:8; 28:15) and is identical to the place of Matthew as author. From this vantage point, the reader is better able to understand those statements in Jesus' great discourses that seem to be out of place in the context of Jesus' earthly ministry (e.g., references to a universal mission [10:17–18; cf. 5:11–12; 7:15–23; 13:38; 18:19–20; 23:34] over against a mission that is supposed to be to "the lost sheep of the house of Israel" [10:5–6; cf. 4:17–9:34; 4:17, 23; 9:35–36]).

65. Howell, *Matthew's Inclusive Story*, 225–29 discusses key elements of Matthew's ending in relation to the reader, including: (i) a backward glance at all that Jesus taught (ἐνετειλάμην) that challenges the disciples and the reader to obey Jesus' teaching in the Gospel; (ii) an open-ended closure to the Gospel that challenges the reader and "carries actual readers forward from the text's conclusion to their own present" in a way that is consistent with the "textual structures and ideological point of view of the plotted story" (see Uspensky, *Poetics of Composition*, 137–40, 146–51, who examines the literary technique of framing and argues that the author assists the reader in transitioning to and fro between real and narrated worlds by adopting a point of view that is external to narrated events; see also Anderson, "Matthew: Gender and Reading,"

minor characters in the story, help to define and shape the role of the reader, but they must be distinguished from the Matthean reader;[66] (x) the author invites the reader to reject the Jewish leaders' outlook, which is one that opposes both Jesus' and the author's ideological points of view; nevertheless, these leaders help to shape the identity of the Matthean reader;[67] and (xi) the reader is a reflection both of the role that the narra-

---

23-24 regarding actual readers assuming the role of the implied reader).

66. Howell, *Matthew's Inclusive Story*, 229-36 explains that: (i) assuming the intended audience of Matthew's Gospel were Christians, then actual readers would more readily identify with the disciples who receive and accept Jesus' teaching [see Tannehill, "Disciples in Mark," 392; Stock, *Call to Discipleship*, 108; also Anderson, "Matthew: Gender and Reading," 20-22, who notes that the consideration of women and other marginal characters in Matthew to be disciples depend upon whether "discipleship" is defined as membership in the character group or the adoption of norms and values of the author and Jesus]; (ii) one must remember, however, that the reader is distinct from, and superior to, the disciples because of having access to the narrator's commentary on a variety of subjects, to which the disciples are not always privy [e.g., the struggles Jesus faces in obeying God's will (3:13-4:11; 26:39); see Bauer, *Structure of Matthew*, 60-62 on Matthew's portrayal of Jesus as the epitome of obedience to the will of God even in trying circumstances] as well as access to information communicated to the story's characters; (iii) other characters who are outside of the disciples' character group also display traits that are approved by the author (e.g., Joseph's obedience to God's will [1:18-25; 2:13-14]; the Roman centurion's [8:5-13] and the Canaanite woman's faith [15:21-28]; the devotion of the woman with the alabaster vial of costly perfume [26:6-13]); and (iv) the disciples as a character group possesses conflicting traits, especially in the matter of their obedience to God's will and their courage to follow the master amidst adversity (see Kingsbury, *Matthew as Story*, 13-14, who remarks that because of their conflicting traits, the reader is invited, depending on the narrator's or Jesus' attitude toward them at any given time, to identify with or against them; also Patte, *Matthew*, 119, 136, 391-93, 397, who distinguishes between Matthew's imperfect "actual" disciples and the "ideal" disciples of Jesus' teaching, the latter of which might be seen as a version of the reader that fully understands and accepts both the author's and Jesus' ideological points of view).

67. In this regard, Howell, *Matthew's Inclusive Story*, 237-42 illustrates that: (i) their opposition to Jesus provides the reader with negative examples that are to be avoided (e.g., not practicing what they preach [23:3-5; cf. 6:1-6, 16-18]; barring entry into the kingdom of heaven [23:13-15]; being blind about the law [23:16-22; cf. 15:1-10]; observing the insignificant, but neglecting the important [23:23-24; cf. 12:1-8]; being full of hypocrisy and lawlessness [23:27-28]); whereas, Jesus' example is to be followed [e.g., facilitating entry into the kingdom of heaven [4:17; 12:28]; exhibition of mercy and justice [12:1-2, 15-21]; loving God and neighbor [22:37-40]; striving after spiritual perfection [5:48]; practicing obedience [7:21f.; 12:46-50] and humility [6:1-6; 16:18]; see Senior, *Passion of Jesus*, 36 on the portrayal of discipleship in negative terms; also Bauer, *Structure of Matthew*, 65-71 on Matthew's repetition of contrast between Jesus and his opponents); (ii) unlike the reader, who is aware of Jesus' identity because of having access to narrative commentary, the Jewish leaders are

tive implies and the processes and actions of actual readers in the reading process—e.g., through anticipation and retrospection, consistent interpretation, and the ability to predict correctly as a result of the author's use of redundancy.[68]

In summary, the (implied) reader is not to be regarded as Matthew's historical community or even as Jesus' disciples, but is superior to them because of having access to the narrator's commentary as well as to information communicated to the characters in the story. Jesus' message is not limited to the story's characters either but extends beyond them to everyone who reads or hears the Gospel by means of commentary, rhetorical questions, inclusive language, and irony. The reader evaluates

---

unable to recognize Jesus as the Messiah and are therefore the primary victims of irony in Matthew (e.g., they are ignorant about the Messiah despite having the Scriptures [2:5-6]; they unwittingly help Jesus accomplish God's will at the right "time," through Judas's search for "opportunity" [26:16, 18]; they wrongfully accuse Jesus but unwittingly point out certain aspects of his true character—e.g., as destroyer of the temple [26:61-62; cf. 27:40]; as the Son of God [26:63; 16:16]; as blasphemer who speaks the truth [26:65]; as prophet [26:68]; as "King of the Jews" [27:11]; as "king" whom they coronate [27:27-29]; as savior [27:39, 42; cf. 1:21; 16:25; 26:28]; as provider of a sign [i.e., the resurrection] that they do not understand [27:42; cf. 12:38; 16.1]; as resurrected Lord [27:64; cf. 28:11-15]); for further discussion about irony, see O'Day, "Narrative Mode and Theological Claim," 657-68, esp. 663; Muecke, *Compass of Irony*, (at various places throughout the text); and Booth, *Rhetoric of Irony*, (at various places throughout the text).

68. The notion of reader "incorporates both the prestructuring of the potential meaning by the text, and the reader's actualization of this potential through the reading process" (Iser, *Implied Reader*, xii); Howell, *Matthew's Inclusive Story*, 243-47 highlights the following to be among the important strategies that a text utilizes to educate the reader: (i) the temporal dimension of reading forces the reader to look forward and back in successive iterations and results in early information being retained and used to interpret later information unless or until newer material undermines it; for this reason, Mathew's focus on Jesus in the beginning of the Gospel—as the obedient Son of God (3:15, 17), the fulfillment of God's plan (1:22-23; 2:6), and the Messiah of Israel (1:1)—gives the reader a frame of reference for interpreting subsequent events (see Iser, *Implied Reader*, 288; Perry, "Literary Dynamics," 47-61; Mailloux, "Learning to Read," 93-108, esp. 95-96; and Mailloux, *Interpretive Conventions*, 67-90 for discussions about temporal based reading); (ii) readers try to interpret the diverse elements of an developing narrative in a way that fits everything into a consistent pattern because they expect the literary text to be coherent (see Iser, *Implied Reader*, 283); and (iii) the author's use of redundancy—i.e., the repetition of information from multiple sources—helps to form coherent interpretations by increasing predictability and reducing alternatives (see Suleiman, "Readable Text," 119-42; Anderson, "Double and Triple Stories," 71-89; and Burnett, "Matthew's Eschatological Discourse," 91-109 for discussions of the use of redundancy in narrative).

various character groups in the story by their response to the ideological point of view of Jesus and the author.[69]

Gospel Relationships

This research incorporates IBS and narrative critical methods, supported by the examination of evidence provided by the historical background of Matthew insofar as it helps to explain the broader implications of the author's use of social and cultural terms or themes regarding Matthean discipleship. But how should I treat the issue of Gospel relationships and *redaction criticism*?[70] If I were to use a strictly IBS approach, then redaction criticism would have to be considered—i.e., the comparison of the Gospel accounts—at least for heuristic purposes. However, by using the narrative-critical approach, which emphasizes literary constructs (e.g., plot, conflict, character, setting, event, narrator, point of view, etc.), I must be careful about including redaction-critical elements into the discussion. In this research, I propose to footnote relevant and important comparisons between the Synoptic Gospel accounts, but I plan to do so without making any claims about specific redaction editorial work vis-à-vis earlier sources. Joel B. Green describes this kind of intermediate approach as "new redaction criticism":

> The comparison of narratives of the same story—not with an interest in source-usage, but in order to allow the distinctives of each to be highlighted by way of comparison. Juxtaposing parallel accounts would lead now not to decisions about bedrock historicity or to solutions of a source-critical nature, but rather to discussion of how locating this account within this narrative sequence leads to fresh horizons of meaning.[71]

---

69. Howell, *Matthew's Inclusive Story*, 248.

70. This refers to a type of criticism that focuses on the "alterations made in the traditional material used by the writer as key to his/her theological point of view" (Aune, *Westminster Dictionary*, 398–99).

71. Green, "Narrative and New Testament Interpretation," 153–66, esp. 162–63.

2

Survey of Literature

Chapter Summary

THIS CHAPTER EXPLORES RELEVANT secondary literature from the early centuries of the Common Era to the twenty-first century thereof for the purpose of determining: (i) how scholars have utilized the Matthean Commission (28:16–20) in their writings; (ii) more specifically, how they have interpreted μαθητεύσατε (28:19a); and (iii) what specific research needs might emerge therefrom.

Approach

I have anchored this survey of literature around contemporary Matthean scholarship,[1] which I am using as a point of departure for incorporating the interpretations of earlier scholars into the discussion. Overall, I have examined the work of several hundred authors, spanning the period from the late first century CE to the present day. This scope of coverage incorporates over 2,300 writing events, each of which represents a writing extract that incorporates one or more elements of the Matthean Commission as the basis for its author's argument. Therefore, each citation in

---

1. This includes work of the following scholars: David R. Bauer, Jeanine Brown and Kyle Roberts, Ulrich Luz (d. 2019), W. D. Davies (d. 2001) and Dale C. Allison, Donald A. Hagner, R. T. France (d. 2012), Craig S. Keener, John Nolland, David L. Turner, John P. Meier, Robert H. Smith (d. 2006), Craig L. Blomberg, and Michael J. Wilkins.

this survey corresponds with a scholar's utilization of the Commission on a specific theme for a precise purpose.

In presenting my findings, I first note the general comments that scholars have set down about the Great Commission in its entirety. I follow this with separate discussions, on a verse-by-verse basis, about specific issues that scholars address with the help of the Commission. Along the way, I highlight the key findings from my review of the literature, a summary of which follows.

Key Survey Findings

It is noteworthy that scholars have utilized the Matthean Commission to write about numerous topics[2] for a variety of reasons.[3] It is equally astonishing that amidst the vast quantity of words expended by scholarship on the Commission, a significant effort has not to date been given to discovering the full meaning of μαθητεύσατε (28:19a), the passage's main imperative, beyond what has already been supplied by its three adjacent participles—"going," "baptizing," and "teaching."

Several scholars correctly identify 28:16–20 as a summary of the entire Gospel of Matthew, acknowledging that: (i) several major themes come to full realization therein, and (ii) the passage is heavily reliant on what comes before. This supports the idea that earlier passages throughout Matthew up to the climactic 28:19 supply the readers with vital information to inform their judgment about the meaning of μαθητεύσατε.

Scholars speak about the meaning of μαθητεύσατε both directly and implicitly: (i) some substitute "make disciples of all nations" with "preach the gospel," "preach to all nations," or "preach the kingdom," or they even conflate the Matthean and Markan Commissions—generally correlating "making disciples" with preaching and evangelism in some general way;

---

2. The themes addressed include: (i) Jesus as the new Moses; (ii) Christian faith—e.g., "little faith" or faith mixed with doubt; (ii) Jesus' authority in relation to his Father's; (iv) the importance of foreign missions; (v) the identity of "all nations"—Jews and Gentiles, or Gentiles only; (vi) the nature and purpose of Christian baptism (including infant vs. believer baptism); (vii) the nature and composition of the Trinity—one essence, three persons; (viii) the preferred teaching content for new disciples; (ix) the forms of God's presence with his church; and (x) the Parousia.

3. The purposes include: (i) being a proof text in support of a theological argument; (ii) administering the sacraments in the church; (iii) protecting the church against heresies; and (iv) preparing for and discussing matters at the church's ecumenical councils over the centuries.

(ii) others make similar exchanges between "make disciples of all nations" and "baptize all nations" or "teach all nations," suggesting that the meaning behind these phrases are readily interchangeable; (iii) a handful of scholars employ a conquest motif as they address the missionary component of the Commission, which, according to two scholars, may have more to do with colonial expansion than with discipling an indigenous church; nevertheless, for those who utilize that motif, "make disciples" may imply a form of conquest of the human soul; (iv) the majority of scholars, however, who directly address the meaning of μαθητεύσατε, suggest that its meaning is spelled out by one, or by a combination of two or more, of its adjacent participles; at the same time, some of them appear ready to embrace the possibility that the rest of Matthew's Gospel has much to offer in terms of illuminating the meaning of μαθητεύσατε, which is especially true in light of Matthew's portrayal of Jesus' modeling of disciple-making for the Twelve throughout his entire Gospel.

Specific Research Needs

Taking these key research findings into consideration, the following specific research needs have emerged: (i) I must examine the Commission text to determine which earlier Matthean passages it recalls, and how these passages might help readers to develop a fuller sense of the meaning of μαθητεύσατε as they move through the narrative to its climax in 28:16–20; (ii) in light of the scholarly claim that Jesus teaches by action as well as by speech (and even by silence), all of which intuitively seems to be correct, I must let my research determine whether Matthew intends his readers to combine Jesus' spoken commands and his actions to interpret διδάσκοντες αὐτοὺς τηρεῖν πάντα ὅσα ἐνετειλάμην ὑμῖν (28:20a); failing that, in attempting to decipher the full meaning of μαθητεύσατε, I may be constrained to focus my attention not on what Jesus does throughout Matthew, but solely on what he commands, particularly in the five great discourses of the Gospel; and (iii) I must also let my research determine the accuracy of the claim that the adjacent participles of μαθητεύσατε have such broad meanings that they incorporate most of the features of Matthean discipleship therein; for, if this assertion is correct, it demonstrates that the meaning of μαθητεύσατε is already spelled out by its adjacent participles.

Recent research that has been undertaken on the Commission text does not appear to fully satisfy the research needs that I have identified. ProQuest lists twenty-eight results for dissertations published during the period 2001–2020 whose titles include the terms "Matthew 28:16–20" or "Great Commission."[4] The majority of them are praxis oriented, focusing on assorted themes, including: (i) church planting; (ii) developing a missional church culture; (iii) preaching and evangelism; (iv) spiritual disciplines and mission; (v) training for missions; (vi) application of church resources towards missions; (vii) Christian discipleship strategies; and (viii) baptismal theology. However, only three of these dissertations focus on the meaning of various elements of the Great Commission text. Ernest Munachi Ezeogu, for example, argues that the apparent contradictions between the Great Commission and the rest of the Gospel are occasioned by a traditional reading of the passage as a missionary text. Ezeogu finds that there are no textual grounds for reading 28:16–20 as a missionary mandate because, among other things, πορευθέντες (28:19a) is not an imperative and the characteristic vocabulary of missionary discourse is missing from Matthew's Commission. Instead, Ezeogu proposes a new model for reading the Commission as a magisterial commissioning whose purpose is to authorize the admission of Gentiles to the teaching office of Matthew's Jewish Christian church.[5]

Scott Allan Gilbert contends in his 2017 published dissertation that preaching the Great Commission requires every believer to go and intentionally engage in evangelism and in discipling less mature believers. Using linguistic analysis, rhetorical criticism, and narrative criticism, Gilbert reasons, *inter alia*, that disciple-making: (i) is contingent upon following Jesus—hearing his instruction and seeing his example;[6] (ii) includes an evangelistic component of proclaiming the gospel so that others might become followers of Christ;[7] (iv) requires instruction in word

---

4. As found in a global search of dissertations and theses in ProQuest on March 17, 2021.

5. Ezeogu, "Great Commission," 179 writes that "Μαθητεύω [28:19a] in the active sense in which it is used here, means to make someone else a disciple; in modern vernacular, to enrol somebody as a student. That they [the eleven disciples] are here being invested with the power to admit others as their students indicates a change in their own status. It means that they are no longer disciples, since disciples cannot have their own body of disciples, but teachers. They have undergone a transition from being disciples or scribal students to becoming scribes in their own right."

6. Gilbert, "Go Make Disciples," 181.

7. Gilbert, "Go Make Disciples," 181.

and deed;[8] and (v) includes *mimesis* of Jesus—imitation being inherent in the Greek concept of μαθητής, where a disciple would learn from a master.[9] Gilbert rightly concludes that "making disciples includes both baptism and teaching, but disciple-making does not entail *only* baptism and teaching."[10] However: (i) he does not utilize the evidence from the Commission text itself to explain why the instrumental participles ("baptizing" and "teaching") do not fully explain the meaning of μαθητεύσατε; rather, he bases his assertion on D. A. Carson's argument that the two participles "do not syntactically function as means for discipleship, but rather 'characterize it'"; and (ii) in support of another claim that disciple-making requires instruction in word and deed, he fails to address an inherent problem in the phrase διδάσκοντες αὐτοὺς τηρεῖν πάντα ὅσα ἐνετειλάμην ὑμῖν (28:20a)—i.e., that Matthew's prior use of ἐντέλλω (4:6; 17:9; 19:7) and ἐντολή (5:19; 15:3; 19:17; 22:36–40) are associated with spoken or written commands and not with someone's actions,[11] and that prior uses of τηρέω (19:17; 23:3) are connected with keeping the commandments and the requirements of the Mosaic law, not with abiding by someone's prior actions.

Michael Brands considers, among other things, whether Jesus' followers actually "make disciples," which is a common translation of μαθητεύω (28:19a). Brands has doubts about the appropriateness of the use of the English concept of "making," which may suggest the idea of "force, manipulation, pounding inanimate material into shape, or creating something new from nothing." He opines that "none of these notions faithfully describe discipleship in Matthew, or how Jesus relates to people, or what his followers are called (or able?) to do in mission," and adds that "to understand μαθητεύω (*mathēteuō*; Matt 28:19a) and its hope for multiplication, we need to press further into how related dynamics in the Matthean context disclose fuller and clearer definition."[12]

---

8. Gilbert, "Go Make Disciples," 182–183 borrows from Mortimer Arias and Alan Johnson (1992), who note that Matthew's didactic structure alternates between Jesus' teaching (chapters 5–7) and his actions (chapters 8–9), integrating his word and deed.

9. Gilbert, "Go Make Disciples," 183–184.

10. Gilbert, "Go Make Disciples," 168.

11. France, *Matthew*, 1118–19.

12. Brands, "Kingdom Commission," 192 n. 44. On the theme of "multiplication" in discipleship, which he believes is present in Jesus' metaphor of God's kingdom harvest (9:35–38) and in his banquet imagery (9:9–13; 22:1–14; 26:26–29), Brands reckons that Jesus' own model best shows his followers how to "fish for people" (4:19).

Brands summarizes that "Jesus commissions his followers to serve in God's eschatological messianic kingdom as light to all the nations," which is fulfilled through "wholistic integrated word-and-deed service."[13]

In this book, I hope to build on recent scholarship and address the various research needs: (i) by allowing the Commission text itself to point to earlier passages in Matthew that might help to develop a fuller sense of the meaning of μαθητεύσατε, (ii) by permitting Matthew's text to explain if and why the author intends his reader to combine Jesus' spoken commands with his actions in interpreting διδάσκοντες αὐτοὺς τηρεῖν πάντα ὅσα ἐνετειλάμην ὑμῖν (28:20a), and (iii) by letting the Commission text either confirm or deny the accuracy of the claim that the adjacent participles of μαθητεύσατε are sufficient to explain the meaning of that imperative.

General Comments

In a recent essay, David R. Bauer offers a detailed exegesis of Matthew 28:16–20 as he explores the theology of mission in the Gospel of Matthew through the lens of the Great Commission.[14] This scholar, agreeing with Christopher Wright, posits that "mission stands at the center of the Bible from beginning to end," and, citing David Bosch, he notes that the Gospel of Matthew is essentially a missionary text, in spite of the absence of the term therein.[15]

Bauer reckons that the Commission comprises 28:16–20. He indicates that there is more to Matthew's concept of discipleship than what the Gospel writer explicitly describes in the passage, and he acknowledges that it "sets forth the essential task of disciples in the church during the

---

13. Brands, "Kingdom Commission," 267.

14. Bauer, "Mission in Matthew's Gospel," 240–76, esp. 240; Smith, *Matthew*, 338 points to features that are missing in the Commission if it is to be "understood primarily in terms of a summons to missionary and evangelistic activity."

15. Bauer, "Mission in Matthew's Gospel," 241 also notes that many Matthean scholars who pay attention to mission focus primarily on the tension between Jewish particularism and Gentile universalism; see also Betz, "Heresy and Orthodoxy," 144–47 concerning the backdrop of early Christian debates about heresy and orthodoxy, against which Matthew writes; Tennent, *World Missions*, 450–52 regarding two theological problems that hindered the Reformers from reflecting on 28:18–20 missiologically for over two centuries; and Ferdinando, "Mission," 46–59, esp. 55–58, on mission taking place in the absence of social action, but never in the absence of discipling.

post-Easter period."¹⁶ In defense of the view that Matthew is essentially a missionary text, Bauer emphasizes that: (i) one of the Gospel's five great discourses is devoted to the theme of mission (9:35—11:1), and (ii) the structure of Matthew's narrative moves towards the resurrection and culminates with the missionary commissioning, representing a climax to the climax of the resurrection.¹⁷ For this and other reasons, Bauer concludes that the Commission must be interpreted in light of its overall function within the entire Gospel.¹⁸

Jeannine Brown and Kyle Roberts posit that the Commission is indeed heavily reliant on what comes before.¹⁹ They explain:

> Mission permeates all of Matthew, as Jesus calls disciples to join him and 'fish for people' (4:19) and to pattern their ministry after his own mission to Israel (10:1–8). Jesus' God-given mission is the restoration of Israel as the first stage in God's redemption of all peoples. This perspective reminds us of the importance

---

16. Bauer, "Mission in Matthew's Gospel," 245.

17. Bauer, "Mission in Matthew's Gospel," 241–42; see Bauer, *Gospel of the Son of God*, 227-28 on the climax of Matthew being the complex of Jesus' passion and resurrection—two aspects of a single overarching reality, presented in five alternating blocks of narrative between Jesus' followers and his opponents that (i) form a chiasm around 28:1–10, (ii) signal the essentiality of the resurrection within the passage, (iii) point (along with 28:7, 10) to the climactic encounter between Jesus and his disciples in 28:16–20, and (iv) stimulate the reader to reflect on how the disciples will eventually respond to Jesus' announcement (28:18–20).

18. Bauer, "Mission in Matthew's Gospel," 243; see Luz, *Matthew 21–28*, 619–20 relating to the biblical language of the final commission signaling Matthew's understanding of Jesus' proclamation on the mountain in Galilee in terms of God's dealings with his people, and the resulting logical inference that Matthew's readers interpret the text primarily from their reading of the entire Gospel.

19. Brown and Roberts, *Matthew*, 264; see Davies and Allison Jr., *Matthew (III)*, 678–79, 687–88 about the Matthean commission being "the key to the Gospel and even a table of contents placed at the end"; and Luz, *Matthew 1–7*, 161–62 relating to the correlation between the Matthean Jesus' call of the disciples at the sea of Galilee (4:18–22) and his final commission (28:16–20): "He calls them away from their work and wants to make them 'fishers of people.' With this promise a space is created and a future horizon is opened up that in later parts of the Gospel will be filled with content... In the disciples' discourse [9:36–11:1], whose beginning refers back to our text, the disciples receive their first commission to 'fish' for people (Matt 10:5–16). With the parable of the fishnet the expression is clearly understood to refer to missionary activity (cf. 13:47). The missions command of 28:19–20 will finally make plain what Jesus means."

of understanding mission in Matthew within the frame of the divine mission for this world.[20]

The Matthean Jesus' mission is holistic and attends comprehensively to people's needs, involving mercy and justice, gospel proclamation, and enactment,[21] which implies that μαθητεύσατε involves teaching others to observe what Jesus says and does.

Additional considerations point to the significance of 28:16–20 within the Gospel: (i) major themes—including Jesus' authority, his relationship to the Father, and the role of the nations—come to full realization therein,[22] (ii) the ministry of Jesus and the disciples that was once restricted to Israel (10:5–6; 15:24) is now refocused towards "all the nations,"[23] and (iii) the inclusio around the theme of *with-ness* or *Mitsein* (1:23; 28:20) underlines the climactic character in the Commission.[24] Additionally, three prominent structural features in the passage express a christological focus that mirrors the entire Gospel: (i) a cause-and-effect relationship between 28:18 and 28:19–20a that is accentuated by the conjunction "therefore" (οὖν),[25] (ii) the repetition of inclusive scope that is marked by four occurrences of πᾶς,[26] and (iii) a causal link between the Commission (28:19–20a) and Jesus' promise to be with his disciples until

---

20. Brown and Roberts, *Matthew*, 264.

21. Brown and Roberts, *Matthew*, 264.

22. Bauer, "Mission in Matthew's Gospel," 242, 243; see Brown and Roberts, *Matthew*, 261–62 on the Commission being a "large terminal railway station in which many lines converge," bringing together themes and plot motifs from across Matthew's Gospel.

23. Bauer, "Mission in Matthew's Gospel," 242–43; see Saunders, "Matthew," 873 on the unresolved tension in Matthew revolving around the implications of Jesus' death for the Jewish people—i.e., whether God has turned away from Israel toward the Gentiles, or Jesus has died to save the Jews also; and Luter Jr., "Great Commission," 2:1091 about the universality of the Commission representing a shift from Jesus' focus on Israel (10:5–6; 15:24) towards "all nations" (28:19).

24. Bauer, "Mission in Matthew's Gospel," 243.

25. Bauer, "Mission in Matthew's Gospel," 244; see also Schnabel, *Early Christian Mission*, 1:352–55 on the presupposition of missionary work being the risen Lord with his authoritative word; and Luz, *Matthew 21–28*, 625 about: (i) the disciples' proclamation being intended to be the instrument of the resurrected Jesus' universal authority; and (ii) the risen Jesus' spoken word of authority (28:18) confirming and deepening their faith, and enabling them to undertake the new commission.

26. Bauer, "Mission in Matthew's Gospel," 244 also notes that Jesus' all-inclusive authority is described both spatially (28:18b), and temporally (28:20b).

the end of the age (28:20a)—a relationship that may involve either the movement from effect to cause, or from cause to effect.[27]

Ulrich Luz describes the Commission as the *summa* of the Gospel that is in christological, ecclesiological, and ethical balance.[28] Matthew concludes his Gospel with a manifest of the risen Jesus—comprising a word of authority (28:18b), a commissioning (28:19a-20a), and a promise (28:20b)—that abandons the narrative text by ceasing to tell the story in his own words and that includes Jesus' view of the present and future of this epoch until the Parousia.[29] Furthermore, only Matthew and John merge Jesus' post-resurrection appearances to his disciples with a Commission (28:16-20; John 20:19-23). John connects the event with a granting of the Spirit (John 20:22), which is missing from Matthew. Nevertheless, I know that Matthew is familiar with the presence of the Spirit with the church (10:19-20), but in the Commission he emphasizes Jesus' promise of his ongoing presence with them (28:20).[30] Luz also calls attention to two textual forms of Matthew that have recently become known: (i) a Hebrew text of the Gospel that is of Jewish Christian origin and contains neither the Trinitarian baptismal command nor the mission command to all nations; and (ii) the middle Egyptian text of the Codex Schøyen.[31]

W. D. Davies and Dale C. Allison recognize the diverse opinions regarding the Commission's sources, noting that it may: (i) be redactional,[32] (ii) be based on a pre-Matthean pericope, or (iii) preserve several sayings of different origin that were possibly conjoined before Matthew.[33] Never-

---

27. Bauer, "Mission in Matthew's Gospel," 244; Schnabel, *Early Christian Mission*, 1:353 emphasizes that the present tense of Jesus' word of promise underlines the duration of the promise.

28. Luz, *Matthew 21-28*, 636.

29. Luz, *Matthew 21-28*, 615-16.

30. Luz, *Matthew 21-28*, 302.

31. Luz, *Matthew 1-7*, 60; see Howard, "Matthew," 4:642-43 on the Hebrew Matthew's treatment of the Gentile mission and the trinitarian baptismal formula.

32. Davies and Allison Jr., *Matthew (III)*, 679-80 reckon that four items in the Commission may be attributed to Matthew's hand: the setting on a mountain, the command to go and make disciples, the order to do all that Jesus has commanded, and the assurance of Christ's presence, which together combine to give the passage a distinctive Mosaic atmosphere and quality; Keener, *Matthew*, 715 concurs, but also reckons that "the different forms of the commission suggest its essential accuracy by multiple attestation."

33. Davies and Allison Jr., *Matthew (III)*, 677-78.

theless, the similarities of the form and content between the Commission and other canonical appearances of the resurrected Jesus to his eleven disciples seem to demonstrate the passing on of a tradition.[34] The Commission relates two periods—the time of Jesus' earthly ministry and the time of the post-Easter church—which, though different, have the same Lord and mission.[35] Matthew's Commission comprises elements that are frequently attested in the OT commission narratives, including the reference to "the observance of all that God has commanded."[36] Davies and Allison note that, like 1 Chronicles 22:1–16 and Jeremiah 1:1–10, the Commission intentionally borrows from the traditions about Moses as well as from the account of Romulus Quirinus's ascension.[37] They believe that 28:16–20 is key to the entire Gospel and expresses the meaning of the Matthean Jesus' resurrection, namely: (i) the universalization of his cause that results from his exaltation as Lord of all; (ii) the end of an old and the beginning of a new time; (iii) the vindication of the words and deeds of earthly Jesus; and (iv) the acts by which Jesus becomes the ever-present divine assistance to his present and future disciples.[38] They conclude that the Commission offers a christological concentration of Matthew's Gospel—Jesus as the Son, the Son of Man, Lord, Teacher, son of Abraham, and Immanuel, "God with us."[39]

John P. Meier contends that Matthew's final form reveals a mature theological development on such issues as salvation history, eschatology,

---

34. Davies and Allison Jr., *Matthew (III)*, 678.

35. Davies and Allison Jr., *Matthew (III)*, 678. The two scholars correlate "all I have commanded you" (28:20a) with Jesus' earthly ministry as a whole; however, Schnabel, *Early Christian Mission*, 2:1495 argues that the first Gospel comprises much more than the "commandments of Jesus" that the disciples are directed in 28:20a to teach, and that it cannot be reduced to Jesus' commandments.

36. Davies and Allison Jr., *Matthew (III)*, 679; see Luz, *Matthew 21–28*, 617–19, who contemplates the genre possibilities of the Matthean commission in terms of: (i) "appearance story" that climaxes in a commissioning (cf. 28:9–10; Mark 16:14–18; John 20:19–23; Luke 24:36–49; Acts 1:4–8); and (ii) "commissioning" that is representative of the genre throughout the Bible (i.e., calling stories; e.g., Gen 11:28–12:4a; Exod 3:1–4:16; Jer 1:1–10), appointments of a successor (e.g., Josh 1:1–11; 1 Chr 22:1–16) and other commissionings (e.g., Gen 41:37–45; 2 Chr 36:22–23)].

37. Davies and Allison Jr., *Matthew (III)*, 680.

38. Davies and Allison Jr., *Matthew (III)*, 673, 688; see Larkin Jr., "Acts," 349–668, esp. 379, who describes the "exaltation" of Jesus Christ as a three-stage process, comprising bodily resurrection, ascension, and enthronement or session at God's right hand to commence his perpetual reign and intercession for his people.

39. Davies and Allison Jr., *Matthew (III)*, 688.

and world mission, which argues for a post-AD 70 dating of the Gospel. Evidence of this resides in: (i) the Gospel's affirmation of a mission to all nations;[40] (ii) baptism with a triadic formula instead of circumcision as the initiation rite of the people of God; (iii) the commandments of Jesus instead of the Torah as the object of teaching; and (iv) the abiding presence of the resurrected Lord in his church as the center of gravity in Matthew's eschatology.[41] The Gospel stands on the borderline between the Jewish and Gentile world; however, its superior Greek vis-à-vis Mark's, its Greek play on words, and the pointers throughout toward the climactic missionary charge (2:1-12; 8:5-13; 15:21-28; 27:54) in the Final Commission argues for its composition in Antioch, a predominantly Greek-speaking metropolis with the largest Jewish population in Syria.[42]

Robert H. Smith marvels at what Matthew chooses to eliminate from his account of the final scene of the Gospel. For Smith, it is a "deceptively simple scene" that omits Jesus' assumption of power, and how the disciples break bread with Jesus or touch his body. Instead, Matthew focuses on the words of Jesus, the master-teacher, in a way that harmonizes with what has gone before in the Gospel.[43] Jesus' meeting with his disciples is "a marvel of reserve" that says nothing about Jesus' posture or gestures, the time or season, or even about the names of specific disciples that are present.[44]

Michael J. Wilkins comments that Matthew provides for his church a practical and realistic portrayal of what it means to be called a "disciple,"[45] the most commonly used term to designate the followers of Jesus.[46] Matthean disciples are not meant to be an idealistic paradigm, since the author shows both positive and negative traits.[47] From Matthew's

---

40. Meier, "Matthew," 4:632.

41. Meier, "Matthew," 4:623-24.

42. Meier, "Matthew," 4:624; see White, "Christianity," 1:930-31 regarding a Matthean community, probably being situated in the Galilee or nearer Syria, attempting to "work out the strictures of both an internal church order (18:15-20) and an external gateway for non-Jewish converts (28:18-20) in the period after the First Revolt."

43. Smith, *Matthew*, 334-35.

44. Smith, *Matthew*, 335.

45. For a comprehensive sweep of ancient discipleship literature, including classical and Hellenistic sources, the LXX, and the New Testament, see Wilkins, *Discipleship in the Ancient World*.

46. Wilkins, "Disciples," 176-81.

47. Wilkins, "Discipleship," 182-88, esp. 182.

perspective, the disciples are "with" Jesus, the Jewish leaders are "against" Jesus, and the crowds are required to make a decision about whether to be with or against him (cf. 12:30; Mark 9:40; Luke 9:50; 11:23).[48] While the Commission is given to the eleven remaining disciples (28:16), they are indeed models for all disciples, whom Jesus commands to "make disciples," or "to continue the work he [Jesus] began with them."[49] Bauer acknowledges that Matthew introduces the discipleship theme in 4:18–22 and later develops it throughout the Gospel.[50]

Matthew's salvation history, according to Scot McKnight, must carefully consider various Matthean texts, including the Commission, which speak in salvation-historical terms.[51] McKnight identifies six basic periods in Matthew's scheme, viz., the time of: (i) anticipatory revelation and promise; (ii) transition with John the Baptist; (iii) the Messiah's inauguration of the kingdom of heaven and his revelation of ethical standards;[52] (iv) Israel's decision; (v) all nations; and (vi) consummation. For McKnight, Jesus is at the center of Matthew's outline of salvation history. All nations are now just as privileged as Israel was, and the occasional reception of Gentiles in Jesus' ministry culminates in his final Commission to all nations.[53]

Colin Brown emphasizes the miraculous nature of events surrounding the Commission, and he records the resurrection appearances and ascension of Jesus in his list of miracle stories relating to events in the

---

48. Wilkins, "Discipleship," 183; see Watson, "People, Crowd," 605–9 on Matthew's distinction between the disciples and the crowds.

49. Wilkins, "Discipleship," 188; see also Hertig, "Great Commission Revisited," 347 on "making disciples" not meaning merely adding new church members into a congregation nor expanding the church numerically. Hertig views Matthean discipleship to be costly. He notes that: (i) disciples must understand Jesus' words and apply them uncompromisingly (7:24–27); and (ii) the goal of making disciples refers to "the process of transforming into the likeness of Jesus, as demonstrated by Jesus' own example of making disciples. Disciple making is not a performance; it is total submission to God's reign."

50. Bauer, *Gospel of the Son of God*, 310–11.

51. According to McKnight, "Matthew," 537, these texts include 1:1–17; 3:1–12; 5:17–20; 9:14–17; 11:2–19; 16:13–28; 21:33–22:14; 23:1–25:46; 27:51–53; 28:1–10; 28:16–20.

52. McKnight, "Matthew," 534 remarks that Jesus inaugurates the kingdom of heaven in three phases—his public ministry, his Passion, and his vindicating resurrection.

53. McKnight, "Matthew," 537–38.

Gospels.⁵⁴ Meanwhile, Allison Trites views Jesus' post-resurrection appearances as evidence of the authenticity of the resurrection miracle itself.⁵⁵ Several scholars discuss elements of Matthew's Commission vis-à-vis those of the other Gospels, including: (i) Graham Twelftree, who observes that Jesus' temptations on the pinnacle of the temple and on a high mountain are in reverse order in Matthew and Luke;⁵⁶ (ii) Gary Shogren, who perceives that Jesus' teaching receives more attention in Matthew and Luke than in Mark;⁵⁷ and (iii) George W. E. Nickelsburg, who remarks that Jesus' appearance in Jerusalem (Luke 24:36–53) permits the Lord to commission his disciples to "preach to all nations in his name, as in Matt 28:16–20."⁵⁸ Nickelsburg's remark is noteworthy in that it equates "*preach* [κηρύσσω] to all nations" (Luke 24:47) with "*make disciples* [μαθητεύω] of all nations" (28:19). Over the centuries, several scholars seem inclined to substitute "make disciples of all nations" with "preach the gospel," "preach to all nations," or "preach the kingdom." Others conflate the Matthean and Markan Commissions entirely,⁵⁹ and there are those who generally exchange "make disciples" with "preach," "evangelize,"⁶⁰ "baptize,"⁶¹ or

---

54. Brown, "Miracle," 3:371–81, esp. 374.

55. Trites, "Luke," 317–18; for other perspectives on the Commission as "miracle story," see Remus, "Miracle (New Testament)," 4:856–69; and Yang, "Miracles," 903–4.

56. Twelftree, "Temptation," 821–27, esp. 823–25; Stein, *Luke*, 144–45 asserts that variations in Gospel writers' accounts reflect their theological interests.

57. Shogren, "Authority and Power," 50–54; see also Stein, *Luke*, 619 as regards the juxtaposition of Luke's commission with those of the other Gospels.

58. Nickelsburg, "Resurrection," 5:690.

59. Several early scholars make this substitute, including Tertullian, Aphrahat, Bonaventure, Luther, Menno Simon, Calvin, and John Owen; more recently, however, Davies and Allison Jr., *Matthew (III)*, 680 writes, "Jesus . . . told his disciples to go into all the world and to teach the observance of all the commandments"—an apparent conflation of the Markan and Matthean commissions.

60. Ferdinando, "Mission," 54–55 distinguishes between evangelism ("bringing people to faith") and discipling (or making disciples), "which signifies . . . fostering spiritual growth in terms of relationship with God and his people, and of obedience in all areas of life," which is not divorced from social action; however, several scholars, ancient and modern, appear not to make this distinction: Novatian, Eusebius, Menno Simon, Calvin, John Bunyan, Wesley, Ridderbos, Schnabel, Blomberg, and Craig Evans just to name a few.

61. A selection of these scholars includes Hilary of Poitiers, Athanasius, Basil the Great, Ambrose of Milan, Jerome, Augustine, Peter Chrysologus, Peter Damian, and Luther.

"teach."⁶² Hans Kvalbein calls attention to this lax treatment of μαθητεύω (28:19), noting that, while much has been written over the years on various elements of the Great Commission—e.g., the character of Jesus' authority, "going" as crossing borders to proclaim the gospel, the meaning of baptism, teaching the Christian faith, and Jesus' promise to be present with his church—by comparison, little has been said and written on the meaning of the imperative of the Commission, and "the biblical concept of discipleship has in our church tradition been replaced by other concepts and other words."⁶³

Matthew 28:16

Bauer notes that Matthew describes the disciples' arrival in terms of their identity, number, and destination. For him, "the disciples" represent "the whole of the post-Easter church," since Matthew typically presents them in this way.⁶⁴ Until recently, they were "the Twelve,"⁶⁵ but now they are "the eleven disciples," which calls the readers' attention not only to Judas's betrayal and the danger of falling away from the faith without return, but also to Peter's denial, repentance, and subsequent reinstatement.⁶⁶ Their destination is the mountain in Galilee,⁶⁷ a place of revelation⁶⁸ for the disciples

---

62. Recognizing that several ancient scholars made this substitution, Wesley, *Works*, 10:198–99 writes "Go and teach all nations, baptizing them,—teaching them to observe all things" makes plain tautology, vain and senseless repetition, and notes that it ought to be translated, "Go and make disciples of all nations, by baptizing them" (28:19); Luz, *Matthew 21–28*, 625 confirms that the Vulgate translates μαθητεύσατε (28:19) as *docete* ('teach') and then has another *docents* ('teaching') follow in 28:20.

63. Kvalbein, "Go Therefore and Make Disciples," 49.

64. Bauer, "Mission in Matthew's Gospel," 245 n. 23; see Bauer, *Gospel of the Son of God*, 196 on Matthew's use of the indefinite subject, τὶς (e.g., 16:24), indicating that the Twelve are representative of those who will made disciples through them in the post-Easter period.

65. Matt 10:1, 2, 5; 11:1; 20:17; 26:14, 20, 47; possibly also 19:28, which refers to the disciples' "sitting on twelve thrones, judging the twelve tribes of Israel."

66. Bauer, "Mission in Matthew's Gospel," 246 n. 29 argues that Judas "does not repent, but experiences remorse (μεταμέλομαι, 27:3), i.e., a different feeling over against a changing of the mind or alteration of intention (μετανοέω, cf. 4:17); see Michel, "μεταμέλομαι, ἀμεταμέλητος, κτλ," *TDNT* 4:626–29; Rengstorf, "κλαίω, κλαυθμός, κτλ," *TDNT* 3:722–26.

67. See also Luz, *Matthew 8–20*, 411; and *Matthew 21–28*, 621–22 on the portrayal of Galilee in Matthew.

68. Bauer, "Mission in Matthew's Gospel," 248 (n. 38); moreover, "we [the entire

and the reader that has a threefold significance: (i) pointing to the comparison between the mission of the post-Easter church and the ministry of the earthly Jesus,[69] (ii) signaling the eschatological character of the mission of the church,[70] and (iii) emphasizing the mission to the Gentiles—i.e., all the nations of earth—which Jesus subsequently makes explicit (28:19).[71] From a practical viewpoint, however, the disciples' meeting with Jesus in Galilee is fitting; they are Galileans and they would normally return home after a pilgrimage to Jerusalem for Passover and the Feast of Unleavened Bread.[72]

Brown and Roberts highlight that Jesus' resurrection is first revealed to the women who followed him from Galilee. They are commissioned to tell Jesus' disciples about his resurrection, even before he commissions the Eleven to disciple the nations.[73] It is noteworthy that Matthew 26–28 is framed by the presence of women, who appear at important points and fill key roles in the passion narrative; however, because the commissioning of the Eleven (28:16–20) receives such prominence in Matthean studies, it is easy to miss the importance of women in Matthew's final chapters.[74] Brown and Roberts conclude that Jesus' commission to the women is so important to the overall narrative that one should speak of two commissionings in Matthew: female (28:1–10) and male (28:16–20).[75]

---

post-Easter church] are there on the mountain, experiencing and reacting to the presence of the Resurrected One; and he is speaking to us all" (245); see also Brown and Roberts, *Matthew*, 262 (cf. 57, 157–58, [357 n. 10]); Luz, *Matthew 1–7*, 182–83 on the geographic and theological meaning of "mountain" in Matthew; and Rogers, "Great Commission," 383–98, who perceives the mountain scene in 28:16–20 as "the culmination of the convergence of the Son of God and Moses themes throughout the Gospel in which Matthew argues that Jesus, Son of God is the only one to whom the community owes worship and obedience."

69. Bauer, "Mission in Matthew's Gospel," 246–47.

70. Bauer, "Mission in Matthew's Gospel," 247; see Bauer, *Gospel of the Son of God*, 231.

71. Bauer, "Mission in Matthew's Gospel," 247.

72. Turner, *Matthew*, 688.

73. Brown and Roberts, *Matthew*, 232–33.

74. Brown and Roberts, *Matthew*, 424.

75. Brown and Roberts, *Matthew*, 427 (cf. 259–260); see also Wainwright, "Feminist Criticism," 116; and Luter Jr., "Women Disciples," 171–72, who seeks to determine whether there is a special kind of discipleship related to women that is evident in the NT and suggests several ways that women disciples can be recognized, beyond the obvious discipleship terminology. Luter notes, among other things, that only one woman is out-and-out called a "disciple" ($μαθήτρια$) in the NT (Acts 9:36); however, he adds that "'disciples' is essentially interchangeable with 'church,' 'saints,' 'believers,' and other

Luz reckons that "to the mountain" stands out for Matthew's readers because no mountain was mentioned in 28:7 or 28:10. Accordingly, they are likely to reflect on the phrase and in the process recall the previous mountain scenes in the Gospel: the temptation of Jesus (4:8), Jesus' preaching on the mountain (5:1; 8:1), the mountain of the second feeding (15:29), and the mountain of the transfiguration (17:1, 9). Luz adds, "It is clear that the readers, who now have arrived at the end of the Matthean story of Jesus, have available to them a great variety of possible connotations and allusions from what they have thus far read or heard."[76]

Davies and Allison hesitate to render εἰς τὸ ὄρος οὗ ἐτάξατο αὐτοῖς ὁ Ἰησοῦς (28:16) as "to the mountain which Jesus had designated." Instead, because (i) the Matthean Jesus had not previously directed the disciples to a mountain, and (ii) in 2:9 and 18:20 οὗ means "where," not "whither," they suggest that τάσσω may mean "give commands"; hence, they read "to the mountain where Jesus gave them commands"—a redactional reference to the mountain on which Jesus preaches the Sermon (5:1).[77] Some scholars hesitate to embrace Davies and Allison's view on this matter.[78]

Craig S. Keener takes note of the various themes, including faith and unbelief (28:16–17), that the Commission narrative teaches. Keener

---

terms [e.g., Acts 8:1; 9:1; 11:26]," and that "some of the other ways to determine that people are, in fact, being viewed as disciples in the NT when these expected terms don't appear are: 1) the use of the word 'follow' (ἀκολουθέω) in relation to Jesus; 2) the expression 'with him' (i.e., Jesus, in Luke 8:1–3); and 3) a comparison of the individual's level of commitment to what Christ laid out as 'the cost of discipleship' in Luke 14:26–33." However, Luz, *Matthew 21–28*, 606, argues that: (i) the women are not given a commission to preach; (ii) they are not present for Christ's decisive appearance on the mountain in Galilee; and (iii) their meeting with Jesus serves only to prepare for the concluding scene.

76. Luz, *Matthew 21–28*, 616–17; see also Nolland, *Matthew*, 1261–62 on the argument that, in light of the adjoining reference to "all that I have commanded you" (28:20), "the mountain" (28:16) refers to that on which the Sermon was delivered (5:1–8:1); and Allison Jr., "Mountain and Wilderness," 563–65 about the several Gospel texts that place Jesus on a mountain, and the uncertainty of linking many events with known mountains with any degree of probability.

77. Davies and Allison Jr., *Matthew (III)*, 681.

78. France, *Matthew*, 1110 n. 11 describes Davies and Allison's assertion as "a unique and misleading way to refer to Jesus' teaching," since, "if that were the sense we would rather have expected διδάσκω, and probably also some indication that the reference is to the more distant past"; see Hagner, *Matthew 14–28*, 883–84 on the idea that Matthew's concern might be to situate this revelatory expression of Jesus at an appropriately holy mountain, as elsewhere in the Gospels—e.g., mount Tabor, the mount of the transfiguration.

emphasizes that, within the logic of Matthew's account, the disciples had enough faith to believe the women and proceed to Galilee without them. He recognizes, however, that Matthew's audience is probably so familiar with the resurrection tradition that they would know that other events intervened.[79]

Walter Elwell and Barry Beitzel call attention to the nineteenth-century argument that the transfiguration was originally a resurrection account that was inadvertently or deliberately read back into the ministry of Jesus because of issues relating to vocabulary and the form of the account.[80] Pre-mid-twentieth-century scholars employ 28:16 in their writings in various ways, including: (i) commenting that this meeting seems to be Jesus' last appearance in Galilee, when he sends them forth to baptize;[81] and (ii) compiling lists of appearances of the Lord after his resurrection, including his appearance on the mountain in Galilee.[82]

Matthew 28:17

Bauer takes note of the disciples' paradoxical response to seeing Jesus on the mountain in Galilee: "worship" (προσκυνέω) and "doubt" (διστάζω). He reasons that their act of worship, when viewed alongside previous references to worship that are directed towards Jesus,[83] points to the deity of Christ and emphasizes the continuity between the earthly Jesus who ministered in Galilee and the now resurrected Lord.[84] Bauer perceives that the statement "some doubted" refers to the Eleven, and whether all or some of the disciples' doubt is secondary to "the fundamental claim that post-Easter discipleship is characterized by both worship and doubt."[85] The term

79. Keener, *Matthew*, 715–16.
80. Elwell and Beitzel, "Transfiguration," 2:2098–99.
81. Chrysostom, *Hom. Matt.*, 90.2 (NPNF1 10:530–532).
82. Augustine, *Cons.*, 3.25.83 (NPNF1 6:223–224). For a selection of earlier scholarly writings that include significant discussion regarding 28:16, see Cyril of Alexandria, "Emmaus Disciples," ACCS 383; Aquinas, *Catena Aurea: Matthew*, 1:985–86; Lightfoot, *Commentary (Luke-John)*, 3:449; *Commentary (Acts-1 Corinthians)*, 4:8–10, 119–21.
83. Matt 2:2, 11; 8:2; 9:18; 14:33; 15:25; 20:20; 28:9; cf. 2:8; Mark 5:6; John 9:38.
84. Bauer, "Mission in Matthew's Gospel," 248; Nolland, *Matthew*, 111 indicates that Matthew employs προσκυνέω "in a manner which seems designed to blur, in the case of response to Jesus, the distinction between deferential respect and religious worship."
85. Bauer, *Gospel of the Son of God*, 231–32; see Hagner, *Matthew 14-28*, 884,

appears only once elsewhere in the New Testament (14:31), the episode of Jesus walking on the water (14:22–33), where it is connected with the disciples' worship of Jesus as well (14:33).[86] There, Jesus labels Peter's failure as "doubt" that is characterized by "little [or weak] faith" (ὀλιγόπιστος), which might explain the meaning of the disciples' doubt in 28:17:

> It is precisely people who both adoringly worship and often only haltingly believe that Jesus commissions. He does not wait for, nor does he require, a perfection of faith before he sends them out. The church is sent precisely in its weakness. Yet the existential problem of doubt, which has the power to diminish and even nullify mission, is potentially solved by Jesus' presence and word (vv. 18–20).[87]

Brown and Roberts acknowledge that Matthew's final scene brings together themes and plot motifs from across the entire Gospel, and they propose that the disciples' initial response of worship and doubt upon seeing the resurrected Jesus is thematic.[88] The Matthean Jesus is unique among humanity.[89] He embodies God's presence (1:23; cf. 18:20; 28:20) and he is to be worshipped, which is a connection that Matthew repeatedly affirms. This theme reaches a climax in the final scene of the Gospel, where Jesus participates in the divine privilege of universal rule (28:18) and is rightly worshipped by his disciples, signaling a high Christology.[90] Brown and Roberts posit that Matthew's intended readers are to take the worship scenes at 14:33; 28:9; and 28:17 "as paradigmatic anticipations of the reverence for Jesus that they offered in their worship gatherings."[91] Furthermore, it is not the resurrection alone that makes Jesus worthy of

---

885–86, who indicates that there are two issues of importance here: (i) what the definite article οἱ is referring to; and (ii) the shade of meaning of ἐδίστασαν, "they doubted." Hagner is of the view that διστάζω amounts to hesitation that occurs because of recent events, which Jesus addresses in 28:18–20.

86. Bauer, "Mission in Matthew's Gospel," 248–49 also explains that Matthew intends the reader to interpret 28:17 in light of 14:22–33 ("the second boat scene") because of its connection with 8:23–28 ("the first boat scene"), in which Jesus calms the storm; see Nolland, *Matthew*, 1253 n. 35, who associates the fear in 28:10 and the doubt in 28:17 on the basis of the undisputed relationship between fear and doubt in 14:30–31.

87. Bauer, "Mission in Matthew's Gospel," 249–50.
88. Brown and Roberts, *Matthew*, 262, 339.
89. Brown and Roberts, *Matthew*, 326.
90. Brown and Roberts, *Matthew*, 35.
91. Brown and Roberts, *Matthew*, 306–7.

worship; rather, it is "Jesus' resurrection *as his vindication and enthronement* by God (in light of Daniel 7) that suggests worship is the right response to this risen Jesus."[92] Additionally, by implicitly connecting the disciples' doubtful response (28:17) with Peter's wavering during "the second boat scene" (14:22–33), Matthew is signaling that they have not progressed in faith across the story.[93] As a result, Matthew's church's mission might rest more in Christology and in Jesus' presence among his followers (28:20) than in discipleship.[94]

Scholars up to the mid-twentieth century utilize the text of 28:17 in a variety of ways, including: (i) arguing that the Father, along with the Son and the Holy Spirit, is to be worshipped because the Trinity is to be worshipped;[95] and (ii) admiring the evangelist's truthfulness when he admits that some of the disciples doubted, determining not to conceal their shortcomings.[96]

Matthew 28:18

Bauer emphasizes Jesus' christocentric declaration about his authority, which includes both the power (capability; e.g., 10:1) and the right (legitimacy; e.g., 21:23–27) to act. This new "all-inclusive" authority, which leads to a commission that transcends what he previously demands of

---

92. Brown and Roberts, *Matthew*, 262.

93. See Barnes, *1-2 Kings*, 152, who notes the sobering contrast of worship and doubt found in 28:17 and suggests that "miracles are sources of encouragement, but only to those who already have a predisposition to believe (cf. Luke 16:31)."

94. Brown and Roberts, *Matthew*, 262 (cf. 140, 149–50, 453–454) emphasize Matthew's repeated characterization of the disciples as possessing "little faith" (6:30; 8:26; 14:31; 16:8; 17:20), which the scholars define as "wavering in faith because of fear": (i) despite realizing the Jewish leadership's rejection of Jesus (e.g., 12:1–14; 19:3; 26:3–5) and their negative influence on the people (21:33–46; 23:1–4, 13; 27:20; cf. 9:36), they are able to move beyond their "little faith"; (ii) they frequently misconstrue Jesus' mission and teachings (e.g., 16:22–23; 18:1–5; 19:13–15; 20:20–24); and (iii) they doubt and waver even as they worship (28:17; cf. 14:31, 33).

95. Ambrose, *Spir.*, 3.11.85 (NPNF2 10:147).

96. Chrysostom, "Risen Lord," ACCS 312–13. A selection of other early scholars that reflect on the contributions of 28:17 include Jerome, *Comm. Matt.*, 327; Leo the Great, *Sermons*, 322–23; Wright, *Proverbs, Ecclesiastes, Song of Solomon*, 307 re Nilus of Ancyra; Wycliffe, *Select English Works*, 2:140; Barsanuphius and John, *Barsanuphius and John: Letters (II)*, 323; Fructuosus and Braulio, *Iberian Fathers (2)*, 93–94.

them,⁹⁷ includes, but is not limited to, his earthly authority.⁹⁸ For Bauer, the verse echoes Daniel 7:13-14 LXX⁹⁹ and signals Jesus' exaltation, which Matthew correlates with the time of the resurrection¹⁰⁰—the time at which God grants comprehensive authority to Jesus,¹⁰¹ who is now enthroned over the cosmos.¹⁰²

Brown and Roberts perceive echoes of Daniel 7 in Matthhew 28:18, and they acknowledge that in granting authority to Jesus (cf. 11:27), God gives authority to human beings also (9:8), Jesus being the representative human being for Israel and humanity. However, they recognize that Jesus is also "the one to whom God has given an authority beyond what humans possess."¹⁰³ Jesus does not explicitly hand over his authority to his disciples, even though he promises them various kinds of authority

---

97. Bauer, "Mission in Matthew's Gospel," 250 n. 57 observes that Jesus' declaration (28:18) leads, for the first time, to commands to "make disciples," "baptize," and "teach"; additionally, the Commission marks the broadening of ministry beyond "Israel alone" to "all nations."

98. Bauer, "Mission in Matthew's Gospel," 250 n. 56 spells out several components of Jesus' earthly authority.

99. Bauer, "Mission in Matthew's Gospel," 250 n. 58 explains that Daniel's "Son of Man" represents the righteous remnant of Israel (Dan 7:22, 25, 27a), but the writer's use of third-person masculine singular pronouns in Dan 7:27b may for the basis for finding fulfillment in a specific individual; see also *Gospel of the Son of God*, 232–33. Keener, *Matthew*, 716 (n. 339), 716–17, 718–19 posits that: (i) there are some differences between 28:18–20 and Dan 7:13–14, but concedes that an allusion to Dan 7 and other OT texts is likely; and (ii) the climax of Jesus' deity (cf. 1:23) is in his authority (28:18)—including the authority to tell his subordinates to "go" (cf. 8:9)—and in the baptismal formula (28:19b).

100. Bauer, "Mission in Matthew's Gospel," 251 n. 61 notes that several NT writers ascribe greater status or authority to Jesus at the point of his exaltation (e.g., Acts 2:29–36; Rom 1:1–4; Phil 2:5–11; Heb 1:1–5); Bauer notes, however, that "some [e.g., von Dobbeler, Barth, and Moberly] have argued on the basis of 11:27 that 28:18 does not describe a new authority, but is a confirmation of the authority he had all along"; see also Keener, *Matthew*, 716 n. 339 on Ἐδόθη ("has been given") being an *ingressive aorist*, suggesting that Jesus' reign could have begun at the resurrection; and Wallace, *Greek Grammar*, 558–59 about the *ingressive aorist*.

101. Bauer, "Mission in Matthew's Gospel," 251 n. 60 asserts that the verb ἐδόθη ("has been given") is a divine or theological passive—i.e., God is the obvious agent—therefore, one understands that the authority was "given by God"; see Wallace, *Greek Grammar*, 437 on the theological passive.

102. Bauer, "Mission in Matthew's Gospel," 251 n. 62 submits that Jesus' new range of authority—esp. "in heaven" (ἐν οὐρανῷ)—is wider than that which he previously enjoyed (contrast 9:6); it is a cosmic "co-authority" with the Father.

103. Brown and Roberts, *Matthew*, 91.

(16:19; 18:18-19); instead, the connection between his authority and his disciples' commissioning resides in his promise to be present with them (28:20). They derive their authority for mission by participating in his authority as they remain with him and follow his lead.[104] Jesus gives authority for healing and exorcism to the Twelve (10:1), but they are not effective in drawing on this power (14:16-17; 17:16-17), and he points to their "little faith" as the reason for their lack of efficacy (17:19-20; 21:21-22; cf. 6:30; 8:26; 14:31; 16:8). Brown and Roberts suspect that Matthew uses the motif of "little faith" to underscore Jesus' authority (11:27; 17:18; 28:18) and the importance of his presence with his followers (28:20).[105] They also explain that Matthew's accenting of Jesus' universal lordship in 28:18 affirms Jesus' inclusion in the "unique divine identity."[106]

John Nolland questions whether Jesus is speaking about a newly acquired authority or about one that has been challenged by the passion events. Nolland argues that the motivation to find here a newly acquired authority comes from: (i) a strong Christian impulse to see everything differently after Jesus' death and resurrection, and (ii) the echoes of Daniel 7 in the text that may imply newly gained authority if the allusion is to the status of the "one like a son of man" (Dan 7:13) having just been acquired. The command to go to all the nations (28:19), which contrasts "nowhere among the Gentiles" (Matt 10:5), is new and could imply new authority that is linked to a fresh beginning in Galilee that is grounded in the achievement of Jesus' death and resurrection. However, the vindication of authority, rather than new authority, is the likely way that Jesus' death and resurrection undergirds his authority claim. It represents, therefore, a reaffirmation of authority after being rejected by the Jerusalem establishment.[107] Nolland also observes that: (i) while many people in Matthew "come/go to" or "approach" (προσέρχομαι) Jesus, only here and after the transfiguration (17:7) does Jesus approach someone;[108]

104. Brown and Roberts, *Matthew*, 151, 453-54, 473-74, 481-82.
105. Brown and Roberts, *Matthew*, 100, 336.
106. Brown and Roberts, *Matthew*, 306.
107. Nolland, *Matthew*, 1264-65.

108. Nolland, *Matthew*, 1263; also distinctive in a nearby text is that the resurrected Jesus "meet" (ὑπαντάω) with the women (28:9); France, *Matthew*, 650-51 reckons that Matthew uses προσέρχομαι with Jesus as the subject to describe situations in which the disciples are overwhelmed by a supernatural event (17:7; 28:18); see also Penner, "Revelation and Discipleship," 201-10, who contends that Matthew's account in 17:7 centers on the revelation of Jesus as the Son of God and on the expected response of that revelation being: (i) discipleship to someone who is greater that Moses and Elijah;

and (ii) the phrase "in heaven and on earth," found only four times in Matthew,[109] is likely to be an echo of the authority that Jesus gives to the church—i.e., Peter (16:19) and the community (18:18).[110]

David Turner reckons that echoes of Daniel 7 in Matthew 28:18–20 are clearest from the LXX, which includes such terms as ἐδόθη, ἐξουσία, πάντα τὰ ἔθνη, γῆς, οὐρανός, and αἰῶνος; furthermore, mention of the oppressed but ultimately vindicated saints (Dan 7:22, 25–27) fits well with Jesus' teaching on discipleship in Matthew (cf. 5:11–12; 10:17–42; 16:24–28; 23:34; 24:9–31).[111] Additionally, Turner perceives the irony of Jesus' crucifixion: that all of Jesus' claims are eventually shown to be true, although unknown to the other characters in the story. "After his resurrection, Jesus was exalted as the glorious Son of Man and given all authority (28:18) . . . Things are not always as they seem, and sometimes things are exactly the opposite of what they seem."[112] On Matthew's high Christology that culminates in the vindication of a resurrected Christ, Turner notes that:[113] (i) the religious leaders mock Jesus' kingship (27:42), but he is subsequently vindicated and he, as their exalted king, sends his apostles into the world (28:18; cf. 26:64; Dan 7:13–14);[114] (ii) Matthew employs "Son of Man" language that underscores Jesus' authority and glorious return, the background of which is Daniel 7:13;[115] (iii) the Gospel writer presents Jesus as Immanuel—"Jesus as God's Son is also God himself with his people, effecting their deliverance";[116] (iv) Matthew portrays as unique the relationship between the Father and the Son in redeeming God's people; he demonstrates this through the Father's

---

(ii) discipleship that requires uncompromising obedience to Jesus; and (iii) discipleship to someone who demonstrates compassion and loving care for his disciples.

109. Matt 6:10; 16:19; 18:18; 28:18; Matthew frequently places "heaven" and "earth" side by side—5:18; 6:10; 11:25; 16:19; 18:18, 19; 24:35; 28:18; cf. 24:30.

110. Nolland, *Matthew*, 1265.

111. Turner, *Matthew*, 689.

112. Turner, "Gospel of Matthew," 361.

113. For exploration of Matthew's christological titles ("King," "Son of Man," "Immanuel," "Son of God," and "Servant"), noting that Jesus of the Gospels avoids "Messiah," opting to refer to several figures of OT prediction as fulfilled in his ministry, see France, "Jesus Christ," 573.

114. Turner, "Gospel of Matthew," 19, 56.

115. Turner, "Gospel of Matthew," 20–21.

116. Turner, "Gospel of Matthew," 45 cites Hill (1972:80) to claim that Immanuel is "more of a title signifying the character and mission of Jesus as God with his people to save them from their sins. It is not just that God is present in Jesus to help his people."

delegation of all things to the Son (11:27) and the Son's unparalleled authority;[117] and (v), citing Isaiah 42 in Matthew 12:15-21, Matthew indicates that Jesus, the Servant, has a ministry to the Gentiles, who are already receptive to his message (cf. 1:3, 5-6; 2:1-2, 11; 4:15-16; 8:10-12; 15:28; 27:54); therefore, Jesus' followers anticipate being involved in a worldwide ministry to the nations (cf. 22:9; 24:14; 25:32).[118] Finally, Turner explores the significance of the text's "heaven and earth" language, noting that: (i) Matthew often spotlights the theological significance of the "earth,"[119] which must be salted and illumined;[120] and (ii) disciples long for the realities of heaven to be realized on earth (6:10), and the Father gives Jesus universal authority in both (28:18).[121]

Davies and Allison, not unlike most modern commentators, detect an allusion in the text to Daniel 7:13-14, and add that "the common affirmation, that the resurrected Lord has fulfilled or proleptically realized the promise of the Son of man's vindication, commends itself."[122]

R. T. France points out that some scholars dispute the allusion to Daniel in Matthew 28:18, perceiving that the Matthew text transcends the limits of the Daniel text.[123] Nonetheless, for France, "that Matthew's vision goes far beyond the Danielic model does not in the least conflict with Dan 7:14 being the source (or at least a source) of its language and imagery."[124] France also comments that: (i) by means of a "rather fulsome introductory clause" of the verse that is aimed at restoring the broken relationship with the disciples, Matthew emphasizes the climactic role of Jesus' speech and his response to the disciples' hesitation by employing a combination of three verbs—"came to" them, "spoke to" them, and

---

117. Turner, "Gospel of Matthew," 165-67.

118. Turner, "Gospel of Matthew," 171-72; Turner also emphasizes that: (i) Matthew is the only Gospel that uses the word 'church' (16:18; 18:17); and (ii) the community of the Messiah is formed from unexpected sources, which eventually creates tension between the Matthean Jesus' exclusive ministry to Israel (10:5-6; 15:24) and his subsequent mandate for global mission (24).

119. Turner, "Gospel of Matthew," 76-77; cf. 5:13, 18, 35; 6:10, 19; 9:6; 10:34; 11:25; 16:19; 18:18-19; 23:9; 24:30, 35; 28:18.

120. Turner, "Gospel of Matthew," 84; cf. "earth" (5:13; 6:10; 16:19; 18:18-19); "world" (5:14; 13:38; 24:14; 26:13).

121. Turner, "Gospel of Matthew," 100.

122. Davies and Allison Jr., *Matthew (III)*, 682-83.

123. France, *Matthew*, 1112 n. 22; see Bauer, *Structure of Matthew's Gospel*, 111-12.

124. France, *Matthew*, 1112-13 (cf. 395-98).

"said";[125] (ii) the Gospels inform their readers that Jesus' authority, which he derives from God and is the basis of his claim to be the Son of God, is the dominant impression of all aspects his ministry;[126] (iii) the realization of the future coming of the kingdom of God begins with the resurrected Christ's receipt of the power and dominion of the Son of Man;[127] and (iv) Jesus' vision of the future heavenly enthronement of the Son of Man (24:30) is achieved in 28:18 and leads to the gathering of his people from all over the earth, but the agents of the ingathering are not angels (24:31), but his own disciples (28:19–20).[128]

Robert H. Smith explains that "authority" is what Hellenistic religion promised to its adherents (Acts 8:19; 1 Cor 6:12; 8:9; 10:23; 2 Cor 10:8; 13:10), and is what qualifies teachers in Judaism to judge legal matters.[129] Jesus' universal authority is explained in part by the other three uses of "all" in 28:18–20, and what teachers and scribes saw at the time in Torah or Wisdom, and what priests saw in the temple, is what Matthew sees in Jesus.[130] Indeed, because of his authority, the Matthean Jesus says, "You have one teacher, one master" (23:8-10).[131]

While some scholars discuss Jesus' resurrection authority in terms of new authority vis-à-vis the vindication or reaffirmation of previously rejected authority, Craig Blomberg approaches the issue from the perspective of newly delegated authority, some of which was previously voluntarily relinquished (cf. Phil 2:6–8) by the Son of God at the time of his incarnation.[132]

Luz incorporates 28:18 into his writings in several ways. First, from a source-critical point of view, he compares Matthew's use of γῆ in this passage with other applications throughout the Gospel.[133] Second, on

---

125. France, *Matthew*, 1112.
126. France, "Jesus Christ," 568.
127. France, "Jesus Christ," 574.
128. France, *Matthew*, 1114.
129. Smith, *Matthew*, 336–37.
130. Smith, *Matthew*, 337.
131. Smith, *Matthew*, 337–38.
132. Blomberg, *Matthew*, 307; Walker, "Isaiah," 1–291, esp. 49, reminds that "the eternal Son was not born (i.e., did not have his beginning) that first Christmas, although a human child appeared at that time."
133. Luz, *Matthew 1–7*, 310 n. 10 considers the use of γῇ (6:10) without the article to be evidence against Matthean authorship of the Lord's Prayer (6:9–13), and claims that, although text-critically uncertain, 28:18 is to be regarded as one of Matthew's

the validity of the Torah, Luz rejects Balch's theory that there is a break between 5:17, 19 and 16:19 that is similar to the one between 10:5–6 and 28:18–20: "Jesus promises the disciples that after Easter they will have the freedom to 'loosen' 'even a great commandment, for example, circumcision.'"[134] Luz regards it improbable that 5:18b intends to place a time limit on the Torah's validity; rather, he proposes that "until heaven and earth pass away" focuses on universal time and the Torah will remain in force.[135] Third, concerning the risen Lord's universal authority: (i) the earthly Jesus' renunciation of power offered by the Satan (4:8–10) prefigures the authority of the risen Jesus over heaven and earth[136] and unfolds what obedience to God means;[137] (ii) Matthew's theology is to be measured by the standard of commandments of the risen Christ, whose authority extends to proclaiming judgment upon God's enemies (23:13–36), even if it seems to betray a previous command to love one's enemies (5:44);[138] (iii) because Christ is the Lord of the universe, one must go against the grain of Matthew's apocalyptic pessimism (24:4–28), which ignores the presence of Immanuel in the world;[139] (iv) Matthew's readers recall all they have read or heard of the earthly Jesus' power, which leads them to understand that next to the power of the risen Jesus no other power matters;[140] and (v) the ancient church understood the risen Jesus' claim to power in light of the doctrine of the Trinity.[141] Fourth, concerning Jesus' earthly demonstration of power: (i) the people are astonished because Jesus teaches with ἐξουσία (7:28–29), which is also seen in his

---

exceptions to the rule that γῆ is always determinate when it carries the meaning 'world' or 'land'; *Matthew 21–28*, 150–151 (cf. 150–151, 301, 620) regards ἐπὶ τῆς γῆς (23:35) similarly to be a Matthean redaction.

134. Luz, *Matthew 1–7*, 218 n. 74.

135. Luz, *Matthew 1–7*, 217–18; see also *Matthew 1–7*, 218–19 concerning the validity of the Torah and the complications of interpreting 5:18 christologically to mean that in Christ's death and resurrection everything predicted in the OT has happened.

136. Luz, *Matthew 1–7*, 153.

137. Luz, *Matthew 1–7*, 155; Bauer, "Son of God," 769–75, esp. 774, attributes Jesus' receipt of all authority from the Father to his obedience as Son until the end.

138. Luz, *Matthew 21–28*, 175.

139. Luz, *Matthew 21–28*, 206.

140. Luz, *Matthew 21–28*, 624.

141. According to Luz, *Matthew 21–28*, 625 the Chalcedonians solve the problem of the bestowal of power upon someone who always had the power by saying that 28:18b speaks of the "human nature of the Son of God that after his death is finally united with the Logos."

deeds (4:23:25) and will later be transferred to his disciples (10:1), which anticipates the risen Jesus' universal authority that he will receive from God;[142] (ii) forgiveness of sins is an important Matthean theme; Jesus forgives sins as the Son of Man with the last judgment of the world in mind (9:6), and the crowds are amazed not because Jesus heals the paralytic, but because God has given authority to "people" (i.e., the church) to forgive sins (9:8);[143] and (iii) Matthew's readers already know the answer to the religious leaders' presumptuous question about the source of Jesus' authority (21:23); they know that everything has been given to Jesus from the Father (11:27; cf. 28:18).[144] Fifth, as regards Jesus' granting of authority, Matthew's concern in 10:1-2, 5 is not with the constitution of the circle of the twelve apostles, but with Jesus' authorization of the Twelve, who share in his own authority, and which determines the church's activity. Matthew understands their power to be an expression of the power of the risen Lord, who remains with the church, and their mission to be the prototype of the continuing mission of the church.[145] Sixth, concerning the Matthean "Son of God" Christology, there is no distinction between "Son" and "Son of God" (cf. 11:25-27; 28:19).[146] Finally, on Matthew's "Son of Man" Christology, Luz: (i) discusses the distinction that scholarship makes between the "Son of Man" and "Son of God," along with opposing views to that claim;[147] (ii) examines alternatives for the interpretation of παραδίδοσθαι (11:27a);[148] (iii) expresses that the "kingdom of the Son of Man" (13:41) will not come about only with the Parousia, but already exists in the world;[149] it is "the reign of the exalted one over heaven and earth that he now makes visible primarily through the proclamation and the life of his disciples" in a community that practices and proclaims Jesus' commandments;[150] (iv) argues that, since many of Matthew's sayings about the coming Son of Man do not originate in Daniel 7, Matthew and his readers' knowledge of ὁ υἱὸς τοῦ ἀνθρώπου "was deepened with the aid

---

142. Luz, *Matthew 1-7*, 389-90.
143. Luz, *Matthew 8-20*, 28-29.
144. Luz, *Matthew 21-28*, 29.
145. Luz, *Matthew 8-20*, 66-67.
146. Luz, *Matthew 8-20*, 169; see also Matt 1:21-23; 2:15; 3:17; 4:1-11; 16:16-17; 17:5 for God's revelation of Jesus as his Son.
147. Luz, *Matthew 8-20*, 164-66 (see also 165 n. 81).
148. Luz, *Matthew 8-20*, 166.
149. Luz, *Matthew 8-20*, 434-35.
150. Luz, *Matthew 8-20*, 269-70.

of the Book of Daniel but did not primarily originate there";[151] (v) claims that Jesus is Son of Man in his total activity (16:13), earthly and heavenly; the "Son of Man" therefore is a horizontal title that describes Jesus' way through history, and it is a universal title that designates Jesus' path to rule and judge the entire world;[152] (vi) asserts that 22:41–46 reminds Matthew's readers of the entire Matthean Christology—Messiah, Son of Man, Son of God, the "God-with-us" to whom the Father has given everything, and Lord—and helps them understand the larger scope of his Davidic sonship;[153] (vii) emphasizes the horizontal (Son of Man) and vertical (Son of God) dimensions of the Matthean Christology;[154] and (viii) emphasizes the destiny of the Son of Man—temporarily accused, abused, condemned, and crucified—to be the exalted judge of the world who is seated at the right hand of God (26:64).[155]

Scholars up to the mid-twentieth century employ the text of 28:18 variedly with regard to Jesus' authority, including: (i) making a connection between God's absolute authority to heal "former acts of ignorance" with the unlimited authority that is given to the resurrected Jesus (Herm. Sim. 5.7.3 [60.3]);[156] (ii) correlating Jesus' absolution of the thief on the cross (Luke 23:43) with the removal of the flaming sword that was placed to guard the tree of life and the gates of paradise, which only the one with universal power could remove;[157] and (iii) commenting that despite Christ's claim to universal authority, "even to this day he does not yet possess all power on earth . . . For example, he does not yet rule over those who are sinners. When all power is given to him, his power will be complete, and all things will be subject to him."[158]

---

151. Luz, *Matthew 8–20*, 389–90.

152. Luz, *Matthew 8–20*, 391.

153. Luz, *Matthew 21–28*, 90–91.

154. Luz, *Matthew 21–28*, 91.

155. Luz, *Matthew 21–28*, 430.

156. Lake, *Apostolic Fathers in Greek*, 168–70 re Shepherd of Hermas; see Tertullian, *Against Praxeas*, 2.7.16 (ANF 3:611–612); *Against Praxeas*, 2.7.17 (ANF 3:612–613); and *Works*, 279–80.

157. Just, *Luke*, 365 re Origen.

158. Wilken, Christman, and Hollerich, *Isaiah: Interpreted*, 66 re Origen; A selection of other early scholars who contribute their thoughts on the theme of Jesus' authority in relation to 28:18 include Novatian, *Trinity*, 76; Hilary of Poitiers, *De. Trin.*, 11.29 (NPNF2 9a:210–212); *Comm. Matt.*, 285–86; Athanasius, *C. Ar.*, 3.26 (NPNF2 4:407–408); *C. Ar.*, 3.36 (NPNF2 4:413–414); *C. Ar.*, 4.6 (NPNF2 4:435).

Matthew 28:19

Bauer asserts that the nature of Christ's universal authority is dynamic, lunging into the present age to achieve God's redemptive purposes through the church by means of the mandate expressed in 28:19–20a, the substance of which is represented by the finite verb of the passage (μαθητεύσατε, "make disciples"), preceded by an aorist participle (πορευθέντες, "going"), and followed by two present participles (βαπτίζοντες, "baptizing"; and διδάσκοντες, "teaching").[159] "The disciples are to make disciples of others in the same way that Jesus made disciples of them throughout the Gospel." Bauer bases this viewpoint on: (i) the etymological links between μαθητεύω, its noun form, μαθητής, and μανθάνω; (ii) Matthew's comparison of Jesus' earthly ministry with that of his disciples; and (iii) the connection between the eleven μαθηταὶ (28:16) and μαθητεύω (28:19).[160] Jesus models for the disciples what making disciples is to look like—teaching, preaching, healing, correcting, warning, encouraging, and sharing ministry tasks with them—which "may form, at least in part and in some measure, the content of discipling in 28:19."[161] Jesus is, however, not just a model for making disciples, or a facilitator of discipleship, but he is "the one final discipler" who initiates all discipleship (cf. 4:18–22; 9:9; 11:28–30), which is an offer to enter into relationship with himself.[162]

The scope of the discipling work is πάντα τὰ ἔθνη ("all the nations"), which refers to persons within these nations and not to nation-states or people-groups.[163] It represents an expansion of the ministry of Jesus

---

159. Bauer, "Mission in Matthew's Gospel," 251.

160. Bauer, "Mission in Matthew's Gospel," 251; see "μαθητεύω," BDAG, 609; "μαθητής," BDAG, 609–10; "μανθάνω," BDAG, 615; and "μαθητής," LSJ, 1072.

161. Bauer, "Mission in Matthew's Gospel," 251–52; furthermore, "those who are made disciples will form local congregations characterized by nurture, discipline, and forgiveness (5:1–7:28; 12:46–50; chapter 18), in analogy to the circle of the twelve that Jesus established during his earthly ministry."

162. Bauer, "Mission in Matthew's Gospel," 252; so also Keener, *Matthew*, 719.

163. Bauer, "Mission in Matthew's Gospel," 252 n. 69 (so also Keener, *Matthew*, 719; and Hagner, *Matthew 14–28*, 887); see Brands, "Kingdom Commission," 89–90, who asserts that "the common rendering of 'make disciples of all nations' (Matt 28:19) most naturally yields the particular, or constricted, understanding of making individual persons drawn from the populations of the nations into individual disciples. While it can be demonstrated easily from Matthew's gospel that the heart of this mission includes an intensely personal purpose, this rendering of Matt 28:19 can limit the object of mission to an individualism in which the concept of nations bears no further

and his disciples beyond Israel to "all nations," and, while it emphasizes Gentiles, it should not be interpreted to mean an end of the mission to the Jews,[164] since Matthew sometimes uses ἔθνος in the sense of "nation" (e.g., 21:43; 24:7, 9, 14; 25:32) as opposed to "Gentiles" (e.g., 4:15; 6:32; 10:5, 18; 12:18, 21; 20:19, 25), and the Matthean Jesus refers to a mission to Israel in the post-Easter period (e.g., 10:23; 23:34–36).[165] Matthew repeatedly juxtaposes Jewish particularism and Gentile inclusion "to indicate that from the beginning God has intended that all peoples would have the opportunity of God's salvation, but that such opportunity would come specifically through Israel."[166] This explains the temporal priority

---

relevance. Such mission would tend to focus only on isolated individuals. It would follow that mission carries little or no hope for broader social or cultural crises... The object here is not simply individuals, which would be represented more naturally in Greek by ἄνθρωπος (*anthrōpos*, human being/person). Rather, the text requires that we take seriously the fact that it is the nations who are identified as the object of mission."

164. Bauer, *Gospel of the Son of God*, 179 n. 38 interacts with Axel von Dobbeler's argument that both the restrictive command of 10:5–6 and the demand of universal mission in 28:16–20 remain in force because the mission in chapter 10 pertains to Israel and the Commission pertains to Gentiles, both of which are to continue until the end. Matthew, according to von Dobbeler, calls for two separate missions: (i) a "restitution of Israel," which involves an affirmation of the faith that has always been theirs; and (ii) the conversion of the Gentiles through a process of discipleship, which requires them to turn away from paganism to faith in Israel's God, as Jesus has fulfilled it; see also von Dobbeler, "Die Restitution Israels," 18–44 on the major views regarding the relationship between Matthew's missionary discourse (esp. the restriction of 10:5–6) and the Commission.

165. Ezeogu, "Great Commission," 179–180 translates ἔθνη (28:19a) as "Gentiles" for two reasons: "Firstly, the issue at stake is whether or not Gentiles could become disciples. That Jews could become disciples was not in question at all, it is taken for granted. So we could translate ἔθνη as 'Gentiles' and still maintain inclusivity and universal access to discipleship. Secondly, ἔθνη is best understood as individuals ('Gentiles') and not as collectivities ('nations'). The ἔθνη in verse 19 are subjects of baptism. 'Gentiles,' therefore, is preferable to 'nations' since you could baptize a Gentile but how do you baptize a nation?"; see also Levine, "To All the Gentiles," 146, who posits that "Hare and Harrington are thus correct in translating 28:19 as 'make disciples of all the Gentiles.' This specific rendering of *ethne* deliberately recalls not only the gentile characters throughout the gospel, it also directly expands the initial mission charge. Whereas Hare and Harrington are thus correct in translating 28:19 with 'Gentiles' rather than 'nations,' they overstate their case by concluding that Matthew abrogates the mission to the Jews."

166. Bauer, "Mission in Matthew's Gospel," 252–53 highlights Matthew's emphasis on Jesus being the "son of Abraham" (1:1) through whom "all the nations of the earth will be blessed" (Gen 12:3; 18:18; 22:18; cf. Matt 1:1–17; 2:1–12; 8:11; 10:18; 12:18–21; 15:21–28; 21:43; 22:1–10; 24:14 [cf. 26:13]; 26:28 [cf. 20:28]; 27:54).

given to the exclusive evangelization of Israel (10:5-6), prior to fulfilling her global mission in 28:18-20.[167]

Bauer describes the aorist participle πορευθέντες as a "participle of attendant circumstance" that should be understood as coordinate with the main verb and as a command—"Go and make disciples." Disciples can accomplish their task of making disciples "*only* by moving away from where they are to the space inhabited by others."[168] Such movement involves crossing the geographical, cultural, religious, and ethnic boundaries that often separate human beings. Matthew's repeated reference to the gospel being preached throughout "the whole world" (24:14; 26:13) requires such movement. Elaborating on the idea of going, Bauer concludes that the servants of Jesus, the ruler of the world, must pursue "an aggressive conquest of the peoples of the earth through a discipling that involves going to them."[169]

Bauer opines that βαπτίζοντες and διδάσκοντες are two instrumental participles that spell out the substance of the main verb, μαθητεύσατε.[170] Supporting this view is Matthew's use of μαθητεύω (13:52) in the sense

---

167. Bauer, "Mission in Matthew's Gospel," 254.

168. Bauer, "Mission in Matthew's Gospel," 254 (my emphasis) (cf. *Gospel of the Son of God*, 233); see also Wallace, *Greek Grammar*, 640-45, esp. 640, on "the attendant circumstance participle [being] used to communicate an action that, in some sense, is coordinate with the finite verb . . . It is translated as a finite verb connected to the main verb by 'and'"; and Keener, *Matthew*, 718-19 about "making disciples" involving "going" (cf. 10:7), which is presupposed (i.e., "having gone") because the participle is aorist and may represent part of the aorist imperative command, "make disciples."

169. Bauer, "Mission in Matthew's Gospel," 254; cf. *Gospel of the Son of God*, 215 who argues, in the context of 25:31-46, that by the end of the age the church will be found among the nations of the world (cf. 24:14; 28:18).

170. Bauer, "Mission in Matthew's Gospel," 254 (see Porter, *Idioms*, 192; and Wallace, *Greek Grammar*, 628-30); contra Malina, "Literary Structure and Form," 87-103, esp. 90-91, who opines that both participles meet the conditions of a "participial imperative," and the command of 28:19-20a is paratactic—i.e., "make disciples and baptize and teach" (so also Meier, "Matthew," 4:637); Brown and Roberts, *Matthew*, 263-264, 473, France, *Matthew*, 1115, Smith, *Matthew*, 338-339, Blomberg, *Matthew*, 431, and Luz, *Matthew 21-28*, 625 concur with Bauer's assessment that "baptizing" and "teaching" indicate the means of discipling the nations; however, Davies and Allison Jr., *Matthew (III)*, 686 see a partial filling out by "baptizing" and "teaching" only; meanwhile, Turner, *Matthew*, 689-690, Tennent, *World Missions*, 138, and Keener, *Matthew*, 718, 720 are of the view that "make disciples" comprises all three elements of "going," "baptizing," and "teaching"; and Carter, "Acts," 492 reckons that the Commission sets forth a twofold objective: "make disciples" and "teach" observance of Jesus' commands.

of "teaching" or "training,"[171] and the Matthean Jesus' use of teaching as a major disciple-making technique. Bauer also claims that "'baptizing' and 'teaching' have such broad ramifications that *most* of the aspects of discipling that Matthew presents otherwise in his Gospel are herein included";[172] however, Bauer does not specify which aspects of discipling that Matthew presents otherwise in his Gospel are not included in "baptizing" and "teaching" (28:19b–20a).[173] Such elaboration would be important if I am to determine whether "baptizing" and "teaching" spell out the substance of "make disciples" as Bauer contends. To be clear, Bauer agrees that preaching, for example, is a significant discipling practice that the Matthean Jesus models,[174] and he also acknowledges that preaching is distinct from teaching (and most certainly also baptizing);[175] therefore, preaching (and possibly other practices also) is an important aspect of the content of discipling in 28:19 that is not included within the broad ramifications of baptizing and teaching. This means that the two instrumental participles, by themselves, may not fully explain the meaning of μαθητεύσατε.

Bauer recognizes that 28:19 makes the only reference in Matthew's Gospel to Christian baptism, and that the nondevelopment of its meaning there suggests that Matthew's implied reader brings his[176] understanding of baptism to bear upon this statement.[177] For Bauer, however, "baptizing" "in the name of the Father, and the Son, and the Holy Spirit" (i) is

171. Bauer, "Mission in Matthew's Gospel," 254; Brown and Roberts, *Matthew*, 135 comment that the unusual combination of a 'scribe' and one 'discipled for the kingdom' invites the reader to adopt a learning stance toward Jesus' kingdom teachings (11:29).

172. Bauer, "Mission in Matthew's Gospel," 254–55 (my emphasis).

173. Bauer, "Mission in Matthew's Gospel," 254 comments, but without elaborating, that "One might object that the Gospel of Matthew in its entirety indicates that discipling involves more than 'baptizing' and 'teaching.' And this claim contains some truth."

174. Bauer, "Mission in Matthew's Gospel," 251.

175. Bauer, "Mission in Matthew's Gospel," 254 n. 82 (cf. 4:23; 9:35; 11:1).

176. I have already footnoted in chapter 1 of this book that the implied reader in Matthew is male; for this reason, I use the masculine pronoun throughout my work to refer to the implied reader or "the reader."

177. Bauer, "Mission in Matthew's Gospel," 255 observes that as one looks to the rest of the NT and (with qualification and care) to John's baptism (3:1–17) to appreciate the significance of baptism in 28:19, one finds that Christian baptism involves various factors, including response to preaching, confession of sin, repentance, faith in Christ, forgiveness of sins, reception of the Holy Spirit, and incorporation into the faith community.

an act of transfer that moves someone from being "in Adam" to being "in Christ"; (ii) means "to be brought existentially into the sphere of, and in submission to, the active powerful presence of the Father, Son, and Spirit, so that one belongs to the Father, Son, and Spirit (e.g., 1 Cor 1:10–17)"; and (iii) represents the initiation into discipleship, whereas "teaching" refers to the ongoing process of discipling.[178]

Brown and Roberts utilize 28:19 to make various claims. On the Holy Spirit, they assert that: (i) the Spirit's involvement in the early chapters of Matthew is significant (1:18, 20; 3:11, 16; 4:1), but is mentioned relatively little thereafter (10:20; 28:19);[179] (ii) the Spirit, who dwells among Christians, was known from the inception of the church along with Christ and the Father, and converts were consistently baptized "in the name of the Father and the Son and the Holy Spirit," a practice believed to be derived directly from the Matthean community;[180] (iii) John the Baptist's reference to Jesus baptizing persons ἐν πνεύματι ἁγίῳ (3:11) is resolved by the risen Jesus' command to his disciples in the Commission;[181] (iv) Matthew emphasizes Jesus' obedience to and reliance on the Father as well as his empowerment by the Spirit for ministry, which provides a pattern for Jesus' disciples to follow;[182] and (v) the language of "proceeding" and "sending" in relation to the Holy Spirit contributes to a focus on who sent or proceeded from whom, resulting in the Spirit becoming "the subordinate and even overlooked third."[183]

On Trinitarian theology, Brown and Roberts explain that: (i) Matthew's baptismal or Trinitarian formula plays an important role in the development of early Christian theology, as theologians struggled to define the nature of God;[184] (ii) the practice of baptism along Trinitar-

---

178. Bauer, "Mission in Matthew's Gospel," 255; see also Bauer, *Gospel of the Son of God*, 233, who notes that ὄνομα ("name") is singular, although it is followed by Father, Son, and Holy Spirit, which suggests a fundamental unity among them.

179. Brown and Roberts, *Matthew*, 102; later references to the Spirit in Matthew are 12:18, 28, 31, 32; 22:43; additionally, *Matthew*, 319, 431 n. 116 detects that the Spirit is most active in Matthew's storyline when the main character, Jesus, is most passive—in his infancy and prior to the inauguration of his ministry.

180. Brown and Roberts, *Matthew*, 316–17.

181. Brown and Roberts, *Matthew*, 42, 322.

182. Brown and Roberts, *Matthew*, 326; Jesus is empowered in his messianic ministry by the Spirit of God, and the authority he displays is evidence, not of his divinity, but of his inauguration of the kingdom in the power of the Spirit (*Matthew*, 45).

183. Brown and Roberts, *Matthew*, 431.

184. Brown and Roberts, *Matthew*, 398–99.

ian lines appears to be firmly established by the time Matthew writes his Gospel; the lack of an explanation about it in 28:19 suggests that the author assumes the reader's understanding and practice;[185] (iii) the text of 3:16–17 provides a first glimpse of a Trinitarian theology that prefigures the baptismal formula;[186] and (iv) the long tradition of monotheism that is echoed in the Jewish Shema (Deut 6:4) had to be reconciled with 28:19 and numerous other NT texts that announce Jesus' divine origin and identity.[187]

Concerning postcolonial perspectives, Brown and Roberts raise awareness about: (i) the ways the Commission has been used in recent centuries that appear to clash with the purposes of the Matthean Jesus by focusing more on colonial expansion than on discipling the indigenous church;[188] and (ii) an undue emphasis by postcolonial interpreters on teaching over other activities, such as social justice, in traditional interpretations and applications of the Commission; whereas, Matthew highlights justice, mercy, and covenant loyalty (23:23; cf. 9:13; 12:7, 18–21; 25:31–46), which should not be isolated from activity of teaching, which is a component of discipling and is not the whole of it.[189]

Nolland emphasizes that, while Jewish itinerant mission even to fellow Jews is something of a novelty (23:15), Jesus' final Commission to his disciples is based on the conviction that a fresh initiative of God is underway and it will be proclaimed by Christian disciples.[190] Matthew does not innovate Jesus' universal mission, as the equivalent material in Luke 24 (esp. v. 47) demonstrates. Instead, Matthew and Luke "merge

---

185. Brown and Roberts, *Matthew*, 322–23.
186. Brown and Roberts, *Matthew*, 45.
187. Brown and Roberts, *Matthew*, 399–400.
188. Brown and Roberts, *Matthew*, 451–52; some authors have utilized language associated with "conquest" in their writings, including: (i) Hutcheson, "Reformed Presbyterian Church," 1013 portrays the members of the Presbyterian Reformed Church as conquerors, who, because of Christ's "uncontrolled dominion over all things," are destined to subdue their enemies in heathen countries; (ii) Warfield, *Lord of Glory*, 94–96, who writes that members of the Presbyterian Reformed Church are destined to subdue their enemies in heathen countries; and more recently (iii) Bauer, "Mission in Matthew's Gospel," 254, who comments that the servants of Jesus, the ruler of the world, need to pursue "an aggressive conquest of the peoples of the earth through a discipling that involves going to them."
189. Brown and Roberts, *Matthew*, 453.
190. Nolland, *Matthew*, 1266.

things together, some of which clearly came to be recognized as the will of the risen Jesus only with the passage of time."[191]

Turner speaks about Matthew's use of οὖν to emphasize that "'Universal Lordship means universal mission' . . . Having been exalted, Jesus is now in a position to send out his disciples in mission. Mission is possible because Jesus is potent."[192] Regarding Jesus' divine Sonship, Turner reckons that: (i) the disciples' worship and confession of Jesus as the Son of God (14:33) and Peter's answer concerning Jesus' identity (16:16) anticipate 28:19;[193] (ii) Jesus' transcendent Sonship is prominently featured in Matthew as well as OT texts;[194] and (iii) the soldiers' understanding of Jesus' divine Sonship (27:54), in stark contrast with the mocking of the crowds and the religious leaders (27:40, 43), paves the way for his final Commission and the requirement of confessing his Sonship in baptism.[195] Finally, Turner outlines the implications of a *preterist* understanding of 24:29–31, including what it means to equate the "sending of the angels to gather the elect" with the "mission of the church in discipling all the nations."[196]

Davies and Allison contrast the word given by the religious authorities to the guards (28:11–15) with "the word of the kingdom" (13:19) and Jesus' proclamation in 28:19–20.[197]

Blomberg comments that no greater challenge faces Jesus' followers than their obedience to the charge to make disciples in every part of the world.[198] Jesus anticipates their living in community and provides for their maintenance by giving rules for community discipline (18:15–20) and a commission to bring new members thereinto.[199]

---

191. Nolland, *Matthew*, 1266–67.
192. Turner, *Matthew*, 689.
193. Turner, "Gospel of Matthew," 205, 220.
194. For example: Matthew 1:23; 2:15; 3:17; 4:3, 6; 7:21; 8:29; 11:25–27; 16:16; 17:5; 21:37–39; 22:2; 24:36; 26:29, 39, 42, 53, 63–64; 27:40, 43, 46, 54; 28:19; Old Testament texts: Ps 45:6–7; 110:1; Isa 9:6; 11:1, 10; Jer 23:5–6; 33:15–16; Zech 12:10 (Turner, "Gospel of Matthew," 289).
195. Turner, "Gospel of Matthew," 368.
196. Turner, "Gospel of Matthew," 315–16; "preterist"—adj. pertaining to a person who holds that the prophecies of the Apocalypse have been already fulfilled.
197. Davies and Allison Jr., *Matthew (III)*, 672.
198. Blomberg, *Matthew*, 21–22.
199. Blomberg, *Matthew*, 33.

Luz makes several noteworthy claims about the present text. On baptism, he comments that: (i) Matthew's theology is grounded in the worship of his community, and he offers as evidence the Lord's Prayer (6:9–13), the Eucharist (26:26–28), and the baptism formula that probably reflects the church's use of title Son of God, which is Matthew's most important title of confession (14:33; 16:16; 27:54; cf. Mark 15:39);[200] (ii) the Matthean community's understanding of the Torah, their marked distance from Pharisaic-protorabbinic Judaism, and their celebration of similar rituals to Gentile Christian communities—including the Lord's Supper and the baptism of new members in the name of the triune God—demonstrate the kind of Jewish Christian community from which Matthew's Gospel emerged;[201] (iii) by the baptism with the Spirit, which is not the same as the baptism with fire that speaks of annihilating judgment (3:10–12), Matthew sees Jesus himself as the bearer of the Spirit (12:18, 28) and the triadic baptism formula is commanded by him;[202] (iv) attempts have been made to integrate the baptism of Jesus (3:13–17) into other Christologies, including being a witness for the Trinity, being a material inauguration of Christian baptism, being connected with Jesus' atoning death or incarnation, and being associated with salvation history, since Christ opens heaven for his followers;[203] (v) baptism in the triadic name is a confession of the whole church that expresses the new identity of the baptized persons and reminds them that these three names were "proclaimed" over the persons being baptized;[204] and (vi) since the baptismal command does not go back to Jesus himself, and, contrary to John 4:1, baptism as a sacrament cannot be traced back to Jesus, then one's authority for Christian baptism is the church and tradition because baptism was probably practiced everywhere in the church from the beginning and was legitimated secondarily by the risen Lord in 28:19.[205]

---

200. Luz, *Matthew 1–7*, 43–44.

201. Luz, *Matthew 1–7*, 48.

202. Luz, *Matthew 1–7*, 138.

203. Luz, *Matthew 1–7*, 145; Dau, "Baptism (Lutheran View)," 425 argues that the evidence shows there to be no essential difference between John's baptism and the baptism which the risen Christ (28:19).

204. Luz, *Matthew 21–28*, 631–32; Motyer, "Name," 799–802 explains that baptism in the name of the Trinity emphasizes the totality of the divine nature, purpose, and blessedness designed for the recipient.

205. Luz, *Matthew 21–28*, 633.

On the Gentile mission, Luz advances that: (i) Matthew's decision to champion this mission is one of his most important concerns and is demonstrated by the rupture between the mission commandment of the risen Lord (28:16-20) and that of the earthly Jesus (10:5-6);[206] (ii) Matthew's presentation of statements that limit salvation to Israel and are negative towards Gentiles, and his presentation of other testimony with positive judgments towards the Gentiles, may be explained in one of five ways;[207] (iii) Jesus begins his ministry in "Galilee of the Gentiles," or, more specifically, "Israelite Galilee," prefiguring the movement of salvation to the Gentiles, which for Matthew is a biblical, prophetic perspective;[208] (iv) the explanation that "not giv[ing] what is holy to dogs" and "not throw[ing] your pearls before pigs" (7:6) means that "refraining from proclaiming the law and its 'pearls' to the Gentiles" is not in keeping with Matthean theology, and the saying might possibly have been included by Matthew because it appeared in his copy of Q;[209] (v) Matthew's reference to the Gentiles moves outside the framework of the disciples' preaching to the Jews and reminds the readers of what they are presently experiencing (cf. 10:17-20);[210] (vi) the Lord responds to Israel's unbelief by calling the Gentiles (28:16-20), which Matthew signals in advance with the testimony of two Gentiles against Israel (12:41-42);[211] (vii); the Parable of the Two Sons (21:28-32) polemicizes only against Israel's leaders (21:45) and not against Israel as a whole; the interpretation that Israel, because of its lack of faith, will miss the kingdom of God and the Gentiles will enter therein because of their obedience is possible only later in Matthew's narrative (22:8-10; 27:25; 28:11-20);[212] (viii) in light of his interpretation of the Woes Discourse (ch. 23), Matthew's Jewish Christian

---

206. Luz, *Matthew 1–7*, 50.

207. Luz, *Matthew 1–7*, 52-53 presents the five hypotheses as follows: (i) the Gospel of Matthew is representative of the Petrine church tradition in Antioch; (ii) the Matthean community is rooted in a community that is culturally and ecumenically open, comprising Jews and Gentiles; (iii) Matthew's community is still within the walls of Judaism and its conflict with the Pharisees and scribes is an inner-Jewish conflict; (iv) Matthew is already looking back on a rupture between his church and the local synagogues; and (v) the Gospel of Matthew is reflecting on the story of Jesus and on the separation of church and synagogue from the theology-of-history perspective.

208. Luz, *Matthew 1–7*, 158.

209. Luz, *Matthew 1–7*, 354-56.

210. Luz, *Matthew 8–20*, 88-89.

211. Luz, *Matthew 8–20*, 217-18.

212. Luz, *Matthew 21–28*, 32-33.

community was probably compelled to separate from the synagogue in the not-too-distant past;[213] (ix) the absence of an article in παρὰ Ἰουδαίοις (28:15b) is "unusual and hardly insignificant" and recognizes that not all "the Jews" believe the rumor and that "all Jews" are not being contrasted with "all the nations" (πάντα τὰ ἔθνη) at this point in the narrative;[214] and (x) the Commission, which is already underway for the Matthean church (24:9–14), is "fundamentally universal" and does not exclude a continuing mission to Israel, but "Matthew probably no longer has great hopes for it (22:8–10; 23:39–24:2; and 28:15)."[215]

On discipleship, Luz links Jesus' first call for persons to follow him (4:18–22) with his first commission to the Twelve to fish for people (10:5–16), and later with the Parable of the Fishnet (13:47–50), where the expression is understood to refer to missionary activity, and finally with the Commission, which clarifies what Jesus means.[216] While Luz does not use the term "inclusio," he reasons that Matthew's readers are likely to perceive "Follow me, and I will make you fishers of men" (4:19) and "Go therefore and make disciples of all nations" (28:19) as bookends for the intervening portion of the Gospel. Luz also affirms that Matthew's readers probably understand "the lowliest of my brothers" (25:40, Luz's translation) to mean itinerant radicals who are outsiders and poor, who depend on hospitality as they face trials and risk their lives (ch. 10; cf. 28:19).[217]

Meier perceives salvation history to be a component of Matthew's process view of kingdom, which he orders into three major periods: (i) the Law and the prophets, which pointed forward to and prophesied the time of Jesus (11:13); (ii) the earthly Jesus, during which time Jesus was "sent only to the lost sheep of the house of Israel" (15:24) and enjoined the Twelve to observe the same restriction (10:5–6); and (iii) the time of the church, which is marked by different rules for mission (28:19–20).

---

213. Luz, *Matthew 21–28*, 168–74 perceives such proof to be Matthew's: (i) "frequent and emphatic references to 'their' (or 'your') synagogues, 'their' scribes,' and 'your house' (23:38)"; (ii) emphasis on "the connection of the hostile scribes, chief priests, and elders with the nation Israel (2:4; 21:23; 26:3, 47; 27:1)"; (iii) threats of judgment to Israel (23:34–39; cf. 27:24–25); and (iv) climax of the Gospel by contrasting 'Jews' and 'Gentiles' (28:11–15, 16–20).

214. Luz, *Matthew 21–28*, 611–12.

215. Luz, *Matthew 21–28*, 628–31.

216. Luz, *Matthew 1–7*, 161–63.

217. Luz, *Matthew 21–28*, 279–81.

This outline of salvation history "aids Matthew in resolving the tension between his 'conservative' Jewish-Christian and 'liberal' gentile-Christian traditions."[218] It is Matthew's task to reinterpret and synthesize the competing traditions of his community and to provide a smooth transition from a Jewish past to a Gentile future. He achieves this by preserving both "new things and old" (13:52)—extolling Peter as the "rock" on which he builds his church (16:18–19), while at the same time being wary of the trappings of power and titles (23:1–12).[219]

Powell and colleagues utilize the Commission text to highlight: (i) the elements of Christian worship found in the NT, including the chief rituals of baptism (28:19; Rom 6:1–11) and the eucharistic meal (Mark 14:16–26; 1 Cor 11:23–26);[220] (ii) that while some eschatological expectations expressed in the Synoptic Gospels had not been fulfilled at the time of writing, some events had occurred or were occurring—e.g., the gospel was being preached throughout the nations;[221] and (iii) that God's identification as "Father" is prominent in the Gospels, where writers present him as a caring parent and an authority figure whose unilateral decisions are to be respected by the entire family of believers (cf. Matt 23:9).[222]

Mark D. Futato employs 28:19 against the backdrop of the book of Psalms to highlight: (i) the coming judgment of the earth by the Lord (Ps 98:7–9), who has commissioned Christians to make disciples in a world that is not yet in right order;[223] (ii) the hope and prayer of the ancients for the well-being of the individual, the family, the city, and the nation, which is now expanded because of the scope of the new covenant to include the blessing of all nations (Ps 128:5–6; cf. 72:17);[224] (iii) that the sovereign Lord took one nation to be a "special treasure" for himself to ultimately bless all nations in the fullness of time (Ps 135:4–18; cf. Ps 47:9; Gen

---

218. Meier, "Matthew," 4:639.

219. Meier, "Antioch," 34–35; so also Wogaman, "Faith and Discipleship," 111, who opines in the context of Matt 13:52 that among NT writings "the Gospel of Matthew is especially careful to avoid the impression that the inherited traditions did not matter [cf. 5:17, 21–22, 27–28, 31–32]." For Wogaman, however, "we have encountered in scripture the basis of dramatic new forms of obedience to the God whom we meet in Christ."

220. Powell, "Worship, New Testament," 1391–92.

221. Hiers and Powell, "Eschatology," 254–56.

222. Kingsbury and Powell, "Lord's Prayer," 566–67.

223. Futato, "Psalms," 316.

224. Futato, "Psalms," 391.

12:3);²²⁵ and (iv) that it was always God's intention that Israel would be the channel through which Scripture's revelation of himself would go to the nations (Ps 147:12–20).²²⁶

Eckhard J. Schnabel submits that: (i) Jesus' commission to go to "all nations" probably reminded his disciples about the geographical and ethnographical implications of the table of nations in Genesis 10 because of its ongoing significance in Israelite and Jewish tradition as a valid description of the world;²²⁷ (ii) noncanonical and patristic texts of the second century CE still reflect awareness of the worldwide missionary program of the church that one sees in the Gospels and in Acts;²²⁸ however, church(es) of the second and third centuries seem not to have had an operating program of world mission;²²⁹ and (iii) despite scholars' inclination to determine the relationship between 24:14 and 28:19, one may safely conclude that "the timing of Jesus' second coming does not depend upon the missionary activity of the church or upon the obedience of Christians to the Commission";²³⁰ yet, the command to "make disciples of all the nations" is in fulfillment of the previous prediction of worldwide evangelism.²³¹

Wilkins recognizes that μαθητεύσατε implies both a call to discipleship and the process of becoming a disciple, which he links to baptism and teaching—"the activities through which the new disciple grows in discipleship."²³² The Gospel writers show how Jesus teaches, corrects, admonishes, supports, comforts, and restores his disciples, and Wilkins quite rightly acknowledges that, in turn, the disciples become examples of what Jesus wants to do for the church.²³³ The Matthean disciples are

---

225. Futato, "Psalms," 403–4.

226. Futato, "Psalms," 433–34.

227. Schnabel, *Early Christian Mission*, 1:364–65; see Schnabel, "Mission," 754.

228. Schnabel, "Mission," 770.

229. Schnabel, "Mission," 771 cites four possible reasons: (i) the conviction that world mission was the task of the twelve apostles given by Christ (28:18–20; Acts 1:8); (ii) the idea that conversion of people was the sovereign work of God; (iii) the missionary commission of the Lord had already been fulfilled with the universal geographic distribution of Christians; and (iv) the reasoning that the primary task of the churches was their holy appearance before the world.

230. Schnabel, *Early Christian Mission*, 1:367.

231. Schnabel, "Mission," 753.

232. Wilkins, "Discipleship," 188.

233. Wilkins, "Discipleship," 188.

not portrayed as models of special Christians, but in their own role as disciples they are paradigms for all future disciples,[234] just as the Lord in his earthly life modeled disciple-making for them.

Thomas D. Lea observes that there is no specific form for the ordination ceremony provided by the NT, but he refers to the Matthean Commission and the early church's prayer and laying on of hands (Acts 13:3) as the two closest examples thereof.[235] "The work of an evangelist" (2 Tim 4:5) involves spreading the gospel, and while some Christians may have this gift more evidently than others, "witnessing" is the responsibility of all believers, not just ordained leaders, as the Commission and the book of Acts explain.[236]

W. H. T. Dau claims that: (i) the addition of the Word of God to the external element of "the water" makes baptism a sacrament;[237] (ii) the effects of baptism are regeneration, remission of sins, establishment of a spiritual union with Christ, and the sanctifying gifts of the Holy Spirit, all of which are supported by Christ's absolute authority and his personal presence;[238] (iii) baptism is universal in scope and must incorporate all persons regardless of nationality, race, age, sex, social or civil status (cf. Col 3:11; 1 Cor 12:13);[239] and (iv) baptism's all-embracing nature therefore begs the question, "Why should infants not be baptized?"[240]

Charles W. Carter perceives Pentecost to be evidence of: (i) the culmination of the divine plan of redemption, (ii) the preparation of the disciples to receive the Holy Spirit, and (iii) the beginning of the worldwide witness of Christ by his disciples.[241] On speaking in other tongues (cf. Acts 2:4), Carter argues that it is the work of the Holy Spirit in the lives of the disciples that initiates and facilitates the great missionary evangelistic program to which Christ commissions his disciples.[242] The gift of tongues at Pentecost, which makes possible the proclamation of the gospel

---

234. Wilkins, "Discipleship," 188.

235. Lea, "1 Timothy," 141–43.

236. Lea, "1 Timothy," 245–46.

237. Dau, "Baptism," 1:423–24.

238. Dau, "Baptism," 1:424.

239. Dau, "Baptism," 1:424.

240. Dau, "Baptism," 1:425; early proponents of infant baptism included Zwingli, Luther, Calvin, and Owen; whereas, Menno Simon was an outspoken critic thereof.

241. Carter, "Acts," 504.

242. Carter, "Acts," 726.

message in different languages, anticipates the fulfillment of the Commission of Christ.[243]

Scholars up to the mid-twentieth century utilize the text of 28:19 in a variety of ways. On foreign mission, one scholar explains that prophets are without honor in their own country (13:57), so Jesus' apostles leave Israel as they are commanded by the Lord (28:19; Acts 1:18).[244] Concerning the sacrament of baptism, some scholars: (i) correlate the baptismal formula with the unity of the Trinity—"not unto one having three names, nor into three who became incarnate, but into three possessed of equal honor";[245] (ii) utilize hidden traces of the formula, even if not the full formula, in their works;[246] and (iii) argue that persons who have been washed in the name of the Lord Jesus Christ ought not to be rebaptized.[247] Regarding the Trinity, certain scholars: (i) identify the Spirit who descends upon Christ as a dove (3:16; cf. Mark 1:10; Luke 3:22; John 1:32) as the one about whom the prophet Isaiah speaks (Isa 11:2-3; 61:1) and who is mentioned in Matthew's Gospel (10:20; 28:19);[248] (ii) attempt to demonstrate that the Trinity, which operated figuratively in Noah's days through the dove (Gen 8:6-12), now operates in the church spiritually through the disciples;[249] and (ii) argue, against the Arians, that Jesus Christ, the Son, is not a creature, but is God by nature like the Father.[250] In

---

243. Carter, "Acts," 729; see Levy et al., *Romans*, 255 re Aquinas on the gift of tongues.

244. Origen, *Comm. Matt.*, 10.18 (ANF 9:425-426).

245. Pseudo-Ignatius, *Ps.-Ign. Phil.*, 2 (ANF 1:116); several church fathers and other scholars through to the nineteenth century utilize 28:16-20 as a proof text for the Trinity.

246. Taylor, *Witness of Hermas*, 55 notes that The Shepherd of Hermas makes use of "the short form from the Book of Acts" in Herm. Vis. 3.7.3 (15.3): "These are they that heard the word, and were willing to be baptized into the name of the Lord."

247. Anonymous, *Treatise on Re-Baptism*, 1 (ANF 5:667-678). A selection of other early scholars who incorporate the baptism theme in their writings in relation to 28:19 include Anonymous, *Apostolic Constitutions*, 7.40 (ANF 7:476); Origen, *Homilies on Genesis and Exodus*, 189; Cyprian, *Cyp. Ep.*, 73.2 (ANF 5:386-387); *Baptism of Heretics*, (ANF 5:565-572); Augustine, *Bapt.*, 1.11.15 (NPNF1 4:418); Gregory of Nazianzus, *Orat.*, 40.45 (NPNF2 7:376-377); Chrysostom, *Hom. Eph.*, 20 (NPNF1 13:143-152); Chrysostom, *Hom. Col.*, 9 (NPNF1 13:300-303).

248. Irenaeus, *Haer.*, 3.17.1 (ANF 1:444); see Wilken, Christman, and Hollerich, *Isaiah*, 144, 477.

249. Anonymous, *Against Novatian*, 3 (ANF 5:657-663, esp. 658).

250. Athanasius, *C. Ar.*, 1.59 (NPNF2 4:340-341); see M'Clintock and Strong, "Arianism," 1:388-93; Athanasius, *C. Ar.*, 4.32 (NPNF2 4:445-446); Basil of Caesarea,

the matter of the Gentile mission (including preaching and evangelism, and teaching), a number of scholars: (i) urge people to repent and turn again to God while there is still time (2 Clem. 17.1), especially in light of being called by God to proselytize others to save them from perishing;[251] (ii) establish the patterns and dignity of every order of the clergy appointed by God, given Jesus' previous commission to his disciples;[252] and (iii) connect the breaking and crushing of "the hammer of the whole earth" and the demolition of Babylon (Jer 50:23–24) with the "preaching of the gospel" to all the nations.[253]

Matthew 28:20

Bauer emphasizes that the teaching of new disciples to observe what Jesus commanded involves instructing them about: (i) the need to obey Jesus' commands,[254] and (ii) the substance of those commands.[255] All of

---

Against Eunomius, 93–94; Gregory of Nyssa, *Cont. Eun.*, 2.1 (NPNF2 5:101); Ambrose, *Spir.*, 1.4.48 (NPNF2 10:100); Reventlow, *Biblical Interpretation*, 2:13–14 re Theodore of Mopsuestia; *Biblical Interpretation*, 4:163.

251. Holmes, *Apostolic Fathers*, 160–61 re 2 Clement.

252. Anonymous, *Apostolic Constitutions*, 2.26 (ANF 7:410).

253. Origen, *Homilies on Jeremiah and 1 Kings* 28, 250–51. A selection of other early scholars who utilize 28:19 on the theme of Gentile mission include Athanasius, *Ep. encycl.*, 1 (NPNF2 4:92–93); Orosius and Pacian, *Iberian Fathers*, 51–52; Ambrose, *Seven Exegetical Works*, 124–25; Didymus the Blind, *Zechariah*, 244–45; Chrysostom, *Hom. Jo.*, 66.2 (NPNF1 14:245–246); Leo the Great, *Leo Ep.*, 9.2 (NPNF2 12:7–8); Theodoret, *Psalms 1–72*, 55–56, 183, 281, 381; Andrew of Caesarea, *Apocalypse*, 165.

254. Bauer, "Mission in Matthew's Gospel," 255–256 remarks that the need to obey is connected to Matthew's emphasis on righteousness that results in: (i) salvation from a life of sinning and its consequences; and (ii) a transformed life that is governed by Jesus' twofold love command (22:34–40); see also *Gospel of the Son of God*, 217–218 on the extraordinary events of Jesus' Passion requiring a radical alteration of normally acceptable, and even demanded, practices; and Hagner, "Law, Righteousness, and Discipleship," 369, who notes that "For Matthew, discipleship is a calling to fulfill the righteousness of the Torah, but in a new way. Unlike the former Judaism of Matthew's first readers, the obedience of discipleship is now centered not upon the commandments but upon Jesus and his teaching [28:20a]."

255. Bauer, "Mission in Matthew's Gospel," 256 emphasizes that they are to teach only Jesus' commands (cf. 23:8), the content of which are both stable and dynamic—i.e., they are found written within the Gospel of Matthew, but they must also be reapplied to new situations in which the church finds itself (cf. 16:19); see also *Gospel of the Son of God*, 230–31 on the women disciples who are the first to "teach" the resurrected Jesus' commands (28:8–10) contra the religious leaders' spreading of lies (28:11–15).

the Matthean Jesus' commands must be taught, the critical core of which are the five great discourses that punctuate the Gospel (chs. 5–7; 10; 13; 18; 24–25), which are relevant to the entire church in the post-Easter period.[256] Bauer admits, however, that such teaching must not be limited to Matthew's five great discourses, but should incorporate "the entirety of Jesus' instructions throughout the Gospel," and must include, not only what Jesus says, but also what he does, because "in Matthew's Gospel, Jesus instructs as much through actions as through speech."[257] Of course, the idea that the Matthean Jesus teaches by action as well as by speech is intuitively credible. However, Bauer provides no concrete evidence that Matthew wants his reader to combine Jesus' actions and speech as he interprets διδάσκοντες αὐτοὺς τηρεῖν πάντα ὅσα ἐνετειλάμην ὑμῖν (28:20a). This proof is important because: (i) Matthew's prior use of ἐντέλλω (4:6; 17:9; 19:7) and ἐντολή (5:19; 15:3; 19:17; 22:36–40) are especially associated with spoken commands and not actions,[258] and (ii) until now, τηρέω (19:17; 23:3) has been connected with keeping the commandments and the requirements of the Mosaic law, not with abiding by someone's prior actions. Furthermore, Bauer does not explain which of Jesus' actions are to be interpreted as commands to be kept by his disciples. This too is important given the general understanding that some of Jesus' actions must never be observed, for example: (i) allowing oneself to be the focal point of worship by others (2:2; 14:33; 28:9, 17), and (ii) giving one's life to save people from their sins (1:21; 16:21; 26:2).

Bauer adds that the church's mission, whether by word or example, is possible only because of Jesus' presence (28:20b).[259] Additionally, he reckons that ἐγὼ μεθ' ὑμῶν εἰμι echoes several OT passages in which God promises to be with Israel or her chosen leaders, saving them from

---

256. Bauer, "Mission in Matthew's Gospel," 256–57; see also Keener, *Matthew*, 720 on the five great discourses working well as a discipling manual for young believers.

257. Bauer, "Mission in Matthew's Gospel," 257 submits that: (i) proof of Jesus' instruction by action may be found in the passage: "From that time Jesus began to show (δείκνυμι) his disciples that he must go to Jerusalem, suffer many things ... and be killed ... " (16:21); and (ii) the church's proclamation of the gospel is to be received by the world not only as something heard with the ears, but also as something seen with the eyes; so also Bauer, *Gospel of the Son of God*, 234; Chrysostom, *Hom. Matt.*, 15.1 (NPNF1 10:91).

258. France, *Matthew*, 1118–19.

259. Bauer, "Mission in Matthew's Gospel," 257; see Keener, *Matthew*, 718, who notes that Jesus' continuing presence with his followers even after his departure suggests his omnipresence—an attribute that is limited to deity alone.

destruction (e.g., Josh 22:31; 1 Sam 17:37; Isa 41:10) and empowering them to fulfill an assigned task (e.g., Gen 28:15; Exod 3:11–12; Josh 1:5; Judg 6:12, 16; Hag 2:4–5).[260] Jesus' declaration of his ongoing presence with his disciples: (i) forms an inclusio with "Immanuel . . . God with us" (1:23), and therefore frames the entire Gospel with the theme of God's with-ness or *Mitsein*, which describes someone being in relationship with others; and (ii) involves a new kind of presence that is both continuous and discontinuous with Jesus' physical presence among his disciples.[261]

Brown and Roberts observe that Jesus does not transfer his teaching ministry to the Twelve when he sends them out to the lost sheep of the house of Israel (10:5–8; cf. 4:23; 5:2), but he does so at the end of the Gospel (28:20) after completing his own teaching ministry, and after his resurrection.[262] The Matthean Jesus is the consummate teacher, interpreter, and fulfillment of the Torah[263] whose teaching shapes the implied reader as he attends to it with the purpose of hearing and obeying (17:5).[264] However, learning obedience goes beyond learning the content of Jesus' teachings and involves learning practices—centered around justice, mercy, and loyalty—that are patterned after Jesus' life, and that

---

260. Bauer, "Mission in Matthew's Gospel," 257–58.

261. Bauer, "Mission in Matthew's Gospel," 258 emphasizes five (5) types of *Mitsein* that are present throughout Matthew's Gospel: (i) soteriological (or salvational) (1:23; cf. 1:21); (ii) ecclesial (18:20); (iii) eschatological (26:29); (iv) provisional (26:38, 40); and (v) missional (28:20); see also Bauer, "Mission in Matthew's Gospel," 258 n. 116 on the continuity and discontinuity of Jesus' ongoing presence with his disciples; and *Gospel of the Son of God*, 221, 227, 232, 315–16 about: (i) the resurrected Jesus being the locus of God's presence among his people, which was the function of the temple (1:23; 18:20; 28:20); (ii) the disciples' ability to fulfill their mission because of Jesus' promise to be with them; (iii) Matthew's omission of an account of Jesus' ascension being connected with his ongoing presence; (iv) the assurance of Jesus' ongoing existence pertaining only to the global church (Matt 16:18) and not to individual Christian congregations (cf. Rev 1–3); and (v) God's presence in Jesus, who is God with us.

262. Brown and Roberts, *Matthew*, 101, 234, 263–64, 334–35, 473–74 on: (i) Matthew's five great discourses summarizing Jesus' teaching; and (ii) Matthew's readers' recall of said major discourses when Jesus commissions his disciples to teach the nations "to observe all [πᾶς] that I commanded you" (28:20; cf. πᾶς ["all"] 26:1) (so also Turner, *Matthew*, 690).

263. Brown and Roberts, *Matthew*, 142–44, 263–64, 304–5; see also *Matthew*, 398 on Jesus being the καθηγητής ("master-teacher," 23:8–10), and his elimination of status distinctions within the community of faith.

264. Brown and Roberts, *Matthew*, 334–35, 347.

can sometimes be overlooked because of an undue emphasis on teaching over other activities.[265]

Jesus' ongoing presence is vital to believing communities as their source of power and hope for ministry, and as they seek to obey Jesus' teaching and ways.[266] Because of his presence: (i) the risen Jesus' universal authority accompanies them for mission,[267] (ii) they continue to worship him until the end of the age,[268] and (iii) they have access to his wisdom because he is God's own wisdom.[269] The two scholars agree that "God with us" (1:23; 18:20; 28:20) is a key theme in Matthew's Gospel,[270] framing the entire narrative as an inclusio (1:23; 28:20)—one of author's important structural markers.[271] For them, Christology rather than pneumatology is Matthew's preferred way of emphasizing God's presence among Jesus' disciples;[272] therefore, Jesus, as "God with us," corresponds to the Holy Spirit's role in the life of the believing community, shaping believers towards wholeness and holiness.[273]

According to Nolland, Matthew's paradigm text for Jesus as a teacher of disciples is 5:1–2. These verses introduce the Sermon on the Mount, which Nolland believes takes pride of place in what is taught to new disciples. Jesus' teachings are to be set alongside, and be interpretative of, the commandments of the Mosaic law (cf. 5:18–48), and Matthew's use of ἐντέλλω (28:20) probably echoes "keep the commandments" of 19:17.[274]

265. Brown and Roberts, *Matthew*, 263–64, 453.

266. Brown and Roberts, *Matthew*, 66, 80–81, 100, 108–9, 255–56, 281, 283, 300, 336, 469.

267. Brown and Roberts, *Matthew*, 151, 453–54, 481–82.

268. Brown and Roberts, *Matthew*, 339.

269. Brown and Roberts, *Matthew*, 367.

270. Brown and Roberts, *Matthew*, 264, 302–3, 338.

271. Brown and Roberts, *Matthew*, 19–20, 31–32, 355; Nolland, *Matthew*, 1271 notes the added emphasis of καὶ ἰδού ("and behold"), which strengthens ἐγώ (emphatic 'I'); thus, the risen Jesus (himself), manifesting God's presence, is now present with them (cf. 1:23; 18:20).

272. Brown and Roberts, *Matthew*, 315.

273. Brown and Roberts, *Matthew*, 326, 334.

274. Nolland, *Matthew*, 1270 (cf. 1261–1262); so also Thomas, "Great Commission," 9, who posits that "in light of changes in Jesus' teachings caused by a changing theological environment regarding ministry to Gentiles as reflected in the Great Commission, students of the Gospels would do well to investigate other commands and teachings of Jesus more carefully to see how further light can come to bear on their meanings. As a sample of such an investigation, his Sermon on the Mount with its setting furnishes appropriate excerpts to consider."

The command to obey all of Jesus' teachings is first directed to the disciples who receive the Commission and also to others as they pass them on.[275] The phrase πάσας τὰς ἡμέρας (28:20b) is without parallel in the NT, and it might either be referring to the perilous days that will precede the end of the age (cf. ch. 24), or to some Jewish-Greek idiom that is derived from the LXX.[276] "The end of the age" is distinctive to Matthew (13:39, 40, 49; 24:3; 28:20) in the NT, and it calls to mind Jesus' eschatological role as the Son of Man.[277]

Davies and Allison judge that the full meaning of the resurrection becomes apparent only in 28:16–20, where Jesus becomes an illustration of his own teaching about: (i) persecution for God leading to great reward in heaven, (ii) finding one's life after losing it, and (iii) becoming great by serving, or the last becoming the first.[278] Teaching all that Jesus has commanded is not only about his imperatives, but also his proverbs, blessings, parables, and prophecies, which makes Jesus' entire life a command and so recalls the whole Gospel of Matthew.[279] They agree that the phrase "I am with you" recalls 1:23 and 18:20, but they perceive that its dominant sense may be more about divine assistance than divine presence.[280]

France asserts that Jesus' new commandments are the basis of living as the people of God, and stand in the same place as authority.[281] Christ's promised ongoing presence with his disciples is focused not on individual personal comfort, but on the successful completion of the mission by his disciple community as a whole.[282] The risen Lord convinces the Eleven

---

275. Nolland, *Matthew*, 1270–71.

276. Nolland, *Matthew*, 1271; see Earle, "Matthew," 123.

277. Nolland, *Matthew*, 1271; see also Keener, *Matthew*, 720–21 on the text's specification of "the end of the age," at which time the Son of Man would return in his kingdom after the nations will have heard the gospel (24:14) and be prepared for the judgment (25:32–36).

278. Davies and Allison Jr., *Matthew (III)*, 673.

279. Davies and Allison Jr., *Matthew (III)*, 686.

280. Davies and Allison Jr., *Matthew (III)*, 686–87.

281. France, *Matthew*, 1118 n. 46.

282. France, *Matthew*, 1119 adds that: (i) in OT commissioning scenes, God gives assurance of his divine presence to inadequate servants (e.g., Exod 3:12; 4:12; 23:20–23; Josh 1:5, 9; Judg 6:16; Jer 1:8); and (ii) while the Johannine Jesus promises his disciples the continuing presence of the Spirit (John 14:16–17, 25–26; 16:7), the Matthean Jesus promises his own presence to "the end of the age"; see also Keener, *Matthew*, 720–21 on contemporary Christians losing a sense of Jesus' presence and purpose among them because of having lost sight of their Lord's mission.

that his bodily presence is no longer necessary for them to continue their mission; nevertheless, he will be spiritually present with them.[283]

Hagner opines that the Commission's emphasis is not so much on the initial proclamation of the gospel, but is on the difficult task of nurturing into the experience of discipleship as explained by the instruction to teach new disciples Jesus' commands.[284] This recalls his previous instruction about obeying his teaching (5:17-20; 7:21-27), and his being the one teacher (23:8, 10) in whom "righteousness" finds its final and authoritative definition.[285]

Luz engages the text of 28:20 to argue for the possibility of Mary's perpetual virginity, noting that the phrase "until she gave birth to a son" (1:25) does not indicate that something changed thereafter (cf. 5:25; 16:28; 28:20).[286]

On redaction criticism, Luz: (i) submits that the emphatic "I' (ἐγώ) is frequently redactional in Matthew" (10:16; 23:34; 28:20);[287] (ii) cites Πάντα οὖν ὅσα (23:3; cf. 7:12; 28:20 with τηρέω), ποιέω, τηρέω, ἔργον, γάρ as clearly being redactional;[288] (iii) considers it noteworthy that 18:20 uses ἐν μέσῳ rather than μετά with the Genitive (cf. 1:23; 28:20);[289] and (iv) regards μεθ' ὑμῶν (1:23; 18:20; 28:20) to be a Matthean expression.[290]

Concerning teaching new disciples to observe all of Jesus' commands, Luz remarks that: (i) the linguistic connection between Matthew's account of the guards' deception (28:11-15) and the Commission revolves around the verb "teach" (28:15, 20);[291] (ii) from their traditional usage, κηρύσσω and διδάσκω have different connotations, but in Matthew the subject matter of both activities is the same — i.e., the gospel of the kingdom;[292] and (iii) when Jesus charges his disciples to teach the na-

---

283. France, "Jesus Christ," 571.
284. Hagner, *Matthew 14-28*, 886-87.
285. Hagner, *Matthew 14-28*, 888.
286. Luz, *Matthew 1-7*, 97-99.
287. Luz, *Matthew 1-7*, 227-28.
288. Luz, *Matthew 21-28*, 97-98.
289. Luz, *Matthew 8-20*, 448-49.
290. Luz, *Matthew 21-28*, 365.
291. Luz, *Matthew 21-28*, 609.
292. Luz, *Matthew 1-7*, 168-69; see also Belleville, "1 Timothy," 1-123, esp. 102, on the distinction between "teaching" (i.e., imparting the truths of the Christian faith) and "preaching" (i.e., applying these truths to everyday life).

tions, the thought is probably on the Sermon on the Mount—the first extensive proclamation of Jesus in Matthew.[293]

Luz considers Jesus' ongoing presence with his disciples as he reflects on: (i) Matthew's inclusive account of Jesus that engages his readers, who hear it as insiders and experience God's continuing presence among them;[294] (ii) Jesus' calls on his disciples to decide about being with or against him (12:30)—Jesus being "God with us" and discipleship being "us with him";[295] (iii) the correlation between God's presence and prayer,[296] faith,[297] miracles,[298] judgment,[299] the kingdom of heaven,[300] and the Lord's Supper;[301] (iv) the church's need to rouse itself and shake off

---

293. Luz, *Matthew 1–7*, 176–177 (cf. 174 n. 10, 209, 223–24, 383–84, 391–94, 397–398); *Matthew 21–28*, 633–34.

294. Luz, *Matthew 1–7*, 18; see also *Matthew 8–20*, 11–12 on the granting of the centurion's request (8:5–13) being important for Matthew's readers, who receive courage in their own faith, having seen themselves in the story in terms of their post-Easter conflict with Israel, their movement into the Gentile world, and their proclamation of the gospel to the Gentiles.

295. Luz, *Matthew 8–20*, 205–6; see also *Matthew 8–20*, 225–26 on: (i) Jesus' disciples, his true family (12:46–50), standing under his protection until the end of the world; and (ii) the important feature of being a disciple—doing the will of the Father (12:50; cf. 26:42), who is with his Son (1:23) and, in him, is with his church.

296. For Matthew, confidence in prayer arises from the understanding that the Lord is present with his church (Luz, *Matthew 1–7*, 359–61).

297. "Little faith" results when disciples stop thinking about and trusting in the power and presence of their Lord and can no longer act (Luz, *Matthew 8–20*, 22, 409–10).

298. The earthly, miracle-working Jesus is, for Matthew, always present with his church; therefore, as his disciples proclaim his message, they continue his miracles, and are defined by his presence (Luz, *Matthew 8–20*, 54, 58, 67).

299. Jesus assures his church of his presence until the end of the world (28:20); however, he becomes the judge who deprives for the scribes, the Pharisees, and their followers (23:13–33) of God's presence even before the end of the world (Luz, *Matthew 21–28*, 175).

300. Luz, *Matthew 21–28*, 234 detects several Christian metaphors in 25:10, including "with him," which suggests the Immanuel motif (1:23; 28:20b).

301. Luz, *Matthew 21–28*, 374–78 examines Calvin's mystical vs. Luther's literal position on the doctrine of transubstantiation; Calvin explains that: (i) Christ is no longer physically present in this world (26:11); but (ii) he is present until the end of the age (28:20) according to his divine nature; and (iii) the bond which connects Christ's body and blood with the elements of the bread and wine is the Spirit of Christ (see Cairns, "Mass," 273–74 for more on the doctrine of transubstantiation; and "Consubstantiation," 110).

complacency because it can be certain only of Jesus' reliability and of his presence;[302] and (vi) matters connected with "the end of the age."[303]

Meier considers Jesus' "coming" to his eleven disciples (28:18a) to be a "proleptic Parousia." His promise to remain with and empower them (his church) for mission extends, therefore, from "proleptic" to "fully realized" Parousia at the end of the age (28:20b).[304]

Schnabel remarks that Jesus' promise to be with his disciples takes the place of YHWH and assumes his function with regard to the new people of God. Noting that both the formulation in the present tense (ἐγὼ . . . εἰμι) and the reference to "all the days" (πάσας τὰς ἡμέρας) promises permanence, Schnabel adds that missionary work lasts until the Parousia, until which time Jesus' disciples experience their risen Lord as they undertake his commission. "This is the christological dimension of missions, the grounds and the final reality of missionary work," Schnabel says.[305]

The Gospels provide differing pastoral perspectives for Wilkins: (i) Jesus as the Shepherd of his sheep (Matt 26:31; John 10:1-18; 21:15-19; cf. Heb 13:20; 1 Pet 5:1-5); (ii) the evangelists, with the Gospel accounts themselves becoming records of pastoral care; and (iii) the church as a teaching community (28:20).[306] It is noteworthy, too, that Matthew concludes with the crucial element of discipleship, namely, the presence of the Master with his disciples—Jesus having exchanged physical for spiritual presence.[307]

---

302. Luz, *Matthew 8-20*, 250-251 (cf. 363-64, 450-51, 458-59, 459-61, 478-79); see also *Matthew 21-28*, 283, 635.

303. Luz, *Matthew 1-7*, 160 comments that, in Matthew, the kingdom of heaven is a future reality, and not until 11:12 and 12:28 does the reader learn that it is already dawning; see Kingsbury, *Matthew: Structure*, 128-49 on: (i) the present and future aspects of the kingdom of heaven being of equal value; and (ii) the kingdom of heaven being in a stage of growth during the period from Jesus' birth to the Parousia (28:20) ; Luz, *Matthew 8-20*, 36-37 about the absence of Jesus, the "bridegroom" (9:14-17), during the period between resurrection and Parousia, which coincides with his presence with the church; *Matthew 21-28*, 204 concerning Matthew's view of "end of the age" being shaped around Immanuel's (1:23; 28:20b) proclamation of the gospel of the kingdom to the nations through the church (cf. 28:19), before the end comes (24:14).

304. Meier, "Matthew," 4:637.

305. Schnabel, *Early Christian Mission*, 1:367; see Carter, "Acts," 498, 666 on Christ's ongoing presence being conditioned upon his disciples' obedience to his command to make disciples of all nations.

306. Wilkins, "Pastoral Theology," 876-82, esp. 877.

307. Wilkins, "Discipleship," 188.

Gerald F. Hawthorne calls attention to the insertion of ἀμήν (28:20b), noting that only in English versions of the Bible that are based on the Textus Receptus (KJV and NKJV) is it translated as "amen" rather than "verily," "truly," "solemnly," or translated only in a way to emphasize what is being said.[308]

Robert H. Mounce confirms that teaching was an ancient and honorable profession in the Jewish culture, and that in the New Testament world teaching was primarily but not exclusively moral instruction.[309] However, teaching was not simply doctrinal, but included guidance in ethical conduct, with its goal being "a changed life as well as an informed mind," for which reason the Matthean Jesus connects teaching and obedience (28:20).[310]

Scholars from the first to the mid-twentieth century employ the text of 28:20 in diverse ways. On teaching obedience to Jesus' commands, scholars: (i) appeal to Scripture concerning the Lord's Day, the repeal of Sabbatical ordinances, and Christ's granting of plenary authority to his apostles to lead his church (Matt 16:19; 28:20; John 14:26) when certain persons tried to revive the Jewish Sabbath over observance of "the Christian Sabbath" and the first day of the week as a weekly Easter;[311] (ii) reason that Christ's command to teach only those things that he committed to his disciples[312] is based on their knowledge of everything that he said;[313] and (iii) affirm that through God's grace Christians accomplish Jesus' commission to baptize and to teach observance of his commands.[314] Concerning God's presence with his people, scholars: (i) address the possible identities of the "two or three gathered together" in the name of Christ with the Lord in their midst (18:20), and they

---

308. Hawthorne, "Amen," 7–8. For comments on the textual variant in this verse, see Comfort, *Text and Translation Commentary*, 90.

309. Mounce, *Romans*, 233–35.

310. Mounce, *Romans*, 235 n. 27.

311. Roberts, Donaldson, and Coxe, "Polycrates Bishop of Ephesus," (ANF 8:773–74; see also 773 n. 4).

312. Pseudo-Clement, *Recognitions of Clement*, 2.33 (ANF 8:106).

313. Pseudo-Clement, *The Clementine Homilies*, 17.7 (ANF 8:319–320).

314. Basil of Caesarea, "Concerning Baptism," 380–82. A selection of other early scholars who similarly utilized the text of 28:20 include Chrysostom, *Hom. Matt.*, 15.2 (NPNF1 10:91–92); Jerome, *Comm. Matt.*, 327; Augustine, *Faust.*, 5.3 (NPNF1 4:163); Wilken, Christman, and Hollerich, *Isaiah*, 464 re Cyril of Alexandria; Nicetas of Remesiana et al., *Writings*, 379; Aquinas, *Catena Aurea: Matthew*, 1:989; Luther, *Luther's Works*, 41:199–205.

conclude that the reference may be to "the one church" that is formed by the gathering of two peoples—Jews and Gentiles;[315] (ii) utter a blessing of God's presence[316] and urge every Christian to diligently attend church, knowing that Christ is present and is communicating with them;[317] and (iii) explain that there is no need to partake of the leaven (teaching) of the Pharisees and Sadducees (16:11) because Jesus is with his church always.[318] With regard to the end of the age, certain scholars: (i) interpret Psalm 119:105 mystically, proposing that Christians are in the evening and night of "the end of the age," and until the new light of the future age shines forth, they must let "the lamp of the Law" burn to provide light in proportion to the oil that they supply by the richness of their works;[319] (ii) invite an explanation from Arius and Eunomius about the apparent ignorance of God the Father, represented by the landowner in the Parable of the Tenants (21:33-46), concerning the tenants' future response to his son (21:37), realizing that their explanation of the Father's ignorance must also be extended to the Son, who claims to be ignorant about the timing of the end of the age (24:36; cf. 28:20);[320] and (iii) differentiate between the Roman Catholic and the Protestant understanding of catholicity—the Roman church claiming that only those who are united to the pontiff at Rome belong to the Catholic Church, while Protestants are of the view that the Christian church comprises all churches of all nations for all time.[321]

---

315. Clement of Alexandria, *Stromateis*, 298-99.

316. Anonymous, *Apostolic Constitutions*, 7.46 (ANF 7:477-478).

317. Anonymous, *Apostolic Constitutions*, 2.59 (ANF 7:422-423).

318. Origen, *Comm. Matt.*, 12.6 (ANF 9:453-454). A selection of other early scholars who have written on the theme of God's presence in 28:20 include Aquinas, *Catena Aurea: Matthew*, 1:821, 853; Simonetti, *Matthew 14-28*, 257; Origen, *Cels.*, 2.9 (ANF 4:433-434); *Cels.*, 5.12 (ANF 4:548); *Comm. Jo.*, 10.7 (ANF 9:385); *John's Gospel, Books 13-32*, 143; *Homilies on Joshua*, 32-33.

319. Origen, Homilies on Leviticus 1-16, 235.

320. Jerome, *Comm. Matt.*, 245-46, 277-78.

321. M'Clintock and Strong, "Church," 2:322-29, esp. 325; see "Indefectibility of the Church," 4:542-43 on the perpetuity of the church, which frees it from failure in succession of members, promises of which are made in Scripture (e.g., Isa 61:8, 9; Dan 2:44; Matt 16:18; 28:20; John 14:16, 17).

3

Inductive Study of Matthew 28:16–20

Chapter Summary

THIS CHAPTER EXAMINES HOW Matthew guides his reader's understanding of μαθητεύσατε (28:19) by pointing from the Great Commission to passages within the broader context of the Gospel that illuminate the meaning of that imperative.

Approach

First, I make general observations about the Commission as a whole. Then, proceeding on a verse-by-verse basis: (i) I identify and discuss the important narrative structures of the text, using Bauer and Traina's inductive Bible study as my primary discussion partner; (ii) I comment on those narrative elements—i.e., events, characters, settings, and discourse—that contribute to the reader's understanding μαθητεύσατε; (iii) along the way, I examine any evidence provided by the historical background of Matthew that might be significant in forming the reader's interpretation of the imperative; and (iv) I explain the implications of the reader's findings on the overall goal to discern the meaning of μαθητεύσατε. In the next chapter, I will use the results emanating from this analysis to select and analyze passages from the broader context of Matthew (1:1—28:15) to determine how those passages might contribute to the reader's interpretation of the meaning of μαθητεύσατε.

Key Findings

The Commission requires the reader to look beyond its boundary to gain a fuller understanding of its meaning and that of its imperative, μαθητεύσατε.

An examination of the Commission as a whole reveals the following findings: (i) the characterization of 28:16–20 as the *climax*[1] and/or *summarization*[2] of Matthew requires the reader to make judgements about the Commission vis-à-vis the entire Gospel; (ii) the blended temporal setting of the Commission—i.e., historical, but also timeless—permits the reader to participate in a historical event, but also experience the Matthean Jesus' ongoing (spiritual) presence with his community in terms of divine assistance, empowerment, hope, cohesion, and protection as they undertake the assigned mission; and (iii) the reader determines the meaning of the Commission and its elements in ways that are sympathetic with the evaluative point of view that the implied author espouses throughout the entire Gospel; this requires him[3] to look beyond the Commission's boundary and incorporate the broader context of Matthew to comprehend what may not be readily apparent from within its border.

On 28:16, it is apparent that: (i) the author uses *contrast*[4] to juxtapose two themes that pervade the Gospel and that are familiar to Matthew's reader—i.e., opposition of the religious authorities and outreach to the nations; (ii) the *preparation/realization*[5] structure helps the reader to converge on the author's primary focus in the material that follows

---

1. Bauer and Traina, *Inductive Bible Study*, 99 explain, "Climax is the movement from lesser to greater, towards a high point of culmination" and "readers are encouraged to ask how the material that leads up to the climax . . . illumines the climactic passage."

2. Bauer and Traina, *Inductive Bible Study*, 110 write, "Summarization is an abridgement or compendium (summing up) either preceding or following a unit of material."

3. I have already footnoted in chapter 1 of this book that the implied reader in Matthew male; for this reason, I use the masculine pronoun throughout my work to refer to the implied reader or "the reader."

4. Bauer and Traina, *Inductive Bible Study*, 97 define contrast as "the association of opposites or of things whose differences the writer wishes to stress."

5. Bauer and Traina, *Inductive Bible Study*, 114 explain, "Preparation/realization, or introduction, is the inclusion of background or setting for events or ideas. Preparation pertains to the background or introductory material itself, while realization is that for which the preparation is made."

the *introduction*; it prompts specific questions and recalls certain facts from the wider Gospel about the background details provided—e.g., Jesus' planned meeting, the disciple's state of mind, and Jesus' initiation of contact with the disciples; (iii) the reader perceives the disciples (28:16) to be, *inter alia*, adherents to the Matthean Jesus; he calls them into discipleship and determines the nature of their adherency; they follow him in a surrogate family arrangement, which brings them into close proximity with his verbal teaching and his actions; narratively, they represent every post-resurrection Christian;[6] (iv) the disciples' reduced number recalls specific passion events, including Judas's betrayal, Peter's denial, and male disciples' flight to relative safety; (v) Galilee represents for the reader recent memories and future possibilities as a place of refuge, new beginnings, preparation for public ministry, economic livelihood, and opportunity for global ministry; and (vi) "the mountain" symbolizes a place of revelation, which requires the reader to reflect on other Matthean events in similar settings in order to make inferences about the profoundness of the commissioning event.

On 28:17, the reader: (i) is aware that the disciples' worship of the risen Jesus implies the deity of Christ; therefore, his commissioning of the disciples takes on special meaning because of its divine attributes; and (ii) being a post-resurrection disciple, the reader identifies with the character group of the disciples, whose faith is marked by worship mixed with doubt and who are presented elsewhere in Matthew as struggling with the kinds of issues and experiences that are relevant to post-resurrection Christians.

Concerning 28:18, Matthew's reader recognizes that: (i) the author's repetition of inclusive scope, which is expressed by πᾶς ("all"), requires that every aspect of the Commission is interpreted in the widest possible range—i.e., Jesus' *universal* authority; his command to make disciples of *everyone, everywhere*; his ongoing presence with his disciples *every day*; as well as his command to teach new disciples to obey *all* his commands, both verbal and nonverbal; (ii) Matthew's use of *introduction* (28:18a) facilitates the reader's transition from the disciples' present circumstances, which recall recent passion events, to a new set of circumstances that outlines where the risen Lord wants them to be; and (iii) the God of Matthew's Gospel has given to Jesus all authority, which represents the climax of an irony-filled passion event, out of which the Matthean Jesus

---

6. I make several assertions here that I support in my analysis of 28:16 in the body of this chapter.

is vindicated and proven to be, *inter alia*, the Son of Man who would destroy the temple and rebuild it in three days, the Messiah, the Son of God, and the King of Israel.

With regard to 28:19, the reader is aware that: (i) Matthew utilizes a structure of hortatory *causation*[7] to signal that the disciples are empowered to undertake their assigned mission because of Jesus' receipt of unlimited authority, which is also the basis for his command to make disciples of *everyone, everywhere*, to teach them *everything* that he has commanded, and to be assured of his presence *every day*; (ii) with the help of this same structure, the Matthean Jesus clarifies in "Go therefore and make disciples of all the nations" (28:19) what he means by "I will make you fishers of men" (4:19); (iii) Matthew's use of *cruciality*[8] draws attention to what precedes the pivot (i.e., a pre-resurrection ministry that is marked primarily by Jewish particularism) vis-à-vis what follows the pivot (i.e., an expanded post-resurrection ministry that is characterized by Gentile inclusion); (iv) the possibility of explaining the movement from the general command μαθητεύσατε (28:19a) to its adjoining participles—πορευθέντες (28:19a), βαπτίζοντες (28:19b), and διδάσκοντες (28:20a)—by means of ideological *particularization*,[9] which develops or unpacks that command without necessarily exhausting its meaning, requires the reader to look towards the remainder of Matthew to discover additional meaning that may reside there; and (v) because 28:19 contains the only reference in Matthew to Christian baptism, the meaning of which the author does not develop there, he must look beyond the Commission—perhaps to John's baptizing work (3:1–17) and to the rest of the NT—to comprehend the significance of Christian baptism.

---

7. Bauer and Traina, *Inductive Bible Study*, 105–6 comment that "Causation is the movement from cause to effect . . . Hortatory causation occurs when a writer moves from a statement in the indicative (i.e., a claim or statement of fact) to a command, or exhortation, in the imperative: because A is so, therefore you ought to do B."

8. Bauer and Traina, *Inductive Bible Study*, 108 disclose, "Cruciality involves the device of pivot. Elements on each side of the pivot differ from those on the other side because of the pivot. It involves a change of direction, a radical reversal, a total turning around of the material because of the pivot passage. In cruciality, the movement following the pivot virtually cancels out what preceded the pivot passage."

9. Bauer and Traina, *Inductive Bible Study*, 100–101 explain, "Ideological particularization involves a general statement that the writer spells out or unpacks or develops in the material that follows."

Finally, in the matter of 28:20, the reader understands that: (i) Matthew utilizes logical *substantiation*[10] to explain that, because of the Lord's ongoing presence, the disciples are able to disciple all the nations in the way that he prescribes; alternatively, this narrative progression from the discipling activity of 28:19–20a to the risen Jesus' promise of 28:20b may be viewed in terms of logical *causation*,[11] which perceives Jesus' ongoing presence not in terms of its empowerment for discipling activity, but in terms of the disciples' relationship with their Lord; (ii) the arrangement of Matthew's Gospel according to *climax* by inclusio indicates the importance of God's presence (with-ness or *Mitsein*) throughout the entire story of Jesus; (iii) the implications of broadening the universe of the Matthean Jesus' prior commands to include both verbal and nonverbal commands are that the reader explores beyond the Great Commission and the five great discourses of Matthew and allow the entire life of the Matthean Jesus to be the template for making disciples; and (iv) being a disciple-maker himself, the reader is enjoined to think more broadly about teaching obedience to Jesus' commands than simply telling others what Jesus commands; rather, he models Jesus' character and actions for others to follow.

General Observations

Before proceeding with a detailed analysis of the Great Commission using IBS tools supported by narrative criticism, let me make a few general observations about the Commission as a whole.

Matthean scholars typically use the terms "climax" and/or "summarization" to refer to the structural relationship between 28:16–20 and the entire Gospel of Matthew. Bauer reckons that Matthew's plot—i.e., the interaction of events, characters, and settings[12]—moves towards and reaches its climax in the resurrection, the climax of which is the

---

10. Bauer and Traina, *Inductive Bible Study*, 107 remark, "Logical substantiation occurs when a writer moves from declaration(s) or claims to the reasons why (i.e., the cause) the declaration or claim is true or ought to be accepted: the reason I say (and why you should believe) A is B."

11. Bauer and Traina, *Inductive Bible Study*, 106 comment, "Logical causation occurs when one statement logically causes, or leads to, another statement, when a writer draws an inference from what he has just said."

12. Powell, *Narrative Criticism*, 23; see also Resseguie, *Narrative Criticism*, 197–240 for more about "plot": definition, elements, types, patterns, and arrangement.

missionary commissioning itself. This results in 28:16–20 being "the climax of the climax" of the Gospel.[13]

Davies and Allison portray the Commission as "the grand denouement" (or climax), but they also advance that the passage is in such harmony with the entire Gospel that, despite its brevity, it is almost a summary of Matthean theology.[14] Bauer asserts that *summarization* represents a deliberate attempt to either preview or recapitulate, in point-by-point format, the components of what is being summarized. The interpretive significance of *summarization* is at least threefold; the reader: (i) recognizes that the implied author selectively incorporates material from the wider text into the summary statement; (ii) understands that the writer chooses a mix of terms and structures to employ in his summary statement, reflecting how he wishes the larger presentation to be interpreted; and (iii) is aware of the writer's emphases in the summary statement to better understand the material being summarized.[15] Acknowledging that "several major themes in the Gospel come here to ultimate expression,"[16] Bauer tentatively agrees with Günther Bornkamm (1971) that 28:16–20 "is a summary of the entire Gospel of Matthew," but cautions that "it is not a summarization in the narrow, technical sense, since it does not contain a point-by-point retelling of the Gospel."[17]

David C. Sim argues that the Great Commission does not summarize the Gospel of Matthew or provide the key that unlocks its meaning. For Sim, the Commission introduces new elements—e.g., the Trinitarian formula of baptism and the command to evangelize all the nations—that are

---

13. Bauer, "Mission in Matthew's Gospel," 242.

14. Davies and Allison Jr., *Matthew (III)*, 687–688; so also Krentz, "Missionary Matthew," 24, who argues that Matthew's "conclusion is the goal toward which the entire text trends, designed to pick up earlier motifs of the Gospel, thus making the entire text a missionary text."

15. Bauer and Traina, *Inductive Bible Study*, 110–11.

16. Bauer, "Mission in Matthew's Gospel," 242; see also Brown and Roberts, *Matthew*, 261–62 on the final scene bringing together themes and plot motifs from across Matthew's Gospel, providing an apt summary of some of the evangelist's key messages; and Keener, *Matthew*, 715 about the closing pericope's recapitulation and development of the most important themes of Matthew.

17. Bauer, "Mission in Matthew's Gospel," 242 n. 14; see Smith, *Matthew*, 334–35 on the Commission being in harmony with the larger story of Jesus in the Gospel, but also being a deceptively simple scene that is a tribute to Matthew's economic use of words to describe the meeting between Jesus and his disciples.

to be viewed as deviations from what has gone before in the wider text.[18] Additionally, Sim contends that several important Matthean themes are missing from 28:16–20, namely: (i) the eschatological judgment and its aftermath; (ii) the conflict with formative Judaism—i.e., the coalition of forces (dominated by the scribes and Pharisees) that came together after the destruction of Jerusalem and its temple (70 CE); and (iii) the Mosaic law (cf. 5:17–19).[19] Sim observes correctly that the Commission is not a detailed replica of Matthew's Gospel, but he fails to recognize that in *summarization* the author selectively incorporates material from the wider text, chooses a mix of terms and structures to employ, and emphasizes certain themes over others.

The implications of 28:16–20 being characterized in terms of *climax* and/or *summarization* are twofold: (i) as *climax*, the passage represents the pinnacle of the Gospel, its foundation being everything that has gone before; and (ii) as summary, it outlines and points to the important Matthean themes that are laid out in the main body of the Gospel. These two structural relationships hold 28:16–20 to be an important pericope in Matthew, and they require the reader to make judgments about the Commission vis-à-vis the entire Gospel.

Setting may be described as "the adverb" of literary structure, designating when, where, and how narrative action occurs.[20] It relates to the spatial, temporal, social (including cultural and political), and religious environment of the story. One aspect of setting that deserves immediate attention is the temporal setting of 28:16–20: its historical yet timeless characteristics, the effects of which are perceived by the reader both within and beyond the boundary of the Commission. On the one hand, Matthew wishes his readers to consider this passage to be historical;[21] therefore, he

---

18. Sim, "Matthew 28:16–20," 3–4.

19. Sim, "Matthew 28:16–20," 4–5, however, acknowledges: (i) the suggestion of Davies and Allison (2004, 3:688) that the reference to the "end of the age" is meant to recall Jesus' teaching about end, but he responds that "end of the age" addresses the presence of Jesus during the time of the church, more so than the eschatological events themselves; (ii) the argument that Jesus' promise to be with his followers until the end of the age could possibly be referring to the problems that they are currently enduring at the hands of the scribes and Pharisees; and (iii) that the Mosaic Law is necessarily tied in with the demand of the risen Christ to observe all of his teachings.

20. Powell, *Narrative Criticism*, 69; see also Resseguie, *Narrative Criticism*, 87–120 on setting and its application in the New Testament.

21. Bauer, "Mission in Matthew's Gospel," 245 remarks that 28:16–20 seamlessly connects with the immediately preceding historical account, and "it contributes to

employs an abundance of aorist indicative verbs throughout the entire resurrection narrative (28:1–20), including the Commission (28:16–20): the disciples "proceeded" to where Jesus "designated" (28:16); they "worshipped," but some "doubted" (28:17); Jesus "said" he "was given" all authority (28:18); and he previously "gave commands" to his disciples (28:20).[22] On the other hand, the passage possesses a timeless quality: (i) it lacks closure because the risen Jesus does not physically depart from his disciples, and there is no reference to his ascension to the Father; and (ii) it concludes with Jesus' promise to be with them (ἐγὼ μεθ' ὑμῶν εἰμι, present active indicative) until "the end of the age," which incorporates a view of time beyond the lifespan of the eleven disciples, right up to the Parousia.[23] The Commission's blended temporal setting—i.e., historical, but also timeless—permits the reader to participate in a historical event, but also experience the Matthean Jesus' ongoing (spiritual) presence with his community in terms of divine assistance, empowerment, hope, cohesion, and protection as they undertake the assigned mission.

Moreover, Matthew influences the reader's understanding of the Commission by insisting that he adopts an evaluative point of view—norms, values, and general worldview—that the implied author establishes as operative in the story.[24] Throughout the Gospel, Matthew chooses to make normative the evaluative point of view that belongs to God (cf. 16:23), which means that every perspective espoused therein is to be adjudged right or wrong, true or false, depending upon whether it aligns itself with the evaluative point of view of God. The implied author portrays Jesus as the supreme agent of God (cf. 1:1, 23; 3:17; 16:16–17), and the reader is assured that the evaluative points of view of Matthew as narrator and Jesus are in complete alignment with the evaluative point of view of God.[25] Therefore, Matthew's reader determines the meaning of the Commission and its elements in ways that are sympathetic with

---

Matthew's concern throughout 27:55–28:20 to provide historical evidence for Jesus' resurrection."

22. Bauer, "Mission in Matthew's Gospel," 245 n. 25 notes that although many contemporary scholars reject the notion of temporality in Greek verbs in favor of 'aspect' and 'space,' others counter their position, insisting that "the indicative mood, at least, grammaticalizes time."

23. Bauer, "Mission in Matthew's Gospel," 245; see Davies and Allison Jr., *Matthew (III)*, 688–89 on the "open-ended" ending of 28:16–20.

24. Powell, *Narrative Criticism*, 23–24.

25. Kingsbury, *Matthew as Story*, 34.

the evaluative point of view that the implied author espouses throughout the Gospel. This requires the reader to look beyond the Commission's boundary and incorporate the broader context of Matthew to comprehend what may not be readily apparent from within it border—e.g., the meaning of μαθητεύσατε (28:19).

Matthew 28:16

Matthew introduces the Great Commission with a postpositive δέ, a common Greek particle that is used to connect one clause to another and that may express either *contrast* or simple continuation, depending on the context.[26] Matthew concludes the story of Jesus' resurrection (28:1–10) with two contrasting outcomes: (i) a conspiracy that is perpetrated by the religious authorities and the guards to conceal the truth about the resurrection (28:11–15), vis-à-vis (ii) Jesus' mandate to his disciples to reveal the truth to all the nations (28:16–20).[27] The use of δέ in 28:16 juxtaposes the bribery, concealment, and deceit of the conspiracy that precedes it with virtue, revelation, and truth of the commissioning that follows it, creating two contrasting themes that pervade the Gospel and that are familiar to Matthew's reader: opposition of the religious authorities[28] and outreach to the nations.[29] It is also noteworthy that the *contrast* presented in 28:16 is the second of two sets of contiguous contrasting scenes, which together demonstrate God's intervention against all attempts to obstruct his salvific plan.[30] In the first scene, Matthew differentiates between: (i) the religious authorities' plot to seal the tomb to hinder Jesus'

---

26. "δέ," BDAG, 213; see also Wallace, *Greek Grammar*, 671; Porter, *Idioms*, 208; and Levinsohn, *Discourse Features*, 71–80.

27. So Turner, *Matthew*, 679; and Davies and Allison Jr., *Matthew (III)*, 680–81.

28. For opposition of the religious authorities, see: 2:4; 3:7; 5:20; 9:3, 11, 34; 12:2, 14, 24; 15:1–2; 16:1, 6, 21; 19:3; 20:18; 21:15–16, 23, 45–46; 22:15, 34–35; 23:13–33; 26:3–4, 14–15, 57–68; 27:1, 12, 20, 41, 62–64; 28:11–15.

29. For outreach to the nations, see: Gentile women in Jesus' genealogy (1:1–17); Gentile magi and infant Jesus (2:1–12); Gentiles reclining at table in the kingdom of heaven (8:11); Jesus' disciples bearing witness to the Gentiles (10:18); Gentiles hoping in Jesus' name (12:18–21); the faith of the Gentile woman (15:21–28); the kingdom of heaven being given to a nation (21:43); Gentiles being invited to the marriage feast (22:1–10); the gospel being preached to all the nations (24:14; cf. 26:13); Jesus' blood being poured out from many (26:28; cf. 20:28); and the Gentile centurion's confession that Jesus is the Son of God 27:54.

30. So Osborne, "Resurrection," 673–88, esp. 679–80.

resurrection (27:62–68) and (ii) God's sovereign act of raising Jesus from the dead (28:1–10). Across the wider swath of text from 27:62 to 28:20, this semantic structure may be classified as a *recurrence*[31] of *contrast*.

Also evident in 28:16 is the structure of *preparation/realization* or *introduction*, which represents "the inclusion of background or setting for events or ideas. Preparation pertains to the background or introductory material itself, while realization is that for which the preparation is made."[32] The reader might consider 28:16–18a to be the preparation for the final words of Jesus in the Gospel that follow immediately thereafter. The background material provided comprises three elements that describe: (i) the disciples' arrival at the scene of the meeting (28:16), (ii) the disciples' initial state of mind (28:17), and (iii) the moment of contact between Jesus and the disciples (28:18a). Bauer is correct that, although this introductory material is relatively brief, when it is read in light of the earlier chapters of the Gospel, it provides significant insight into 28:16–20 and, by extension, into mission.[33] Additionally, the reader might consider Jesus' final words (28:18b–20) to be the *realization* or the purpose for which the preparation is made. Its basic composition is also threefold: (i) Jesus' declaration of his authority (28:18b), (ii) his charge to the disciples (28:19–20a), and (iii) his promise to be present with them (28:20b). The likely consequence of Matthew's imposition of this *preparation/realization* structure upon 28:16–20 is that, *inter alia*: (i) it helps the reader to converge on the author's primary focus in the material that follows the introduction—i.e., Jesus' authority, his commission, and his promise of his ongoing presence; and (ii) it provides essential context that guides the reader's understanding by prompting specific questions and recalling certain facts from the wider Gospel about the background details provided—e.g., Jesus' planned meeting (cf. 26:32; 28:7, 10), the disciple's state of mind (cf. 14:31), and Jesus' initiation of contact with the disciples (cf. 17:7).

In 28:16, Matthew relates the story of the eleven disciples proceeding to Galilee to "the mountain which Jesus had designated," providing details about characters, events, and settings that guide the reader's understanding of the passage. The author immediately brings the disciples

---

31. Bauer and Traina, *Inductive Bible Study*, 95 disclose, "Recurrence is the repetition of the same or similar terms, places, or other elements, which may involve motifs, concepts, persons, literary forms, or other structural relationships."

32. Bauer and Traina, *Inductive Bible Study*, 114.

33. Bauer, "Mission in Matthew's Gospel," 243.

into narrative focus. The Greek term used in the text for "disciple" is μαθητής ("pupil, apprentice"; "disciple, adherent"), a cognate of μαθητεύω ("to be a pupil, with the implication of being an adherent of the teacher," or "to cause one to be a pupil, teach"), both of which derive from μανθάνω ("to learn, be instructed, be taught").[34]

In Matthew's historical account of Jesus' life, "the disciples" comprise a group of persons whom Jesus calls to follow him (e.g., 4:18; 9:9). He names them "apostles" (ἀπόστολος, 10:2-4)[35] before sending them out as his messengers with extraordinary status. For the duration of the earthly relationship with their master, the disciples experience: (i) Jesus' ministry in Galilee and in the region of Judea and beyond the Jordan, where he preaches, teaches, and heals every kind disease and sickness;[36] (ii) his teaching and explanations directed at them only,[37] to them and the crowds combined (e.g., 5:1-7:39; 19:16-22), to the crowds in parables while in the disciples' presence (e.g., 13:1-9, 24-30, 31-32, 33-35), and to the religious authorities in parables while in the disciples' presence (e.g., 21:28-32, 33-44; 22:1-14)]; (iii) his miracle-working faith (e.g., 8:23-27; 14:22-33; 21:18-22); (iv) his defense of them against unjust criticism by others (e.g., 9:14-17; 12:1-7; 15:1-14, 15-20); (v) his compassion for the people (9:36-38); (vi) his empowerment of them for ministry (10:1); (vii) his redefinition of family relationships (12:46-50); (viii) his provision for those who follow him (e.g., 14:13-21; 15:32-39); (ix) his forewarnings about future dangers (e.g., 16:1-12, 20, 21; cf. 17:22-23; 20:17-19; 26:1-2, 21-25, 31-35); (x) his interrogation of them to verify their understanding of certain matters (e.g., 15:16-17; 16:9-11, 13-20); (xi) his occasional rebuke (e.g., 16:22-23; 20:20-28); (xii) his transfiguration

---

34. "μαθητής," BDAG, 609-10; "μαθητεύω," BDAG, 609; "μανθάνω," BDAG, 615; cf. Rengstorf, "μανθάνω, μαθητής, μαθητεύω, κτλ," *TDNT* 4:390-461.

35. "ἀπόστολος," BDAG, 122.

36. Jesus' Galilean ministry: (i) teaching and preaching (4:22-23; cf. 9:35; 13:54); and (ii) healing (8:14-17, 28-34; 9:1-8, 18-26, 27-31, 9:32-33; 12:9-21, 22-29; 14:34-36; 15:21-28, 29-31; 17:14-18). Jesus' Judean ministry: 19:2; 20:29-34.

37. Jesus' teachings in the following Matthean passages are received firsthand by his disciples only: (i) "lost sheep of the house of Israel" (10:5-11:1); (ii) parables about the kingdom (13:10-17, 18-23, 36-43, 44, 45-46, 47-50; 18:23-35; 19:23-26; 20:1-16; 25:1-13, 14-30); (iii) the return of the Son of Man (24:1-14, 15-28, 29-31, 32-35, 36-44, 45-51; 25:31-46); (iv) discipleship (13:52; 16:24-28; 19:27-30); (v) John the Baptist (17:10-13); and (vi) assorted teachings about faith, tribute money, rank in the kingdom, stumbling blocks, lost sheep, and discipline and prayer (17:19-21, 24-27; 18:1-20).

on the mountain (17:1–13), including God's approval of him (17:5–6); (xiii) his testing and rejection by the religious authorities,[38] sometimes going on the offensive against them (e.g., 21:23–27; 22:41–46; 23:1–12; 23:13–36); (xv) his triumphant entry into Jerusalem (21:1–11), where they obey his commands despite being aware of what is to follow (21:1, 6–7; cf. 26:17–19); (xvi) his cleansing of the temple (21:12–17); (xvii) his lament over Jerusalem (23:37–39); (xviii) his intentional interaction with society's marginalized persons, often being rebuked by his own disciples and others (e.g., 9:10–13; 19:13–15; 26:6–13); (xix) his institution of the Lord's Supper (26:26–35); (xx) his passion event (26:36—27:66), though they follow from a distance (26:56, 58; 27:55–56); and (xxii) his resurrection event (28:1–10), having been alerted by the women disciples, who remain close by (27:55, 61; 28:1) and are told by an angel of the Lord and by the risen Jesus that he will meet them in Galilee (28:7, 10).

Matthew typically refers to Jesus' closest followers as "the disciples" (e.g., 13:10; 14:26; 26:45), "his disciples" (5:1; 8:23; 12:1), or "the Twelve" (20:17; 26:14, 20, 47; cf. 10:1), but they are part of the wider group of adherents who follow Jesus (cf. 8:19, 21; 27:55, 57).[39] Moreover, the reader knows that they are not the only group of disciples in first-century CE Palestine. Gospel writers also refer to "disciples" who follow other leaders: John the Baptist (9:14; 11:2; cf. Luke 5:33; John 4:1), the Pharisees (Luke 5:33), and Moses (John 9:28).

Bauer extends the term "the disciples" to incorporate the entire post-resurrection church because throughout his narrative Matthew typically portrays the disciples in ways that foreshadow the post-resurrection experience of the church to the point where they appear to represent the post-resurrection church.[40] Bauer's point of view is supported by the idea that the implied reader responds to the text at every point with whatever emotion, understanding, or knowledge the text ideally calls for.[41]

---

38. The religious authorities: (i) accuse Jesus and his disciples (9:1–3); (9:34; 12:24); (12:1–2); (15:1–2); (ii) conspire against Jesus (12:14; cf. 16:21; 20:18–19; 21:45–46; 22:15–22; 26:3–4, 14–16, 47, 57–68; 27:1–2, 12, 20, 41, 62–66; 28:11–15); (iii) demand Jesus to prove his credentials (12:38; 16:1); (iv) test Jesus' knowledge (19:3); (22:23–33); (22:34–36); (v) are jealous of Jesus (21:15); and (vi) challenge Jesus' authority (21:23–27).

39. Another Gospel writer speaks about Jesus appointing seventy others and sending them out in pairs "ahead of him to every city and place where he himself was going to come" (Luke 10:1).

40. Bauer, "Mission in Matthew's Gospel," 245 n. 23.

41. Kingsbury, *Matthew as Story*, 37–40.

His argument, therefore, is that "the disciples" represent more than the historical figures who closely follow Jesus around in the story, and that their characters represent every post-resurrection Christian.

Wilkins's survey of the use of μαθητής in classical and Hellenistic literature reveals a historical progression. The term was used in three ways in early classical period: (i) in the general sense as a *learner*; (ii) in the technical sense as an *adherent* of a great teacher, teaching, or master; and (iii) more restrictedly by Sophists to refer to one of their *institutional pupils*. Μαθητής continued to be used in late Hellenistic period in the general sense of learner and adherent, but more generally to refer to the latter. The type of adherence in question, which was determined by the master, ranged from being the pupil of a philosopher, to the follower of a great thinker and master of the past, to the devotee of a religious figure. Wilkins writes that by the third century CE the term was used by one prolific writer to refer exclusively to an adherent. At the time of Christ, μαθητής had become a convenient term to designate the followers of Jesus as persons who adhered to their master.[42]

"The disciples" "follow" (ἀκολουθέω) Jesus closely and consistently.[43] Within this close social setting, Jesus instructs them and models a type of behavior before them that is vital for achieving his objective: to replicate themselves throughout the nations. It is a surrogate family environment, in which the disciples observe as well as participate actively in their own discipling process. Bruce Malina and Richard Rohrbaugh describe the "surrogate family," or "fictive kin" group, as "the household or family [that] provided the early Jesus-group members with one of their basic images of social identity and cohesion."[44]

The reader, therefore, perceives "the eleven disciples" (28:16) as: (i) adherents to the Matthean Jesus, who calls them into discipleship and determines the nature of their adherency (4:19; 8:22; 9:9; 10:38; 16:24; 19:21, 28–30); (ii) followers of their master in a surrogate family

---

42. Wilkins, Discipleship in the Ancient World, 11–42.

43. "ἀκολουθέω," BDAG, 36–37. This term has varied usage in the NT: "come behind," "accompany," "be a disciple of," "obey," and "follow behind" someone. Thirteen of its twenty-five appearances in Matthew refer to following Jesus as a disciple (4:20, 22; 8:19, 22; 9:9 [x2]; 10:38; 16:24; 19:21, 27, 28; 20:34; 27:55); the others relate either to persons accompanying Jesus as he ministers (4:25; 8:1, 10; 9:27; 12:15; 14:13; 19:2; 20:29), or to following a person who is ahead (8:23; 9:19; 21:9; 26:58).

44. Malina and Rohrbaugh, *Social-Science Commentary*, 373–74, 414. For more on kinship and the early Christian community acting as a surrogate family, see also Hanson, "Kinship," 62–79; and Neyrey, *Honor and Shame*, 54.

arrangement, bringing them into close proximity with his teaching and his actions; and (iii) representing more than the historical figures who closely follow the earthly Jesus; their narrative significance extends to every post-resurrection Christian.

"The disciples," who previously comprised twelve persons, are now only eleven in number. This is the only occurrence of the term ἕνδεκα in Matthew (cf. Mark 16:14; Luke 29:9, 33). Their reduction in number recalls the disciples' surrogate family arrangement that has gone awry in at least three ways: (i) Judas betrays Jesus and, though feeling remorseful, commits suicide and is no longer among their group;[45] (ii) Peter denies knowing Jesus; his weeping implies repentance that leads to restoration;[46] nevertheless, his temporary falling away (cf. 26:31-33) recalls Jesus' previous pronouncement about the consequences of failing to confess him publicly (cf. 10:32); and (iii) all the male disciples leave Jesus and flee at the time of his betrayal and arrest (26:56), following only from a distance thereafter (26:58; cf. 27:55 on the women disciples). Except for Judas, the falling away of the disciples is temporary, as the Lord forewarns in the comment that after his resurrection he will go ahead of them to Galilee and meet them there (26:32; cf. 28:7, 10).

Matthew adds that the destination of the eleven disciples is Galilee, a location with which the reader is familiar: (i) Jesus occasionally withdraws there, seeking refuge from political and religious authorities (e.g., 2:19-23; 4:12-16; cf. Isa 9:1, 2; 60:1-3);[47] (ii) he arrives from Galilee to be baptized by John (3:13-17); (iii) Jesus calls his first disciples by the Sea of Galilee (4:18-22) and undertakes the majority of his public ministry there (e.g., 4:17, 23, 25; 15:29-31; 11:20-24);[48] (iv) he forewarns his dis-

---

45. The reader's remembrance of Judas's betrayal serves as a warning about the danger of permanently "falling away" (Bauer, "Mission in Matthew's Gospel," 246).

46. Bauer, "Mission in Matthew's Gospel," 246 n. 29 contrasts Peter's denial, followed by weeping (κλαίω) as a sign of repentance, with Judas's remorse (μεταμέλομαι) that does not lead to a change of mind or alteration of intention (μετανοέω, cf. 4:17).

47. See also "ἀναχωρέω," BDAG, 75; and Riesner, "Archeology and Geography," 34-46, esp. 40, on the "Withdrawal Areas around Galilee."

48. See also Riesner, "Archeology and Geography," 36-39 on "The Public Ministry of Jesus in Galilee," including Nazareth, Cana (John 2:1, 12; 4:46; 21:2), Nain (Luke 7:11-12), the Sea of Galilee (John 21:1; cf. 6:1), Tiberias (Luke 13:31-33), Magdala (Mark 8:10), Gennesaret (Matt 8:18-27; 14:22-24, 34; Mark 6:53-56), The Sermon on the Mount (Matt 5:1-7:29; Luke 6:17-71), the First and Second Miraculous Feeding (14:13-21; 15:32-39), Jesus' Appearance by the Sea (John 21), Capernaum (Matt 8:5; 11:20-24; 17:24), Chorazin (Matt 11:20-24), and Bethsaida (Matt 11:20-24; Mark 8:22-26).

ciples on two occasions, while in Galilee, that he must go to Jerusalem, be betrayed, killed, and will be resurrected on the third day (17:22; cf. 16:21); (v) on his triumphant entry into Jerusalem, the crowds recognize him to be "the prophet Jesus, from Nazareth in Galilee" (21:11); (vi) he forewarns his disciples that they will all fall away, but that after he is resurrected, he will go ahead of them into Galilee (26:31–32), where they will meet again (cf. 28:7, 10); and (vi) many women disciples, who follow Jesus from Galilee, are present at his crucifixion, looking on from a distance (27:55–56).

Bauer perceives that the disciples' Galilean destination has a threefold significance for the disciples and the reader: (i) it points to the comparison between the mission of the post-resurrection church and the ministry of the earthly Jesus; (ii) it signals the eschatological character of the mission of the church by fulfilling Scripture (Matt 4:12–16; cf. Isa 9:1–2) and heralding God's long-awaited end-time rule over the earth; and (iii) it emphasizes the mission to the Gentiles—i.e., "all the nations"—which Jesus subsequently makes explicit (28:19; cf. 4:12–16).[49]

Seán Freyne advises that the name Galilee has been interpreted to mean "the circle" or "the district," and notes that Josephus defines the boundaries of Jewish Galilee of his day in terms of its surrounding states: Carmel, Ptolemais, and Gaba on the west; Samaria and Scythopolis to the south; Hippos, Gadara, and the Gaulanitis on the east side; and the territory of Tyre to the north completing the circle. Evidence suggests, however, that it had once been more extensive. Galilee was an administrative territory throughout the Hellenistic-Roman period, comprising, according to Josephus, 204 cities and villages when he assumed responsibility for its administration in 66 CE. This suggests a rural lifestyle, even though Galilee comprised large thriving city centers—e.g., Tarichaeae, Gischala, and Gamala—each with its own city walls, hippodrome, and adjoining land.[50]

Galilee represents, for the reader, recent memories and future possibilities as a place of: (i) refuge from enemies; (ii) new beginnings—the life of discipleship and the church; (iii) learning for public ministry; (iv) preparation for future trial and persecution; (v) economic resources and livelihood; (vi) ministry opportunity where "the nations" (Jews and Gentiles) already converge for trade and commerce, coalescing around

---

49. Bauer, "Mission in Matthew's Gospel," 246–47.

50. For additional information on the commercial, political, judicial, economic, and social framework of Hellenistic/Roman Galilee, see Freyne, "Galilee," 2:895–99.

a *lingua franca* that facilitates communication; and (vii) administrative structure and order. It is conceivable, therefore, that the risen Lord would designate Galilee as the location for meeting his disciples immediately after his passion and resurrection, with a view towards issuing his commission to them there.

The disciples are to meet the risen Jesus at "the mountain which [he] had designated to them"; however, Matthew makes no prior reference to this specific mountain in Galilee. This has created speculation about the identity of the mountain, which several scholars associate with the mountain of Jesus' Sermon (5:1),[51] and others with the Mount of Transfiguration (17:1) or Mount Tabor.[52] Matthew's reader is familiar with mountain locations in his story. They are places of: (i) supernatural revelation (4:8; 17:1-2, 9); (ii) teaching (5:1-2; 8:1); (iii) prayer (14:23); (iv) healing (15:29-30); (v) opportunity to exercise faith (17:20; 21:21); (vi) safety and provision (18:12); and (vii) refuge (24:16).

Scholars generally agree that most of the mountains in the Gospels are theologically significant and can be related to Sinai, Zion, or the Mount of Olives.[53] Christian tradition links several events of the Gospels to known mountains, but only three named mountains are identified therein: (i) the Mount of Olives (Matt 21:1 parr.; 24:3 par.; 26:30 parr.); (ii) the hill on which Nazareth is situated (Luke 4:29); and (iii) Mount Gerizim (John 4:20-21). The Gospel writers draw parallels between Jesus, who fulfills the prophecy of Deuteronomy 18:15, 18 (cf. Acts 3:22-23), and Moses. Jesus' transfiguration on a "high mountain" (Matt 17:1-13 // Mark 9:2-8 // Luke 9:28-36) closely parallels Moses' encounter with God at Sinai (Exod 24:1-18; 34:1-35).[54] Additionally, Jesus' going up on a mountain and sitting down (5:1) and his coming down from the mountain (8:1) are perceived to be illuminated by Sinai, and they render the Sermon on the Mount to be "some sort of counterpart to the giving

---

51. Powell, "Sermon on the Mount," 936-38; Nolland, *Matthew*, 126-1262; Blomberg, *Matthew*, 429-30; Smith, *Matthew*, 335-36.

52. Hagner, *Matthew 14-28*, 883-84; Riesner, "Archeology and Geography," 39; Wesley, *Explanatory Notes*, 98.

53. On the theological significance of mountains in the Gospels, see Allison Jr., "Mountain and Wilderness," 563-64; see also Donaldson, *Jesus on the Mountain*, 31-49 concerning mountain symbolism in Israel's experience.

54. See Allison Jr., "Mountain and Wilderness," 563 on the similarities between Jesus' and Moses' transfigurations; see Broyles, "Moses," 560-62 regarding the mountain typology in the Gospels.

of the Law on Sinai."[55] Some perceive a Zion typology in the Matthean Jesus' ministry of gathering, healing, and feeding on the mountain (15:29–39)—an event that may project Jesus' ministry as the fulfillment of Jewish hopes about Zion. In 15:30–31, one could argue for an allusion to Isaiah 35:5–6, which is a prophecy about Zion—the location of Israel's eschatological gathering (Jer 31:1–25; Tob 14:5–7), a place of healing (Isa 35:5–6), and the venue of the messianic feast (Isa 25:6–10).[56] The location of Jesus' eschatological discourse (Matt 24 // Mark 13) links the Parousia with the Mount of Olives (cf. Acts 1:11) and may represent an allusion to Zechariah 14:4, which some scholars consider to be connected with the splitting of the temple veil in two (Matt 27:51–53).[57] Finally, the mountain in Matthew 4:8 serves the literary function of connecting Jesus' renunciation of power that the Satan offers to him on a "very high mountain" with the risen Jesus' declaration on a mountain in Galilee of possessing universal power (28:18). The underlying moral of the story is that only by obedience to his Father, and not by usurpation, does Jesus acquire legitimate authority which comes only from God.[58]

The phrase "the mountain which Jesus had designated" is pregnant with implications for the reader, who understands that: (i) the Matthean Jesus' advance choosing of a mountain venue to meet with his disciples adds to the significance of the setting, since it is reasonable to assume that he selected it for a specific reason; (ii) the mountain setting in Matthew is associated with divine revelation; therefore (iii) whatever activity occurs there must take on supernatural significance, and the reader will recall Matthew's accounts of events in similar settings and make inferences about the profoundness of Jesus' commission that follows.

---

55. Allison Jr., "Mountain and Wilderness," 564 also contends that John 6:3 ("Jesus went up on the mountain, and there he sat down with his disciples") closely resembles Matt 5:1–2 and is reminiscent of Exod 24:2; 34:3 LXX.

56. Allison Jr., "Mountain and Wilderness," 564.

57. Allison Jr., "Mountain and Wilderness," 564 notes that both texts feature: (i) a resurrection of the dead that occurs immediately outside Jerusalem; (ii) an earthquake; (iii) use of σχίζω ("to split") in the passive voice; and (iv) the resurrected ones being called οἱ ἅγιοι ("the holy ones").

58. See also Donaldson, *Jesus on the Mountain*, 193–202 on the mountain motif in Matthew's Gospel—i.e., a place of temptation, teaching, feeding, transfiguration, and eschatological discourse.

Matthew 28:17

Matthew utilizes *contrast* once more, but on this occasion he emphasizes the difference between two actions of the disciples: they worship Jesus, but some are doubtful about some aspect of their experience.

The reader is familiar with the term προσκυνέω ("worship, do obeisance to, prostrate oneself before, do reverence to"[59]), which Matthew typically uses with Jesus as the object of other people's worship or reverence: (i) the magi follow a star in the East and come to worship the one who is born king of the Jews (2:2, 11); (ii) persons seeking Jesus' assistance worship him—e.g., a leper needing to be cleansed (8:2), a synagogue official whose daughter has just died (9:18), and a Canaanite woman whose daughter is cruelly demon possessed (15:25); (iii) the disciples worship Jesus, recognizing that he is God's Son after he walks on water and calms a storm (14:33); (iv) the mother of the sons of Zebedee bows down before Jesus while requesting her sons' preferment in his coming kingdom (20:20); and (v) the women disciples take hold of the feet of the resurrected Jesus and worship him near the tomb where he was buried (28:9).

On occasion, Matthew employs προσκυνέω with Jesus not being the object of worship. In one such instance, the Matthean Jesus describes the response of a slave who prostrates himself before his lord, who forgives him the debt that he owes and could not immediately repay (18:26). It is noteworthy, however, that the master to whom deferential respect is paid by the slave possesses qualities that are similar to Jesus—he is a forgiving, compassionate king (18:21–35). In the two other episodes, Jesus is also involved: (i) Herod pretends to want to worship Jesus (2:8), and (ii) the devil invites Jesus to worship him in return for all the kingdoms of the world (4:8–9). Both situations represent the intentional wrongful application of worship, but in the end the evaluative point of view of God is reinforced: in the former, the magi truly worship the infant Jesus (2:11) and are warned by God in a dream not to return to Herod to provide the whereabouts of the child (2:12); in the latter, Jesus rebukes the Satan, telling him that the Scriptures preclude such behavior because only God is to be worshipped (4:10; cf. Deut 6:13; 10:20).

The Gospels employ various Greek terms relating to worship (προσκυνέω, σέβω, λατρεύω, λειτουργέω, etc.), and while references thereto typically occur in connection with some other activity—e.g., healing, the temptation of Jesus, etc.—worship itself is not peripheral to

---

59. "Προσκυνέω," BDAG, 882–83.

the narrative.⁶⁰ The Gospels provide examples of early church worship: (i) Luke's infancy narratives comprise three psalms of praise (Luke 1:46–55, 68–79; 2:29–32); (ii) the victory shouts of the crowd at the time of Jesus' triumphant entry into Jerusalem represent another example of praise in the Gospels (Matt 21:9 parr.); (iii) the Prologue to the Fourth Gospel (John 1:1–18), in which some scholars opine is embedded a hymn that may have functioned as a poem of praise to God for the Johannine community; (iv) the Lord's Prayer (Matt 6:9–13 par.) appears in an almost identical form in the Didache (Did. 8.2), an early Christian manual of instruction that urges Christians to pray in this manner three times a day (Did. 8.3); and (v) the Gospels' accounts of the Last Supper (Matt 26:26–30 and par.; cf. 1 Cor 11:23–25) may reflect not only the events of the night before the crucifixion, but also the eucharistic practices of the Evangelists' communities.⁶¹

The implications of καὶ ἰδόντες αὐτὸν προσεκύνησαν for the reader may be twofold. Bauer rightly contends that: (i) the disciples' act of worshipping the risen Jesus implies the deity of Christ, who has previously declared that only God is to be worshipped (4:10; cf. Deut 6:13; 10:20); and (ii) the fact that Jesus has previously been the object of worship in the Gospel accentuates the continuity between the earthly Jesus and the resurrected Lord;⁶² therefore, the reader understands that Jesus' communication that follows is authoritative because of its divine origin.

The other side of Matthew's *contrast* regarding the disciples' behavior is that "some were doubtful" (28:17b). This latter half of the verse raises two important issues that several scholars have already addressed, namely: (i) what the definite article οἱ is referring to—whether to some of the Eleven, or to others who are present with them on the mountain; and (ii) the shade of meaning of ἐδίστασαν—whether some of them "doubt," "waver," or "hesitate." Matthew uses διστάζω ("doubt, waver; hesitate"⁶³) on only one previous occasion—i.e., when Peter attempts to walk on the

---

60. For more on the three focal points of Jewish worship in first-century Palestine—i.e., the home (sharing of bread, observing feasts, private prayer); the synagogue (Sabbath services), and the Temple (the main hub of Jewish worship)—see Farris, "Worship," 891–94; see also Reid, "Sacrifice and Temple Service," 1036–50 on access to worship in the Temple; and Aune, "Worship, Early Christian," 973–89 for a comprehensive assessment of early Christian worship.

61. Farris, "Worship," 892–93.

62. Bauer, "Mission in Matthew's Gospel," 248.

63. "διστάζω," BDAG, 252.

water towards Jesus, but becomes afraid and begins to sink on seeing the wind, to which Jesus responds, "You of little faith, why did you *doubt*?" (14:31).[64] In this event, Jesus labels Peter's failure as "doubt" that is characterized by "little [or weak] faith" (ὀλιγόπιστος), which might explain the meaning of the disciples' doubt in 28:17b. Elsewhere, Matthew uses two additional terms, ἄπιστος and διακρίνω, that fall within the semantic range of διστάζω.[65] First, the author recounts the story of the disciples' inability heal a boy who is demon possessed (17:14–21). Jesus instructs them to bring the young man to him, he rebukes the demon, and the boy is immediately healed. In the process of solving the problem, Jesus refers to his disciples as "You *unbelieving* [ἄπιστος] and perverted generation" (17:17), and later explains that they were unable to exorcize the demon because of their "little faith" (ὀλιγοπιστία, 17:20). Second, Matthew reports that Jesus curses a barren fig tree, which withers immediately (21:18–22). His disciples are amazed by what they see and Jesus responds, "If you have faith and do not *doubt* [διακρίνω], you will not only do what was done to the fig tree, but even if you say to this mountain, 'Be taken up and cast into the sea,' it will happen" (21:21). In both episodes, the Matthean Jesus correlates the quality of his disciples' faith with their (in)ability to achieve desired results.[66] Not unlike the episode concerning Peter's attempt to walk on the water, it is the littleness of their faith that causes unbelief or doubt and leads to their inability to respond favorably to circumstances as they unfold.

It is notable that: (i) all of the disciples that are present "see" (εἶδον) the risen Jesus with their own eyes; (ii) indeed, they see him well enough to worship him; however, (iii) some are doubtful—perhaps a reflection of the post-resurrection church experience, which Bauer believes is present in Matthew's portrayal of the disciples.[67] The evangelist's contrast between the disciples' worship and doubt is compelling, and it urges the readers, who are post-resurrection disciples, to associate themselves with

---

64. This episode, too, is marked by a contrast between "worship" and "doubt," but it is addressed in reverse order: first Peter "doubts" (14:31), then the disciples "worship" Jesus (14:33).

65. See Louw and Nida, *Greek-English Lexicon*, 1:369–71 on the "Believe to be True" (31.35–31.39) subdomain of the "Hold a View, Believe, Trust" semantic domain.

66. Bauer, *Gospel of the Son of God*, 199 describes ὀλιγόπιστος as faith contaminated by an element of doubt (cf. 14:31).

67. Bauer, "Mission in Matthew's Gospel," 245 n. 23; cf. *Gospel of the Son of God*, 231–32, who argue that post-resurrection discipleship is characterized by both worship and doubt.

the character group of "the disciples," whose faith is marked by worship that is mixed with doubt and who are presented as struggling with the kinds of issues and experiences that are relevant to post-resurrection Christians, which are described elsewhere in Matthew.[68]

Matthew 28:18

Matthew employs a *recurrence* structure that begins in 28:18 and continues to the end of the Commission. Recurrence is usually employed to indicate emphasis, to develop a theme, or to develop depth and richness of presentation by inviting the reader to interpret individual occurrences in light of the other occurrences or the recurring pattern as a whole.[69] The reader observes the repetition of inclusive scope that is expressed by the term πᾶς ("all"): (i) "all authority" (28:18b); (ii) "all the nations" (28:19a); (iii) "all that I have commanded you" (28:20a); and (iv) "all the days" (28:20b). The Matthean Jesus' repetition of πᾶς emphasizes the comprehensiveness of the Commission: he possesses *universal* authority; he commands his disciples to make disciples of *everyone, everywhere*; they are to teach new disciples to observe *everything* that he has commanded; and he promises to be with them *every day* until the Parousia.

The author's use of *recurrence* of the same term has implications for the reader, who must, henceforth, interpret everything about the Commission in terms of the widest possible scope. The reader discovers in the commissioning proper (28:19–20a) that the risen Jesus' unlimited authority (28:18b) becomes the basis for later references to "all" (28:19a, 20a, 20b). In other words, the disciples can accomplish their assigned mission because of the Lord's unlimited authority. Additionally, given the reader's inclination to interpret individual occurrences of a recurring element in light of the other occurrences thereof or in light of the recurring pattern as a whole, he will interpret "*all* I have commanded you" with the same intensity of scope that he interprets "*all* authority," "*all* the nations," and "*all* the days." This means that the disciples are to teach new disciples to obey *all* of Jesus' commands, inclusive of his verbal and nonverbal

---

68. For example: "little faith" (6:25–34; 8:23–27; 14:28–32; 16:5–12; 17:14–21); "taxation" (17:24–27); "persecution and opposition" (24:9–14; 26:31–35; 28:11–15); and the need to "keep watching and praying," but being weighed down by "weak flesh" (26:36–46).

69. Bauer and Traina, *Inductive Bible Study*, 96.

commands (i.e., what he says, does, and even commands from silence); nothing is to be omitted.

Matthew makes use of *preparation/realization* as he introduces the risen Jesus' final words. The reader determines that the narrator's "And Jesus came up and spoke to them, saying" (28:18a) is the *preparation* for those final words, the *realization*, that follow immediately thereafter (28:18b-20). In the preparatory material, the author utilizes a "rather fulsome introductory clause," comprising three verbs—"came up", "spoke", and "said"—to describe the moment immediately prior to the verbal contact between Jesus and the disciples (28:18a), which might be aimed, *inter alia*, at relieving the disciples of recent anxiety and discomfort.[70] One scholar refers to this introductory event as a "proleptic Parousia."[71]

Matthew's use of *introduction* at this point facilitates the reader's transition from the tension of worship mixed with doubt (28:17) to the guidance, hope, and assurance that proceed from Jesus' declaration of authority (28:18b), his commissioning statement (28:19-20a), and his promise to be with them always (28:20b). That is to say, the reader progresses from the disciples' present circumstances to a new and desired situation that describes where the risen Lord wants them to be.

Jesus' declaration, which centers upon his receipt of universal authority (28:18b), immediately follows the narrator's introductory comments. The announcement, which utilizes a divine or theological passive (ἐδόθη), implies that the authority was given to him by God,[72] and it represents the climax of an irony-filled passion event: (i) he was mockingly called "Messiah" by the members of the Sanhedrin (26:68); (ii) the Roman guard dressed him up as a king and pretended to pay homage to him (27:27-32); (iii) they put up a charge against him that read, "This is Jesus the King of the Jews" (27:37; cf. 27:11); and (iv) now, after his resurrection, Jesus is exalted as the glorious Son of Man and is given all authority in heaven and on earth. His declaration proves that all of his previous claims (e.g., 26:64; 27:11) are now shown to be true, though unknown to

---

70. France, *Matthew*, 1112; see also Nolland, *Matthew*, 1263 on people in Matthew typically "coming/going to" or "approaching" (προσέρχομαι) Jesus; whereas, only here (28:18) and after the transfiguration (17:7) does Jesus approach someone; and France, *Matthew*, 650-51 about Matthew's use of προσέρχομαι with Jesus as the subject being connected with the description of situations in which the disciples are overwhelmed by a supernatural event (17:7; 28:18).

71. Meier, "Matthew," 4:637.

72. Wallace, *Greek Grammar*, 437.

other story characters at the time. "Things are not always as they seem, and sometimes things are exactly the opposite of what they seem."[73]

Matthew's reader is familiar with the term ἐξουσία ("authority; power"[74]), which the author typically uses with regard to Jesus throughout the Gospel: (i) the crowds reckon that Jesus teaches as one having *authority*, and not as one of their scribes (7:29); (ii) "the Son of Man has *authority* on earth to forgive sins" (9:6); (iii) the crowds are awestruck and glorify God, who had given *authority* to men to forgive sins (9:8); (iv) Jesus summons his disciples and gives them *authority* to cast out unclean spirits and to heal every kind of disease and sickness (10:1); and (v) the chief priests and elders question the source of Jesus' *authority* to do the things that he does (21:23, 24, 27). On a single occasion, Matthews uses the term in connection with someone other than Jesus—i.e., the centurion, "a man under *authority*," requests Jesus to heal his sick servant (8:9).

Scholars express a variety of views about Jesus' claim to universal authority, including: (i) it is a new "all-inclusive" authority that incorporates, but is not limited to, his earthly authority;[75] (ii) the claim echoes Daniel 7:13-14 LXX and signals Jesus' exaltation, which Matthew correlates with the time of the resurrection, when God grants comprehensive authority to Jesus;[76] (iii) the connection between Jesus' authority and his disciples' commissioning resides in his promise to be present with them (28:20), not in his explicit handing over of authority to them;[77] (iv) Jesus' universal authority is explained in part by the other three uses of "all" in

---

73. Turner, "Gospel of Matthew," 361.

74. "ἐξουσία," BDAG, 352-53.

75. Bauer, "Mission in Matthew's Gospel," 250; so also Brown and Roberts, *Matthew*, 91; Nolland, *Matthew*, 1264-65, however, perceives that Jesus' death and resurrection results in the vindication of authority rather than new authority; Blomberg, *Matthew*, 307 approaches the issue from the perspective of newly delegated authority, some of which was previously voluntarily relinquished (cf. Phil 2:6-8) by the Son of God at the time of his incarnation.

76. Bauer, "Mission in Matthew's Gospel," 250-51; so also Brown and Roberts, *Matthew*, 102, 156, 245, 262, 302-3; Turner, *Matthew*, 689; Davies and Allison Jr., *Matthew (III)*, 682-83; however, France, *Matthew*, 1112-13 notes that while some scholars argue that the Matthew text transcends the limits of the Daniel text, that argument does not conflict with Dan 7:14 being the source (or at least a source) of the language and imagery of 28:18; Luz, *Matthew 8-20*, 189-90 argues that Matthew and his readers' knowledge of ὁ υἱὸς τοῦ ἀνθρώπου "was deepened with the aid of the Book of Daniel but did not primarily originate there."

77. Brown and Roberts, *Matthew*, 151, 453-54, 473-74, 481-82.

28:18–20;[78] and (v) the earthly Jesus' rejection of Satan's offer of power (4:8–10) prefigures the risen Jesus' receipt of authority over heaven and earth,[79] and unfolds what obedience to God means.[80]

Jesus' authority includes both the power (capability; e.g., 10:1) and the right (legitimacy; e.g., 21:23–27) to act.[81] G. S. Shogren defines "authority" as the "the right to effect control over objects, individuals or events. While human authority may be delegated, God's authority arises from himself alone."[82] God reveals his authority and power in the person of Jesus: (i) Scripture foreshadows that the Messiah was to be anointed with the Spirit of God (Isa 9:6–7; cf. Pss. Sol. 17:22–25), and Jesus claims to be that anointed one at the launch of his ministry (Luke 4:16–21); (ii) Jesus's power is unparalleled—he heals diseases, forgives sins, and exercises power over nature; (iii) he teaches with authority, and pronounces judgment on entire cities (Matt 11:20–24; 23:37–39), but he has no authority to assign seats on his left and right in his kingdom (20:20–28 par.); (iv) he delegates authority to his disciples (10:1; 18:18), even to pronounce symbolic judgment on persons who reject their message (10:14); and (v) he exercises power in humility and submission to the cross.[83]

Matthew's treatment of Jesus' revelation of his universal authority has implications for the reader's understanding of the Commission. The use of irony reinforces the prior claims of the implied author that the Matthean Jesus is indeed: (i) the Son of Man who would destroy the temple and rebuild it in three days (26:61; cf. 12:40; 27:40; 27:63; John 2:19–21), (ii) the Messiah and the Son of God (26:63–64; cf. 4:3, 6; 8:29; 16:16; 27:40, 43, 54), and (iii) the King of Israel (27:11; cf. 2:2; 27:29, 37, 42). Additionally, Jesus' declaration of having received universal authority does not mean that he hands over that authority to his disciples; rather, they derive their own authority for mission by following him—i.e., his commands and his actions.

---

78. Smith, *Matthew*, 337.

79. Luz, *Matthew 1–7*, 153.

80. Luz, *Matthew 1–7*, 155.

81. Bauer, "Mission in Matthew's Gospel," 250; so also Arnold, "Power," 5:444–46, esp. 444.

82. Shogren, "Authority and Power" distinguishes "authority" (ἐξουσία) and "power" (typically δύναμις), the latter referring to "the ability to bring about what one desires."

83. Shogren, "Authority and Power," 51–53; see Arnold, "Power," 5:445 regarding the contrast between Christ's power and that of Satan, the prince of this world.

Matthew 28:19

One of the semantic structures that the author utilizes in 28:19 is hortatory *causation*. The key term οὖν ("therefore") suggests the occurrence of causation on two levels in the passage. On one level, Matthew expresses the cause: that Jesus claims to have been given all authority in heaven and on earth (28:18b); then, he outlines its effect: that the disciples must "go . . . *make disciples* [imperative] . . . baptizing . . . teaching" (28:19–20a), which refers to the discipling activity of bringing persons under Christ's authority. On another level, "all authority" (28:18b) that Jesus receives is the cause that results in the later references to "all" in the passage ("all the nations," 28:19a; "all that I commanded you," 28:20a; and "all the days," 28:20b). The author's use of hortatory causation requires the reader to recognize that: (i) the disciples are able to carry out their assigned mission because of the Lord's receipt of unlimited authority; and (ii) his unlimited authority (28:18b) is the basis for his command to make disciples of *everyone, everywhere*, teaching them *everything* that he has commanded, and being assured of his ongoing presence *every day*.

Matthew's use of hortatory causation in 28:19 is also the result of a more remote context. Once the reader encounters "Go therefore and make disciples of all the nations" (28:19), he immediately recalls "Follow me, and I will make you fishers of men" (4:19), the first declaration the Matthean Jesus issues to his disciples, after which they immediately leave their livelihoods and family and follow him (4:20, 22). Luz connects Jesus' first call for persons to follow him (4:18–22) with his first commission to the Twelve to "fish" for people (10:5–16), and to his subsequent Parable of the Fishnet (13:47–50), where the expression is understood to refer to missionary activity, and ultimately with the Commission, which, Luz argues, "finally makes plain what Jesus means." [84]

The two declarations in 4:19 and 28:19 incorporate discipleship language that includes semantically related terms—ὀπίσω, marker of position behind an entity that precedes; "after" (i.e., "come after/follow someone as a disciple," e.g., 4:19);[85] and μαθητεύω, "cause one to be a pupil; teach" (i.e., "make a disciple of, teach someone," e.g., 28:19a)[86]—at

---

84. Luz, *Matthew 1–7*, 161–62.
85. "ὀπίσω," BDAG, 716.
86. "μαθητεύω" BDAG, 609; see also the list of semantically related "discipleship" terms in "Follow, Be a Disciple (36.31–36.43)" in Louw and Nida, *Greek-English Lexicon*, 1:469–70; and Wilkins, *Discipleship in the Ancient World*, 11–42 on the use of

the beginning and end of the Gospel, respectively. The declarations are connected by elements relating to *time* (beginning and end of a journey), *location* (both events occur in Galilee), *characters* (Jesus and his disciples are common to both events), and *semantics* (words of similar meaning are common to both accounts). As a result, the latter command is perhaps best viewed as an extension or development of the former, and Matthew's positioning of them—near the beginning and at the end of his Gospel—suggests that he intends his readers to interpret them in this way. Since the two pronouncements (4:19; 28:19) address the same issue of disciple-making, the reader expects Matthew to use the intervening material (4:20–28:18) to develop the theme of "fishing for men" in the context of Jesus' interaction (in words and actions) with his Twelve, which is exactly what Matthew does. Matthew employs the future tense in "*I will make* you fishers of men" (4:19), which helps the reader connect this declaration with the material in 4:20—28:18. Hearing the command in 4:19, the reader anticipates Jesus' future efforts to fulfill his promise to make his disciples "fishers of men." He perceives all such efforts, as well as the disciples' responses thereto, as described in 4:20—28:18, to be causally linked to Jesus' command to follow him and his promise to equip them to fish for people (4:19).

I agree with Luz's assertion that Matthew clarifies in 28:19 what Jesus means by "I will make you fishers of men" (4:19),[87] and the author attempts to achieve this objective on two levels by means of hortatory causation.[88] On the first level, the causal progression is from 4:19 to 4:20—28:18: Jesus states in the indicative, "I will make you fishers of men" (4:19)—the cause—which he reinforces throughout 4:20—28:18 with commands and exhortations to his disciples (e.g., 5:12, 44; 6:1, 9, 33; 7:7; 10:7–8; 16:6; 19:14; 23:3; 24:4, 6; 26:26–27, 41)—the effect—that are designed to achieve his objective of making them "fishers of men." The usual key words that are associated with causation—"therefore," "so," and "then"—are implied.[89] The reader therefore understands this narrative

---

μαθητεύω and μαθητής by Greek writers in antiquity.

87. Luz, *Matthew 1–7*, 161–62.

88. Alternatively, the structural relationship between Jesus' promise to make his disciples "fishers of men" (4:19) and his earthly ministry as a whole (4:20–28:18) may be described as ideological particularization (Bauer and Traina, *Inductive Bible Study*, 100).

89. Bauer and Traina, *Inductive Bible Study*, 105–6 note that implicit causation can also be present.

progression to mean: "Because I will make you fishers of men, *therefore* you ought to do so and so." Hence, all of Jesus' earthly ministry represents his own efforts to make his disciples "fishers of men."[90] On the second level, the causal progression is from 4:19 directly to 28:19: Jesus states in the indicative, "I will make you fishers of men" (4:19)—the cause—which progresses to his imperative at the end of the Gospel, "Go therefore and make disciples of all the nations" (28:19)—the effect—which is designed to demonstrate the realization or fulfillment of his promise to make them "fishers of men." Consequently, the reader understands this narrative progression to mean: "Because I have already made you fishers of men, *therefore* you ought to go and make disciples of all the nations."

The major implication of utilizing the structure of hortatory causation for the reader is that the initial imperative, "Follow me, and I will make you fishers of men" (4:19), is read in anticipation of all of the Matthean Jesus' future efforts to make his disciples "fishers of men"; additionally, the closing imperative, "Go, therefore and make disciples of the nations . . . " (28:19–20), is interpreted in light of the disciples' past disciple-making experience with their master, which includes all his commands and actions that they hear and see. The underlying unity of Matthew's Gospel around a discipling theme helps to drive this particular argument. The Matthean Jesus embodies perfect alignment between what he commands, promises, and does: (i) he promises to make his disciples ἁλιεῖς ἀνθρώπων (4:19); (ii) he fulfills his promise by teaching special truths and principles, and by modeling certain behaviors before them (4:20—28:18); (iii) he gives them on-the-job training as disciple-makers by sending them, first, to the "lost sheep of the house of Israel" (10:1–41); and (iv) finally, he commissions them into global service of making disciples of all the nations (28:19–20).

Matthew also uses a *cruciality* structure or pivot in this verse. It is important to note, however, that while the pivot (i.e., the total turning around of the material) becomes apparent to the reader in this verse, which he understands in relation to earlier portions of the Gospel, the actual change of direction or radical reversal appears to have occurred at the time of the resurrection: the time of Jesus' exaltation, when God grants comprehensive authority to him; the time at which Jesus' reign

---

90. By "Jesus' earthly ministry," I am referring to all of Jesus' preaching, teaching, healing, explaining, demonstrating, defending, empowering, providing, forewarning, interrogating, rebuking, obeying and praying to the Father, showing compassion for others, and so on that his disciples experience while they are with their master.

could have begun (cf. Acts 2:29-36; Rom 1:1-4; Phil 2:5-11; Heb 1:1-5).[91] The reader knows that until this point in the narrative, the Matthean Jesus has instructed his disciples to focus their ministry on the house of Israel: "Do not go in the way of the Gentiles, and do not enter any city of the Samaritans; but rather go to the lost sheep of the house of Israel" (10:5b-6; cf. 15:24).[92] However, in his final Commission, the scope of the discipling work is πάντα τὰ ἔθνη, which represents an expansion of ministry beyond Israel to "all the nations."[93] The implications of utilizing this structure are at least twofold: (i) it draws the reader's attention to what precedes the pivot—i.e., Matthew's repeated juxtaposition of Jewish particularism and Gentile inclusion, which signals God's intention to save all peoples of the world through Israel;[94] and (ii) it compels the reader to take note of what follows the pivot—i.e., a radical shift of emphasis away from

91. Bauer, "Mission in Matthew's Gospel," 250-51, esp. 251 n. 6; see Keener, *Matthew*, 716 n. 339, who argues that the ingressive aorist,'Εδόθη ("has been given," 28:18), suggests that Jesus' reign could have begun at the resurrection; and France, *Matthew*, 1113, who explains that Jesus' earlier claim of "everything entrusted to me by my Father" (11:27) is now is fully spelled out in 28:18; "indeed Jesus himself now possesses the authority that he attributed to his Father as 'Lord of heaven and earth' in 11:25."

92. The reader is aware of other traces of apparent Jewish particularism in Matthew, for example: (i) Jesus "will save *his people* from their sins" (1:20-21); (ii) Jesus is called "King of the *Jews*" (2:2; cf. 27:11, 29, 37) and "King of *Israel*" (27:42); (iii) the prophet wrote, "For out of you shall come forth a Ruler who will shepherd *My people Israel*" (2:4-6; Mic 5:2-4); (iv) Jesus' saying, "You will not finish going through the cities of Israel until the Son of Man comes," could be interpreted to mean that the disciples' focus would always be on Israel; (v) YHWH is known in the OT as "the *God of Israel*" (15:31; cf. Exod 5:1; 24:10); and (vi) Jesus assures his disciples that their reward in his kingdom will be to judge "the *twelve tribes of Israel*" (19:28).

93. Bauer, "Mission in Matthew's Gospel," 252 interprets πάντα τὰ ἔθνη to mean an expansion of the ministry of Jesus and the disciples beyond Israel, and not to signify a replacement of their previous "Israel only" ministry with a "Gentiles only" ministry. Scholars have for some time debated whether the phrase requires a "Gentiles only" (i.e., a replacement of the "Israel only" ministry) or a "Jews and Gentiles" (i.e., an expansion of the "Israel only" ministry) interpretation; see von Dobbeler, "Die Restitution Israels," 18-44, who argues that both the restrictive command of 10:5-6 and the command for universal mission in 28:19 remain in force until the end of the age.

94. Matthew portrays Jesus as the "son of Abraham" (1:1) through whom "all nations of the earth will be blessed" (cf. Gen 12:3; 18:18; 22:18), which results in overtones of Gentile inclusion throughout the Gospel (e.g., 1:1-17; 2:1-12; 8:11; 10:18; 12:18, 21; 15:21-28; 21:43; 22:1-10, esp. 22:9-10; 24:14; cf. 26:13; 26:28 "for many"; cf. 20:28; 27:54 "Gentile centurion"). See also Bauer and Powell, *Treasures New and Old*, 147 on the role of Gentile women in Matthew's genealogy; Weren, "Five Women," 288-305; and Bauer, "Kingship of Jesus," 306-23, esp. 319-23, regarding the Gentile magi as discipleship figures in Matthew.

the Jewish-only focus of Jesus and his disciples' pre-resurrection ministry towards the Gentile inclusion of their post-resurrection mission.

A third major structural relationship employed by Matthew in 28:19 is ideological *particularization*. The Matthean Jesus commands his disciples to "make disciples" (μαθητεύσατε) and adds three adjoining participles—πορευθέντες (28:19a), βαπτίζοντες (28:19b), and διδάσκοντες (28:20a)—that may develop or unpack the general command of μαθητεύσατε without necessarily exhausting its meaning by themselves.[95]

Daniel B. Wallace provides a detailed explanation of the relationship between the dependent verbal participles and the main verb, μαθητεύσατε.[96] Wallace identifies various types of dependent verbal participles, of which two—*adverbial* and *attendant circumstance*—are likely to be present in the primary text. He explains that adverbial participles are grammatically subordinate to their controlling verbs, and like ordinary adverbs they *modify* main verbs by expressing temporal, emotional or attitudinal, instrumental, causal, conditional, concessive, telic, or resultative ideas.[97] The main verb possesses meaning without the modifying participles being present; however, it takes on additional meaning when it comes into relationship with its modifying participles, and in the same way that ordinary adverbs modify adjectives, verbs, and other

---

95. Some may argue in favor of *instrumentation*, which involves "the movement from means to end . . . [and] may take one of two forms: the statement of purpose or the description of means" (Bauer, "Mission in Matthew's Gospel," 115); I believe, however, that this is not the preferred argument because it confines the reader to look no farther than the adjoining participles—πορευθέντες (28:19a), βαπτίζοντες (28:19b), and διδάσκοντες (28:20a)—to discover the meaning of μαθητεύσατε (28:19a).

96. Wallace, *Greek Grammar*, 622–50.

97. Wallace, *Greek Grammar*, 622; see also Long, "Pragmatics of Circumstantial Participles" who prefers the term "circumstantial" to "adverbial" when describing these participles since it helps to convey the idea that participles do not carry inherent adverbial logical-semantic meanings. Long differentiates between "pre-nuclear" (before the nuclear verb) and "post-nuclear" (after the nuclear verb) participles and emphasizes their basic functions relative to the main verb—i.e., pre-nuclear (transitional, framework, procedural); post-nuclear (redundant, explicating). On post-nuclear participles (e.g., "baptizing" [Matt 28:19b]; "teaching" [28:20a]) and their motivation, Long comments that: (i) grammatical prominence attends the nuclear verb; (ii) post-nuclear participles have a shared nuclear modal salience with the nuclear verb despite the grammatical prominence of the nuclear verb; and (iii) elaborative prominence attends post-nuclear participles due to their presence and relative "final" location, their qualifying nature, and their role in carrying the discourse forward; and *Koine Greek Grammar*, 326–36 for additional information on circumstantial participles.

adverbs without taking over their entire meaning, an adverbial participle modifies its controlling verb.

Some scholars argue that βαπτίζοντες (28:19b) and διδάσκοντες (28:20a) are instrumental participles that "spell out the substance of 'make disciples.'"[98] Several who adopt this stance emphasize the role that these two participles play in explaining the meaning of the imperative μαθητεύσατε. Bauer, for example, claims that "'baptizing' and 'teaching' have such broad ramifications that *most* of the aspects of discipling that Matthew presents otherwise in his Gospel are herein included."[99] This statement implies that there is very little or nothing to be found elsewhere in Matthew that helps explain the meaning of μαθητεύσατε. Nevertheless, Bauer concedes that: (i) preaching is a significant discipling practice that the Matthean Jesus models;[100] and that (ii) preaching is distinct from teaching[101] (and most certainly also from baptizing),[102] although, preaching is not unrelated to either of these two activities. Therefore, the reader must reasonably conclude that: (i) preaching (and possibly other practices also) is an important discipling activity that is not a subset of baptizing or teaching, and (ii) these two instrumental participles by themselves may not fully explain the meaning of μαθητεύσατε. For this reason, he must look to the broader context of Matthew in search of additional meaning of μαθητεύσατε.

Wallace posits that πορευθέντες is best described as an attendant circumstance participle that communicates an action that is coordinate with the main verb. It is to be translated like a finite verb, although it semantically depends on the main verb because it cannot exist without

---

98. Bauer, "Mission in Matthew's Gospel," 254; so also Brown and Roberts, *Matthew*, 263-64, 473; France, *Matthew*, 1115; Smith, *Matthew*, 338-39; Blomberg, *Matthew*, 431; Luz, *Matthew 21-28*, 625.

99. Bauer, "Mission in Matthew's Gospel," 254-55 (my emphasis).

100. Bauer, "Mission in Matthew's Gospel," 251.

101. So Bauer, "Mission in Matthew's Gospel," 254 n. 82.

102. I believe that "preaching" and "baptizing" are two distinct discipling activities: (i) the underlying Greek terms—κηρύσσω and βαπτίζω—reside in different semantic domains (see L&N "Preach, Proclaim [33.256-33.261]" vs. "Baptize [53.41-53.43]"); and (ii) during his earthly ministry, the Matthean Jesus preaches (4:17, 23; 9:35; 11:1) and he urges his disciples to preach (10:7, 27; cf. 24:14); however, he does not baptize or instruct his disciples to baptize others, except at the time of the final Commission (28:19). This is not to suggest that baptizing is not a discipling activity, but simply that the Matthean Jesus does not practice it as he goes about preaching, which makes them two distinct activities.

the main verb.¹⁰³ Wallace concludes that the historical context of the Commission would suggest that πορευθέντες was a command, "Go!," and not a mere temporal idea, "*While* going," since the nature of the task to be undertaken at the time required a firm push as opposed to a gentle nudge.¹⁰⁴ Πορευθέντες, therefore, is semantically dependent on the main verb, μαθητεύσατε. It does not, by itself, or by joining with the two other participles, inevitably express the full meaning of μαθητεύσατε. Instead, the three participles work alongside μαθητεύσατε to develop or unpack its meaning, without necessarily doing so exhaustively, which brings the semantic structure of ideological *particularization* into view.

A major implication of the argument that 28:19 is governed by a semantic structure of ideological *particularization* is that the reader considers the possibility that the Matthean Jesus gives a general command, μαθητεύσατε (28:19a), which he particularizes in the surrounding participles, developing or unpacking that command, without necessarily exhausting its meaning. This permits the reader to examine the remainder of Matthew to discover any additional meaning that may reside there. If this is to be the preferred approach, and I believe that should be, then the reader may find that the proverbial whole (i.e., μαθητεύσατε, 28:19a) is greater than the sum of its parts (i.e., the adjoining participles). Additionally, since the reader knows that words do not have inherent meaning in isolation from their contexts, then he will look to the broader context of Matthew for such meaning. There, he will find Jesus' disciples not only moving from place to place (i.e., "going"), baptizing, and experiencing Jesus' teaching, but also observing him modeling or displaying a wide variety of disciple-making behaviors.

Matthew makes his only reference to Christian baptism (i.e., baptism "in the name of the Father and the Son and the Holy Spirit") in 28:19 (cf. *Did.* 7.1–3). Matthew's reader is familiar with the verb βαπτίζω

---

103. Wallace, *Greek Grammar*, 640; see Robertson, *Grammar*, 1112–13 on the "coincident aorist participle."

104. Wallace, *Greek Grammar*, 645; see also Bauer, "Mission in Matthew's Gospel," 254, who opines that disciples can accomplish their task of making disciples "only by moving away from where they are to the space inhabited by others." This involves crossing the geographical, cultural, religious, and ethnic boundaries that often separate human beings. Matthew's repeated reference to the gospel being preached throughout "the whole world" (24:14; 26:13) requires such movement; and Keener, *Matthew*, 718–19 on "making disciples" involving "going" (cf. 10:7) that is presupposed (i.e., "having gone").

("wash, purify; dip, baptize"[105]) and its cognate noun βάπτισμα ("water-rite, baptism"[106]), which have up to this point been used in connection with John's baptism of persons, including Jesus, in the Jordan River (3:1–17; cf. 21:25).[107] The author does not explain or develop further the meaning of "baptize" in 28:19, which suggests that the sense of the term is known to the implied reader, who brings his understanding of baptism to bear upon the passage. Baptism in the first century CE was not a uniquely Christian idea. Followers of John and of Jesus would have been familiar with this practice (e.g., Matt 3:5–6; Luke 7:29; John 3:22–26; 4:1–2), and John's baptism is believed to be the forerunner of Christian baptism.[108] It is worth paying attention also to the fact that Christian baptism, according to the commissioning statement, is to be undertaken εἰς τὸ ὄνομα ("in the [singular] name"), not "in the [plural] names," although the phrase is followed by a list of three names or titles—Father, Son, and Holy Spirit—which might suggest that there is a underlying unity among these three "persons."[109]

---

105. "βαπτίζω," BDAG, 164–65.

106. "βάπτισμα," BDAG, 165.

107. Matthew correlates John's baptism of Jesus (3:13–17) with Christian baptism (28:19) by incorporating the participation of the Father, the Son, and the Holy Spirit in the baptism process in both passages. However, there are at least two important points of contrast between the two baptisms to be noted: (i) John the Baptist, himself, differentiates between his baptism "with water for repentance" and that of he who is coming after him, who is mightier than him, who will baptize "with the Holy Spirit and with fire" (3:11); and (ii) persons in the early church who receive John's baptism only, have to be baptized "in the name of the Lord Jesus" (Acts 19:5) so that they could receive the Holy Spirit (cf. Acts 19:2).

108. Bauer, "Mission in Matthew's Gospel," 255 recommends that one looks with qualification and care to John's baptism (3:1–17) and to the rest of the NT to appreciate the significance of Christian baptism (28:19), which involves various factors, including response to preaching, confession of sin, repentance, faith in Christ, forgiveness of sins, reception of the Holy Spirit, and incorporation into the faith community; see also Dockery, "Baptism," 55–58 on: (i) background and context, including world religions and Jewish practices; (ii) the baptism of John, including Jewish proselyte baptism and Qumran washings as antecedents to John's baptism; and (iii) the baptism of Jesus and his command to baptize "all the nations"; and Hartman, "Baptism," 1:583–94.

109. Bauer, *Gospel of the Son of God*, 233; see Hartman, "Baptism," 1:590, who expresses this unity in terms of "God the origin and goal, whom Jesus called his Father (7:21; 10:32; 26:42 etc.) and whose will he performed (26:42), was also the Father of the disciples (5:16, 45, 48; 6:9 etc.). He turned to man in the words and works of the Son, but also in the Spirit, the power of the present, active God (1:18; 12:28; cf. 10:20)."

Bauer interprets Christian baptism to be: (i) an act of transfer that moves someone from being "in Adam" to being "in Christ"; (ii) the action of being "brought existentially into the sphere of, and in submission to, the active powerful presence of the Father, Son, and Spirit, so that one belongs to the Father, Son, and Spirit (e.g., 1 Cor 1:10–17)"; and (iii) the initiation into discipleship, which is not to be restricted to conversion, but is to be viewed as a lifetime process of reformation.[110]

Bauer rightly contends that the implication of the baptism command in 28:19 is that the reader looks beyond the Commission passage (28:16–20) to comprehend the significance of Christian baptism because: (i) 28:19 contains the only reference in Matthew to Christian baptism; (ii) the author does not develop its meaning here; (iii) he describes John's baptism (3:1–17), which is not Christian baptism, but which anticipates it; therefore (iv) the reader must consider Matthew's description of John's baptizing work and the description of Christian baptism in the rest of the New Testament (which represents the conceptual background of the reader), both of which require the reader to move outside of the artificial boundary of the Commission passage to derive the meaning of something that lies within its border.

Matthew 28:20

Matthew's use of logical *substantiation* may explain the progression of the narrative between the discipling activity of risen Christ's command to bring all the nations under his authority (28:19–20a)—the effect (i.e., "going," "baptizing," and "teaching")—and his promise to be with them "always, to the end of the age" (28:20b)—the cause. Use of this structure requires the reader to recognize that disciples are able to disciple all the nations in the way that the risen Lord prescribes because of his presence with them always until the end of the age. The reader has discovered in 28:19 that the risen Jesus' universal authority enables the disciples to undertake their mission. Now, he encounters another reason why they are able to carry out the Lord's final command—i.e., his ongoing presence, which is vital to believing communities as their source of: (i) power and

---

110. Bauer, "Mission in Matthew's Gospel," 255. On "baptizing in the name of..." see also Neyrey, *Honor and Shame*, 58–59 who provides additional insight into "commanding in the name of so-and-so," signaling it as an expression of agency, an encoding of power, and a claim that honor resides in the person whose name is thus used.

hope for ministry,[111] (ii) wisdom because he is God's own Wisdom,[112] and (iii) rescue and protection against enemies (cf. Acts 18:9-10; 23:11).[113] Alternatively, the narrative progression from the discipling activity of 28:19-20a to the risen Jesus' promise of 28:20b may be viewed in terms of logical *causation*: because of the disciples' activity to bring all the nations under Jesus' authority (28:19-20a), the *cause*, Jesus promises to be with them always to the end of the age (28:20b), the *effect*. The reader recognizes that this alternative structure views Jesus' ongoing presence not in terms of its empowerment for discipling activity, but in terms of the disciples' relationship with their Lord. Acknowledging Keener's argument that "If many Christians today have lost a sense of Jesus' presence and purpose among them, it may be because they have lost sight of the mission their Lord has given them,"[114] Bauer adds, "The issue here, of course, is whether divine presence is to be understood exclusively in terms of function (salvation and empowerment), or whether it also includes relationship, i.e., interpersonal intimacy."[115]

The entire Gospel of Matthew is structured according to *climax* by inclusio. The book reaches its climax in the Great Commission (28:16-20) and particularly in the risen Lord's promise to be with his disciples always (28:20b). While the semantic structure of climax explains how the author progresses through his story of Jesus from the genealogy of Jesus (1:1) to the promise of his continuing presence (28:20), the rhetorical structure of inclusio illuminates how the material is arranged in the text. At the beginning of the book, the narrator, quoting the prophet Isaiah, makes a declaration about Jesus: "'Behold, the virgin shall be with child and shall bear a Son, and they shall call his name Immanuel,' which translated means, 'God *with us*'" (1:23, emphasis added; cf. Isa 7:14; 8:10). At the end of the Gospel, the risen Jesus himself declares: "And lo, I am *with you* always, even to the end of the age" (28:20b, emphasis added). These two bracketing statements: (i) speak of God's *with-ness*, a theme that permeates the entire Gospel;[116] (ii) frame the entire Gospel; and (iii)

---

111. Brown and Roberts, *Matthew*, 66, 80–81, 100, 108–9, 255–56, 281, 283, 300, 336, 469.

112. Brown and Roberts, *Matthew*, 367.

113. Chrysostom, *Hom. Eph.*, 9 (NPNF1 13:94–98).

114. Keener, *Matthew*, 720–21.

115. Bauer, "Mission in Matthew's Gospel," 244 n. 20.

116. Bauer, "Mission in Matthew's Gospel," 258 notes that God's with-ness or Mitsein describes someone being in relationship with others; moreover, Bauer emphasizes

are so similar in appearance and meaning that, in the original Greek, only one letter separates "with us" (Μεθ' ἡμῶν, 1:23) from "with you" (μεθ' ὑμῶν, 28:20b). Matthew's structure of his Gospel according to climax by inclusio indicates the importance of God's presence throughout: (i) the bracketing statements at 1:23 and 28:20b reinforce the theme of God's with-ness, in the person of Jesus, throughout the narrative; and, (ii) having climaxed the Gospel with Jesus' promise to be present with his church always, even to "the end of the age," a reference to *monumental time*, Matthew brings his audience (the post-resurrection church) into view, since this is the period in which it resides—the time between the Resurrection and the Parousia.[117] They will seek to experience God's presence in terms of both function (i.e., the ability to carry out its mandate) and relationship (i.e., not losing sight of the mission commanded by their Lord).

The phrase "teaching [διδάσκοντες] them to observe all that I commanded you" (28:20a) is another key component of the Commission. The reader has already observed in 28:19 that διδάσκοντες is one of two adverbial participles that may function in a way that particularizes the main verb, μαθητεύσατε, without necessarily doing so exhaustively. By the end of the Gospel, the reader is already familiar with Matthew's use of the term διδάσκω ("tell, instruct; teach") and its cognate noun, διδαχή ("teaching, instruction"):[118] (i) Jesus *teaches* while ministering in the cit-

---

five (5) types of Mitsein that are present throughout Matthew's Gospel: (i) soteriological (or salvational) (1:23; cf. 1:21); (ii) ecclesial (18:20); (iii) eschatological (26:29); (iv) provisional (26:38, 40); and (v) missional (28:20); "Mission in Matthew's Gospel," 258 n. 116 argues that God's with-ness involves a new kind of presence that is continuous and discontinuous with Jesus' physical presence among his disciples; see also Davies and Allison Jr., *Matthew (III)*, 686–87, who agree that the phrase "I am with you" recalls 1:23 and 18:20, but perceive that its dominant sense may be more to do with "divine assistance," echoing various OT passages (e.g., Gen 28:15; Exod 3:11–12; Josh 1:5; 22:31; Judg 6:12, 16; 1 Sam 17:37; Is 41:10; Hag 2:4–5), than "divine presence."

117. Matthew's reference to "the end of the age" (28:20b) brings into view monumental time, which "refers to the broad sweep of time that includes but also transcends history. It cannot be measured by people in the real world or by characters in the story." This temporal setting is in contrast to "mortal time in which the characters of the story live out their lives, just as people do in the real world" (Powell, *Narrative Criticism*, 74); see also Bauer, "Mission in Matthew's Gospel," 245–46 on the "timeless quality" of the Commission passage, which lacks closure because it contains no reference to Jesus' departing or ascending; and Luz, *Matthew 21–28*, 584 concerning the two narrative threads that culminate in 28:15 and 28:20 concluding with references to the narrator's present, "whereby the latter far exceeds the former because it stretches the temporal horizon to the end of the world."

118. "διδάσκω," BDAG, 241; "διδαχή," BDAG, 241; cf. Rengstorf, "διδάσκω,

ies and villages of Galilee (4:23; 5:2; 9:35; 11:1; 13:54) and in the temple (21:23; 26:55); (ii) the crowds are amazed at Jesus' *teaching* (7:28, 29; 22:33); (iii) being called least in the kingdom of heaven is the penalty for *teaching* others that the Law is invalid; conversely, being called great in the kingdom of heaven is the reward for *teaching* others to keep the Law (5:19); (iv) Jesus chastises the Pharisees and scribes, who worship God in vain, for *teaching* the precepts of men as doctrine (15:9); (v) Jesus warns his disciples to beware of the *teaching* of the Pharisees and Sadducees (16:12); (vi) the Pharisees, along with their disciples and the Herodians, plot to trap Jesus while referring to him as a teacher (διδάσκαλος) who *teaches* the way of God (22:16); and (vii) the chief priests *instruct* the guards to say that Jesus' disciples came by night to steal his body from the tomb (28:15).[119]

The risen Jesus commands the disciples to teach "all that I commanded you" (28:20a), which introduces some additional but familiar terms to the reader: (i) ἐντέλλω ("command, order, give orders"[120]) and its cognate noun ἐντολή ("warrant; command, commandment"[121]); and (ii) τηρέω ("keep watch over, guard; reserve, preserve; keep, observe"[122]). To fully comprehend the implications of Matthew's use of διδάσκοντες, the reader must explore the universe of Jesus' prior commands. Scholars have traditionally interpreted the phrase "teaching them to observe all that I commanded you" (28:20a) to mean teaching Jesus' verbal commands in the Matthew's five great discourses. Bauer argues that all of the Matthean Jesus' commands must be taught, "the critical core" of which are the five great discourses that punctuate the Gospel (chs. 5–7, 10, 13, 18, 24–25), and which are relevant to the entire church in the post-resurrection period.[123] Keener concurs, noting that these discourses work well as a discipling manual for young believers.[124] Brown and Roberts advance

---

διδάσκαλος, κτλ," *TDNT* 2:135–59.

119. The reader's interpretation of these texts, comprising Matthew's use of διδάσκω and its cognates, has been formed against the backdrop of Jewish, Christian and classical education systems of the day. See the following authors for more on these matters Drazin, *History of Jewish Education*, 11–23; Marrou, *Education in Antiquity*, 314–29; Jaeger, *Greek Paidea*; Hogan, Goff, and Wasserman, *Pedagogy*.

120. "ἐντέλλω," BDAG, 339.

121. "ἐντολή," BDAG, 340.

122. "τηρέω," BDAG, 1002.

123. Bauer, "Mission in Matthew's Gospel," 256–57.

124. Keener, *Matthew*, 720.

that they summarize Jesus' teaching, and the readers recall them when he commissions his disciples to teach the nations to observe all that he commanded them.[125] Moreover, Brown and Roberts draw attention to Matthew's use of πᾶς ("all") in the transitional formula in 26:1, proffering that this addition, which does not appear in the transitional formulae that conclude each of the four previous discourses (7:28–29; 10:1; 13:53; 19:1), signals that "Matthew understands the Eschatological Discourse to be the final and culminating discourse of the teachings of Jesus in his Gospel."[126] Nolland believes that the Sermon on the Mount takes pride of place in what is to be taught to new disciples. Jesus' teachings are to be set alongside, and be interpretative of, the commandments of the Mosaic law (cf. 5:18–48), and Matthew's use of ἐντέλλω (28:20) probably echoes "keep the commandments" of 19:17.[127] Luz agrees with Nolland, adding that when Jesus charges his disciples to teach the nations, the thought is probably on the Sermon on the Mount—the first extensive proclamation of Jesus in Matthew.[128]

A few scholars, however, argue in favor of extending the meaning of "all that I have commanded you" (28:20a) beyond Jesus' verbal commands and the content of Matthew's five major discourses to all of Matthew. Davies and Allison reckon that:

> ἐνετειλάμην is a constative aorist and refers not to one command or to the Sermon on the Mount but to all of Jesus' teaching—not just imperatives but also proverbs, blessings, parables, and prophecies. But more than verbal revelation is involved, for such revelation cannot be separated from Jesus' life, which is itself a command. ἐνετειλάμην accordingly unifies word and deed and so recalls the entire book: everything is in view. The earthly ministry as a whole is an imperative.[129]

Similarly, Bauer concedes that the Commission requires teaching that: (i) goes beyond the five great discourses, (ii) incorporates "the entirety of Jesus' instructions throughout the Gospel," and (iii) includes what Jesus says and does because "in Matthew's Gospel, Jesus instructs

---

125. Brown and Roberts, *Matthew*, 234, 263–64, 334–35.
126. Brown and Roberts, *Matthew*, 234.
127. Nolland, *Matthew*, 1270 (cf. 1261–1262).
128. Luz, *Matthew 1–7*, 176–177 (cf. 174 n. 10, 209, 223–24, 383–84, 391–94, 397–398); *Matthew 21–28*, 633–34.
129. Davies and Allison Jr., *Matthew (III)*, 686.

as much through actions as through speech."¹³⁰ However, neither Davies and Allison nor Bauer provides any evidence to support the view that Matthew expects or wants the reader to combine Jesus' speech and actions when interpreting διδάσκοντες αὐτοὺς τηρεῖν πάντα ὅσα ἐνετειλάμην ὑμῖν (28:20a). Such evidence is necessary because: (i) Matthew's prior use of ἐντέλλω (4:6; 17:9; 19:7) and ἐντολή (5:19; 15:3; 19:17; 22:36-40) is connected with spoken commands and not actions;¹³¹ and (ii) until now, τηρέω (19:17; 23:3) has been associated with keeping the commandments and the requirements of the Mosaic law, not with abiding by someone's prior actions. Additionally, the author correlates διδάσκω with verbal teaching, with perhaps one possible exception in 5:19.¹³²

There are at least three reasons supporting the view that Matthew wants his reader to combine Jesus' speech and actions in arriving at the universe of his commands to be taught in discipling the nations. First, the reader is aware that the Matthean Jesus exposes the flawed character of persons who teach good habits without actually carrying them out themselves. He says, "therefore, all that [the scribes and the Pharisees] tell you, do and observe, but do not do according to their deeds; for they say things and do not do them" (23:1-3). This command of Jesus elevates for the reader the importance of integrity and the correct alignment of human speech and action. Therefore, the reader expects the disciples to follow this principle as they disciple the nations, teaching from Jesus' entire life—both from what he says and does during his earthly

---

130. Bauer, "Mission in Matthew's Gospel," 257 submits that: (i) proof of Jesus' instruction by action may be found in the passage: "From that time Jesus began to show (δείκνυμι) his disciples that he must go to Jerusalem, suffer many things . . . and be killed . . . " (16:21); and (ii) the church's proclamation of the gospel is to be received by the world not only as something heard with the ears, but also as something seen with the eyes.

131. France, *Matthew*, 1118-19.

132. Teaching is connected to the synagogue (4:23; 9:35; 13:54), the Sermon on the Mount (5:2; 7:29), the cities (11:1), and the Temple (21:23; 26:55). The religious authorities' "teaching as doctrines the precepts of men" (15:9) is linked to "honoring [God] *with their lips*" (15:8; cf. Isa 29:13); their compliment to Jesus about his "teach[ing] the way of God" (22:16) is immediately followed by a request for a speech-act: "*Tell us* [εἶπον] then, what do you think" (22:17); and they conspire by instructing the guards to lie about Jesus' resurrection (28:15). A possible exception to this pattern of connecting διδάσκω with speech occurs in 5:19, where someone invalidates a minor commandment of the Law and *teaches* others to do the same—an act that implies either teaching by speech, or by demonstration.

ministry, because, as far as they are concerned, his words and actions are consistent.[133]

Second, the reader understands the implications of the Matthean Jesus' charge, "But make sure your statement is, 'Yes, yes' *or* 'No, no'; anything beyond these is of evil origin" (5:37), the underlying point of which concerns the need for unity between one's word and one's action. Keener explains that the point of the entire passage (5:33–37) is integrity: "Letting one's 'yes' function as a 'yes' and 'no' as a 'no' seems to employ ancient Jewish figures of speech simply to demand that one be as good as one's word, that one keep one's word."[134]

Third, the reader witnesses the Matthean Jesus' righteousness on full display before the commencement of the five great discourses. Indeed, before he utters a single verbal command to anyone, the reader encounters compelling testimonies about his integrity—i.e., the wholeness, undividedness, and soundness of his character—which elevates him to a status that goes beyond what he says to encapsulate who he is: (i) John the Baptist, whom the reader knows as "one who is more than a prophet" (11:9), the subject of OT prophecy (11:10), and the greatest "among those born of women" (11:11), testifies that Jesus is mightier than he, and that he is not fit to remove his sandals (3:11);[135] (ii) God declares his approval of Jesus through the parting of the heavens (3:16; cf. Isa 64:1; Ezek 1:1), the Holy Spirit descending on Jesus like a dove (3:16; cf. Gen 8:8–12; 4 Bar. 7.8), and a voice out of the heavens saying, "This is My beloved Son, *in whom I am well-pleased*" (3:17; cf. 17:5;[136] Ps 2:7; Isa 42:1), which

---

133. Nevertheless, of the thirteen other times that Matthew uses διδάσκω in his gospel, he does not use it in the context of modeling (4:23; 5:2; 19[x2]; 7:29; 9:35; 11:1; 13:54; 15:9; 21:23; 22:16; 26:55; 28:15).

134. Keener, *Matthew*, 192–95.

135. Keener, *Matthew*, 131–32 remarks that: (i) John recognizes Jesus as the ultimate baptizer (3:11), who expresses his obedience to God's plan revealed in the Scriptures (3:15); and that (ii) Matthew's readers, being familiar with the Scriptures, understand that Jesus fulfills the prophetic Scriptures by identifying with Israel's history and completing Israel's mission (2:15, 18).

136. At the time of Jesus' transfiguration, a voice out of the cloud says, "This is My beloved Son, with whom I am well-pleased; listen to [ἀκούετε] him!" (17:5b). While NT and other early Christian literature typically employs ἀκούω in the context of "hear, listen to," classical and Hellenistic scholarship utilizes the term more broadly to include "be a pupil of." If ἀκούω is the be understood here in the broader sense of being a pupil or disciple of the transfigured Jesus, then the reader will interpret ἀκούετε αὐτοῦ more along the lines of "Follow him!" than simply "Listen to what he says!" (see also "ἀκούω," BDAG, 37–38; and "ἀκούω," LSJ, 53–54).

declares Jesus' identity as well as God's pleasure with his entire being;[137] and (iii) at the time of his temptation by the devil (4:1–11), Jesus testifies about God and about his own character by his actions: he does not yield to the devil's temptation and command that the stones become bread, choosing to live on every word that proceeds from God's mouth (4:3–4); he does not throw himself down from the pinnacle of the temple and put God to the test (4:5–7); and he does not fall down and worship the devil, but reserves worship and service for God only (4:8–10).

The implications of broadening the universe of the Matthean Jesus' prior commands to include both verbal and nonverbal commands are at least threefold: (i) the reader finds this approach to be consistent with the idea of exploring beyond the boundary of the Commission to allow Jesus' entire life to be the template for making disciples who follow and bear resemblance to their one teacher and leader; (ii) the reader is therefore unconcerned about limiting his search for teaching content on discipleship to Matthew's five great discourses, and he explores the entire Gospel for that purpose because, as Davies and Allison reveal, ἐνετειλάμην unifies word and deed and brings the entire book into view; and (iii) the reader, who is a disciple as well as a disciple-maker, is enjoined to think more broadly about teaching obedience to Jesus' commands than simply telling others what Jesus commands; rather, he understands he must also model Jesus' character and actions for others to follow.

---

137. For more on God's approval of Jesus, see Keener, *Matthew*, 132–35.

4

Inductive Study of Other Matthean Passages

Chapter Summary

THIS CHAPTER UTILIZES the results from the inductive study of Matthew 28:16–20 in the previous chapter to select and analyze passages from the broader context of Matthew (1:1—28:15) to determine how those passages might contribute to the reader's interpretation the meaning of μαθητεύσατε (28:19).

Approach

Davies and Allison correctly argue that the term ἐνετειλάμην (28:20a) unifies the words and deeds of the Matthean Jesus and so recalls the entire book of Matthew. For them, everything is in view and the earthly ministry of Jesus as a whole is an imperative.[1] Consequently, the two

---

1. Davies and Allison Jr., *Matthew (III)*, 686. I am of the view that the recall of which Davies and Allision speak applies to Matthew 1–2 also. Matthew makes Jesus' divine origin and purpose known from the outset (1:18–25). The author emphasizes that Jesus is not the natural son of Joseph; rather, he is the Son of God. God speaks and acts on behalf of the infant Jesus (via the Holy Spirit; the angel [1:18–25; 2:12–13, 19–20, 22]; "his star" [2:2, 9–10]; and the prophets [1:22–23; 2:5–6, 15, 17–18]); moreover, the righteous Joseph, motivated by God, facilitates his birth and shelters him from danger (1:19, 24–25; 2:14–15, 21–23). Matthew intends, therefore, for their speech and actions to be attributed to the infant Jesus before he can speak and act for

INDUCTIVE STUDY OF OTHER MATTHEAN PASSAGES 113

scholars extend the universe of Jesus' commands that are to be taught to new disciples to material found outside of Matthew's five major discourses. They are of the view that all of Jesus' earthly ministry—i.e., both what he says and does—is a command to his disciples. In this chapter, I refer to the work of Wolfgang Iser and others to determine the way readers build meaning as they move through a narrative. I do so for the purpose of informing my argument about how Matthew's reader develops a sense of discipleship from all earlier passages in the Gospel to the climactic 28:19. Then, based on the view that the reader arrives at 28:16–20 with intimate knowledge of the preceding story, which shapes his understanding of the Great Commission text, I select several passages from the broader context of Matthew to determine how they contribute to the reader's interpretation of the meaning of μαθητεύσατε (28:19). To accomplish this, I employ three selection criteria to determine which passages to include in my examination.[2] In analyzing each selected passage, I indicate: (i) how it is linked to the Commission text; (ii) where the passage is located in terms of Matthew's overall structure; (iii) what the passage says; (iv) how the major structural relationships within the passage help to reveal the meaning of the passage; and (v) the inferences that I am able to draw from the forgoing analysis about how the passages shape the reader's understanding of the meaning of μαθητεύσατε (28:19).

Key Findings

My analysis of eight selected passages from the broader context of Matthew reveals that the reader understands that the process of "making disciples" includes, *inter alia*:[3] (i) the movement of persons by God (through Jesus) from sin to salvation, and the promise of Jesus' ongoing presence

---

himself; see also Bauer, *Gospel of the Son of God*, 155–56.

2. The selected passages are meant to be samples, for which other passages could also serve. In making my selection: (i) I focus on passages outside of Matthew's five great discourses, since Matthean scholars already agree that these form the basis of the teaching of Jesus' verbal commands; I do not disagree with them on this matter, but I incline to the view that Matthew's reader perceives all his Gospel as teaching material for new disciples; (ii) I concentrate on the existence of terms, themes, and narrative structures that connect the selected passages to the Great Commission text; and (iii) I also pay attention to the existence of other passages in Matthew that support the findings that I discover in the selected passages.

3. I develop these points further in my analysis of the selected passages that follow later in the chapter.

with his disciples as they obediently undertake his mission of discipling the entire world (1:18–23);[4] (ii) the emergence of persons who emulate Jesus as the model of discipleship and demonstrate, like Jesus, the resolve to obey God's will by observing all of Jesus' commands (3:13–17); (iii) the molding of persons into disciples whose words and actions, like Jesus', are mutually consistent, who handle the Scriptures correctly to repel the devil's advances, who unwaveringly obey the Father's will, and who understand that such obedience is the climax of worshipping God (4:1–11); (iv) the need to continuously seek out new disciples in the normal course of daily living, prioritizing teaching them how to reproduce themselves, and making maximum use of (familial and other) relationships and occupational skills to bring persons into Christian discipleship; additionally, disciples respond to such overtures with immediate and ongoing obedience to Jesus' invitation to follow him (4:18–22);[5] (v) the defense and protection of new disciples against opponents who seek to destroy them; the inculcating in disciples of the ability to accurately interpret Scripture in the face of adversity and to appropriately respond to opponents of Christ and his ministry; moreover, disciples recognize the identity of Jesus (i.e., who Jesus is) and his presence and power within themselves (i.e., who they are in Jesus)[6] (12:1–8); (vi) the allowing of opportunity for

---

4. The implication of this revelation for the reader's understanding of μαθητεύσατε (28:19) is that, although the person and number of the imperative is "second person, plural" (i.e., "[You] make disciples"), it is indeed God (through Jesus) who is the principal actor in the disciple-making process. This assigns humans to the role of subsidiary actors or facilitators of the process.

5. Some may argue that a disciple's response to disciple-making overtures relates more so to "being a disciple" than to "making a disciple." However, Matthew's reader is aware of the vital connection between "*being* and *making* a disciple" and he brings that awareness to bear on his interpretation of μαθητεύσατε (28:19) for two important reasons: (i) he is aware that God (through Jesus), not he, is the primary actor in disciple-making (leading to salvation) and that he must therefore recognize, not only how to make a disciple, but also what is God's definition of a good disciple of Jesus; and (ii) he observes that Matthew does not draw a solid line between "*being* and *making* a disciple"; indeed, he depicts the Twelve interchangeably as disciples *of* Jesus and disciple-makers *for* Jesus; similarly, he portrays Jesus both as a model of discipleship (4:1–11; 26:39, 42, 44) and as the master-teacher, -leader (23:8–10) and -disciple-maker (e.g., 4:19; 8:22; 9:9; 10:38; 16:24; 19:21). In summary, Matthean Christians are first and foremost disciples *of* Jesus, who also make disciples *for* Jesus. Disciple-makers never cease to be disciples themselves; therefore, comprehending the fundamentals of "being a disciple" is relevant for every Christian disciple-maker.

6. See previous comment regarding the connection between "being a disciple" and "making a disciple."

new disciples to learn from difficult situations, while the disciple-maker remains watchful over them in order to recognize when they may require immediate assistance, and the provision of explicit guidance to disciples about matters regarding their growth in the Christian faith (14:22–33); (vii) the readiness to minister to the needs of every kind of person, including those who fall outside of one's geographic, ethnic, and cultural boundaries; the willingness to dialogue with divers persons, allowing them to reveal their true selves for the purpose of leading them to the climax of expressing their faith in God (15:21–28); and (viii) the forewarning of disciples about forthcoming dangers to safeguard them against potential spiritual demise, and encouraging in these persons whom they will disciple the recognition of human vulnerabilities and the willingness to forgive and reconcile with other disciples even before they commit an offense (26:31–35).[7] This is not meant to be an exhaustive list of what it means to make disciples; rather, it serves to reinforce the point of view that Matthew presents Jesus in a variety of ways throughout his entire Gospel that are intended to model exemplary disciple-making priorities and explain the meaning of μαθητεύσατε (28:19).

Theory of the Reading Process

Wolfgang Iser is best known for his version of *reader-response criticism*,[8] in which he contends that:

> Every reading moment sends out stimuli into the memory, and what is recalled can activate the perspectives in such a way that they continually modify and so individualize one another. Our example shows clearly that reading does not merely flow forward, but that recalled segments also have a retroactive effect, with the present transforming the past . . . It is clear, then, that

---

7. The act of forgiving others preemptively is especially relevant to disciple-makers, who pour themselves into the process of making disciples of others, only to realize later that new disciples may renege in varying degrees on their commitment to follow Jesus as his disciples.

8. This is "a development within literary studies which focuses on the relationship between text and receiver" (Lategan, "Reader Response Theory," 5:625–28); see also Resseguie, *Narrative Criticism*, on reader-response criticism (at various places throughout the text); Mailloux, "Learning to Read," on the differing assumptions about the relation between the reader and the text (at various places throughout the text); and Fowler, "Who Is the Reader?" 5–23 concerning the array of terms used to describe the reader of the text.

the present retention of a past perspective qualifies past and present. It also qualifies the future, because whatever modifications it has brought about will immediately affect the nature of our expectations. These may radiate in several different directions at once.[9]

Furthermore, Iser makes the claim that what the reader recalls from memory—i.e., from contact with earlier passages in the text, or from previous reading of the text—is not limited to the immediate past but may also be drawn from the distant past. Consequently, Iser reckons that:

> The reciprocal evocation of perspectives does not normally follow a strict time sequence. If it did, what had been read earlier would gradually disappear from view, as it would become increasingly irrelevant. The pointers and stimuli therefore evoke not just their immediate predecessors, but often aspects of other perspectives that have already sunk deep into the past. This constitutes an important feature of the wandering viewpoint. If the reader is prodded into recalling something already sunk into memory, he will bring it back, not in isolation but embedded in a particular context.[10]

If Iser's assessment of a reader's response to a literary text is correct,[11] then it has significant implications for how I might expect Matthew's reader to interact with 28:16-20 in light of the broader Matthean text (1:1—28:15) preceding it. I might conclude that the reader encounters the Great Commission with intimate knowledge of the story that goes before it—both the passages that immediately precede it and those that go right back to the beginning of the Gospel—which modifies his understanding of the text that is presently before him (28:16-20), including the risen Jesus' command to "make disciples [μαθητεύσατε] of all the nations" (28:19).[12]

---

9. Iser, *Act of Reading*, 115.

10. Iser, *Act of Reading*, 116.

11. For more on Iser's theory about "The Reading Process," see Iser, *Implied Reader*, xii, 276-83; and *Act of Reading*, 107-59.

12. Donaldson, "Guiding Readers–Making Disciples," 30-49 opines that "by telling the story of the disciples in their experience with Jesus, Matthew is, in fact, also guiding his readers to an understanding of what discipleship will mean for them" (41-42); see also Edwards, "Uncertain Faith," 41-61, esp. 51, 59, on the reader's involvement in the text being determined by the gaps, where the reader must supply some information.

Selection Criteria of Passages from Matthew 1:1—28:15

Using the following criteria, I select passages from the broader context of Matthew to determine how they contribute to the reader's interpretation of the meaning of μαθητεύσατε (28:19). First, I give priority to passages outside of Matthew's five great discourses (chs. 5–7, 10, 13, 18, 24–25), which have already been exhaustively examined by scholars who argue that these discourses comprise the teaching content of the Commission's command to teach new disciples "to observe all that I commanded you" (28:20a).[13] In other words, it has already been well argued by scholars that discipling others includes teaching them Jesus' verbal commands; therefore, I will not attempt to reproduce such arguments here. Rather, I will examine other passages in Matthew that could shed additional light on what it means to "make disciples." Second, I select passages based on the existence of terms, themes, and structural relationships that may connect those passages to the Commission text.[14] Third, along the way, I identify any additional passages from Matthew that share similarities with the ones selected and that may similarly contribute to the reader's interpretation of the meaning of μαθητεύσατε (28:19).

IBS of Selected Passages

"God with Us" (1:18–23)

The entire Gospel of Matthew is structured according to *climax* by inclusio. The book reaches its climax in the Great Commission (28:16–20) and particularly in the risen Lord's promise to be with his disciples always (28:20b). At the beginning of the book, the narrator, quoting the prophet Isaiah, makes a declaration about Jesus: "'Behold, the virgin shall be with

---

13. See Bauer, "Mission in Matthew's Gospel," 256–57; cf. *Structure of Matthew's Gospel*, 27–35 on "Topical Outlines Based on Alternation of Narrative-Discourse Material" in Matthew; Keener, *Matthew*, 720 about Matthew's five discourses working well as a discipling manual for young believers; Brown and Roberts, *Matthew*, 234, 263–64, 334–35 concerning these discourses summarizing Jesus' teaching, enabling readers to recall them when Jesus commissions his disciples; Nolland, *Matthew*, 1270 regarding the Sermon on the Mount taking pride of place in what is to be taught to new disciples; and Bosch, *Transforming Mission*, 70–71, who prioritize the content of Sermon on the Mount in teaching new believers.

14. I am referring here to structural relationships that are shared between the selected passage and the Commission text—e.g., "inclusio" (1:23; 28:20) and "hortatory causation" (4:19; 28:19).

child and shall bear a Son, and they shall call his name Immanuel,' which translated means, 'God *with us*'" (1:23, emphasis added; cf. Isa 7:14; 8:10). At the end of the Gospel, the risen Jesus himself declares: "And lo, I am *with you* always, even to the end of the age" (28:20b, emphasis added).[15] These two bracketing statements form an inclusio that emphasizes the theme of God's *with-ness* in the person of Jesus, his Son, which permeates the entire Gospel. By examining the passage in which I find the opening bracket of the inclusio (1:18-25), I expect to discover how Matthew's portrayal of Jesus therein contributes to the reader's comprehension of μαθητεύσατε (28:19).[16]

Matthew's account of the conception and birth of Jesus (1:18-25) is located within the first major unit of his Gospel (1:1—4:16), which records the *preparation* for Jesus Christ, Son of God.[17] The entire unit comprises: (i) an account of the genealogy and infancy of Jesus (1:1—2:23); and (ii) a narrative of events concerning the adult Jesus as he prepares to embark on his ministry (3:1—4:16), which comprises the preaching of John the Baptist (3:1-12), John's baptism of Jesus (3:13-17), the temptation of Jesus by the devil (4:1-11), and the positioning of Jesus for ministry in Galilee after John is taken into custody (4:12-16).[18]

After his account of the genealogy of Jesus the Messiah (1:1-17), Matthew provides a record of the conception and birth of Jesus, beginning with his mother Mary's betrothal to Joseph and her impregnation by the Holy Spirit (1:18) before they come together.[19] Joseph plans to divorce Mary privately, but he decides against it after receiving word from an angel of the Lord in a dream about the divine origin of the child that Mary

---

15. For further contrast between "monumental time" (e.g., "end of the age") and "mortal time," see Powell, *Narrative Criticism*, 74; see also Bauer, "Mission in Matthew's Gospel," 245-46 on the "timeless quality" of the Commission passage.

16. While 1:23 illumines 28:20b by emphasizing God's *with-ness* in the person of his Son—a theme that permeates the entire Gospel—it is noteworthy that 1:23 also sheds light on 28:19 by emphasizing that it is God, himself, who is present (in the person of his Son) with the disciples, while they function both as disciples and as makers of disciples of all the nations.

17. In chapter 3 of this book, I explain many of the major structural relationships to which I refer in this chapter. I provide additional explanations in this chapter of those narrative structures that I have not previously explained.

18. Bauer, *Gospel of the Son of God*, 128.

19. Luz, *Matthew 1-7*, 93-94 n. 35 comments that "to come together" (συνέρχομαι) most likely refers to Mary's move to Joseph's house that would take place at the wedding.

is carrying as well as the prescribed name of the child, Jesus (1:19–21).[20] The narrator explains that all these events are taking place to fulfill Isaiah's prophecy: "'Behold, the virgin shall be with child and shall bear a Son,[21] and they shall call his name Immanuel,' which translated means, 'God with us'" (1:23; cf. Isa 7:14).[22] Joseph awakes from the dream and obeys the angel's commands, marrying Mary but keeping her a virgin until she gives birth to a son, whom he calls Jesus (1:24–25).[23]

Matthew employs two narrative structures in his arrangement of 1:18–25 that serve to emphasize the origin, name, and purpose of the Christ child to the reader.[24] First, he utilizes *introduction* (or the *preparation*) to provide the background material (1:18–19) that makes the material that is found in the *realization* (1:20–25) stand out for the reader. In the preparation, the author presents the main characters of the episode: (i) Jesus Christ, the child; (ii) Mary, a virgin, who is betrothed to a man and is found to be with child;[25] (iii) the Holy Spirit, the progenitor or

---

20. For a discussion about two of views concerning Joseph's reaction, see Gnilka, *Das Matthäusevangelium*, 1:17–18.

21. France, *Matthew*, 55–56 explains that Isaiah refers to "the virgin" (παρθένος) in the LXX, while English versions of the Book of Isaiah generally translate the Hebrew as "the young woman" (הָעַלְמָה). France notes that while הָעַלְמָה does not explicitly mean "virgin," it suggests something other than a normal childbirth within marriage; see also Gnilka, *Das Matthäusevangelium*, 1:20–21 concerning modern interpreters' views about the identity of "the young woman" (Isa 7:14)—e.g., "the Prophet's wife, a woman nearby at the time, the king's wife, or a princess who had just entered the harem of Ahaz."

22. Luz, *Matthew 1–7*, 96 reckons that since Greek-speaking readers of the Gospel must know what "Immanuel" means, the translation gives the term additional emphasis.

23. France, *Matthew*, 52–53 judges that Matthew's aorist tenses in 1:19 signal that by the time of the divine intervention Joseph's mind is made up; see also *Matthew*, 58 n. 68 on Joseph's recognition of his wife's son as his own not being "adoption"; for more on Jesus' Davidic sonship, see Gnilka, *Das Matthäusevangelium*, 1:21–22; Davies and Allison Jr., *Matthew (I)*, 220; Brown and Roberts, *Matthew*, 29; and Bauer, "Son of David," 768.

24. Maier, *Evangelium des Matthäus (1–14)*, 70 describes the structure of 1:18–25 as simple and elementary, with its author not skimping on hints for the reader.

25. For more on Jewish marriage and the steps thereof, see Elwell and Beitzel, "Marriage, Marriage Customs," 2:1405–10; Gnilka, *Das Matthäusevangelium*, 1:17 reckons that the normal age for the engagement was between 12 and 13 years for the girl and between 18 and 24 for the man; see also France, *Matthew*, 50–51 on the first-century Jewish concept of "engagement"; and Davies and Allison Jr., *Matthew (I)*, 199–200 about the *halakah* (i.e., Jewish law based on the Talmud) of Galilee differing at certain points from the halakah of Judea—e.g., concerning marriage law.

originator of the child; and (iv) Joseph, to whom Mary is betrothed.[26] From the presentation of this background material emerges the problem of the virginal conception—i.e., Mary, a young woman of marriageable age, who had previously never had a child, would conceive and give birth. Some scholars perceive 1:18-25 to be, in part, an explanation of Matthew's genealogical statement about Jesus' birth through Mary in 1:16. This suggests that the purpose of 1:18-25 is to make clear to the reader that Joseph is in no way responsible for siring Jesus, who is the result of God's creative act in Mary alone.[27] In this regard, it is noteworthy that in 1:16 "the Greek singular relative pronoun used to indicate from whom Jesus was born is feminine in gender and so excludes Joseph."[28] This background material leads to that for which the preparation is made—i.e., the realization—which includes: (i) Joseph's dream,[29] in which the angel of the Lord confirms to Joseph the origin of the child,[30] the name of the child, and the purpose for which he is born, which is to "save his people from their sins" (1:20-21);[31] (ii) a statement of purpose that explains the reason why "all this" is occurring—i.e., to fulfill the prophecy of Isaiah (1:22-23; Isa 7:14);[32] and (iii) a brief description of Joseph's obedient response to God's instructions—i.e., he marries Mary, keeps her a virgin until she gives birth to the child (cf. Isa 7:14), and he calls the child Jesus in agreement with the purpose of his birth (1:24-25). Second, Matthew employs a compound structure of *repetition* of terms with *instrumentation* to emphasize that God is catalyst behind the events described in the

26. Witherington, III, "Birth of Jesus," 60-74 offers several insights into the author's portrayal of Joseph's importance to the broader story of Jesus' birth.

27. Witherington, III, "Birth of Jesus," 71.

28. Brown and Roberts, *Matthew*, 29 n. 16.

29. See Keener, *Matthew*, 95-96 on God's revelations to OT heroes by dreams (e.g., Gen 28:12; 37:5-9; Dan 2:19) and Matthew's emphasis on revelation through dreams (2:12, 13, 19, 22; 27:19); and Black, "Dreams," 199-200.

30. Jesus' divine origin differs to some extent from Greco-Roman supernatural birth stories (Brown and Roberts, *Matthew*, 30); Luz, *Matthew 1-7*, 95 advises us to think here of God's creative intervention by the Spirit and not of the Spirit as Mary's sexual partner.

31. The child's name, *Yeshua* (Heb. יְהוֹשֻׁעַ; Gk. Ἰησοῦς; generally translated "Joshua" in the English OT and "Jesus" in the NT) means "God is salvation" (Keener, *Matthew*, 96); "people" (λαός) here means the OT people of God, Israel (Luz, *Matthew 1-7*, 95).

32. In view of 18:20 and 28:20, Matthew clearly understands "God with us" (Isa 7:14) to mean that Jesus is truly God (1:23); however, Jesus is also the fully human one who will "save his people from their sins" by dying on the Cross (1:21) (Keener, *Matthew*, 97).

passage: (i) the author repeats the phrase "by/of the Holy Spirit" (1:18, 20) to establish the *means* by which Mary is found to be with child,[33] and (ii) he repeats that "the angel of the Lord" (1:20, 24)—i.e., God's *agent*—intervenes via a dream to ensure that Joseph's intended actions would not frustrate God's plan. The blueprint, therefore, originates with God and the action taken to correct Joseph's plan to privately divorce Mary is directed by God. Additionally, God's orchestration is apparent from his naming of the child (1:21), from the narrator's *statement of purpose* that "all this took place to fulfill what the Lord spoke through the prophet" (1:22; cf. Isa 7:14), and from the child's other stated name, Immanuel, which means "God with us" (1:23).

The reader's attention to Matthew's depiction of Jesus in this passage helps to shape his understanding of μαθητεύσατε (28:19). The reader observes that: (i) Jesus' incarnation is for the purpose of saving his people from their sins—first, he saves his people, Israel; then, through them, he saves the entire world; here, the author underlines the reason for Jesus' coming in human form: he wants to make disciples who will follow him, and in so doing he will save them from their sins; Jesus' name (Gk. Ἰησοῦς; Heb. יֵשׁוּעַ) means "God is salvation" and he is the subject of σῴζω ("to save," 1:21b), which makes God (through Jesus) the principal actor in saving persons and also in "making disciples" of persons;[34] (ii) Jesus does not function apart from God; indeed, he is God's very presence—i.e., "God with us"—sent by the Father, by means of the Holy Spirit; he comes to enter into relationship *with* the entire human race;[35] when he

---

33. Hagner, *Matthew 1–13*, 17–18 remarks that the reference to the Holy Spirit points, not only to the divine origin of the child, but also to God's intention to act graciously through the child—i.e., "the promised deliverance and fulfillment of the promises rest upon the coming of an era marked above all by the presence of the Spirit."

34. The implication of this revelation for the reader's understanding of μαθητεύσατε (28:19) is that, although the person and number of the imperative is "second person, plural" (i.e., "[You] make disciples"), it is indeed God (through Jesus) who is the principal actor in the disciple-making process. This assigns humans to the role of subsidiary actors or facilitators of the process. See also France, *Matthew*, 53 on the interpretations of the two names given to the child ("he will save his people from their sins" and "God with us") inviting the reader to reflect on the nature of the Messiah's mission; and Bauer, *Gospel of the Son of God*, 318 for a discussion on discipleship and the experience of salvation from sin, including forgiveness (9:1–9; 6:12; 26:28) and repentance and moral transformation (e.g., 3:1–12; 4:17; 7:17–20; 12:33–37).

35. On the five (5) types of with-ness or *Mitsein* that are present throughout Matthew's Gospel, see Bauer, "Mission in Matthew's Gospel," 258; see also Bonnard, *Saint*

eventually departs, he promises his disciples to remain with them "always, even to the end of the age" (28:20); making disciples, therefore, implies that the one for whom they make disciples is ever-present with them as disciple-makers and also as disciples; indeed, it is God himself who is with them in the person of his Son, Jesus Christ; and (iii) Joseph's obedient response to God is that of a model disciple who is a prototype of Jesus' future disciples, whom he will later call to follow him (cf. 4:19; 8:22; 9:9; 10:38; 16:24; 19:21).[36] From these observations, the reader is aware that the process of "making disciples" involves the movement of persons from sin to salvation (cf. 10:22; 18:11;[37] 24:13) or darkness to light (cf. 4:14-16; 6:20-23), and that disciples receive the promise of Jesus' ongoing presence as they obediently undertake his mission of discipling the entire world.

"This Is My Beloved Son" (3:13-17)

Jesus commands his disciples to baptize new disciples "in the name of the Father and the Son and of the Holy Spirit" (28:19b). By this time, Matthew's reader is familiar with the term βαπτίζω ("wash, purify; dip, baptize") and its cognate βάπτισμα ("water-rite, baptism"), which have up to this point been used in connection with John's baptism of persons, including Jesus, in the Jordan River (3:1-17; cf. 21:25). That the author does not explain or develop further the meaning of "baptize" in 28:19 suggests that the sense of the term is known to the implied reader, who brings his understanding of baptism to bear upon the passage. By examining Matthew's previous use of βαπτίζω (3:13-17), I will attempt to discover how Matthew's portrayal of Jesus in that episode contributes to the reader's comprehension of μαθητεύσατε (28:19).

Matthieu, 21-22, who opines that the Hebrew עִמָּנוּ אֵל (Isa 7:14; cf. 8:8) does not emphasize the idea of divine presence as such, an idea that is often presupposed, but that of active and helpful presence (Gen 21:20; 26:3; 28:20; John 3:2; 8:29; 16:32; Luke 1:28; Acts 7:9; Rom 15:33 etc.); and Davies and Allison Jr., *Matthew (III)*, 686-87 on God's with-ness being "divine assistance."

36. Keener, *Matthew*, 87-95 explains that Joseph models behavior that provides several exhortations for Matthew's reader, including piety, sexual restraint, fidelity, discipline, yielding to God's honor above his own, preferment of others above self, and obedience to God; see also France, *Matthew*, 51 on Joseph's righteousness being more aligned to being careful to keep the law rather than being merciful and considerate; Luz, *Matthew 1-7*, 95; and Davies and Allison Jr., *Matthew (I)*, 202.

37. Many early MSS do not contain this verse.

Matthew's account of Jesus' baptism (3:13-17) forms part of the prolegomena to Jesus' ministry (3:1—4:16), which prepares the reader for the description of that ministry in the remainder of the Gospel.[38] Immediately after Matthew's report on the preaching of John the Baptist in the wilderness (3:1-12),[39] he notifies the reader that Jesus arrives from Galilee at the Jordan to be baptized by John (3:13). Initially, John does not want to baptize Jesus but wants to be baptized by him (3:14);[40] however, Jesus insists that "it is fitting for [them] to fulfill all righteousness," and so John yields to him (3:15).[41] After being baptized, the heavens are opened, Jesus sees the Spirit of God descending on him,[42] and he hears a voice from heaven saying, "This is My beloved Son, in whom I am well pleased" (3:16-17).[43]

Matthew employs three important narrative structures in his arrangement of 3:13-17, which, working together, celebrate Jesus, the Son

---

38. Bauer, *Gospel of the Son of God*, 150.

39. With the account of John the Baptist's ministry (3:1-12), Matthew continues his series of reliable witnesses to the person of Jesus, which includes Matthew himself (1:1-17), the angel (1:18-25), and the magi (2:1-23). John's witness is reliable because he preaches the same message as Jesus and the disciples (3:2; cf. 4:17; 10:7), he fulfills OT prophecy (3:3), and he proclaims God's message fearlessly, remaining steadfast amidst human opposition (3:7-10; 4:12; 11:2; 14:1-12; 17:10-13) (Bauer, *Gospel of the Son of God*, 150-53).

40. Perhaps, his words imply "I need your Spirit-and-fire baptism, not you my water-baptism" (France, *Matthew*, 119).

41. Maier, *Evangelium des Matthäus (1-14)*, 76-77 reckons that "to fulfill all justice" means that the Messiah stands by his people and the servant of God stands up for the many. If one considers that Jesus, the Baptist, and the church are united (as ἡμῖν, 3:15) under the active fulfillment of the law and that justice is a guiding principle of theology, then justice means the divine demand addressed to men.

42. Matthew usually prefers 'Holy' as a modifier of 'Spirit' (e.g., 1:18, 20; 3:11; 12:32; 28:19); therefore, he signals a trinitarian emphasis by adding "of God'" to "Spirit" (cf. 12:28) and establishes continuity between Jesus' baptism and later Christian baptism (28:19) (Gundry, *Matthew*, 52); see Gnilka, *Das Matthäusevangelium*, 1:78-79 on Matthew's preference for "Spirit of God" (3:16).

43. Bauer, *Gospel of the Son of God*, 155 asserts that this declaration represents the climax to 1:1-4:16; Keener, *Matthew*, 132-35 comments that God declares his approval of Jesus through the parting of the heavens (3:16; cf. Isa 64:1; Ezek. 1:1), the Holy Spirit descending on Jesus like a dove (3:16; cf. Gen 8:8-12; 4 Bar. 7.8), and a declaration from the heavens; Patte, *Matthew*, 51 summarizes that it is essential to understand that Jesus, Son of God, is someone who fulfills all righteousness, is totally committed to God's authority, and has an authority comparable to that of God's; France, *Matthew*, 122 proffers that the "voice out of the heavens" (3:17; cf. 17:5) offers Matthew's reader the most unmediated access to God's own view of Jesus.

of God, who perfectly obeys the will of his Father.[44] First, the author employs *recurrence* of *contrast* to emphasize the difference between Jesus' way of thinking and that of John the Baptist, corroborating John's earlier statement, "He who is coming after me is mightier than I, and I am not fit to remove his sandals" (3:11): (i) Jesus comes to John, demonstrating his willingness to be baptized by John (3:13); *but* (ii) on the basis of his own rationale, John tries to prevent Jesus from being baptized by him because he recognizes the supremacy of Jesus; as far as John is concerned, his baptism of Jesus is illogical;[45] *but* (iii) Jesus resists John's rationale, replacing it with his own—i.e., "for in this way it is fitting for [them] to fulfill all righteousness" (3:15a);[46] his is a divine rationale that is based on understanding God's will and is bent on pleasing God. Second, the short passage utilizes *cruciality* to demonstrate that when John, following Jesus, yields to God's will, the tension of the contrasting wills of God/Jesus vis-à-vis John subsides and God testifies of Jesus' perfect obedience as his beloved Son: (i) before the pivot, the author emphasizes John's and Jesus' contrasting ways of thinking about John's baptism of Jesus (3:13–15a); (ii) the pivot occurs when John yields to Jesus (3:15b); (iii) after the pivot, John forsakes his way of thinking and baptizes Jesus, which paves the way for God to testify that Jesus is his beloved Son (3:16–17). The radical reversal occurs with regard to John's way of thinking, which progresses from being an obstacle to their "fulfillment of all righteousness" to their

---

44. Maier, *Evangelium des Matthäus (1–14)*, 166–67 reckons that two narrative highlights stand out in this pericope: the conversation between the Baptist and Jesus and the events after baptism.

45. John has correctly identified Jesus as the one who is "mightier than I" (3:11). He acknowledges Jesus' authority; however, his identification of Jesus leads him to propose a wrong action. For John, Jesus is the eschatological judge who "will baptize you with the Holy Spirit and fire" (3:11); i.e., who will destroy evil people in fire (3:12). This view of Jesus is not incorrect: he will indeed be the eschatological judge. But the text underscores that, "now," in the present (3:15), Jesus should not be perceived in this way. Furthermore, by submitting to John's baptism, Jesus is acknowledging its validity and the validity of John's vocation (Patte, *Matthew*, 50).

46. Jesus submits to baptism, against the objections of John, in order "to fulfill all righteousness" (3:15). Jesus has no sin to confess and repent of, but it is God's will that Jesus identifies with the people in their need so as to deliver them. By identifying with sinners, Jesus demonstrates his righteousness, for the divine declaration of approval comes immediately after Jesus' baptism (Bauer, *Gospel of the Son of God*, 157); for more on the meaning of "to fulfill all righteousness," see Beasley-Murray, *Baptism*, 45–67; Keener, *Matthew*, 132; Patte, *Matthew*, 50–51; Brown and Roberts, *Matthew*, 43; France, *Matthew*, 120; Hagner, *Matthew 1–13*, 56; Luz, *Matthew 1–7*, 142; and Davies and Allison Jr., *Matthew (I)*, 320–43.

accomplishment of the same. Third, the *climax* of the passage represents the final and climactic witness to Jesus, which comes from God himself and occurs when a voice of the heavens says, "This is my beloved Son, in whom I am well pleased" (3:17b). The Father's pleasure in his Son is the result of the Son's obedience to the Father.[47]

Matthew's portrayal of Jesus in this passage shapes the reader's understanding of the meaning of μαθητεύσατε (28:19). The reader notes that Jesus is (in large measure) a model of discipleship in Matthew: (i) he purposefully obeys the will of his Father and does not permit any contrary reasoning to circumvent his knowledge of his Father's will and his desire to fulfill it;[48] (ii) he persists (despite John's objections) in remaining obedient to the will of God, resulting in John's change of thinking, the baptism of Jesus, and God's witness that Jesus is his beloved Son;[49] and (iii) his obedience to the will of his Father climaxes with God's witness of his Sonship and God's pleasure with his entire being.[50] Therefore, the reader understands that from the process of "making disciples" emerges persons who follow Jesus as a model for disciples and demonstrate, like Jesus, the determination or resolve to obey the Father's will by observing all of Jesus' commands.[51]

---

47. For Matthew, the Son of God is not only the one who is revealed from heaven (cf. 2:15; 16:16–17; 17:5); he is above all the obedient one who submits to God's will (Luz, *Matthew 1–7*, 144).

48. The obedience that Jesus demonstrates to his Father's will in 3:13–17 is consistent with his behavior at the times of his temptation: (i) by the devil (4:1–11); (ii) by Peter/Satan to avoid his Passion in Jerusalem (16:21–23; 26:36–46); and (iii) by passersby and the religious authorities to come down from the cross and save himself (27:40–43). In every case, Jesus defers to his Father's will.

49. Jesus also demonstrates persistence in obeying his Father's will by: (i) resisting the devil's temptations (4:1–11); (ii) remaining faithful to his ministry after revisiting his hometown, Nazareth, and finding a lukewarm response thereto (13:53–58); (iii) repeatedly forewarning his disciples about going to Jerusalem to be killed (16:21; cf. 17:22–23; 20:17–19; 26:1–2, 21–25, 31–35); and (iv) remaining on the cross despite the mocking of passersby and the religious authorities (27:40–43).

50. The Father's ultimate witness of Jesus' obedience comes at the time of his resurrection, and results in the risen Jesus' claim, "All authority has been given to me in heaven and on earth" (28:18).

51. See Bauer, *Gospel of the Son of God*, 66, 216, 309–10, 317–18, 323 on Jesus being the model for both discipleship and mission in Matthew.

"You Shall Worship the Lord Your God" (4:1–11)

In 28:17a, the author reports that the disciples worship of the risen Jesus, which most certainly prompts the reader to recall multiple events in the Gospel in which Jesus is the object of other people's rightful worship or reverence: the magi (2:2, 11); a leper (8:2); a synagogue official (9:18); a Canaanite woman (15:25); the disciples (14:33); the mother of the sons of Zebedee (20:20); and two of the women disciples, "Mary Magdalene and the other Mary" (28:9; cf. 28:1). However, the reader also remembers two events that represent the willful and wrongful application of worship. In one instance, Herod pretends to desire to worship the child Jesus (2:8), and in the other, the devil invites Jesus to worship him in return for all the kingdoms of the world (4:8–9). It is the latter event, which Matthew describes more fully in 4:1–11, that I propose to examine to determine the extent to which it contributes to the reader's understanding of μαθητεύσατε (28:19).

Matthew locates 4:1–11 within the first major unit of his Gospel (1:1—4:16), which records the *preparation* for Jesus Christ, Son of God.[52] In the passage, the Spirit leads the newly baptized Jesus into the wilderness to be tempted by the devil (4:1).[53] After fasting for forty days and nights, he becomes hungry and the devil comes and tempts him three times: (i) to turn stones into bread (4:3–4), (ii) to throw himself down from the pinnacle of the temple so that God would save him (4:5–7), and (iii) to fall down and worship him (the devil) in return for all the kingdoms of the world and their glory (4:8–10).[54] Jesus overcomes the devil's temptations, and the devil leaves him (4:11).[55]

---

52. Bauer, *Gospel of the Son of God*, 128.

53. The introduction to the pericope indicates that while the devil is the one who tests/tempts Jesus, the Spirit guides the whole experience and therefore it is according to God's will (France, *Matthew*, 126).

54. Maier, *Evangelium des Matthäus* (1–14), 184 agrees with Davies and Allison that the triple temptation event in 4:1–11 has a parallel in 26:36–46 and in 26:69–75. Matthew seems to be fond of such triple processes (also note the questions of the Jewish teachers in 22:15–40), a pattern that is probably tried and tested in catechesis and that has a parallel in Luke (4:1–13), but not in Mark; see Davies and Allison Jr., *Matthew (I)*, 352.

55. The devil leaves Jesus at the end of this episode (4:11), but Jesus continues to be tempted later in the Gospel by persons and situations that replicate and play the role of the "Satan" (e.g., 16:22–23; 26:36–46; 27:40, 43; 27:42–43) (Bauer, *Gospel of the Son of God*, 161); Hagner, *Matthew 1–13*, 68–69 remarks that Satan tests Jesus and fails; Jesus' command to him to go away calls the reader's attention simultaneously to Jesus'

Jesus encounters two great cosmic powers (God and Satan) in 3:13—4:11, and Matthew combines *recurrence* of *contrast* with *interchange*[56] to emphasize their divergent perspectives on obedience to God: the devil desires Jesus "to express his divine sonship in ways that contradicts God's will" (4:3, 6, 9), whereas God requires Jesus and all of humanity to obey him (4:4, 7, 10).[57] The author arranges this contrast according to a narrative pattern that oscillates between the devil's speech and God's speech: (i) the tempter says, "If you are the Son of God, command that these stones become bread" (4:3), *but* God says, "Man shall not live on bread alone, but on every word that proceeds out of the mouth of God" (4:4; Deut 8:3); (ii) the tempter says, "If you are the Son of God, throw Yourself down; for it is written, 'he will command his angels concerning you' and 'On *their* hands they will bear you up, So that you will not strike you foot against a stone'" (4:6; cf. Ps 91:11–12), *but* God says, "You shall not put the Lord your God to the test" (4:7; cf. Deut 6:16); and (iii) the tempter says, "All these things I will give you, if you fall down and worship me" (4:9), *but* God says, "You shall worship the Lord your God, and serve him only" (4:10; cf. Deut 6:13; 10:20).[58] Furthermore, the reader notices that the contrast between God's and Satan's points of view on obedience begins with humanity's relation to (and dependence upon) God in terms of food (4:3–4; cf. 14:13–21; 15:32–39; Gen 3:1; Deut 8:3–6) and it reaches a *climax* with humanity's relation to God in terms of worship (4:9–10; cf. Exod 20:5; Deut 5:9).[59]

---

victory and authority.

56. "Interchange is the exchanging or alternation of certain elements in an a-b-a-b arrangement" (Bauer and Traina, *Inductive Bible Study*, 116).

57. The background of this passage is Deuteronomy 6–8, which describes the nation of Israel's temptation in the wilderness for forty years and its yielding to that temptation. In Matt 4:1–11, however, Jesus relives the experience of Israel, but he is successful where Israel failed (Bauer, *Gospel of the Son of God*, 158–61); Maier, *Evangelium des Matthäus (1–14)*, 90–91 judges that the imperative, "Go, Satan!" (4:10), which is found only in Matthew, has its parallel in 16:23. Maier is of the view that the parallelization of the two passages is intentional, and that the central idea of suffering and discomfort in 16:23 echoes here, in the sense of the exemplary obedience of Jesus.

58. Jesus, the Son of God, does not follow the ways of OT Israel. He rejects the devil's offer of the world's kingdoms and their glory, seeing through the devil's designs (Davies and Allison Jr., *Matthew (I)*, 373).

59. Twelftree, "Temptation," 824 regards the final temptation to be "the most devilish of all; the call to Jesus to receive his proper inheritance without obedient worship of God"; see Davies and Allison Jr., *Matthew (I)*, 352, who comment that "the three temptations exhibit a spatial progression, from a low place to a high place"; Luz,

Matthew's depiction of Jesus in this passage influences the reader's understanding of the meaning of μαθητεύσατε (28:19). The reader notes that: (i) Jesus testifies about God and about his own character by his actions—he chooses to live on every word that proceeds from God's mouth (4:3–4), not to put God to the test (4:5–7), and to reserve worship and service for God only (4:8–10); (ii) he consistently relies upon and utilizes God's own words to frame all of his responses to Satan's overtures; (iii) he demonstrates an excellent handling of Scripture to correct the devil's misuse thereof for his own needs (4:6b); (iv) he repeatedly and unwaveringly obeys his Father's will;[60] and (v) ultimately, he recognizes the climactic correlation between worshipping God and obedience to God.[61] Consequently, the reader recognizes that the process of "making disciples" seeks to mold persons into disciples whose words and actions, like Jesus', are mutually consistent,[62] who handle the Scriptures correctly to repel the devil's advances, who unwaveringly obeys the Father's will, and who understand that such obedience is the climax of worshipping God.

Matthew 1–7, 153 notes that underlying the narrative is the understanding of divine sonship; however, of greatest importance is the allusion to the Gospel's final pericope. "After Jesus as the obedient Son of God has rejected divine demonstrations of power, has suffered, and has died on the cross, there finally takes place, again on a mountain (28:16), the proclamation of his power not only over all the kingdoms of the world but over heaven and earth (28:18). The renunciation of power by the earthly Jesus points ahead to the authority of the risen Jesus."

60. The temptation narrative encourages Jesus' followers to be, like Jesus the faithful Israelite, faithful to God through temptation (Brown and Roberts, *Matthew*, 49).

61. Matthew repeatedly emphasizes the importance of obeying the Father's will (e.g., 3:13–17; 12:50; 21:28–32; 26:39, 42). Similarly, he reiterates that "hearing" is for the purpose of obeying God's words (7:24, 26; 11:15; 13:9, 43; 13:10–17; 13:18–23; 17:5). Bauer, *Gospel of the Son of God*, 157 argues, "Matthew 4:12 witnesses to Jesus' obedience to the will of his Father in that Jesus embarks on his ministry only after John, the God-appointed preparer, is removed from the scene; therefore, Jesus begins his ministry in accordance with God's timing."

62. Jesus regularly champions the correct alignment of human speech and action: (i) he unmasks the human flaw of teaching good habits to others without actually carrying them out for oneself (e.g., the scribes and the Pharisees, 23:1–3); and (ii) he charges his disciples, "But let your statement be, 'Yes, yes' *or* 'No, no'; anything beyond these is of evil" (5:37), the underlying point of which revolves around the need for unity between one's word and one's action.

"I Will Make You Fishers of Men" (4:18–22)

The Matthean Jesus commands his disciples to "make disciples" in 28:19a. The reader is familiar with Matthew's use of μαθητεύω intransitively in the context of being a pupil or adherent of a teacher (13:52; 27:57) and transitively in terms of causing someone to be a pupil (28:19).[63] He is also aware of the author's use throughout his Gospel of other terms that are within the semantic range of μαθητεύω, namely: (i) ὀπίσω ("after," as in following after someone as an adherent or disciple, 4:19; 10:38; 16:24); (ii) ἀκολουθέω ("follow as a disciple"; e.g., 4:20, 22; 8:22; 9:9); and (iii) μαθητής ("learner; pupil; disciple"; e.g., 5:1; 10:1; 26:20; 28:16).[64] Once the reader encounters "Go therefore and make disciples of all the nations" (28:19), one of the passages that comes to mind is "*Follow* [ὀπίσω] me, and I will make you fishers of men" (4:19), the first declaration that the Matthean Jesus issues to his disciples, after which they immediately leave their livelihoods and family and *follow* [ἀκολουθέω] him as disciples (4:20, 22) and witness him making disciples.[65] Matthew describes Jesus' calling of his first disciples in 4:18–22, a passage I propose to examine to discover the extent to which it contributes to the reader's understanding of μαθητεύσατε (28:19).

This passage (4:18–22) is located at the commencement of the second major unit of Matthew's Gospel (4:17—16:20), which begins Jesus' proclamation of the kingdom to Israel. The wider unit progresses: (i) from Jesus' call of his disciples (4:18–22); (ii) to his announcement of the kingdom through teaching, preaching, and healing (4:23—11:1); and (iii) concludes with the dual response to that announcement of the kingdom—i.e., acceptance by the disciples and rejection by Israel as a whole.[66]

Matthew records that after Jesus overcomes his temptation by the devil (4:1–11), he withdraws to Galilee and begins to preach "the kingdom

---

63. "μαθητεύω," BDAG, 609. Sometimes Matthew uses ἀκολουθέω in the context of the crowds following or accompanying Jesus (e.g., 4:25; 8:1, 10; 12:15; 14:13).

64. See "Follow, Be a Disciple (36.31–36.43)" in Louw and Nida, *Greek-English Lexicon*, 1:469–70.

65. Throughout Matthew, ἀκολουθέω ("following") is practically a designation for discipleship. Bauer, *Gospel of the Son of God*, 317–18 notes that "the primary significance of 'following' Jesus pertains to Jesus' demand that they 'come after' him on the journey to Jerusalem where he will suffer, die, and be raised (16:21–28:20); here they walk behind him, so that he becomes model, motivation, and forerunner of their own destiny. Thus, the language of Matthew 4:18–22 anticipates that fateful journey."

66. Bauer, *Gospel of the Son of God*, 128.

of heaven is at hand" (4:12-17). As he is walking by the Sea of Galilee, he sees two brothers, Simon-Peter and Andrew, casting a net into the sea (4:18)[67] and he commands them, "Follow me, and I will make you fishers of men" (4:19).[68] They immediately leave their livelihood to follow him as disciples (4:20). Further on, he sees and calls another pair of fishermen brothers, James and John, to follow him, and they too immediately leave their livelihood and family and follow Jesus as disciples (4:21-22).

The reader observes that Matthew utilizes several narrative structures in his arrangement of 4:18-22 to underscore the centrality of following Jesus and becoming "fishers of men" to Christian discipleship. First, the *preparation* (4:18) identifies three of the main characters of the passage (Jesus and the two brothers, Simon-Peter and Andrew), the location of the event (the Sea of Galilee), and the occupation of the two brothers (fishermen) in anticipation of the description of Jesus' appeal to them and two other fishermen brothers (James and John) to follow him as disciples and to undertake their new profession of "fishing for men" (4:19-22)—i.e., the *realization*. Second, it is also apparent to the reader that Matthew uses *recurrence of causation with interchange* to describe the exchange between Jesus and the two pairs of fishermen brothers. The passage comprises two call events,[69] each of which involves a command to follow (*cause*) and a positive response (*effect*) that is part of a larger alternating rhythm of *command-response-command-response*, which emphasizes to the reader that immediate obedience is the only correct response to Jesus' command to follow him as his disciple: (i) Jesus calls

---

67. Bonnard, *Saint Matthieu*, 50 considers various possible meanings of the image of the disciples casting their net into the sea (4:18) and concludes that in light of the immediate context (4:12-17) and the connection of this passage to Matt 10, the image of the fishermen casting nets into the sea approximates the idea of Jesus' apostles being effective witnesses of the kingdom of God to people.

68. Jesus' call to follow him is unexpected and commanding, and the author's use of the historical present (καὶ λέγει, 4:19) suggests that it can be repeated at any time and will be repeated (Gnilka, *Das Matthäusevangelium*, 1:101); see Wallace, *Greek Grammar*, 526-32 on the Historical Present (Dramatic Present) frequently being used to describe a past event for the purpose of vivid portrayal; for Maier, *Evangelium des Matthäus* (1-14), 213-14, "Follow me" is analogous to the calling to the prophetic discipleship, but it far surpasses it, this calling being to the service and the church of the Messiah.

69. Keener, *Matthew*, 150 notes that, by seeking out disciples himself, Jesus' calling of them may have represented a serious breach of custom by "coming down to their level" socially; so also Brown and Roberts, *Matthew*, 54; and France, *Matthew*, 147 on the unconventionality of Jesus calling his disciples to follow him.

Simon-Peter and Andrew to follow him (4:19); (ii) they immediately leave their nets and follow him (4:20); (iii) Jesus calls James and John to follow him (4:4:21); (iv) they immediately leave their boat and father and follow Jesus.[70] The *parallelism* between the two call events is itself a *recurrence of structure*, which reminds the reader that Jesus is repeatedly calling new persons to follow him and to become "fishers of men" while they are his disciples.[71] Third, a *recurrence of terms* emphasizes other important elements of the passage regarding Jesus' calling of persons to be his disciples: (i) on relationships, Jesus calls two pairs of "brothers" (4:18, 21); in one instance, a pair of brothers must leave their "father" (4:21, 22) in pursuit of their new calling; (ii) on occupations, both pairs of brothers are "fishermen" (4:18, 19), who fish in the same area and are therefore acquainted with each other, including their network of relatives;[72] (iii) on means of livelihood, the men leave behind the tools of their trade, including fishing nets (4:18, 20, 21) and fishing vessels (4:21, 22); (iv) on commands, Jesus commands both pairs of brothers to follow him as his disciples (4:19, 21);[73] and (v) on responses, the men are united in their individual responses to Jesus' call—"immediately," abandoning everything, "they follow" him as his disciples (4:20, 22).[74] Fourth, Matthew's use of the future tense ("I will make you," 4:19) is noteworthy. With its use, the reader anticipates Jesus' future efforts to fulfill his

---

70. "Fishermen, like tax gatherers, were 'among the more economically mobile of the village culture'... Thus, these fishermen had much to lose economically by leaving their businesses," and they could not easily return to abandoned businesses (Keener, *Matthew*, 149, 151–53); see France, *Matthew*, 148 on the inclusion of the boat and the men's father (4:21) making the radical nature of the disciples' renunciation of their present way of life in favor of "fishing for people" even more pronounced.

71. See Bauer, *Gospel of the Son of God*, 163–64 on the threefold effect of this parallelism (i) by emphasizing repeated elements; (ii) by allowing the stories to interpret each other; and (iii) by stressing the normative and paradigmatic character of these two episodes.

72. See Wilkins, "Disciples," 177 on the early disciples being drawn from an existing network of relatives, business partners, neighbors, and acquaintances.

73. The command to follow Jesus as a disciple (4:21) is implied by the narrator's words, "and he called them."

74. France, *Matthew*, 148 observes that Matthew's use of "immediately" (4:22) emphasizes the extraordinary readiness of these fishermen to abandon all for the sake of following a charismatic stranger as his disciples; Davies and Allison Jr., *Matthew (I)*, 397 compares this story with other call stories (1 Kgs 19:19–21; Judg 6:11–12; 1 Sam 11:5; Amos 7:14–15; Mark 2:14).

promise to make his disciples "fishers of men."[75] All such future efforts and the disciples' responses thereto, which are described throughout the text that follows (4:23–28:20), are causally linked to 4:18–22 and to Jesus' commands to follow him. The reader recognizes this movement from 4:18–22 to the remainder of Matthew's text to be that of hortatory *causation*, which the author attempts to achieve on two levels.[76] On the first level, the causal progression is from 4:19 to 4:20—28:18: Jesus states in the indicative, "I will make you fishers of men" (4:19), the cause, which he reinforces throughout 4:20—28:18 with commands and exhortations to his disciples (e.g., 5:12, 44; 6:1, 9, 33; 7:7; 10:7–8; 16:6; 19:14; 23:3; 24:4, 6; 26:26–27, 41), the effect, that are designed to achieve his objective of making them "fishers of men."[77] The usual key words that are associated with causation—"therefore," "so," and "then"—are implied.[78] The reader therefore understands this narrative progression to mean: "Because I will

---

75. Luz connects Jesus' first call for persons to follow him and to become "fishers of men" (4:18–22) with his first commission to the Twelve to "fish" for people (10:5–16), and to his subsequent parable of the fishnet (13:47–50) where the expression is understood to refer to missionary activity, and ultimately with the Commission, which, the scholar argues, "finally makes plain what Jesus means" in 4:18 (Luz, *Matthew 1–7*, 161–62). As I explained in my analysis of 28:19 in the previous chapter of this book, "Follow me, and I will make you fishers of men" (4:18) and "Go therefore and make disciples of all the nations" (28:19) are connected on several levels: time (beginning and end of a journey); location (both events occur in Galilee); characters (Jesus and his disciples are common to both events); and semantics (words of similar meaning are common to both accounts). I agree with Luz that 28:19 is best viewed as Matthew's explanation of the meaning of 4:19. Therefore, the reader anticipates Matthew's use of the intervening material (4:20–28:18) to develop the theme of "fishing for men" in the context of Jesus' interaction (in words and actions) with his Twelve; Davies and Allison Jr., *Matthew (I)*, 398 perceive an allusion to Jer 16:16 in Matt 4:19, and they conclude, "In any event, in being called by Jesus, the disciples were not being invited to study Torah or practise it. Rather were they (*sic*) being called to rescue the lost, to help in the work of announcing and preparing for the kingdom of God"; Hagner, *Matthew 1–13*, 77 opines that by becoming "fishers of human beings," the disciples join Jesus in proclaiming the kingdom and in encourage those who listen to enter therein.

76. As I have already indicated (in chapter 3 of this book), the structural relationship between Jesus' promise to make his disciples "fishers of men" (4:19) and his earthly ministry as a whole (4:20–28:18) may also be described as ideological particularization (Bauer and Traina, *Inductive Bible Study*, 100).

77. I refer here to Jesus' verbal commands; however, as I have sought to demonstrate in my analysis of 28:20 (in chapter 3 of this book), all of Jesus' life—verbal and nonverbal commands—come into view when making disciples.

78. Bauer and Traina, *Inductive Bible Study*, 105–6 note that implicit causation can also be present.

make you fishers of men, *therefore* you ought to do so and so." Hence, all of Jesus' earthly ministry represents his own efforts to make his disciples "fishers of men."[79] On the second level, the causal progression is from 4:19 directly to 28:19: Jesus states in the indicative, "I will make you fishers of men" (4:19), the cause, which progresses to his imperative at the end of the Gospel, "Go therefore and make disciples of all the nations" (28:19), the effect, which is designed to demonstrate the realization or fulfillment of his promise to make them "fishers of men."[80] Consequently, the reader understands this narrative progression to mean: "Because I have already made you fishers of men, *therefore* you ought to go and make disciples of all the nations."[81]

Matthew's characterization of Jesus in this passage guides the reader's understanding of the meaning of μαθητεύσατε (28:19). The reader observes that: (i) Jesus seeks out and finds new disciples as both he and they go about their normal daily activities—e.g., walking/fishing by the Sea of Galilee; he does not wait for them to come to him;[82] (ii) Jesus invites persons into discipleship for the twofold purpose of following him

---

79. See my analysis of 28:19 (in chapter 3 of this book) for a list of the components of Jesus' earthly ministry that would constitute making his disciples "fishers of men."

80. I have dealt in greater length with the connection between 4:19 and 28:19 in my analysis of 28:19 (in chapter 3 of this book).

81. Luz, *Matthew 1-7*, 161-62 connects Jesus' first call for persons to follow him (4:18-22) with his first commission to the Twelve to "fish" for people (10:5-16), and to his subsequent parable of the fishnet (13:47-50) where the expression is understood to refer to missionary activity, and ultimately with the Commission, which, Luz argues, "finally makes plain what Jesus means"; see Edwards, "Uncertain Faith," 59, who comments, "The narrator keeps the disciples in the forefront of the reader's mind from the opening call of the four fishermen (4:18-22) down to their unsure worshiping (28:17). Jesus himself tells them that their task is to 'disciplize' (28:19)."

82. In the same way, Jesus calls Matthew while he is sitting in his tax collector's booth (9:9); he keeps company with tax collectors and sinners (irreligious Jews), for which reason he realizes the ire of the religious authorities (9:11; 11:19; cf. Mark 2:16; Luke 5:30; 15:2). Davies and Allison Jr., *Matthew (I)*, 401 observe that "James and John, like Peter and Andrew and Elisha of old, are called to discipleship in the midst of their daily activity. They leave one occupation for another."

as disciples[83] and of serving him as disciple-makers or "fishers of men";[84] (iii) the correct response to Jesus' invitation into discipleship is immediate and ongoing obedience (cf. 19:16–22; 28:20);[85] (iv) Jesus repeatedly invites persons into discipleship, continuously calling them to follow him (cf. 8:22; 9:9; 10:39; 16:24; 19:21, 28); (v) Jesus promises to train his disciples to become "fishers of men"—i.e., persons who are committed to making new disciples—therefore, all of his earthly ministry (both in words and actions) encapsulate his efforts to train his disciples for that very purpose;[86] (vi) as Jesus invites persons into discipleship, he seeks to leverage his disciples' existing relationships and occupational skills for the purpose of making new disciples;[87] however, new disciples must be willing to reprioritize existing family and work relationships and obligations;[88] and (vii) Jesus' disciples must adhere to his commands to

---

83. Unlike the classical and Hellenistic concept of discipleship in which teachers made disciples for themselves—i.e., pupils and learners followed the teacher—Jesus' disciples are not to make disciples for themselves (cf. 23:8–10; 18:4); rather, they disciple others to follow Jesus and they are to assume "the egalitarianism of 'brothers,' recognizing that the only status among them is the anti-status attitude of humility" (Bauer, *Gospel of the Son of God*, 208); see also Wilkins, *Discipleship in the Ancient World*, 11–42.

84. Jesus teaches his hearers in terms they can understand—e.g., "fishers of men" (Keener, *Matthew*, 151).

85. The immediacy of the disciples' obedience to Jesus' command to follow him (4:20, 22) may be viewed in contrast to the Rich Young Ruler's reluctance to obey a similar command from Jesus; instead, he walks away grieving (19:16–22).

86. When the Matthean Jesus rebukes his disciples, for example, about the "littleness of their faith" (e.g., 6:30; 8:26; 14:31; 16:8; 17:20), it demonstrates that his time with them is a period of training that he wants to be successful.

87. Jesus calls a network of fishermen into discipleship (4:18–22); similarly, he calls Matthew, a tax collector, into discipleship, after which he accepts an invitation to dine in a house with "many tax collectors and sinners" (9:9–10). Keener, *Matthew*, 151 remarks that Jesus calls artisans and encourages them to recognize that the skills they already had were serviceable in the kingdom. "If God called shepherds like Moses and David to shepherd his people Israel, Jesus could call fishermen to be gatherers of people."

88. In the matter of following Jesus, one of his disciples says, "Lord, permit me first to go and bury my father." Jesus replies, "Follow me, and allow the dead to bury their own dead" (8:21–22); see also 12:46–50 regarding the changed "family" relationships resulting from being disciples of Jesus. Keener, *Matthew*, 153 comments that Jesus' call "cost comfort, challenged the priority of family, and was probably therefore scandalous"; see Carter, "Matthew 4:18–22," 58–59, who argues that diverse material in Matthew's Gospel, including the call of the first disciples (4:18–22) creates "a vision of discipleship that embraces an ambivalent relationship to society consisting of

make disciples of the nations (28:20). Accordingly, the reader is aware that the process of "making disciples" has implications for the disciple-maker as well as the new disciple. Disciple-makers should continuously seek out new disciples wherever they are, prioritizing teaching new disciples how to reproduce themselves, and making maximum use of (familial and other) relationships and occupational skills to bring persons into Christian discipleship. On the other hand, new disciples ought to respond with immediate and ongoing obedience to Jesus' invitation to follow him.

"Look, Your Disciples Do What Is Not Lawful" (12:1–8)

Matthew emphasizes the religious authorities' opposition to Jesus' ministry from the immediate context of the Commission passage by juxtaposing their attempt to conceal the truth about the resurrection (28:11–15) with Jesus' mandate to his disciples to reveal the truth to all the nations (28:16–20). Matthew's reader is familiar with these two contrasting themes that pervade the Gospel. On the religious authorities' opposition to Jesus' ministry, the reader is sure to recall multiple incidents in which members of their ranks are adversarial to Jesus and his disciples in the ordinary course of their activities: (i) conspiring to destroy Jesus (12:14; cf. 16:21; 20:18–19; 21:45–46; 22:15–22; 26:3–4, 14–16, 47, 57–68; 27:1–2, 12, 20, 41, 62–66; 28:11–15); (ii) demanding a sign from him (12:38; 16:1); (iii) testing his knowledge (19:3; 22:23–33, 34–36); (iv) displaying fits of anger about matters concerning him (21:15); and (v) challenging his authority (21:23–27). The reader is also aware of the Matthean Jesus' response to being tested and rejected by them: (i) he resists their attempts to minimize his authority to forgive sins and heal the sick (9:1–8); (ii) he openly rebukes them (12:22–29); and (iii) sometimes he goes on the offensive against them by interrogating them on his own terms (21:23–27; 22:41–46), exposing the inconsistencies between their words and actions (23:1–12), and by pronouncing judgment on them because of their wicked deeds (23:13–36). I would like to examine one of these encounters in which Jesus defends his disciples against the accusations of the

---

detachment from societal ties on the one hand, but of participation in socioeconomic structures, and their use, on the other. Allegiance to Jesus means being a 'voluntary marginal,' living a liminal existence in alternative households."

Pharisees (12:1–8) to determine how it might contribute to the reader's understanding of μαθητεύσατε (28:19).

The author locates 12:1–8 within the second major unit of his Gospel (4:17—16:20), which records the proclamation of Jesus Christ, Son of God, to Israel, and includes, *inter alia*, a dual response to that proclamation: acceptance by the disciples, and rejection by Israel as a whole (including the religious authorities).[89] It is notable that throughout the Gospel both the ministry of Jesus and that of his disciples result in persecution of the kind that is characterized by the events of 12:1–8 and by other previously mentioned conflicts.[90] In 12:1–8, Jesus and his disciples are going through the grainfields on the Sabbath, and his disciples become hungry and pick the heads of grain to eat (12:1). The Pharisees observe the disciples' actions, and they complain to Jesus that such behavior is unlawful on the Sabbath (12:2).[91]

Matthew utilizes three narrative structures to emphasize Jesus' active resistance against the Pharisees' opposition. First, he utilizes *recurrence of interrogation*[92] to repel their objections to the disciples' actions and compel them to reexamine their own interpretation of the Law concerning the Sabbath. On two occasions in this brief episode, Jesus cross-examines them concerning *whether they had read the Law* about: (i) David and his companions, who, when they became hungry, entered the temple and ate the consecrated bread that was meant for the priests alone (12:3–4; cf. 1 Sam 21:1–6);[93] and (ii) the priests in the temple, who desecrated the

---

89. Bauer, *Gospel of the Son of God*, 128. Bauer observes that "Matthew begins with a catalogue of responses in 11:1–12:50, where he indicates that the two major subgroups within Israel, the Jewish crowds (11:2–24) and the religious leaders (12:1–45), repudiate Jesus' proclamation of the kingdom; only the disciples (11:25–30; 12:46–50) accept it" (181).

90. Bauer, *Gospel of the Son of God*, 131 observes "a repeated contrast between Jesus and his opponents, especially the Jewish leaders and, to some extent, the political leaders, and increasingly the Jewish crowds."

91. The Pharisees address Jesus instead of his disciples because a teacher is responsible for his disciples' behavior, and Jesus' reply accordingly focuses on his own authority, not theirs (France, *Matthew*, 457–58); For more on the Tradition of the Pharisees and the Pharisees in the Gospels, see Westerholm, "Pharisees," 609–14 and "Sabbath," 716–19 on Sabbath Law and the Sabbath in the Gospels; and Keener, *Matthew*, 351–59 on "Conflict Narratives."

92. "Interrogation is the employment of a question or a problem followed by its answer or solution" (Bauer and Traina, *Inductive Bible Study*, 113).

93. The Sabbath day is not mentioned in 1 Samuel 21; however, it is likely connected to the story by the command to consecrate bread to Yahweh each Sabbath (Lev

Sabbath and yet were not guilty (12:5; cf. Num 28:9-10).[94] The Matthean Jesus does not wait for the Pharisees to respond to his question; rather, he provides the answer to them, affirming that: (i) in him "something greater than the temple is here" (12:6); (ii) if they knew the real meaning of compassion, they would not have condemned the innocent so quickly (12:7; cf. Hos 6:6); and (iii) he is "Lord of the Sabbath" (12:8).[95] Second, Matthew uses *contrast* to inform the reader that, while the Law makes demands about Sabbath-keeping, Jesus has come to correctly apply the Law to practical situations in which the reader finds himself—e.g., satisfying his hunger on the Sabbath while away from home. The contrast between observing the ritual demands of the Law and Jesus' application thereof is marked in the text by the keyword "but" in: "*But I say to you* that something greater than the temple is here" (12:6, emphasis added)[96] and "*But if you had known* what this means, 'I desire compassion, not a sacrifice,' you would not have condemned the innocent" (12:7, emphasis added; Hos 6:6).[97] In other words, "The Law says A, but I say (and you should know)

24:8). Additionally, the rationale for the exception may center on David's role and mission (21:2-5; cf. 16:12-13), which coincides with Matthew's focus on Jesus as 'Son of David' (Brown and Roberts, *Matthew*, 119); see Davies and Allison Jr., *Matthew (II)*, 307 who emphasizes several points of correlation between the current passage and 1 Sam 21.

94. According to Jesus: (i) the temple, like the Sabbath (12:9-14), exists to help persons (12:3-4); and (ii) the OT itself testifies that the temple sanctifies labor on the Sabbath day (12:5; cf. Num 28:9-10), especially that which satisfies human need (12:7) (Bauer, *Gospel of the Son of God*, 293).

95. As Lord, Jesus expresses his authority over the entire realm belonging to God, including the Sabbath (Brown and Roberts, *Matthew*, 120); so also Hagner, *Matthew 1-13*, 330.

96. The Matthean Jesus' assertion, 'but I say to you,' recalls the antitheses of 5:21-48 and the fulfilling of the law (5:17) in the sense of teaching the will of God that lies behind the letter of the law (Bauer, *Gospel of the Son of God*, 171); Luz, *Matthew 8-20*, 181 comments that "Jesus does not say that he is greater than the temple, nor may we simply insert here the concept of the kingdom of God ... In my judgment the following verse [12:7] gives a further explanation here. With the word θυσία it takes up again the idea of sacrifice on the Sabbath and supersedes it with 'mercy' ... Thus what is greater than the temple is mercy, which in Jesus' interpretation of the will of God has become the greatest thing"; however, Davies and Allison Jr., *Matthew (II)*, 315 incline to the view that "something greater than the temple is here" (12:6) is explained by 'the Son of Man is Lord of the Sabbath' (12:8).

97. Hos 6:6 is a favorite Matthean OT citation, which indicates that "Sabbath laws are to be interpreted in such a way that divine mercy is emphasized rather than strict conformity with ritual prescriptions" (Westerholm, "Sabbath," 718). With the words of 12:7, Jesus implies that the Pharisees do not understand that God prioritizes

B." Third, the author employs logical *substantiation* to apprise the reader that the reason Jesus pronounces that "something greater than the temple is here" (12:6) and that the Pharisees have condemned the innocent by their erroneous interpretation of the Law (12:7) is because he himself is Lord of the Sabbath, who determines what is and is not acceptable Sabbath practice.[98]

Matthew's representation of Jesus in this passage exerts influence on the reader's interpretation of the meaning of μαθητεύσατε (28:19). The reader discerns that: (i) Jesus actively defends his disciples against adversaries, who plot to destroy him and them (e.g., 12:14; cf. 10:16–18; 23:34); indeed, the protective measures that he adopts on this and other occasions (cf. 15:1–20) remind the reader of his desire to "gather [Jerusalem's] children together, the way a hen gathers her chicks under her wings" (23:37b) to protect them from the one who "kills the prophets and stones those who are sent to her" (23:37a); (ii) he demonstrates superior knowledge and authority about matters in which he shares a common interest with his adversary—e.g., the Law concerning Sabbath observation;[99] the reader knows that such an advantage is also available to his disciples when they encounter persecution because the risen Jesus promises to be with them always (28:20b) and he forewarns them not to worry about what to say when they confront earthly authorities because the Spirit of their Father will speak on their behalf (10:16–20); (iii) he uses the power of interrogation to guide the conversation towards a desired conclusion, knowing the appropriate questions to ask and the

---

compassion over ritual sacrifice, but he (Jesus) does.

98. The Son of Man is not only greater than David and the temple, but he is also "Lord" of the institution—i.e., the Sabbath—that is traced in the OT to God's direct command (Gen 2:3; cf. Exod 31:13; Lev 19:3, 30; Isa 56:4 etc.) (France, *Matthew*, 462–63); Davies and Allison Jr., *Matthew (II)*, 315 argue that this concluding statement renders much of the foregoing irrelevant: If Jesus is Lord of the Sabbath, then what he says is law, and there is no need for argument; for Maier, *Evangelium des Matthäus (1–14)*, 660–61, "the Son of Man as the bringer of divine salvation is Lord of the Sabbath. The 'christological title' expresses a 'christological authority.' In this Christian authority, Jesus finally says how to behave on the Sabbath: he has the authority to interpret. However, behind this also indicates the trinitarian mystery that he, together with the Father, is the giver of the Torah, and thus of the Sabbath"; see also Bauer, *Gospel of the Son of God*, 183, 184, 188, 299 on Matthew's comparison of the actions of Jesus, the "Lord of the Sabbath," and those of the religious authorities.

99. All things, including wisdom and authority, have been handed over to the Matthean Jesus by his Father (11:27); therefore, he speaks as one having authority, and not as one of them (7:29).

corresponding answers to them; and (iv) he fully comprehends his identity—he is "Lord of the Sabbath," which entitles him to determine what is acceptable Sabbath practice.¹⁰⁰ As a result, the reader comprehends that the process of "making disciples" requires disciple-makers to defend and protect new disciples against opponents that would seek to destroy them. Disciple-makers must recognize the identity of Jesus (i.e., who Jesus is) and his presence and power within themselves (i.e., who they are in Jesus), demonstrating an accurate handling of the Scriptures in the face of adversity, and harnessing the potential of interrogation to gain the upper hand over those who oppose Christ and his ministry.

"You of Little Faith" (14:22-33)

In 28:17b, Matthew records that, having worshipped the risen Jesus, some of the disciples are doubtful. The reader is aware that the author uses διστάζω ("doubt") only on one previous occasion—i.e., when Peter attempts to walk on the water towards Jesus, but becomes afraid and begins to sink upon seeing the wind, to which Jesus responds, "You of little faith, why did you *doubt*?" (14:31).¹⁰¹ It is this event, which Matthew describes more fully in 14:22-33, that I propose to examine to determine the extent to which it contributes to the reader's understanding of μαθητεύσατε (28:19).

This passage (14:22-33) is located within the second major unit of Matthew's Gospel (4:17—16:20), which documents the proclamation of Jesus Christ, Son of God, to Israel. It forms part of the dual response of the disciples and Israel (11:1—16:20) to Jesus' announcement of the kingdom (4:23—11:1), and it represents an occasion on which the disciples correctly recognize Jesus as the Son of God (14:33; cf. 16:13-20).¹⁰²

Matthew writes that immediately after Jesus and his disciples feed "the five thousand men, besides women and children" (14:13-21), he sends the disciples ahead in a boat to the other side of the Sea of Galilee and he goes up on the mountain by himself to pray (14:22-23). During the night, while the boat is a long distance from land and is being

---

100. Matt 15:1-9 functions in a similar way to 12:1-8 in contributing to the reader's understanding of the meaning of "make disciples" (28:19).

101. In this pericope, "little faith" is defined by wavering in faith because of fear (14:30-31) (Brown and Roberts, *Matthew*, 140).

102. Bauer, *Gospel of the Son of God*, 128.

battered by the waves and the wind,[103] Jesus approaches them, walking on the water (14:24-25).[104] Jesus identifies himself and Peter attempts to walk on the water towards him, but he becomes afraid and begins to sink (14:27-30). Jesus saves him and asks, "You of little faith, why did you doubt?" (14:31). After returning to the boat, the wind stops and the disciples worship Jesus, saying, "You are certainly the Son of God" (14:32-33).

Matthew utilizes multiple narrative structures in this passage to emphasize the importance of a disciple's faith that is not contaminated by doubt. The first half of the passage (14:22-26) serves as the *preparation* or introduction for the *realization* in 14:27-33. The reader observes that in the introductory material the author depicts the extreme fear of the disciples by emphasizing certain details about the setting: (i) initially, Jesus is not present with them in the boat; he goes away into the mountain to pray, so they are alone (14:22-23); (ii) the boat is a long distance from land (14:24a); therefore, the situation cannot be solved simply by going ashore; (iii) the boat is being battered by waves because of high winds (14:24b); (iv) in the darkness of night—i.e., 3-6 a.m.—they see what appears to be a ghost approaching them (14:25); and (v) they become terrified and cry out in fear (14:26). This material leads into the main section of the passage, the realization, in which the author outlines a conversation between the Jesus and the terrified disciples. This exchange combines the structure of *climax* with *interchange*, proceeding in a narrative pattern that oscillates between the Peter's speech that is marked by fear and uncertainty[105] and Jesus' speech that is resolute and unwavering, and reaching a climax with the disciples' declaration that Jesus is God's Son: (i) Jesus says, "Take courage, it is I; do not be afraid" (14:27); (ii) Peter says, "Lord, if it is you, command me to come to you on the water" (14:28); (iii) Jesus replies,

---

103. The Sea of Galilee (or Sea of Gennesaret) is located well below sea level (212 meters), and this low-lying setting results in sudden violent downdrafts and storms (cf. Matt 8:24; Mark 4:37; Luke 8:23; John 6:18). The wind that blows from the east is especially notorious (cf. Matt 14:22-24; Mark 6:45-48), and this typically arises when the seasons are changing—e.g., around Passover (cf. Mark 6:39; John 6:4) (Riesner, "Archeology and Geography," 37).

104. See Luz, *Matthew 8-20*, 319-20 on the OT and extrabiblical significance of "walking on water."

105. Bauer, *Gospel of the Son of God*, 191 notes that in the Gospel of Matthew, Peter often functions as a spokesman for the disciples, and his actions are also representative of them (so also Kingsbury, "Figure of Peter," 67-83; and France, *Matthew*, 999); "Peter is an example of the believer who suffers from lack of faith in Jesus: after taking the first few steps of a difficult endeavor he falters when opposition begins to buffet" (Davies and Allison Jr., *Matthew (II)*, 509).

"Come!" (14:29); (iv) Peter cries out, "Lord, save me!" (14:30); (v) Jesus says, "You of little faith, why did you doubt?" (14:31); and finally (vi) the disciples concede, "You are certainly God's Son!" (14:33).[106] Additionally, Matthew's portrayal of the conversation emphasizes the *contrast* between the differing levels of faith of its participants—Peter and the disciples vis-à-vis Jesus—and it comprises the revelation by Jesus that Peter and the disciples' shortcoming is "doubt" that is characterized by "little [or weak] faith" (14:31).[107]

Matthew's portrayal of Jesus in this passage helps to direct the reader's perception of the meaning of μαθητεύσατε (28:19). The reader discerns that: (i) by sending the disciples ahead to the other side of the Sea of Galilee while he waits behind on the mountain to pray, Jesus gives them the opportunity to experience and learn from a difficult situation that they encounter when they are physically separated from him;[108] (ii) nevertheless, he is not too far away to recognize when they are in difficulty and in need of his assistance;[109] and (iii) by addressing the nature of Peter and the disciples' problem of "little faith," he provides unambiguous guidance about the importance of faith that is not contaminated by

---

106. Matthew emphasizes Jesus' divine sonship throughout his Gospel, within each of the three major divisions—(i) 1:1–4:16; (ii) 4:17–16:20; and (iii) 16:21–28:20—reaching a climax with the declaration that Jesus is God's Son (3:17; 16:16; 27:54; 28:19) (Bauer, *Gospel of the Son of God*, 237–38); see also Brown and Roberts, *Matthew*, 141 on Matthew's progressive revelation of Jesus' identity in 14:22–33.

107. Luz, *Matthew 8–20*, 321 notes that in the passage "faith is 'little faith,' that is, that mixture of courage and fear, of listening to the Lord and looking at the wind, of trust and doubt that according to Matthew remains a fundamental characteristic of Christian existence . . . That is not to say that Matthew declared doubt to be an essential characteristic of faith, but neither does he condemn it"; for Gnilka, *Das Matthäusevangelium*, 2:14, the sinking of Peter exemplifies the meaning of *Kleinglaube* or 'little faith': "a situation in which one's own existence is threatened, and the trust placed in Jesus does not endure."

108. Jesus separates himself from his disciples at other times during their ministry, for example: (i) when he sends them to minister to the "lost sheep of the house of Israel" (10:1–11:1); and (ii) at the time when they unsuccessfully attempt to heal a demoniac and Jesus warns them of the "littleness of [their] faith" as well (17:14–23).

109. The double εὐθύς/εὐθέως (14:27, 31) is characteristic of Jesus. He is immediately ready to help, and he also immediately has the power to turn things around (Maier, *Evangelium des Matthäus (1–14)*, 810–11). On another occasion, the disciples have trouble with a great storm (8:23–27); Jesus is nearby, but he is asleep in the boat and is in a sense absent; nevertheless, he comes to their assistance as soon as difficulty arises (8:25).

doubt.[110] Therefore, the reader understands that in the process of "making disciples," disciple-makers allow their charges the opportunity to safely learn from difficult situations, by remaining at a far enough distance to be able to recognize when they may need immediate assistance, and by providing explicit guidance about matters regarding their growth in the Christian faith.

"O Woman, Your Faith Is Great" (15:21–28)

Jesus commands his disciples to make disciples of "all the nations" (28:19a), which the reader recognizes as a change of direction of the ministry of Jesus and his disciples.[111] Until this point in the narrative, they focus their ministry on the house of Israel (10:5b–6; cf. 15:24). However, in Jesus' final Commission, the scope of the discipling work is πάντα τὰ ἔθνη, which represents an expansion of ministry beyond Israel to "all the nations." The author's utilization of this *cruciality* structure in 28:19 draws the reader's attention to Matthew's juxtaposition of Jewish particularism and Gentile inclusion that precedes the pivot, and to the shift of emphasis of Jesus and his disciples' ministry away from a Jewish-only focus towards the Gentile inclusion that follows the pivot.[112] By examin-

110. The Matthean Jesus repeatedly warns the disciples of their (ὀλιγόπιστος) "little faith" (e.g., 6:30; 8:26; 16:8); Matthew uses two additional terms (ἄπιστος and διακρίνω) in the context of the disciples' "unbelief" and "lack of faith" (17:14–21; 21:18–22). See also Bauer, *Gospel of the Son of God*, 190, 199 on the disciples' "weak faith."

111. As I mentioned in my analysis of 28:19 (in chapter 3 of this book), the reader is also aware that while the pivot becomes more apparent in this verse because of the command to "make disciples of all the nations," which he understands in relation to earlier portions of the Gospel, the actual change of direction or radical reversal appears to have occurred at the time of the Resurrection: the time of Jesus' exaltation, when God grants comprehensive authority to him, and at which time his reign could have begun (cf. Acts 2:29–36; Rom 1:1–4; Phil 2:5–11; Heb 1:1–5).

112. In my analysis of 28:19 (in chapter 3 of this book), I address by way of footnote disclosure specific traces of Jewish particularism in Matthew, the significance of the expansion of the ministry of Jesus and the disciples beyond Israel, and Matthew's juxtaposition of Jewish particularism and Gentile inclusion up to 28:19. However, the role of the Missionary Discourse (Matt 10) and its relation to the Great Commission is central to any discussion about Jewish particularism vis-à-vis Gentile inclusion in Matthew. Von Dobbeler, "Die Restitution Israels," 21–28 argues that both the restrictive mission command to Israel (10:5–6) and the demand of universal mission to the Gentiles (28:16–20) remain in force until the end of the age. According to von Dobbeler, Matthew calls for two separate missions: (i) "the restitution of the people [of Israel], who are lying on the ground, withering away, who will be raised up and thus prepared

ing the *pre-pivot* encounter between Jesus, his disciples, and a Gentile woman whose daughter is in need of healing (15:21–28), I hope to

---

for the reign of their God"; and (ii) the conversion of the Gentiles, "bringing them under the reign of the one God, and that means converting them from dead idols to the living God." Von Dobbeler theorizes that 10:5b–6 and 28:19–20 "do not constitute a contradiction, but rather are in a relationship of complementarity. The mission to the lost sheep of the house of Israel and the mission to 'the nations' are different not only in their addressees but also in their character. Combining them with the term 'mission' is misleading; in Matt 10 and Matt 28 it is much more a matter of missions with different accents." The scholar adds that the Christians of Matthew might have been a community that represented "a group within the renewal movement of Judaism after 70 CE, which saw themselves in stark intra-Jewish opposition, but which was far removed from identifying themselves as 'outside the walls' as regards Judaism." Von Dobbeler provides a helpful discussion on the major scholarly positions regarding the relation between Matt 10 and Matt 28, including: (i) the explanatory model of historical succession, which takes into account the varying phases of the activity of Jesus and of the history of early Christian mission, to which Jesus' instructions are allocated according to Matt 10 and Matt 28; one view that emerges from this model is that the mission to Israel is "practice" for the later mission to the Gentiles (contributors to this model include Adolf Schlatter, Theodor Zahn, Rudolf Bultmann, Schuhler Brown, Ulrich Luz, and Eung Chun Park); (ii) the "substitution model" (Substitutionsmodell), which assumes that in Matthew's view "Israel has ceded its position in salvation-history [heilgeschichtliche Stellung] to the Gentile church and consequently the sending of the disciples by the resurrected Jesus to all peoples supersedes and replaces the mission to Israel [Nach Walker]"; and (iii) the "expansion model" (Entschränkungsmodell), which posits that the mission to Israel is not abolished in Matthew, but its specific limitation to Israel is; this makes it possible to understand 28:19–20 as an expansion beyond Israel of the charge given in 10:6; this may be described in terms of two concentric circles—the narrower circle of the mission to Israel being a permanent prerequisite of the wider circle of the mission to the Gentiles; therefore, without Israel the connecting center to the Gentile church is missing (Ferdinand Hahn). Von Dobbeler goes in a different direction from these models, stating that "the mission to Israel and the mission to the Gentiles stood in a relationship of complementarity to each other; they not only had different target groups in mind, but also pursue differing goals and are therefore characterized by differing charges"; see also Brown and Roberts, *Matthew*, 99–104, 108–9 concerning, *inter alia*, Matthew's reader being drawn to understand the teachings in 10:1–42 as being directed toward himself (e.g., 10:16, 24–42), although Jesus' address in 10:1–42 is to the Twelve; Davies and Allison Jr., *Matthew (II)*, 150, 165–69, 185–86 regarding, among other things, commentators being puzzled by the presence of 10:5–6 in a Gospel that ends with a command to "make disciples of all the nations" (28:19), and on Matthew's belief that the differences between the pre- and post-Easter situations reconcile the tension between 10:5–6 and 28:16–20, with Easter marking the point at which the mission goes beyond the borders of Israel; and Luz, *Matthew 8–20*, 73–74 on Jesus' prohibition in 10:5–6 being emphatic and sounding harshly exclusive, even for early Christian ears, since at the time of Matthew's Gospel the Gentile mission was successful and was being carried out by many churches.

discover how Matthew's portrayal of Jesus in that event contributes to the reader's comprehension of μαθητεύσατε (28:19).

This report of Jesus' encounter with the Syrophoenician woman forms part of Matthew's account of the dual response—i.e., acceptance by the disciples and rejection by Israel as a whole (11:1—16:20)—to Jesus' announcement of the kingdom (4:23—11:1). To emphasize the rejection and hostility toward Jesus by Israel as a whole, Matthew contrasts the worship and abundant faith of a Canaanite woman from Tyre who pleads for healing for her daughter (15:21-28).[113] After repelling opposition from the Pharisees and scribes about his disciples' break with the tradition of the elders by not washing their hands when they eat bread (15:1-14), and having explained to the disciples that it is not what people eat that defiles them, but what comes from their hearts (15:15-20), Jesus withdraws from Gennesaret into the district of Tyre and Sidon (15:21; cf. 14:34).[114] There he meets a Canaanite woman, who begs him to have mercy on her daughter who is demon possessed (15:22). Jesus does not respond to her immediately and his disciples implore him to send her away, but he finally answers, "I was sent only to the lost sheep of the house of Israel" (15:23-24).[115] Nevertheless, the woman persists, bowing down before him and continuing to ask for his help, but only to be told by Jesus, "It is not good to take the children's bread and throw it to the dogs" (15:25-26).[116] By her response, she demonstrates that she is not disheart-

113. According to Maier, *Evangelium des Matthäus* (15-28), 35, this short story, which is widely reported in Matthew and Mark, contains a diverse message: (i) Israel retains its prerogative of the history of salvation; (ii) faith in the Messiah Jesus is true access to God; and (iii) the world mission is already announced in the days of Jesus.

114. This is one of the withdrawal areas around Galilee. Upper Galilee bordered on the territory of the Gentile city Tyre. When threatened, Jesus found this to be a natural place to withdraw (Riesner, "Archeology and Geography," 40).

115. Gnilka, *Das Matthäusevangelium*, 2:30-31 considers it noteworthy that Matthew omits Mark 7:27a: "Let the children be fed first." Gnilka contends that "while Mark already indicates the subordinate mission to the Gentiles, Matthew remains with Israel for the time being. Matthew argues from the Jewish position, Mark from the Gentile Christian position. The image of the lost sheep of the house of Israel must not be restricted. All Israelites are lost sheep. The image of the herd is widespread in OT (Isa 53:6; Mic 2:12; 7:14; Zech 9:16 LXX). As the shepherd of Israel, Jesus shows himself to be the Messiah."

116. Luz, *Matthew* 8-20, 340 explains the importance of understanding that "κυνάριον means not the young or small dog but the dog that is a household pet... Nor was there in Judaism a special hostility to dogs, although there was an obvious fear of the numerous stray dogs ... It is a household image and has nothing to do with the despised wild dogs. Only with the household pet does the contrast between dogs

ened by those words. Jesus commends her great faith and pronounces that her daughter is healed at once (15:27–28).

The reader observes that Matthew employs various structures in his arrangement of 15:21–28 that work together to signal God's intention to save all the people of the world through Israel. First, the introductory material (15:21–22a) identifies the two main characters of the passage (Jesus and a Canaanite woman[117]) and the location of the event (the district of Tyre and Sidon), and it describes the moment of contact between Jesus and the woman; she, in a heightened emotional state, initiates contact with Jesus, crying out (κράζω) to him. This background material is presented in anticipation of the author's portrayal of their dialogue, in which the woman requests Jesus' assistance and he responds to her request (15:22b–28). Matthew's use of *introduction* in the passage focuses the reader's mind on the material for which the preparation is made—i.e., the dialogue between Jesus and the Canaanite woman (15:22b–28). Second, the author utilizes *recurrence* of *contrast* with *interchange* to emphasize

---

and children make sense"; Gnilka, *Das Matthäusevangelium*, 2:31–32 remarks that the Jews liked to refer to themselves as "children of God," and "dog" was a terrible swear word. Whether "dog" refers to the Jewish insult of the Gentiles remains to be seen. The diminutive, little dogs under the table, evidently not loitering street dogs, but house dogs, soften the harshness somewhat; see also Gullotta, "Among Dogs and Disciples," 325–40: a study of Matthew's intentional and strategic redaction of Mark's story of the Syrophoenician woman that attempts to reconstruct the nature of the Matthean community's suspicion, fear, and exclusion of Gentiles barring exceptional displays of faith and submission.

117. The reader is aware that, not only is this person a woman (which, by itself, places certain limitations on her social standing), but she is a Canaanite whose people were to be destroyed from the land (Exod 23:23; Deut 20:17). Furthermore, she is unnamed and is simply "some" Canaanite woman, which serves to intensify the contrast between the rejection of Jesus by his own people who have a name, "Israel," and the acceptance of Jesus by those who have no name in particular, "the Gentiles." Bauer, *Gospel of the Son of God*, 189 notes, "Her distance from the blessings that were promised to Israel is indicated by the fact that she is a 'Canaanite,' thus belonging to a people who, according to the Old Testament, were to be destroyed from the land. Nevertheless, in spite of resistance from the disciples (15:23) and especially from Jesus (15:24–26) she perseveres and validates Jesus' declaration in 11:21 that the people of Tyre would be more receptive of the kingdom than Israelite cities"; see Brown and Roberts, *Matthew*, 145; Davies and Allison Jr., *Matthew (II)*, 547; Scholer, "Women," 880–86; and Wallace, *Greek Grammar*, 244 concerning the anarthrous γυνή (e.g., Matt 15:22; John 4:7), which says nothing about this particular woman. "Thus an indefinite noun is unmarked in that (next to) nothing is revealed about it apart from its membership in a class of others that share the same designation."

the magnitude of the woman's faith.[118] The woman makes several statements that exhibit her deep faith in Jesus to heal her sick daughter. These are followed by his corresponding responses, which, together, form an alternating *request-response* rhythm that juxtaposes her profound faith with obstacles that Jesus seems to present to her in his responses: (i) the woman says, "Have mercy on me, Lord, Son of David;[119] my daughter is severely demon-possessed" (15:22b), *but* Jesus, after a lengthy pause and negative comments from his disciples, who are also present, responds, "I was sent only to the lost sheep of the house of Israel" (15:23–24); (ii) bowing down before him, she continues her pleading, "Lord, help me!" (15:25), *but* Jesus responds, "It is not good to take the children's bread and throw it to the dogs" (15:26);[120] (iii) the woman persists, "Yes, Lord; but even the dogs feed on the crumbs which fall from their masters' table" (15:27),[121] and Jesus concludes, "O woman, your faith is great; it shall be

118. Gundry, *Matthew*, 311–12 argues that "to play up the greatness of the woman's faith (so v. 28 in contrast with Mark), Matthew makes Jesus refuse to answer the woman, makes the disciples ask for her dismissal, makes Jesus tell the disciples that he was sent only to the Jews, makes the woman repeat her plea, and makes Jesus say to the woman only that Gentiles ought not to receive benefits belonging to the Jews, not that the Jews receive benefits "first" (for that would imply the arrival of the Gentiles' time to receive benefits)".

119. The woman recognizes that Jesus is no mere magician, and by hailing him as 'Lord,' and 'Son of David' (15:22; cf. Ps. Sol. 17:21), she acknowledges him as the rightful king over a nation that had conquered her ancestors (Josh 12:7–24; 2 Sam 8:1–15), which is more than many of his own people had done (15:2; 21:15–16; 23:39) (Keener, *Matthew*, 417–18); Hagner, *Matthew* 1–13, 441 (cf. 198) is of the view that by calling Jesus κύριε, 'Lord,' no fewer than three (3) times (15:22, 25, 27), the woman is confessing her "faith in Jesus as God's messianic agent but not necessarily belief in Jesus' deity. (Of course, Matthew's readers understand Jesus as one rightly worshiped as manifesting the very presence of God)." Perhaps, she has come to this conclusion having seen or heard of Jesus' other miracles (cf. 8:2, 6; 17:15; 20:30–31, 33); see also Bauer, "Son of David," 768 on the Matthean Jesus being the Son of David (9:27; 15:22; 20:31), "the Messiah-king in the line of David who has been sent by God specifically to the people of Israel, not in order to exercise oppressive rule over them (20:20–21:17) but to bring them salvation and deliverance by healing them of their diseases."

120. Keener, *Matthew*, 415–17 remarks that Jesus is not cursing, but is putting off the woman, possibly testing her, as teachers sometimes tested their disciples.

121. She does not dispute that Jesus' mission is to Israel first and that her status is secondary to that of Israel; nevertheless, she believes that Jesus possesses so much power that he will have more than enough left over after Israel's need has been met (Keener, *Matthew*, 418); see also France, *Matthew*, 595, who notes that the Canaanite woman turns Jesus' own parable against him and her reply "Yes, Lord; but even the dogs feed on the crumbs which fall from their masters' table" encapsulates the biblical truth (whether she knows it or not) that Israel's election is not for her benefit alone but

done for you as you wish," at which time, her daughter is healed (15:28). Third, Jesus' concluding statement in 15:28 represents the *climax* of the passage—a movement from lesser to greater—which steers the flow of the passage from a starting point that expresses the desperate need of a nameless woman, who represents a people that were to be destroyed from the land and culminates with the celebration of the deep faith of the same woman (and the faith potential of her entire people)[122] by Jesus, the Son of God.

Matthew's depiction of Jesus in this passage shapes the reader's understanding of the meaning of μαθητεύσατε (28:19). The reader observes that: (i) in light of Israel's rejection of his ministry as a whole, Jesus ministers to people who are outside of the typical geographic, ethnic, and cultural boundaries of his stated mission (15:24; 10:5–6); he recognizes the big picture of his Father's purpose, which is to save all the people of the world through Israel; therefore, despite his disciples' objections in the matter (15:23b), he does not limit his immediate ministry to its primary Jewish audience in the traditional stamping ground of Galilee, especially knowing that he will later send his disciples to "make disciples of all the nations" (28:19);[123] (ii) Jesus leverages his conversation with persons to varying degrees, allowing them to express their desires and

---

is to be a means of blessing to all nations, a light to the Gentiles (cf. Gen 12:3; Isa 49:6).

122. The woman possesses faith, not only in a general sense, but "particularly the faith with which Gentiles could approach Jesus, even during his earthly ministry to Israel" (Keener, *Matthew*, 414).

123. Matthew portrays Jesus as the "son of Abraham" (1:1) through whom "all nations of the earth will be blessed" (Gen 12:3; 18:18; 22:18), which results in overtones of Gentile inclusion throughout the Gospel (1:1–17; 2:1–12; 8:11; 10:18; 12:18, 21; 21:43; 22:1–10; 24:14 [cf. 26:13]; 26:28 [cf. 20:28]; 27:54). Bauer, "Mission in Matthew's Gospel," 254 addresses the notion of crossing boundaries in his comment that "the repeated reference [in Matthew] to the gospel being preached throughout 'the whole world' (24:14; 26:13) certainly points to the crossing of geographical boundaries; but the broad context of the Gospel indicates that it involves every bit as much the crossing of all cultural, religious, and ethnic boundaries that typically separate human beings from one another, even in cases where no geographical distance must be spanned"; Luz, *Matthew 8–20*, 340 remarks that "the mission command to go to the Gentiles (28:18–20) will mean a fundamental change in the divine plan. In the hindsight of the Matthean church that has received from the Lord the commission to go to the Gentiles, [15:24] is 'historical,' but not therefore surpassed and meaningless." God remained faithful to his special promises to Israel when he sent the Son of David, Jesus. By rejecting Jesus, Israel has brought on itself guilt toward God, who turned to the Gentiles after Easter in a new, unheard of act of grace on the part of the risen Lord. In 15:21–28, Jesus "signals" this coming, unheard of grace of God.

interests, thus giving them the opportunity to reveal their true selves;[124] in 15:21–28, he could have healed the woman after her first request for help (15:22), which, by itself, displays her eagerness and desperation; instead, he tests her resolve by means of a longer exchange and is able to conclude, not simply that she has faith, but that she possesses *great* faith (in contrast with his disciples, whom he considers to have "little faith," 6:30; 8:26; 14:31; 16:8); and (iii) Jesus seizes every opportunity, especially those in which people express a need, to lead persons to a climax that permits them to express their faith in God, either verbally or by their actions.[125] Consequently, the reader recognizes that the process of "making disciples" involves Christian disciple-makers ministering to all persons, including those who fall outside of their geographic, ethnic, and cultural boundaries. They converse with a diversity of persons, allowing them to reveal their true selves, with an eye toward leading them to the climax of expressing their faith in God.

"You Will All Fall Away Because of Me" (26:31–35)

Matthew describes the disciples by their number: οἱ ἕνδεκα (28:16) in the Great Commission. They were previously known, *inter alia*, as οἱ δώδεκα ("the Twelve," 20:17; 26:14, 20, 47; cf. 10:1);[126] however, a reduction in their ranks has occurred, which the reader perceives as a surrogate family arrangement that has gone awry in at least three ways: (i) Judas betrays Jesus (26:47–56) and, though later feeling remorseful, he commits

---

124. Matthew comprises several examples of this narrative pattern (e.g., 3:13–15; 8:5–13, 18–22; 9:3–6, 11–13; 12:1–7, 9–14, 22–29, 38–45, 46–50; 15:1–9; 16:1–4; 17:24–27; 18:21–35; 19:3–12; 21:15–17, 23–27, 33–46; 22:15–22, 23–40, 41–46; 26:59–64; 27:11–14).

125. Similar interactions occur throughout Matthew, for example: (i) the centurion whose servant is sick (8:5–13); (ii) the woman with a hemorrhage for twelve years (9:20–22); and (iii) the two men who are blind (9:27–31). Examples from elsewhere in the Gospels include the healing of the blind beggar, Bartimaeus (Mark 10:46–52), and the cleansing of the ten lepers (Luke 17:11–19).

126. The Twelve are "disciples" of Jesus—examples of what it means to be believers in (and committed followers of) him. They are also in training as Jesus' "apostles" or commissioned representatives. Jesus calls them into special relationship with him (4:18–22; 9:9; 10:1–4). In Matthew, they are normally mentioned as a group—i.e., "the disciples" (e.g., 13:10; 14:26; 26:45), "his disciples" (5:1; 8:23; 12:1), or "the Twelve" (20:17; 26:14, 20, 47; cf. 10:1)—with occasional focus on individuals. They are found in the Synoptic Gospels as well as the Book of Acts (see Wilkins, "Disciples," 178–81 for more on the Twelve).

suicide (27:1–10);[127] (ii) Peter denies knowing Jesus (26:69–75; cf. 10:32), which triggers the temporary falling away about which their master forewarns (26:31–33); however, his weeping implies repentance that leads to restoration (26:75);[128] and (iii) all the male disciples leave Jesus and flee at the time of his betrayal and arrest (26:56), following only from a distance thereafter (26:58; cf. 27:55 on the women disciples). Amidst the betrayal of Judas, and the denial and flight of Peter and the remaining disciples to relative safety, it does not escape the reader's attention that the Matthean Jesus foresees the frailties of the Eleven, and that he forewarns and forgives them in advance of their future shortcomings. I hope to examine this aspect of the Jesus' behavior towards his disciples (26:31–35) to determine how it contributes to the reader's understanding of μαθητεύσατε (28:19).

Matthew locates 26:31–35 within the third major unit of his Gospel (16:21—28:20), which records the passion and resurrection of Jesus Christ, Son of God.[129] The larger unit progresses: (i) from Jesus' movement towards his death and resurrection, which are anticipated in his journey to Jerusalem (16:21—20:34) and in his encounters of conflict at Jerusalem (21:1—25:46); (ii) to the actual events of his death and resurrection, including his trials and crucifixion (26:1—27:54) and his resurrection and commissioning (27:55—28:20).[130]

The material of 26:31–35 follows immediately after Jesus' institution of the Lord's Supper (26:26–30). Citing Zechariah's "I will strike down the shepherd, and the sheep of the flock shall be scattered" (Zech 13:7), he forewarns his disciples that they will "fall away" (σκανδαλίζω) because of him on that very night (26:31).[131] However, he does not proceed to

---

127. This may serve as a warning to the reader about the danger of permanently falling away about which Jesus forewarns in the context of mission (24:9–10) (Bauer, "Mission in Matthew's Gospel," 246).

128. See Bauer, "Mission in Matthew's Gospel," 246 n. 29 on the contrast between Peter's denial, followed by weeping (κλαίω) as a sign of repentance, and Judas's remorse (μεταμέλομαι) that does not lead to a change of mind or alteration of intention (μετανοέω, cf. 4:17).

129. Although Matthew emphasizes the theme of Jesus' suffering, death, and resurrection in the material following 16:21, the subject pervades the entire Gospel (e.g., 2:1–23; 9:3; [cf. 26:65–66]; 9:15; 10:4, 38; 12:14, 40; [cf. 16:4]; 16:21; 17:22–23; 20:17–19; 26:1–2, 21–25, 31–35).

130. Bauer, *Gospel of the Son of God*, 128.

131. Luz, *Matthew 21–28*, 388 notes that it is God who "strikes down" the shepherd; therefore, the reader knows that God is behind the Passion. The Matthean Jesus now

chastise them because of their forthcoming actions; rather, he reassures them with the statement, "But after I have been raised, I will go ahead of you to Galilee" (26:32).[132] These words are a signal of: (i) *hope*—he, the shepherd, will be raised after being struck down and they will meet him again in Galilee;[133] and (ii) implied *forgiveness*—the nature of their falling away will not preclude them from gathering with him again in Galilee and resuming their ministry activities.[134] Peter vows that he will never fall away (26:33), but the Lord graciously reaffirms his previous forewarning, providing specific details about the exact time and number of Peter's upcoming denials of his master (26:34). Once again, the Eleven repeat that they would never deny Jesus and that they are willing to die with him (26:35). Perhaps seeing no benefit in attempting to convince them any further of the truth, the Matthean Jesus does not rebut their final assertion.

Matthew combines *contrast* with *interchange* to emphasize Jesus' strength in knowledge and pre-positioned forgiveness vis-à-vis the disciples' present lack of insight.[135] On the one hand, Jesus possesses "superhuman" knowledge of events about which he has not been informed: he

---

says it directly through the Scripture; Hagner, *Matthew 14–28*, 777 agrees and adds that, since Matthew introduces the prophet's quotation with the formula γέγραπται ("it is written," 26:31), it is easy to see God as the acting subject.

132. Maier, *Evangelium des Matthäus (15–28)*, 541–42 observes that in 26:31 Jesus addresses everyone's failure (26:31); nobody should think themselves better than the other; however, 26:32 offers a second prophecy concerning a future meeting in Galilee, which surprisingly follows the first in 26:31 about the disciples' falling away. Following 26:31, one could expect a rebuke to the disciples. But 26:32 has a very different character. It is a message of victory; Gnilka, *Das Matthäusevangelium*, 2:407 notes that Galilee, not Jerusalem, is the place of this gathering. According to Jesus (23:37–39), Jerusalem is no longer an alternative as a theme of salvation history. Galilee points in the direction of the region where the church of Matthew is to be found.

133. France, *Matthew*, 999 remarks that Jesus' resurrection will be the preface to a reunion with his disciples; their stumbling will not be terminal, and his restoration will lead to their regrouping; additionally, the fact that the reunion is to be in Galilee—the place of light (4:15–16)—gives the reader new hope.

134. Unlike the Eleven, Judas (who seems to be absent from the group for the events of 26:31–35) is not a beneficiary of Jesus' forgiveness. Instead, his falling away is permanent, as Jesus declares in 26:24.

135. One knows from the wider NT context that once the disciples are baptized with the Holy Spirit on the Day of Pentecost (Acts 2:1–13), they attain a higher level of spiritual insight and understanding (cf. John 16:13–15; Acts 4:8–13, 31; 5:1–11; ; 6:3, 8–10, 18–21; 9:1–19; 10:9–16, 34–48; 13:1–3; 13:6–12; 15:1–35; 16:9–10; 18:9–10; 27:21–26).

divulges his betrayal at the hands of Judas (26:21), he reveals the meaning of his death in the elements of the Lord's Supper (26:26–29), and he accurately predicts the falling away of the disciples and the denials of Peter (26:31–34);[136] additionally, by referring to Jesus' resurrection and hinting at a future meeting with the disciples in Galilee (26:32; cf. 28:16), Matthew signals that Jesus has already forgiven the disciples for their upcoming temporary falling away. On the other hand, the disciples are unaware of what Jesus already knows, and they meet his pre-positioned forgiveness with refusals to admit that his predictions would come to pass; they resort, instead, to emphatic speech to strengthen their refutation (26:33, 35).[137] Therefore, knowledge and insight is met with spiritual ignorance, and forgiveness is met with strong denial of the need therefor.[138] Matthew augments this contrast with a prediction-response pattern: (i) Jesus predicts, *"You will all fall away"* (26:31); (ii) Peter responds, "though all may fall away . . . *I will never fall away*" (26:33); (iii) Jesus predicts, "this *very* night, . . . *you will deny me* three times" (26:34);[139] and (iv) Peter responds, "Even if I have to die with you, *I will not deny you*" (26:35). This structure accentuates the depth of Jesus' insight and forgiveness over against Peter and the disciples' spiritual ignorance and obstinacy.

Matthew's characterization of Jesus in this passage helps to form the reader's understanding of the meaning of μαθητεύσατε (28:19). The reader is aware that: (i) Jesus forewarns his disciples about impending dangers, intending to ensure that they are vigilant and do not fall away permanently after his departure;[140] (ii) Jesus recognizes their human

136. Bauer, *Gospel of the Son of God*, 218–19.

137. The disciples do not always appreciate or fully grasp what Jesus is saying (e.g., 15:16–17; 16:9, 11), and are often overcome by the limitations of their humanity (e.g., 8:26; 14:27; 17:7; 26:40, 43, 45). Bauer, *Gospel of the Son of God*, 312 comments that while they are often slow to understand (e.g., 15:16; 16:11) and weak in faith (e.g., 14:31; 17:20), their fault is a frailty of the flesh and not a rebellion of the spirit (26:41); indeed, they are never guilty of resisting Jesus' authority or disobeying his command.

138. Peter, leaving off the doubt of 26:22 for "the intoxication of human self-confidence" (Calvin), contradicts his Lord (26:33; cf. 16:21–23) and the Scripture (Zech 13:7), making himself out to be more loyal than his fellow disciples. "Where he should have prayed, and have said, 'Help us, that we be not cut off,' he is confident in himself" (Chrysostom) (Davies and Allison Jr., *Matthew (III)*, 486–487); cf. John Chrysostom, *Hom. Matt.*, 82.3 (NPNF1 10:493–494).

139. Jesus' "this *very* night" (26:34) sharply contrasts Peter's blustering "never" (26:33) (Luz, *Matthew 21–28*, 389).

140. On other occasions, Jesus forewarns his disciples about a variety of matters (e.g., 6:1; 7:15; 10:16–18; 16:6, 11, 12; 24:42–43; 25:13; 26:38, 40, 41).

frailty, but he does not immediately reprimand them because of their upcoming temporary falling away;[141] and (iii) he forgives them and provides a sense of hope and restoration even before they commit the offense.[142] Therefore, the reader accepts that the process of "making disciples" involves Christian disciple-makers forewarning their charges of forthcoming dangers to safeguard against their spiritual demise. They recognize the vulnerability of human beings and are willing to forgive others and reconcile with them even before they commit an offense.

Summary

Throughout the broader context of his Gospel, Matthew reveals that the reader understands that the process of "making disciples" incorporates several components that are not explicitly brought to light in 28:16–20. Some of these elements are: (i) the movement of persons by God (through Jesus) from sin to salvation; (ii) the emergence of persons who emulate Jesus as the model of discipleship; (iii) the molding of persons whose words and actions are mutually consistent; (iv) the need to continuously seek out new disciples in the normal course of one's daily life; (v) the need to defend and protect one's newly made disciples from the enemy's hostile attacks; (vi) the requirement to grant spiritually immature disciples the space to face difficult situations by themselves, while the disciple-maker remains alert from a safe distance; (vii) the willingness to disciple persons who fall outside of one's ethnic, social, geographical, economic, and cultural space; and (viii) the inclination to speak truthfully to new disciples about impending dangers, being willing to forgive and reconcile with them in advance of any shortcomings. This is not meant to be an exhaustive list, but it is intended to reveal the possibilities that exist when one opens oneself up to learn more fully from the broader context of the Gospel of Matthew about the component parts of disciple-making.

---

141. Elsewhere in Matthew, Jesus employs a similar strategy of instructing his disciples (amidst their human weaknesses) without breaking them (e.g., 8:26; 15:16–17; 16:9, 11; 14:31; 16:8; 17:20).

142. Jesus' actions in the passage are congruent with: (i) his verbal commands about forgiveness elsewhere in the Gospel—e.g., forgiveness of others in order to receive the Father's forgiveness (6:12, 14, 15); his proclamation to forgive a brother up to seventy times seven (18:21–35); and with (ii) his announcement that his blood is to be poured out for many for the "forgiveness of sins" (26:28).

5

Matthean Discipleship in the New Testament Canon

Chapter Summary

This chapter examines discipleship terminology and patterns of discipleship in the NT canon (outside the Gospel of Matthew) for the purpose of identifying the major points of similarity, difference, and development between Matthean discipleship and that of the broader NT canon.

Approach

The two significant points that affect my overall approach toward realizing my goal in this chapter are as follows. First, it is worth reemphasizing an important principle that I noted in the last chapter—i.e., there is a vital connection between *being* a disciple (or the character of discipleship) and *making* a disciple.[1] Reemphasis of this point is necessary because much of the NT (outside of Matthew) appears to deal with the character of discipleship, whereas this book focuses on "making disciples." However, these two concepts complement each other toward achieving my goal of

---

1. So also Jacob, "Discipleship and Mission," 107, who advances that "discipleship is undoubtedly the way of learning, and of knowing. It is also about being and doing. It has to do with understanding Jesus' words and obeying them just as he acted in obedience to the divine word. To be a disciple means to teach by word and example to observe everything that Jesus had commanded (28:19)."

interpreting the full meaning of μαθητεύσατε (Matt 28:19). It is worth remembering that Matthew's reader is aware that God (through Jesus), not he, is the primary actor in disciple-making (leading to salvation) and that he (the reader) must therefore recognize not only how to make a disciple, but also what is God's definition of a good disciple of Jesus. Furthermore, Matthew's reader observes that the author does not draw a solid line between *being* and *making* a disciple; indeed, Matthew depicts the Twelve interchangeably as disciples *of* Jesus and disciple-makers *for* Jesus; similarly, he portrays Jesus both as a model of discipleship (4:1–11; 26:39, 42, 44) and as the master teacher, leader (23:8–10), and disciple-maker (e.g., 4:19; 8:22; 9:9; 10:38; 16:24; 19:21). Matthean Christians are first and foremost disciples *of* Jesus, who also make disciples *for* Jesus. Disciple-makers never cease to be disciples themselves; therefore, comprehending the fundamentals of being a disciple, or the character of discipleship, is a vital tool for every Christian disciple-maker. For this reason, I cannot ignore NT background material about the character of discipleship as I explore the meaning of "make disciples" (28:19). Indeed, the former is the foundation of the latter, and I must consider the NT characterization of discipleship in general—i.e., what it means to *be* a disciple—if I am to fully understand what it means to *make* a disciple.

Second, there is no doubt that "baptizing" and "teaching" play important roles in the overall process of making disciples. Indeed, Matthew makes this very clear when he attaches the three adjoining participles—πορευθέντες (Matt 28:19a), βαπτίζοντες (28:19b), and διδάσκοντες (28:20a)—to μαθητεύσατε (28:19a), the lone imperative in the Great Commission. As I have explained in chapter 3 of this book, by attaching these three participles to μαθητεύσατε, Matthew employs ideological *particularization*, which develops or unpacks the general command of μαθητεύσατε without necessarily exhausting its meaning by themselves. Therefore, since most scholars already agree that "baptizing" and "teaching" play a significant role in "making disciples," and since their contributions toward disciple-making are evident in the NT outside of Matthew ("baptizing" [e.g., Acts 2:41; 9:18; 18:8; 1 Cor 1:16; Gal 3:27], "teaching" [e.g., Acts 4:2; 5:42; 18:11; Rom 12:6–7; Col 1:28; 2 Thess 2:15; Heb 5:12]), I will not consume additional resources in this chapter, attempting to demonstrate what is already widely accepted. I will focus instead on what other meanings may be attributed to disciple-making in the NT.

In this chapter, I examine the character of discipleship in the broader NT canon, observing the following corpora: Mark; Luke-Acts;

the Johannine tradition;[2] the Pauline Epistles;[3] and the Other Epistles.[4] The steps of my investigation include: (i) identifying a list of discipleship terms that are found in the NT;[5] (ii) examining how NT authors use these terms in varying contexts; (iii) surveying the contributions of contemporary scholarship on the patterns of discipleship in the NT; and (iv) summarizing how the treatment of discipleship by other NT authors might represent a comparison, contrast, or development of Matthew's treatment of discipleship.

Key Findings

My examination of discipleship in the broader NT canon reveals, *inter alia*, the following findings.[6] Mark utilizes μαθητής in a manner that is consistent with Matthew's use of the term—i.e., primarily to describe the activities of Jesus' closest adherents who follow him as their master: going from place to place, obeying his commands, observing his actions, and learning from him. Unlike Matthew, however: (i) Mark's disciples are not restricted from going to the Gentiles when Jesus summons the Twelve and sends them out on an earlier mission (Mark 6:7–13; cf. Matt 10:1–15); (ii) Mark emphasizes the disciples' lack of understanding and hard heartedness; and (iii) Mark, with a possible exception in Mark 4:35–41 (cf. Matt 8:23–27), does not emphasize the disciples' "little faith."

Luke's use of μαθητής is also generally consistent with Matthew's use of the term. However, after Jesus' ascension (Acts 1:9–11), the term becomes synonymous with Χριστιανός ("Christian") and with members

---

2. I include in this literary category the Gospel of John, the Johannine letters (1–3 John), and the Revelation to John.

3. The Pauline Epistles, also called the Epistles of Paul or the Letters of Paul, are the thirteen books of the New Testament, from Romans to Philemon that are attributed to Paul the Apostle, although the authorship of some is in dispute.

4. By the term "the Other Epistles," I am referring to the Letter to the Hebrews, the Letter of James, the First and Second Letters of Peter, and the Letter of Jude.

5. I have compiled and included such a list in the "Table of New Testament Discipleship Terms" in the Appendix. The list is not exhaustive, but it includes the principal discipleship terms found in the New Testament. In its compilation, I have utilized the terms included in "Follow, Be a Disciple (36.31–36.43)" and "Imitate Behavior (41.44–41.49)" in Louw and Nida, *Greek-English Lexicon*, 1:469–70, 508–9, and I have expanded upon them by including additional terms that other scholars have incorporated in their writings on the theme of NT discipleship.

6. I develop these points further in my analysis that follows later in the chapter.

of the ἐκκλησία ("church") in general (Acts 11:26; 26:28). Additionally, Luke uses ἀπόστολος ("apostle") far more frequently than Matthew with reference to the activities of Jesus' closest disciples. In fact, Luke does not refer to them as μαθητής in the book of Acts, and he occasionally widens the scope of ἀπόστολος to incorporate such other persons as Matthias (Acts 1:26) and Saul/Paul and Barnabas (Acts 14:4, 14).[7] Some minor differences exist between the Lukan and the Matthean Jesus' Commission in terms of its setting and timing (Luke 24:46–49; Acts 1:7–8; cf. Matt 28:18–20). However, both commissions emphasize God's sovereignty in missions, including the inability of the disciples to understand spiritual matters and to function apart from God's action.

On Matthean and Johannine discipleship, I note that in both sets of literature Jesus calls persons to follow him as disciples who are able to witness his ministry firsthand as they are following. However, unique to John is that some of Jesus' disciples eventually cease following him because they do not understand some of his pronouncements (e.g., John 6:51–52, 59–61, 66). The general broadening of discipleship terminology in the Johannine literature is a significant point of development between Matthean and Johannine discipleship. John, like Matthew, uses μαθητής to refer to Jesus' disciples.[8] At times, however, John refers to them as "the disciples" (e.g., John 4:31, 33; 13:5; 21:1, 4, 12, 14) or "his disciples" (e.g., John 2:22; 6:3, 60, 61, 66) without specifying whether he is referring to the Twelve or to Jesus' larger group of followers. Additionally, outside of his Gospel, John utilizes such terms as τέκνον ("spiritual child"), τεκνίον ("little child"), and ἀδελφός ("brother") to refer to members of the community of Christian believers rather than to his immediate followers.

Paul's discipleship terminology is different from Matthew's. The former never uses μαθητεύω or μαθητής, but rather the cognate μανθάνω, and he utilizes ἀκολουθέω on one occasion only (1 Cor 10:4), and even then not in a discipleship sense. It is clear, however, that both writers

---

7. Some scholars argue that Paul and Barnabas do not meet the criteria for apostle, according to Acts 1 because: (i) they are not chosen by Jesus himself (1:2); and (ii) according to Peter, they are not "of the men who have accompanied us all the time that the Lord Jesus went in and out among us—beginning with the baptism of John until the day that he was taken up from us—one of these *must* become a witness with us of his resurrection" (1:21). This creates an internal tension within Acts whose author, however, refers to Paul and Barnabas as "apostles" (14:14).

8. In Matthew, μαθητής is limited to the Twelve, although μαθητεύω does point to other persons outside that group, e.g., Joseph from Arimathea (27:57) and others from among "the nations" who will be made disciples (28:19).

speak about similar discipleship themes, sometimes employing different terminology, for example: (i) not following an evil master/leader (1 Tim 5:15; cf. Matt 7:15; 24:11, 24); (ii) learning from a teacher's example (2 Tim 3:14b; Phil 4:9; 1 Cor 4:6; cf. Matt 11:29); (iii) the repercussions of *repudiating* Christ (2 Tim 2:12a; cf. Matt 10:32–33); and (iv) laboring as fellow workers (e.g., Rom 16:3, 9, 21) and soldiers (Phil 2:25; Phlm 2). Pauline discipleship emphasizes, *inter alia*, disciples *imitating* their master. Paul sees himself as playing a critical role in the ongoing discipling of his addressees, wanting to present them "complete in Christ" (Col 1:28). He emphasizes that Christians ought to "imitate" their disciple-maker (e.g., 1 Cor 4:16; Phil 3:17; 1 Thess 1:6–7), and he commands his coworkers to be an "example" for others to follow (1 Tim 4:12; Titus 2:7). Matthew accomplishes the same goal with his exhortations "Follow me!" (Matt 4:19; 8:22; 9:9; 19:21) and "Listen to him!" (Matt 17:5). It is apparent, therefore, that the objectives of the Matthean and Pauline modes of discipleship are very largely congruent.

Finally, like Paul, the authors of the Other Epistles appear at times to stand in discontinuity with Matthean discipleship in terms of their nonuse or limited use of traditional Matthean discipleship terms. However, the terms employed by the writers of these materials and the themes that they address are consistent with Matthean discipleship principles, including: (i) not following *after* the flesh, but pursuing the righteousness of God's kingdom (e.g., 2 Pet 2:10; Jude 7; cf. Matt 5:16, 48; 6:33); (ii) trusting in God (e.g., Heb 2:13; cf. Matt 6:25–33; 7:7–11) and not in ungodly spiritual leaders (e.g., Matt 16:6–12; 23:1–7); (iii) being children of obedience (e.g., 1 Pet 1:14; cf. Matt 1:18–25; 3:13–17; 4:1–11; 16:21–23; 26:36–46; cf. 7:21; 12:50); and (iv) the meaning of discipleship being the student becoming like his teacher and the *slave* like his master (e.g., Jas 1:1; 1 Pet 2:16; 2 Pet 1:1; Jude 1; cf. Matt 10:24–25; cf. 23:10b). Once again, it appears that the objectives of the modes of discipleship in the Other Epistles and in Matthew are largely compatible.

Patterns of Discipleship in the Remainder of the New Testament

Gospel of Mark

Discipleship Terminology in Mark

The term μαθητεύω (cf. Matt 28:19) does not occur in Mark. However, the following analysis of Markan discipleship terms includes several that are common to Matthew. Mark uses μαθητής in various contexts:[9] (i) Jesus' disciples encounter opposition from the religious authorities on various issues (2:15, 16, 18, 23); (ii) the disciples withdraw with him amidst the religious authorities' conspiracy to kill him (3:7); (iii) the disciples follow Jesus around, witnessing his ministry—healing (3:9; 5:31; 10:46-52); teaching (6:1; 8:34-38; on the kingdom of God, 10:23-31; about the poor widow's mite, 12:43-44); miracles (6:35, 41, 45-52; 8:1-9); repelling the attacks of the religious authorities (8:10); his transfiguration (9:1-13); cursing of the fig tree (11:14); prophesying about the coming destruction of the temple buildings (13:1-2); administering the Lord's Supper (14:22-25); and his grief experience in Gethsemane (14:32-42); (iv) Jesus speaks vaguely (in parables) to the crowd, but explains everything privately to his disciples (4:10, 34; 7:17; 9:28-29; 10:10-12; 13:3-4); (v) John's disciples bury John's body (6:29); (vi) Jesus defends his disciples against opposition from the religious authorities (7:2, 5); (vii) Jesus questions his disciples about his identity (8:27); (viii) Jesus forewarns his disciples about his impending suffering, crucifixion, and resurrection (8:31; 9:31); (ix) Jesus rebukes his disciples for not setting their mind on God's interests (8:33) and for chiding the people who bring children to him for a blessing (10:13-16); (x) the disciples fail to drive out an evil spirit (9:14, 18); (xi) Jesus sends two of his disciples to fetch him a colt for his triumphal entry into Jerusalem (11:1-10) and to make preparations for "eating the Passover" (14:12-16); and (xii) after Jesus' resurrection, an angel commissions the three women at Jesus' tomb to inform Jesus' disciples to meet their master in Galilee (16:7).

Mark utilizes additional discipleship terms in his Gospel as follows: (i) ἀδελφή—person or thing viewed as a sister in relation to another entity, *sister* (i.e., "of a female who shares beliefs of the reference person or

---

9. "μαθητής," BDAG, 609-10.

of others in a community of faith"; 3:35; cf. Matt 12:50);¹⁰ (ii) ἀδελφός—person viewed as a brother in terms of a close affinity, *brother, fellow member, member, associate* (i.e., "one who shares beliefs," 3:35; cf. Matt 12:50; 25:40; 28:10);¹¹ (iii) ἀκολουθέω—follow someone as a disciple, *be a disciple, follow* (i.e., "persons following Jesus as his disciples" [1:18; 2:14; 9:38; 10:28; 10:52; cf. Matt 4:20, 22; 8:19; 9:9; 10:38; 19:21, 27, 28; 20:34; 27:55]; "Jesus issuing commands to persons about following him as his disciples" [2:14; 8:34; 10:21; cf. Matt 8:22; 9:9; 16:24]);¹² (iv) ἀπόστολος—of messengers with extraordinary status (i.e., "group of highly honored believers with a special function as God's envoys," 6:30; cf. Matt 10:2);¹³ (v) ἀρνέομαι—disclaim association with a person or event, *deny, repudiate, disown* (i.e., "repudiating Christ," 14:68, 70; cf. Matt 10:33; 26:70, 72);¹⁴ (vi) διάκονος—one who gets something done, at the behest of a superior, *assistant* (i.e., "servant in the kingdom," 9:35; 10:43; cf. Matt 20:26; 23:11);¹⁵ (vii) δοῦλος—one who is solely committed to another, *slave, subject* (i.e., "in a positive sense"; e.g., in relation to a superior human being, 10:44; cf. Matt 6:24; 18:23, 26–28; 20:27; 22:3f., 6, 8, 10);¹⁶ (viii) ἐπακολουθέω—happen as result or appropriate event in connection with something, *follow* (i.e., "signs," 16:20);¹⁷ (ix) μανθάνω—gain knowledge by instruction (i.e., "learn," 13:28; cf. Matt 9:13; 11:29; 24:32);¹⁸ (x) ὀπίσω —marker of position behind an entity that precedes, *after* (i.e., "come after/follow someone as a disciple"; e.g., Jesus commands persons to follow him as disciples [1:17; cf. Matt 4:19] and persons follow Jesus as his disciples [1:20; 8:34 cf. Matt 10:38; 16:24]);¹⁹ (xi) περιπατέω—to conduct one's life, *comport oneself, behave, live* (i.e., "the sphere in which one lives or ought to live"; e.g., tradition of the elders, Mark 7:5);²⁰ and

10. "ἀδελφή," BDAG, 18.
11. "ἀδελφός," BDAG, 18–19.
12. "ἀκολουθέω," BDAG, 36–37; see also Lange, *Mark*, 34 who reckons that "the 'following' [of the multitude from Galilee, 3:7] does not merely indicate external following; it includes a moral element also."
13. "ἀπόστολος," BDAG, 122.
14. "ἀρνέομαι," BDAG, 132–33.
15. "διάκονος," BDAG, 241.
16. "δοῦλος," BDAG, 259–60.
17. "ἐπακολουθέω," BDAG, 358.
18. "μανθάνω," BDAG, 615.
19. "ὀπίσω," BDAG, 716.
20. "περιπατέω," BDAG, 803.

(xii) τέκνον—one who is dear to another but without genetic relationship and without distinction in age, *child* (i.e., "spiritual child in relation to a master, apostle, or teacher," 10:24).[21]

Pattern of Discipleship in Mark

Larry Hurtado posits that both Mark's teaching on discipleship that is directed to the disciples/readers and his portrayal of the Twelve, which seems to have a strongly instructive purpose, reflect the author's interest in Christian discipleship. For Hurtado, the themes of Christology and discipleship in Mark's Gospel are strongly connected.[22]

Concerning Mark's teaching on discipleship, the disciples' behavior triggers criticism and the Markan Jesus' response to that criticism seems intended to inform the reader. Jesus defends his disciples against their critics (e.g., 2:17, 18–22, 23–28; 7:1–23), providing important teaching (by example) on discipleship to Mark's readers. Additionally: (i) he identifies his followers seated around him as his true family (3:31–35),[23] and (ii) his reply to the scribe's question about the chief commandment (12:28–34) puts total love for God and for one's neighbor as the critical marker of nearness to the kingdom of God. These episodes define Christian discipleship over against Jewish definitions of religious responsibility.[24]

The passion predictions in 8:22—10:52 emphasize that: (i) discipleship that is shaped by Jesus himself—his death and self-sacrificing service—requires his disciples' allegiance to his name;[25] (ii) the circle of disciples needs to be open and inclusive (9:38–50);[26] and (iii) disciples must be willing to forfeit everything for Jesus' sake (e.g., 10:1–27).[27] The Olivet Discourse (13:5–37) focuses on the disciples' responsibility for

---

21. "τέκνον," BDAG, 994–95.

22. Larry W. Hurtado, "Following Jesus," 9–29.

23. Doing the will of God is fundamental for discipleship (cf. Matt 6:10; 7:21–23). It is not primarily related to "obeying the Torah," but is rather connected with "being in kinship with Jesus" (Bayer, *Markus*, 179–80).

24. Hurtado, "Following Jesus," 10.

25. References to "anyone" (8:34; 9:35) and "whoever" (8:35; 9:37; 10:43–44) signal the broader intended reach of Jesus' teaching (Hurtado, "Following Jesus," 11–12).

26. Hurtado, "Following Jesus," 13–14; see Bayer, *Markus*, 349 on the disciples' feeling of importance due to Jesus' growing popularity; so also Lange, *Mark*, 89.

27. Hurtado, "Following Jesus," 14; see Bayer, *Markus*, 367 on the sharp antithesis between trusting in wealth and trusting in God (cf. Matt 7:3–5, 13–14; 23:24).

proclaiming the gospel with its attendant opposition (13:9-13) and on the importance of being watchful (13:33-37), since no one knows the time of the eschatological denouement.[28]

Scholars generally recognize the negative way in which the Twelve are portrayed in Mark's Gospel. Some argue that Mark discredits the Twelve as representatives of a heretical type of Christianity and/or Christology; others incline to the view that Mark uses the Twelve to provide readers with lessons on discipleship.[29] On the prominent and positive role of the Twelve, the reader notes, *inter alia*, that: (i) the calling of its first four members (1:16-20) occurs immediately after the introductory statement of Jesus' Galilean ministry (1:14-15); (ii) Mark frequently uses plural verbs ("they") that combine the movement and activities of Jesus and his disciples (e.g., 1:21; 5:1-2, 38); (iii) three of five controversy stories in 2:1—3:6 concern the disciples (2:13-17, 18-22, 23-28); (iv) Jesus' appointment of the Twelve (3:13-19) contains a fuller definition of their purpose than contained in the Synoptic parallels (cf. Matt 10:1; Luke 6:13);[30] (v) the disciples do God's will in following Jesus (3:35); and (vi) they extend Jesus' ministry in word and powerful deed (6:7-13), bringing Jesus to Herod's attention (6:14).[31]

Mark introduces certain topics that result in the reader's ambivalence toward the Twelve, including their: (i) lack of understanding (4:10-13, 33-34; 9:10); (iii) panic, fear, lack of faith, and awe and bewilderment (4:35-41); (iv) hardened hearts (6:45-52; cf. 8:14-21);[32] (v) state of being overwhelmed and terrified (9:2-8); (vi) inability to heal the demoniac boy (9:14-29); and (viii) betrayal (Judas), denial (Peter), and desertion of Jesus (chs. 14-15).[33] Conversely, the Markan Jesus is

28. Hurtado, "Following Jesus," 15-17.

29. Hurtado, "Following Jesus," 17-18.

30. See Witherington, III, *Mark*, 421-22 on the Markan Jesus' call to follow and be with Jesus perhaps being the primary characteristic of a disciple (cf. 1:16-20; 2:14; 3:14).

31. Hurtado, "Following Jesus," 18-19; see Lange, *Mark*, 37 on Jesus' call of the Twelve perhaps suggesting that he first makes a larger selection and then makes a narrower choice in 3:14.

32. A hardened heart (6:52; cf. 8:17) does not respond to God's will and work, but it opposes reaching insight and trusting Jesus as the Father's Messenger (Bayer, *Markus*, 265).

33. Hurtado, "Following Jesus," 19-21; for more on Mark's disciples' hardness of heart, see Matera, "Incomprehension of the Disciples," 153-72; Hur, "Disciples' Lack of Comprehension," 41-48; Lee and Van der Watt, "Hardening of the Disciples'

presented as the model (i.e., the basis for and pattern) of discipleship (e.g., 8:34; 10:43-45; 14:24).³⁴ Mark's Christology emphasizes the cross as the disclosure and meaning of Jesus, which harmonizes with Mark's emphasis on Jesus' crucifixion as the paradigm of faithful discipleship. Together, Markan accounts of Jesus and the Twelve combine to illustrate the definition of a faithful disciple and the dangers the reader must avoid. Markan discipleship means following Jesus, with no rival, no distraction, and no competition for the allegiance of the disciples.³⁵

Markan vis-à-vis Matthean Discipleship

Mark utilizes μαθητής in a manner that is consistent with Matthew's use of the term—i.e., primarily to describe the activities of Jesus' closest adherents who follow him as their master: going from place to place, obeying his commands, observing his actions (e.g., Mark 11:14b), and learning from him. They are a work in progress and the Markan Jesus rebukes them on occasion for setting their mind on human interests and for being intolerant of others (8:33; 10:13-16), though never like Matthew for being men of "little faith" (cf. Matt 6:30; 14:31; 16:8; 17:20), in spite of their inability to reproduce their master's miraculous achievements (e.g., 9:14-29; possibly also 11:19-23).

Markan and Matthean discipleship comprises similarities in terms of: (i) Jesus being a model of discipleship—e.g., his call to follow him as disciples and his promise to make them "fishers of men" (1:17; cf. Matt 4:19); (ii) the disciples' urgent response to Jesus' call (1:18, 20; cf. Matt 4:20, 22; 9:9); (iii) the surrogate family arrangement (e.g., 2:15; 3:7, 33-35; 6:1; cf. Matt 8:23; 12:48-50); (iv) the disciples' imitation of Jesus (3:14-15; cf. Matt 10:1), though sometimes unsuccessfully (9:14-29; cf. Matt 17:14-21); (v) their promotion of his ministry (3:14-15; 6:7-13; cf. Matt 10:1);³⁶ (vi) the cost of discipleship (8:34; cf. Matt 10:38; 16:24);

Hearts," 145-49; Gibson, "Rebuke of the Disciples," 31-47; Tyson, "Blindness of the Disciples," 261-68; Lane, *Mark*, 281-82; and Wilkins, "Discipleship," 183-84. For a comparative study of the portrayal of the Matthean disciples, see Brown, *Disciples in Narrative Perspective*.

34. Hurtado, "Following Jesus," 25.

35. Hurtado, "Following Jesus," 25-26; see Boomershine, "Mark: Forming Disciples," 405-11 on Mark's redefinition of what it means to be Jesus' disciple: from a traditional warrior who takes up his sword to one who takes up his cross.

36. For additional comments on Jesus' branching out into Galilee from his more

(vii) the obstacles encountered (e.g., 2:16, 23–38; 7:1–5; cf. Matt 12:1–8; 15:1–20); and (viii) the required allegiance to Jesus (1:17; 2:14; 8:34; cf. Matt 23:8–10).[37]

Markan and Matthean discipleship differ in certain ways, including: (i) Mark's non-restriction of the disciples from going to the Gentiles (cf. Matt 10:1–15); (ii) Mark's emphasis on the disciples' lack of understanding and hard heartedness;[38] (iii) Mark's lack of emphasis on the disciples' "little faith" (cf. Matt 6:30; 8:26; 14:31; 16:8; 17:20; cf. 28:17);[39] and (iv) the Markan Jesus' command to his disciples, according to Mark's longer ending, to "preach the gospel to all creation" (Mark 16:15),[40] vis-à-vis the Matthean Jesus' command to "make disciples of all the nations" (Matt 28:19).[41]

Luke-Acts

Discipleship Terminology in Luke-Acts

Luke utilizes μαθητεύω in the term's only occurrence in the NT outside of Matthew. Luke explains that Paul and Barnabas, while on their first missionary journey, go to the city of Derbe, where they preach the gospel and "make many disciples" (Acts 14:21). Afterwards, they return

---

restricted work in Capernaum, including the practical instructions to his disciples, see Gould, *Mark*, 105–6.

37. See also Wilkins, "Discipleship," 187–88 on Jesus' particular form of discipleship.

38. For a contrast of Matthew's and Mark's treatments of the disciples' understanding in their respective Gospels, see Wilkins, "Discipleship," 182; see also Peter-Ben Smit, "A Question of Discipleship - Remarks on Matthew 8:18–23," *RB* 123.1 (2016): 79–92, who notes (against the backdrop of the narrative "gaps" in Matt 8:18–23) that, rather than always teaching something in a direct way (e.g., 'this is a good or bad disciple'), Matthew sometimes edits his source and inserts it into the Markan narrative sequence, thereby inviting his audience to reflect on its own discipleship by pondering the question of discipleship in the sense of following Jesus in a radical way.

39. Mark refers to their lack of faith on one occasion (Mark 4:35–41; cf. Matt 8:23–27).

40. Most scholars agree that Mark 16:9–20 is non-Markan and subscribe to the view that either the original ending has been lost, Mark was prevented from finishing his Gospel, or Mark intended for his Gospel to end the way that it does at 16:8. For a detailed discussion about Mark's secondary ending (16:9–20), see Marcus, *Mark 8–16*, 1088–96.

41. I have noted by way of footnote in the Survey of Literature in chapter 2 that several ancient and contemporary scholars have at times conflated the Matthean and Markan commissions in their writings.

to Lystra, Iconium, and Antioch, strengthening the souls of the disciples (which presumably they had already made) and encouraging them to continue in the faith (14:21b–22a). In this present context, Luke correlates μαθητεύω with preaching the gospel (εὐαγγελίζω) and with the strengthening (ἐπιστηρίζω) and encouraging (παρακαλέω) of the disciples (μαθητής).[42] Matthew's use of μαθητεύω (Matt 28:19) connects the term to "going" (πορευθέντες), "the nations" (τὰ ἔθνη), "baptizing" (βαπτίζοντες), and "teaching" (διδάσκοντες); however, he also links it to the broader context of Matthew through his use of key narrative elements in Matthew 28:16–20—e.g., events, characters, setting, and rhetoric—that unite the Commission to the rest of the Gospel. Therefore, when I consider that the Matthean Jesus proclaims the gospel (e.g., Matt 4:17; 11:1, 5), and that he strengthens and encourages his disciples throughout Matthew (e.g., Matt 5:3—7:27; 19:27–30) as he teaches them the art of fishing for people (4:23—28:20), it becomes apparent that both Matthew and Luke use μαθητεύω in contexts that are largely congruent.[43]

The following is an analysis of other discipleship terms that appear in Luke-Acts, several of which are also common to Matthew. Luke uses μαθητής in the Gospel of Luke to speak concerning: (i) the opposition from the religious authorities towards Jesus' disciples on various matters (5:30, 33; 6:1; 19:39–40);[44] (ii) Jesus' choosing of twelve of his disciples and his naming of them as apostles (6:13); (iii) the disciples' following Jesus around, witnessing his ministry—healing (6:17–19); teaching (Beatitudes, 6:20; pupil and teacher, 6:40; seek first the kingdom, 12:22–32; discipleship, 14:25–33; the unrighteous steward, 16:1–9; stumbling blocks, 17:1–2); raising the dead (7:11–17); miracles (8:22–25; 9:12–17); grief experience in Gethsemane (22:39–46); (iv) Jesus' fielding of questions from John's disciples (7:18–23); (v) Jesus' vague speech (in parables) to the crowd, but his explanation of everything privately to his disciples

---

42. See Bruce, *Acts*, 279–80 on the connection between the strengthening and encouraging of the disciples and the persecution that first-century Christians encountered (e.g., Acts 14:5, 6, 19; cf. Rom 8:17; 2 Tim 2:12a); Barrett, *Acts*, 685–87; Keener, *Acts*: 3:1–14:28, 2:2178–79; and Schneider, *Apostelgeschichte*, 2:165–66.

43. Detwiler, "Great Commission in Acts 14," 33, 40–41 explores the possibility that Acts 14:21–23 is an outline of, and a brief commentary on, the discipleship process that Jesus calls his followers to pursue in their own lives and to encourage in the lives of others.

44. See Coleman, "Boundary-Shattering Table Fellowship," 128–42, for an exploration of the Pharisaic criticisms of Jesus in Luke, including how his choice of table companions consistently offends them and incites their puzzlement and hostility.

(8:9-15; 10:23); (vi) Jesus' questioning of his disciples about his identity (9:18);[45] (vii) the disciples' failure to drive out an evil spirit (9:40); (viii) Jesus' forewarning of his disciples about: his impending passion (9:43-45); the leaven of the Pharisees (12:1); the second coming of the Son of Man (17:22-37); and the prideful manner of the scribes (20:45-47); (ix) Jesus' rebuke of his disciples for wanting to destroy certain persons who do not receive him (9:51-56) and for hindering the children from coming to him (18:15-17); (x) Jesus' teaching his disciples how to pray (11:1-4); (xi) Jesus' sending two of his disciples to fetch him a colt for his triumphal entry into Jerusalem (19:28-35) and to make preparations for the eating the Passover (22:7-13); and (xii) the crowd of disciples' praising God at Jesus' triumphant entry into Jerusalem (19:37). In the book of Acts, Luke uses μαθητής in connection with the activity of: (i) all persons who come to believe the apostles' proclamation and teaching of the gospel (Acts 6:1, 2, 7; 9:1, 10, 19, 38; 11:26, 29; 13:52; 14:20, 22, 28; 15:10; 16:1; 18:23, 27; 19:1, 9, 30; 20:1, 30; 21:4, 16), and (ii) the disciples of Saul/Paul (9:25).

Luke utilizes additional discipleship terms in Luke-Acts as follows: (i) ἅγιος—a pure substantive, the holy (thing, person) (i.e., "the holy ones"; e.g., *believers, loyal followers, saints* of Christians as consecrated to God, Acts 9:13, 32, 41; 26:10; cf. Matt 27:52);[46] (ii) ἀδελφός—person viewed as a brother in terms of a close affinity, *brother, fellow member, member, associate* (i.e., "one who shares beliefs," Luke 8:2; 22:32; Acts 1:15, 16; 6:3; 9:17, 30; 10:23; 11:1, 12, 29; 12:17; 14:2; 15:1, 3, 7, 13, 22, 23ab, 32, 33, 36, 40; 16:2, 40; 17:6, 10, 14; 18:18, 27; 21:7, 17, 20; 22:13; 28:14, 15, 17, 21; cf. Matt 12:50; 23:8; 25:40; 28:10);[47] (iii) ἀκολουθέω—follow someone as a disciple, *be a disciple, follow* (i.e., "persons following Jesus as his disciples" [Luke 5:11, 28; 9:49, 57, 61; 18:28, 43; cf. Matt 4:20, 22; 8:19; 9:9; 10:38; 19:21, 27, 28; 20:34; 27:55] and "Jesus issuing commands to persons about following him as his disciples" [Luke 5:27; 9:23, 59; 18:22; cf. Matt 8:22; 9:9; 16:24]);[48] (iv) ἀπόστολος—of messengers with extraordinary status; (i.e., "of prophets," Luke 11:49); "of a group of highly honored believers with a special function as God's envoys" (Luke 6:13; 9:10; 17:5; 22:14; 24:10; Acts 1:2, 26; 2:37, 42, 43; 4:33, 35, 36, 37; 5:2, 12, 18, 29, 40; 6:6;

---

45. See Green, *Luke*, 352, 366 on the correlation between Christology and discipleship in Luke 9:1-50.

46. "ἅγιος," BDAG, 10-11.

47. "ἀδελφός," BDAG, 18-19.

48. "ἀκολουθέω," BDAG, 36-37.

8:1, 14, 18; 9:27; 11:1; 14:4, 14; 15:2, 4, 6, 22, 23; 16:4; cf. Matt 10:2);[49] (v) ἀρνέομαι—disclaim association with a person or event, *deny, repudiate, disown* (i.e., "repudiating Christ," Luke 12:9; 22:57; Acts 3:13, 14; cf. Matt 10:33; 26:70, 72); to refuse to pay any attention to, disregard, renounce (i.e., "in a wholly selfless way," Luke 9:23);[50] (vi) δικαίως—pertaining to being just or right in a juridical sense, *justly, in an upright manner* (i.e., "of treatment in a deserving manner for one's way of life *uprightly, justly, in (all) justice*," Luke 23:41);[51] (vii) δοῦλος—one who is solely committed to another, *slave, subject* (i.e., "in a positive sense"; e.g., in relation to a superior human being [Luke 14:17, 21-23; 16:13; cf. Matt 18:23, 26-28; 20:27; 22:3f., 6, 8, 10]; e.g., of the relationship of humans to God [Luke 2:29; Acts 2:18; 4:29; 16:17]);[52] (viii) ἐκκλησία—people with shared belief, *community, congregation* (i.e., "of OT Israelites *assembly, congregation*" [Acts 7:38]; "of Christians in a specific place or area" [Acts 2:47 v.l.;[53] 5:11; 8:1, 3; 9:31; 11:22, 26; 12:5; 13:1; 14:23; 15:3, 4, 22, 41; 16:5; 18:22; 20:17; cf. Matt 18:17]; "the global community of Christians, *(universal) church*" [Acts 9:31; 12:1; 20:28; cf. Matt 16:18]);[54] (ix) μαθήτρια—"a female disciple" (Acts 9:36);[55] (x) ὀπίσω—marker of position behind an entity that precedes, *after* (i.e., "come after/follow someone as a disciple"; e.g., following Jesus as a disciple [Luke 9:23; 14:27; cf. Matt 4:19; 10:38; 16:24] and following others as disciples [Luke 21:8; Acts 5:37; 20:30]);[56] (xi) πείθω—"to be a disciple or follower of someone" (Acts 5:36, 37);[57] (xii) περιπατέω—conduct one's life, *comport oneself, behave, live* (i.e., "of 'walk of life', go about," Acts 21:21);[58] (xiii) τέκνον—one who has the

49. "ἀπόστολος," BDAG, 122.

50. "ἀρνέομαι," BDAG, 132-33.

51. "δικαίως," BDAG, 250.

52. "δοῦλος," BDAG, 259-60.

53. For comments regarding this textual variant, see Comfort, *Text and Translation Commentary*, 336; and Omanson and Metzger, *Textual Guide to the Greek New Testament*, 222-23.

54. "ἐκκλησία," BDAG, 303-4.

55. "μαθήτρια," BDAG, 610. Matthew refers to Jesus' female disciples as γυναῖκες ("the women," 27:55; 28:5).

56. "ὀπίσω," BDAG, 716.

57. "πείθω," BDAG, 791-92; See Louw and Nida, *Greek-English Lexicon*, 1:469 n. 6 regarding the proximity of πείθομαι (Acts 5:36) to μαθητεύω and ἀκολουθέω because of the way it is used in Acts 5:36.

58. "περιπατέω," BDAG, 803. In Acts 15:1, Codex Bezae (D) and a few other witnesses have "and walk"; i.e., instead of τῷ ἔθει τῷ Μωϋσέως they read καὶ τῷ ἔθει τῷ

characteristics of another being, *child* (i.e., "of those who exhibit virtues of ancient worthies," Luke 3:8);⁵⁹ (xiv) υἱός—person related or closely associated as if by ties of sonship, *son* (i.e., "of a pupil, follower, or one who is otherwise a spiritual son"; e.g., "sons" of the Pharisees, Luke 11:19; cf. Matt 12:27);⁶⁰ and (xv) Χριστιανός—one who is associated with Christ, Christ-partisan, *Christian* (Acts 11:26; 26:28).⁶¹

Pattern of Discipleship in Luke-Acts

Richard Longenecker reckons that while Luke uses μαθητής less frequently and in a less nuanced way than the other canonical evangelists, he treats the theme of discipleship in a manner that is more extensively developed, more radically expressed, and more consistently sustained.⁶²

On the structure of Luke-Acts vis-à-vis discipleship, Longenecker emphasizes the parallels of event and expression between what Jesus does and says in Luke's Gospel and what the disciples (i.e., primarily Peter and Paul) do and say in the Acts of the Apostles.⁶³ For Longenecker: (i) Luke and Acts should be read together, interpreting each other; (ii) Acts' depiction of the ministry of early church must have been shaped by Jesus tradition of Luke's Gospel; and (iii) Jesus' ministry and the church's mission together constitute the fullness of God's redemptive activity on behalf of humanity.⁶⁴

Longenecker observes that: (i) Luke portrays the Twelve more positively than Mark; (ii) Luke refers to the Twelve as "apostles" (Luke 6:13; 9:10), perhaps prefiguring their role as church leaders later in Acts; (iii) Luke (like Matthew and John) refers to the broader category of Jesus followers as "disciples"; and (iv) each evangelist means for readers to

---

Μωϋσέως περιπατῆτε; this variant focuses more strongly on obedience to the Law; see also Eberhard Nestle and Erwin Nestle, *Nestle-Aland: NTG Apparatus Criticus*, ed. Barbara Aland et al., 28th ed. (Stuttgart: Deutsche Bibelgesellschaft, 2012), 429 for the text critical data relating to Acts 15:1.

59. "τέκνον," BDAG, 994–95.
60. "υἱός," BDAG, 1024–27.
61. "Χριστιανός," BDAG, 1090.
62. Longenecker, "Discipleship in Luke-Acts," 50.
63. Longenecker, "Discipleship in Luke-Acts," 52; see Talbert, "Discipleship in Luke-Acts," 62–75; and Edwards, "Parallels and Patterns," 485–501.
64. Longenecker, "Discipleship in Luke-Acts," 53.

identify with and learn from the successes and failures of the disciples—i.e., to learn what it means to be follower of Jesus.[65]

The travel narrative in Luke's Gospel (9:51–19:27) comprises numerous references to Jesus and his disciples.[66] The major topics addressed therein are: (i) loving and helping others (10:25–37); (ii) prayer (11:5–13; 18:1–8); (iii) possessions and true riches (12:13–34; 16:19–31); (iv) service to God (13:1–9; 17:7–10; 19:11–27); (v) the importance of response to God (14:15–24;[67] 16:19–31); (vi) God's love for the lost (15:1–7; 15:8–10; 15:11–32); (vii) humility (18:9–14; 14:7–14); and (viii) shrewdness in one's affairs (16:1–12). Each topic is intended to teach about the meaning of following Jesus and to provide pictorial patterns for Christian discipleship.[68]

With Jesus and his disciples' departure for Jerusalem (9:51–62), Luke emphasizes that "following" Jesus is connected with joining him in the journey and in proclaiming the kingdom of God. To achieve this, Luke pushes the disciples' boundaries beyond Israel (e.g., 9:52; 10:1–24, 30–37).[69] Once Jesus arrives in Jerusalem, following the lengthy travel narrative, the Twelve recede more and more into the background. Their earlier distinction from the other disciples become blurred with nonspecific references to "the disciples" (e.g., 19:29, 37) and there is an increasing christological focus in the text (18:35–43; 19:11–27, 38).[70]

Luke portrays Jesus' passion and the cross "in exemplary fashion as the culmination of Jesus' unconditional obedience to God and so as patterns for the lives of his followers" (e.g., service [22:27],[71] prayer against

---

65. Longenecker, "Discipleship in Luke-Acts," 54–56.

66. For a contrast between Luke's Galilean section (4:14–9:50) and his Travel Narrative (9:51–19:48), see Green, *Luke*, 394–99.

67. Jesus introduces the possibility that ties to possessions and family might be impediments to authentic discipleship (Green, *Luke*, 563–64).

68. Longenecker, "Discipleship in Luke-Acts," 64–67; see Green, *Luke*, 23–24 concerning the Lukan call to discipleship being an invitation to align oneself with Jesus, and thus with God; and Fitzmyer, *Luke I–IX*, 235–57 on the primary ways that humans react to the proclamation of Christ and his disciples: (i) faith (e.g., Luke 8:11–15; Acts 6:7; 10:43); (ii) repentance and conversion (e.g., Luke 3:3, 8; 5:32; 10:13; Acts 2:38; 3:19; 5:31); and (iii) baptism (e.g., Luke 3:16; Acts 1:5; 2:38; 8:12).

69. Green, *Luke*, 400–401.

70. Green, *Luke*, 680–81.

71. In the narrative of the Last Supper (22:1–38), Luke embeds a discipleship motif within the narrative: (i) pointing to Satan's influence that lies behind the faltering of the disciples (22:3–6, 31–34); (ii) highlighting the struggle and misunderstanding

falling into temptation [22:40, 46], carrying one's cross [23:26; cf. 9:23]). Of course, suffering, sacrifice, and soteriology are part of Luke's portrayal of Jesus' passion (e.g., "his departure" [9:31] and "Passover meal" [22:7, 8, 13, 15, 19–20]); however, by omitting Mark's "to give his life a ransom for many" (Mark 10:45b; cf. Matt 20:28b) in Luke 22:24–30, Luke indicates that he wants his readers to think about Jesus' passion and cross as exemplary of Christian living and service.[72]

In Acts 1–2, three basic themes of Luke's Nazareth pericope (Luke 4:14–30) are highlighted: (i) the presence of God's Spirit on his servants,[73] (ii) the proclamation of the good news of God's redemptive activity, and (iii) the universality of God's grace as expressed in the gospel (Acts 2:21). These themes are meant to characterize every Christian disciple. Other discipleship themes appearing in Luke and recurring with greater explication in Acts include: (i) being shaped in the apostolic tradition (e.g., Acts 2:42);[74] (ii) dependency on God in prayer (e.g., Acts 1:14, 24–25; 2:42; 6:4; 12:5); (iii) priority allegiance to Jesus (addressed at various points throughout the text); and (iv) concern for the disenfranchised (e.g., Acts 4:32–5:11).[75]

Longenecker also observes that in Acts Luke does not refer to the Twelve (Judas having been replaced by Matthias) as οἱ μαθηταὶ ("the disciples");[76] instead, he refers to believers as ἀδελφοί ("brothers," Acts 1:16), and he uses μαθητής (e.g., Acts 6:1, 2, 7; 11:26, 29; 15:10; 16:1; 19:1,

---

among Jesus' followers (22:24, 38); but also (iii) portraying two disciples, Peter and John, as adopting Jesus' role as "table servant" (22:8–13); and (iv) announcing the disciples' stability and loyalty in the face of diabolic testing (22:28) and their ability to share regal authority (22:29–30) (Green, *Luke*, 748–50).

72. Longenecker, "Discipleship in Luke-Acts," 67–70.

73. Being filled with the Spirit will be repeated on several occasions (cf. Acts 4:8, 31), "but the baptism in the Spirit which the believing community now experienced [Acts 2:42] was an event which took place once for all" (Bruce, *Acts*, 51–53).

74. The apostolic fellowship found expression in various practical ways, two of which are mentioned in Acts 2:42—the breaking of bread and prayers (Bruce, *Acts*, 73).

75. Longenecker, "Discipleship in Luke-Acts," 71–72.

76. Οἱ δώδεκα ("the Twelve") is used for the apostles only in Acts 6:2 (cf. "the Eleven" in 1:26; 2:14), although it is quite common in the Gospels of Mark and Luke (Mark 3:16; 4:10; 6:7; 9:35; 10:32; 11:11; 14:10, 17, 20, 43; Luke 8:1; 9:1, 12; 18:31; 22:3, 47; cf. 1 Cor 15:5). Matthew uses "the Twelve" also (Matt 20:17; 26:14, 47), but sometimes adds "apostles" (Matt 10:2) or "disciples" (Matt 26:20 v.l.) to it. For comments on the textual variant in Matt 26:20, see Omanson and Metzger, *Textual Guide to the Greek New Testament*, 46.

9, 30; 21:4, 16) and ἀδελφός (e.g., Acts 6:3; 11:1; 15:1; cf. Luke 8:21; 22:32) interchangeably for believers in Jesus. Luke's use of these terms may be the result of μαθητής being commonly used by philosophical schools of the day and only recently becoming acceptable in religious associations.[77] The evolution of the use of μαθητής to incorporate all believers in Christ means that a disciple of Jesus is no longer limited to persons who are physically present with Jesus and who literally follow him around from place to place.

Finally, Luke's development theme is expressed more fully in Acts: (i) the Lukan Jesus grows and becomes strong (Luke 2:40, 52), and (ii) in Acts, the word of God progresses from Jerusalem Christians to Gentiles to Rome itself (Acts 28:31). Herein lies the author's exhortation to believers in Christ to develop in lives of faith and service.[78]

Lukan vis-à-vis Matthean Discipleship

Luke utilizes μαθητής in a manner that is consistent with Matthew's use of the term—i.e., primarily to describe the activity of persons who come to believe the gospel message preached by Jesus. Sometime after Jesus' ascension (Acts 1:9-11), the term becomes synonymous with Χριστιανός ("Christian") and with members of the ἐκκλησία ("church") in general (Acts 11:26). Additionally, Luke uses ἀπόστολος ("apostle") far more frequently than Matthew with reference to the activities of Jesus' closest disciples. Indeed, Luke does not refer to them as μαθητής in the book of Acts, and he occasionally widens the scope of ἀπόστολος to incorporate Matthias (Acts 1:26) and Saul/Paul and Barnabas (Acts 14:4, 14).

Additionally, Lukan and Matthean discipleship comprises similarities in terms of: (i) Jesus being a model of discipleship—e.g., his call to follow him as disciples and his promise that they will be catching men (Luke 5:10, 27; 9:23, 59; 18:22; cf. Matt 4:19); (ii) the cost of discipleship (e.g., Luke 5:11, 28; cf. Matt 4:20, 22); (iv) the sense of immediacy about following (e.g., 18:43; cf. Matt 4:20, 22; 9:9); (v) the surrogate family arrangement (e.g., 9:51–19:27; cf. Matt 8:23; 12:48–50); (vi) the demands of discipleship (Luke 9:23, 57–62; cf. Matt 8:19–22; 10:38; 16:24); (vii) the

---

77. Longenecker, "Discipleship in Luke-Acts," 72; see also Wilkins, *Discipleship in the Ancient World*, 11–42 on the classical and Hellenistic use of μαθητής and its historical progression as a convenient term to designate the followers of Jesus.

78. Longenecker, "Discipleship in Luke-Acts," 74.

obstacles encountered (e.g., 5:30, 33; 6:1–5; 15:2; cf. Matt 9:14; 12:1–8; 15:1–20); and (viii) the required allegiance to Jesus (Luke 5:27; 9:23, 59; 18:22; cf. Matt 8:22; 16:24; 23:8–10).[79]

Luke's general broadening of the terminology of discipleship in the book of Acts—in terms of the interchangeable use of μαθητής and ἀδελφός for Christian believers—is a significant point of development between Lukan and Matthean discipleship. Additionally, the reader observes the use of new terms (e.g., Χριστιανός, Acts 11:26) and the maturation of others (e.g., ἐκκλησία; e.g., Acts 5:11; 8:1, 3; 9:31).[80]

Lukan and Matthean discipleship differ in terms of the setting and timing of Jesus' commission of his disciples (Luke 24:46–49; Acts 1:7–8; cf. Matt 28:19–20). In spite of this, however, the universal scope of both commissions and their emphasis on God's sovereignty in missions are evident.[81]

The Johannine Literature

Discipleship Terminology in the Johannine Literature

The term μαθητεύω (cf. Matt 28:19) does not occur in the Johannine tradition;[82] however, the following examination of Johannine discipleship terms includes several that are common to Matthew. John uses μαθητής in various contexts in the Gospel of John. He writes, for example, concerning: (i) matters relating to the disciples of John the Baptist (1:35, 37; 3:25); (ii) the disciples' personal interactions with Jesus—e.g., traveling together (2:12; 6:22–25; 11:54); undertaking miscellaneous tasks such as

---

79. Fitzmyer, *Luke I–IX*, 257–58 argues that Luke's portrait of Jesus comprises qualities that Luke thinks should dominate the lives of Christians themselves and the Christian church—i.e., the qualities of mercy, love, charm, joy, and delicacy that tend to soften the starker reality that is at times portrayed in the other Gospels.

80. In the Book of Acts, Luke uses ἐκκλησία ("church, congregation, assembly") twenty-two (22) out of twenty-three (23) times in the context of the body of Jesus followers in Jerusalem, Judea, Galilee, Samaria, and among the Gentiles—i.e., "to the remotest part of the earth" (Acts 1:8). He uses the term once only in reference to "the congregation in the wilderness" (Acts 7:38).

81. See Tennent, *World Missions*, 142–43, 149–51 for a comparison of the Matthean and the Lukan commissions, and a discussion about God's sovereignty in missions.

82. See John's use of ποιέω + μαθητής rather than μαθητεύω to convey the notion Jesus "making and baptizing more disciples than John" (John 4:1). The construction does not appear elsewhere in the NT.

buying food (4:8); showing concern for Jesus' personal well-being (4:31, 33); witnessing his ministry (e.g., healing [6:2; 9:1-12]; teaching [e.g., "a difficult statement," (6:59-65); "a new commandment" (13:33-38); the vine and the branches (15:1-11); Jesus comes from God (16:23-33)]; baptizing [3:22; 4:1, 2]; interacting with women [4:27; 12:1-8]; raising the dead [11:1-46]; serving others [13:5-20]; other signs or miracles [2:2, 11; 6:1-14, 15-21; 20:30-31]; predicting his betrayal [13:21-30] and his death and resurrection [16:16-22]); (iii) matters regarding the larger group of Jesus' disciples beyond the Twelve (6:60, 66; 7:3; 8:31); (iv) Peter's confession of faith (6:66-71); (v) the Pharisees calling themselves disciples of Moses (9:27-28);[83] (vi) the disciples' future reflection on Jesus' words (2:17, 22; 12:16); (vii) Jesus' betrayal by Judas (18:1-11); (viii) Jesus before the priests (18:12-24); (ix) Peter's denial of Jesus (18:25-27); (x) Jesus' crucifixion (19:16-30); (xi) Joseph of Arimathea's claim of Jesus' body (19:38-42); (xii) the empty tomb (20:1-10); (xiii) Mary Magdalene's encounter with the resurrected Jesus, followed by her announcement to the disciples (20:11-18); (xiv) the resurrected Jesus' first two appearances to his disciples—first without and then with Thomas (20:19-29); and (xv) Jesus' third appearance to his disciples by the Sea of Tiberias (21:1-25). John does not use μαθητής in the remainder of the Johannine literature; however, his use to the term in John's Gospel is generally consistent with Matthew's use thereof—i.e., primarily to describe the activity of persons who come to believe the gospel message preached by Jesus and follow him around as his adherents. The Johannine Jesus calls persons to follow him as his disciples and many respond in agreement with his command, although some later withdraw and cease walking with him because they do not understand some of his harsh statements (e.g., 6:51-52, 59-61, 66).

John utilizes additional discipleship terms in his literature as follows: (i) ἅγιος—a pure substantive, the holy (thing, person) (i.e., "the holy ones"; e.g., *believers, loyal followers, saints* of Christians as consecrated to God, Rev 5:8; 8:3, 4; 11:18; 13:7, 10; 14:12; 16:6; 17:6; 18:20, 24; 19:8; 20:9; cf. Matt 27:52);[84] (ii) ἀδελφός—a person viewed as a brother in terms of a close affinity, *brother, fellow member, member, associate* (i.e., "one who shares Christian beliefs," John 20:17; 21:23; 1 John 2:9, 10, 11; 3:10, 13, 14, 15, 16, 17; 4:20, 21; 5:16; 3 John 3, 5, 10; Rev 1:9; 6:11; 12:10; 19:10;

---

83. See Muderhwa, "Blind Man of John 9," 1-10 on an examination of John 9 that seeks to compare Christian discipleship with Mosaic discipleship.

84. "ἅγιος," BDAG, 10-11.

22:9);⁸⁵ (iii) ἀκολουθέω—follow someone as a disciple, *be a disciple, follow* (i.e., "persons following Jesus as his disciples" [John 1:37, 38, 40; 8:12; 10:27; 12:26; Rev 14:4;⁸⁶ cf. Matt 4:20, 22; 8:19; 9:9; 10:38; 19:21, 27, 28; 20:34; 27:55]; "Jesus issuing commands to persons about following him as his disciples" [John 1:43; 21:19, 22; cf. Matt 4:19; 8:22; 9:9; 16:24]);⁸⁷ (iv) ἄμωμος—pertaining to being without fault and therefore morally blameless, *blameless* (Rev 14:5);⁸⁸ (v) ἀξίως—worthily, in a manner worthy of, suitably (i.e., "of God," 3 John 6);⁸⁹ (vi) ἀπόστολος—of messengers without extraordinary status, *delegate, envoy, messenger* (i.e., "one who is sent," John 13:16); of messengers with extraordinary status (i.e., "of prophets" [Rev 18:20; cf. 2:2]; i.e., "of a group of highly honored believers with a special function as God's envoys" [Rev 21:14; cf. Matt 10:2]);⁹⁰ (vii) ἀρνέομαι—disclaim association with a person or event, *deny, repudiate, disown* (i.e., "repudiating Christ," John 13:38; 18:25, 27; 1 John 2:23; Rev 2:13; 3:8; cf. Matt 10:33; 26:70, 72);⁹¹ (viii) διάκονος—one who gets something done, at the behest of a superior, *assistant* (i.e., "in service of Jesus," John 12:26);⁹² (ix) δοῦλος—one who is solely committed to another, *slave, subject* (i.e., "in a pejorative sense" [John 8:34]; "in a positive sense," e.g., of the relationship of humans to God [John 15:15; Rev 1:2; 2:20; 7:3; 15:3; 19:2, 5; 22:3, 6]);⁹³ (x) ἐκκλησία—people with shared belief, *community, congregation* (i.e., "of a specific Christian group *assembly, gathering*" [3 John 6]; "*congregation* or *church* as the totality of Christians living and meeting in a particular locality or larger geographical area" [3 John 9, 10; Rev 1:4; 2:1, 7, 8, 11, 12, 17, 18, 23, 29; 3:1, 6, 7, 13, 14, 22; 22:16]);⁹⁴ (xi) μανθάνω—gain knowledge by instruction (i.e., "learn"; e.g., from the Father [John 6:45], elementary knowledge [John 7:15], and a song [Rev

---

85. "ἀδελφός," BDAG, 18–19.

86. Rev 14:1–5 refers to "the one hundred and forty-four thousand who had been purchased from the earth," who have not been defiled with women and who follow the Lamb wherever he goes; no lie is found in their mouth and they are blameless.

87. "ἀκολουθέω," BDAG, 36–37.

88. "ἄμωμος," BDAG, 56.

89. "ἀξίως," BDAG, 96.

90. "ἀπόστολος," BDAG, 122.

91. "ἀρνέομαι," BDAG, 132–33.

92. "διάκονος," BDAG, 241.

93. "δοῦλος," BDAG, 259–60.

94. "ἐκκλησία," BDAG, 303–4.

14:3]; cf. Matt 9:13; 11:29; 24:32);⁹⁵ (xii) μιμέομαι—use as a model, *imitate, emulate, follow* (3 John 11);⁹⁶ (xiii) ὀπίσω—marker of a position in back of something *behind* (i.e., "draw back, withdraw"; e.g., from walking with Jesus, John 6:66; cf. Matt 24:18); marker of position behind an entity that precedes, *after* (i.e., "come after/follow someone as a disciple"; e.g., following Jesus as a disciple, John 12:19; Rev 13:3; cf. Matt 4:19; 10:38; 16:24);⁹⁷ (xiii) ἀπέρχομαι εἰς τὰ ὀπίσω—"to go back to what lies behind" or "to cease being a disciple or follower of someone" (John 6:66);⁹⁸ (xiv) περιπατέω—go here and there in walking, *go about, walk around* (i.e., "go about with someone," e.g., walking [worthily] with Jesus [Rev 3:4] or not walking with Jesus anymore [John 6:66]; "in imagery, nonliteral use of the word," e.g., walk in light/darkness [John 8:12; 11:9, 10; 12:35ab; 1 John 1:6, 7; 2:11; Rev 21:24]); conduct one's life, *comport oneself, behave, live* as habit of conduct (i.e., "by a comparison," e.g., walk as Jesus walked, 1 John 2:6ab); "sphere in which one lives or ought to live, so as to be characterized by that sphere" (e.g., walk in truth; 2 John 4, 6ab; 3 John 3, 4);⁹⁹ (xv) συμμαθητής—"fellow pupil, fellow disciple" (John 11:16);¹⁰⁰ (xvi) σύνδουλος—a subordinate in total obedience to a ruler, *slave* (i.e., "of a relationship to the heavenly κύριος" [Rev 6:11]; "of the revealing angel" [Rev 19:10; 22:9]);¹⁰¹ (xvii) συνεργός—pertaining to working together with, *helping*, as substantive (i.e., "helper, fellow worker," 3 John 8);¹⁰² (xviii) τεκνίον—"little child," used by Jesus in the context of disciples, or by a Christian apostle or teacher to his spiritual children (John 13:33; 1

---

95. "μανθάνω," BDAG, 615.
96. "μιμέομαι," BDAG, 651.
97. "ὀπίσω," BDAG, 716.
98. Matthew does not employ this phrase to refer to a disciple's withdrawal from walking with Jesus; however, he engages with related themes in: (i) the Parable of the Sower (13:3–9), where the word is sown in the heart of the hearer, but is "snatched away" (ἁρπάζω, 13:19) , or the hearer "falls away" (σκανδαλίζω, 13:20–21), or the word is "choked" (συμπνίγω, 13:22) ; (ii) the rich young ruler's "turning away" (ἀπέρχομαι) from Jesus (19:16–26); (iii) Jesus' disciples' temporary flight from him (φεύγω, 26:56); (iv) Peter's denial of Jesus, after which he "goes out" (ἐξέρχομαι, 26:75) and weeps bitterly; and in (v) Judas's betrayal of and permanent separation from Jesus (Matt 10:4; 26:14–16, 25, 47–50; 27:3), finally "going away" (ἀπέρχομαι, 27:5) to hang himself.
99. "περιπατέω," BDAG, 803.
100. "συμμαθητής," BDAG, 957.
101. "σύνδουλος," BDAG, 966–67.
102. "συνεργός," BDAG, 969.

John 2:1, 12, 28; 3:7, 18; 4:4; 5:21);[103] and (xix) τέκνον—one who is dear to another but without genetic relationship and without distinction in age, *child* (i.e., "a spiritual child in relation to master, apostle, or teacher" [3 John 4; Rev 2:23]; "of the members of a congregation" [2 John 1, 4, 13]); one who has the characteristics of another being, *child* (i.e., "of those who exhibit virtues of ancient worthies" [John 8:39], "of those who exhibit characteristics of transcendent entities"; e.g., believers are [τὰ] τέκνα [τοῦ] θεοῦ [John 1:12; 11:52; 1 John 3:1, 2, 10a; 5:2]; e.g., people who do not practice righteousness are τὰ τέκνα τοῦ διαβόλου [1 John 3:10b]).[104]

Pattern of Discipleship in the Johannine Literature

Melvyn Hillmer perceives Thomas's confession, "My Lord and my God" (John 20:28), to be the climax of John's Gospel. For Hillmer, Thomas's confession is the proper response of every Christian disciple to the revelation in Christ.[105]

John's Gospel speaks about discipleship in terms of the disciples' identity: (i) they are with Jesus during his earthly ministry and they comprise all believers in Jesus; (ii) John's meaning is often unclear when referring to "Jesus' disciples"—i.e., whether the Twelve or the larger group of followers;[106] (iii) Jesus' disciples come from among the disciples of John the Baptist (1:35-51);[107] (iv) John does not provide a complete list of Jesus' disciples; (v) John, unlike the Synoptics and Acts, does not use the term

103. "τεκνίον," BDAG, 994; see also "Persons for Whom There Is Affectionate Concern (9.46-9.48)" in Louw and Nida, *Greek-English Lexicon*, 1:109-10.

104. Neither Matthew nor Luke-Acts uses τέκνον in a discipleship sense, but the authors of both writings deploy the term in other contexts; see previous comments in this chapter, under the subheadings "Discipleship Terminology in Mark" for an analysis of the deployment of τέκνον in Matthew, Mark, and Luke-Acts.

105. Hillmer, "Discipleship in the Johannine Tradition," 77. On Thomas's confession (John 20:28), see also Bernard, *John*, 2:683; Brown, *John (XIII-XXI)*, 1026-27; and Schnackenburg, *Johannesevangelium*, 1:395-98 on Thomas's expression being ultimately about the change of Thomas's attitude, from unbelief to faith because of Jesus' appearance and words.

106. John sometimes specifies that he is speaking about Jesus' closest disciples— i.e., "the Twelve" (6:67, 70, 71; 20:24); however, he most often refers to Jesus' disciples simply as "the disciples" (e.g., 4:31, 33; 13:5) or "his disciples" (e.g., 2:22; 6:3, 60, 61, 66), without specifying whether he is referring to the Twelve or to the larger group of disciples. Sometimes, however, John is clearly referring to the larger group of disciples (e.g., 6:60, 66; 7:3; 8:31).

107. Not all of John the Baptist's disciples changed their allegiance (cf. Acts 19:1-7).

"apostle" in the technical sense in his Gospel,[108] and he never explicitly refers to the women as "disciples," though they are present and they believe in Jesus (11:27–28; 19:25; 20:1, 11–18);[109] (vi) the Johannine disciples stand over against the Ἰουδαῖος ("Jews")[110] who reject Jesus; (vii) little distinction is made between the various sects of Judaism; (viii) believers in Jesus are sometimes removed from the synagogue (9:22; 12:42; 16:2); (ix) Johannine discipleship is separation from the κόσμος ("world,"),[111] of which Jesus and his disciples are not a part (17:14);[112] (x) the distinction between the larger group of Jesus' followers and the Twelve emerges out of the former's negative response to Jesus' claim to be the bread of life (6:32–35); (xi) in contrast, the Twelve believe in Jesus (6:67–68); and (xii) there are secret or crypto-disciples in the Gospel (e.g., 3:1–21; 7:50–52; 24:42; 19:38).[113]

The Fourth Gospel also expresses discipleship in relational terms: (i) those who "believe" (πιστεύω)[114] Jesus are his true disciples, despite not understanding everything (cf. 4:33; 13:1–11, 37); (ii) those who "know" (γινώσκω)[115] Jesus (6:69);[116] (iii) the sheep and the good shepherd (10:4, 11, 14; cf. 10:15); (iv) the vine and the branches (15:1–17); (v) Jesus and his friends (15:14–15);[117] and (vi) Jesus and the Beloved Disciple, who is

---

108. The term appears only once in John's Gospel (John 13:16), referring generally to "one who is sent," and again in the Book of Revelation (Rev 2:2; 18:20; 21:14).

109. See Beirne, *Women and Men in the Fourth Gospel*, 1–2 on the equal treatment of women and men in John's Gospel.

110. This term appears 71 times in John (cf. Matthew [5]; Mark [7], Luke [5]).

111. This term appears 78 times in John (cf. Matthew [8]; Mark [3], Luke-Acts [3]).

112. See Borchert, *John 12–21*, 199–200; and Segovia, "Discipleship in the Fourth Gospel," 76–102 on the divergence between Jesus' disciples and the world.

113. Hillmer, "Discipleship in the Johannine Tradition," 78–84.

114. "πιστεύω," BDAG, 816–18. John uses πιστεύω over one hundred times in his Gospel.

115. "γινώσκω," BDAG, 199–200. John utilizes γινώσκω approximately one hundred and seven times in his Gospel, and he climactically expresses "knowing," as with "believing," in terms of eternal life (17:3).

116. See Morris, *John*, 344–45 on John's use of the emphatic "we" and the perfect tense of "believe" and "know" in John 6:69, giving Peter's expression full force.

117. See Borchert, *John 12–21*, 149–50 on John's use of φίλος ("friend") to spell out the implications of such friendship, which has the same obedience requirements as those for abiding in his love (ἀγάπη, 15:10).

regarded as John's ideal disciple (e.g., 18:15–16; 19:26; 20:3–10; 21:20–24; cf. 19:35).[118]

The Fourth Gospel also speaks of discipleship in action terms.[119] The disciple is to: (i) "follow" (ἀκολουθέω) Jesus; (ii) "bear fruit" (φέρω καρπός, 15:2, 4, 5, 8, 16; cf. 12:24); (iii) "love one another" (ἀγαπάω ἀλλήλων, 13:34, 35; 15:12, 17)];[120] (iv) "serve" others (e.g., 21:15, 16, 17); (v) "keep" (τηρέω) Jesus' commands, words, etc. (e.g., 8:51, 52; 14:15, 21, 23, 24; 15:10); and (vi) "abide" or "remain" (μένω) in Jesus and in his love (e.g., 15:4–10).[121]

On discipleship in the Johannine Letters (1–3 John), Hillmer notes that the author does not emphasize the actions of the immediate followers of Jesus; rather, he draws attention to the responsibilities of the members of the Johannine community, who are to: (i) "love one another" (e.g., 1 John 3:11, 23; 4:7, 11, 12; 2 John 5; cf. 1 John 2:9, 11; 3:15; 4:40); [122] (ii) "know the truth" (e.g., 1 John 2:21; cf. 2:4; 3:18–19; 1 John 4:6); (iii) "keep [τηρέω] Jesus' commandments" (e.g., 1 John 2:3, 4,5; 3:22, 24; 5:3);[123] and (iv) "abide in Jesus" (e.g., 1 John 2:6, 10, 24, 27, 28; 3:6; 2 John 2, 9). The followers of Christ are called "children" (τέκνον; 1 John 3:1, 2, 10; 5:2; 2 John 1, 4, 13; 3 John 4) and "little children" (τεκνίον; 1 John 2:1, 12, 21, 28; 3:7, 18; 4:4; 5:21),[124] and members of Johannine community are referred

---

118. Hillmer, "Discipleship in the Johannine Tradition," 84–88; Zhakevich, "Compensatory Benefits of Discipleship," 1–2 groups certain Johannine themes that may be viewed as compensatory benefits under three overarching umbrellas: (i) membership in the divine family; (ii) abiding with the Father, Son, and Spirit; and (iii) royal friendship with Jesus.

119. Hillmer, "Discipleship in the Johannine Tradition," 89–93.

120. See Baffes, "Christology and Discipleship in John 7," 144–50 on disciples being obedient followers of Jesus acting in love.

121. For more on the language of "abiding" in John, see Brosend, "Abiding Love," 565; and James, *Salvation and Discipleship Continuum in Johannine Literature*, 134–35.

122. Yarbrough, *1–3 John*, 103 comments that "the nature of John's message that God is light (1:5) carries with it the corollary command to love, which is both old and new (2:7–8).

123. See Brown, *Epistles of John*, 250–51 on the variation between singular and plural ("commandment[s]") not being of clear theological significance, and the alternation of number (like variety of tense) being, in part, a stylistic device; cf. Brown, *John (XIII–XXI)*, 638, 641.

124. For additional information on the significance of the three words for "children"—τεκνίον, παιδίον, παῖς—in the Johannine letters, see Akin, *1–3 John*, 75 n. 138; and Marshall, *Epistles of John*, 115.

to as "brothers" (ἀδελφός; 1 John 2:9, 10, 11; 3:10, 13; 3 John 3, 5, 10).[125] The term "disciple" (μαθητής) is absent from the Johannine Letters.

On discipleship in the Revelation of John, David Aune focuses on three groups on text that address the theme: 5:1–14; 14:1–5; 12:1–17.[126] Revelation 14:1–5 refers to 144,000 persons who have the name of the Lamb and of God written on their foreheads. They "*follow* [ἀκολουθέω] the Lamb wherever he goes" (14:4b),[127] and are described as "first fruits" (ἀπαρχή)[128] and "blameless" (ἄμωμος, 14:4c–5).[129] Aune summarizes that: (i) Christians who have given their allegiance to God and are marked with the name of God and of Lamb on their foreheads "follow the Lamb wherever he goes"; (ii) they are willing to suffer and die as a consequence of faithfulness to God and the Lamb; and (iii) their designations as "first fruits" for God and the Lamb and "blameless" underscore their sacrificial calling.[130]

In Revelation 5, the universal quest for someone who is worthy to open the scroll that is sealed with seven seals concludes with the introduction of "the Lion of the tribe of Judah" by one of the twenty-four elders (5:5).[131] The reason the Lamb alone is worthy to open the sealed scroll is that he was slain, ransoming God's people (5:9). Jesus' death, under the metaphor of the Lamb, is understood as his victory.[132] Aune concludes that: (i) the concept of victory in the Apocalypse refers to triumph that is accomplished through apparent defeat and death; (ii) the exalted Jesus is paradigmatic for Christian disciples; (iii) Jesus' victory is based on his

---

125. For Akin, 1–3 *John*, 98, "The term ἀδελφός, translated 'brother,' could mean any neighbor, in line with the command of Lev 19:18 ... From the context [of 1 John 2:9, 10, 11] it may be better to conclude that John is here referring only to those who have believed that Jesus is the Christ, the Son of God."

126. Aune, "Following the Lamb," 283–84.

127. "This number [144,000] is symbolic of perfection and appears to be in obvious contrast to 666, the number of the second monster in chapter 13, the figure of imperfection in all three digits" (Ford, *Revelation*, 233); see Fiorenza, "The Followers of the Lamb," 144–65 on possible identities of the 144,000.

128. "ἀπαρχή," BDAG, 98.

129. "ἄμωμος," BDAG, 56.

130. Aune, "Following the Lamb," 283.

131. This epithet is based on Gen 49:9, a passage which later Judaism applied to the Messiah (Ford, *Revelation*, 85–86).

132. Aune, "Following the Lamb," 278.

sacrificial death; and (iv) the one who overcomes as he overcame will sit with him on his throne (3:21).[133]

In Revelation 12, the dragon (i.e., the serpent or the devil) is enraged because his attempts to destroy the woman (i.e., the people of God) have been unsuccessful. He turns his anger toward the woman's offspring (i.e., Christians), "who keep [τηρέω] the commandments of God and hold to the testimony of Jesus" (12:17; cf. 3:10; 14:12).[134] For Aune: (i) John's view of a Christian disciple is one who obeys the God's commands and bears witness to the salvific significance of Jesus; (ii) there is no divergence between law and grace in the Johannine Apocalypse; and (iii) obedience to God's will (mediated by Torah) complements the demands of faith in Christ.[135]

Johannine vis-à-vis Matthean Discipleship

On the key points of similarity and dissimilarity between Matthean and Johannine discipleship, I observe that: (i) in both sets of literature, Jesus calls persons to follow him as his disciples (e.g., John 1:43; 21:19, 22; cf. Matt 4:19; 8:22; 9:9; 16:24);[136] (ii) Jesus' disciples follow their master (John 1:37, 38, 40; 8:12; 10:27; 12:26; Rev 14:4;[137] cf. Matt 4:20, 22; 8:19; 9:9; 10:38; 19:21), observing his earthly ministry from close range; (iii) some of the Johannine Jesus' disciples fall away for lack of understanding (e.g., John 6:51–52, 59–61, 66);[138] and (iv) John alone records Jesus' washing his disciples' feet (John 13:5–20); however, having washed their

---

133. Aune, "Following the Lamb," 283.

134. See Ford, *Revelation*, 193 on the meaning of "the rest of her children" (Rev 12:17) and the "son" (12:5).

135. Aune, "Following the Lamb," 283.

136. John, however, makes no reference to the notion of "catching or fishing for people" as the disciples' new occupation (cf. Matt 4:19; Mark 1:17; Luke 5:10), nor does he explicitly refer to the idea of the disciples leaving everything to follow Jesus (cf. Matt 4:20, 22; 19:27; Mark 10:8; Luke 5:11, 28) and their immediacy of doing so (cf. Matt 4:20, 22; 9:9; Mark 1:18; Luke 18:43).

137. Rev 14:1–5 refer to "the one hundred and forty-four thousand who had been purchased from the earth," following the Lamb wherever he goes.

138. The Matthean Jesus, too, has to address the issue of disciples turning away from him, having first received his message (cf. the Parable of the Sower [Matt 13:3–9] and the Sower Explained [Matt 13:10–23]; Jesus disciples' temporary flight from him [26:56]; Peter's denial of Jesus [26:75]; and Judas's betrayal of and permanent separation from Jesus [Matt 10:4; 26:14–16, 25, 47–50; 27:3, 5]).

feet, Jesus reminds them to do the same to one another (John 13:12-17), which is a fundamental Matthean theme (Matt 10:24; cf. 23:8-12).

The general broadening of discipleship terminology in the Johannine literature is a significant point of development between Matthean and Johannine discipleship. John, like Matthew, uses μαθητής most often to refer to all disciples. On occasion, he refers to Jesus' closest disciples as "the Twelve" (John 6:67, 70, 71; 20:24; cf. Matt 10:2; 24:16, 47); however, he often refers to them as "the disciples" (e.g., John 4:31, 33; 13:5; 21:1, 4, 12, 14) or "his disciples" (e.g., John 2:22; 6:3, 60, 61, 66), without specifying the disciples to whom he is referring. John does not use μαθητής outside of his Gospel; instead, he utilizes such terms as τέκνον ("spiritual child"; e.g., John 1:12; 1 John 3:1; 2 John 1; 3 John 4; Rev 2:23), τεκνίον ("little child"; e.g., John 13:33; 1 John 2:1, 12), and ἀδελφός ("brother"; e.g., John 20:17; 1 John 2:9, 10, 11; 3 John 3; Rev 1:9; 12:10), in which cases he is referring to members of the community of believers in Jesus Christ rather than to his immediate followers.

The Pauline Epistles

Discipleship Terminology in the Pauline Epistles

Paul does not use the terms μαθητεύω ("be a disciple; make a disciple") and μαθητής ("disciple, follower, learner") in the Pauline Epistles, although he uses μανθάνω ("learn"); however, the following examination of Pauline discipleship terms shows that some are familiar to Matthew in various degrees: (i) ἅγιος—reference to a Christian as a "saint or holy one" (e.g., Rom 1:7; 8:27; 12:13; 15:25; 1 Cor 1:2; 6:1, 2; 2 Cor 1:1; 8:4; 9:1; Eph 1:1, 15, 18; 2:19; 3:8; Phil 1:1; 4:21; Col 1:2, 4; 1 Thess 3:13; 2 Thess 1:10; 1 Tim 5:10; Phlm 5, 7);[139] (ii) ἀδελφή—"a female who shares beliefs of the reference person or of others in a community of faith" (Rom 16:1; 1 Cor 7:15; 9:5; Phlm 2; cf. Matt 12:50);[140] (iii) ἀδελφός—person viewed as a brother in terms of a close affinity ("one who holds Christian beliefs"; e.g., Rom 1:13; 7:1, 4; 8:12; 1 Cor 1:1, 10, 11, 26; 2:1; 2 Cor 1:1, 8; 2:13; 8:1; Gal 1:2, 11; 3:15; Eph 6:21, 23; Phil 1:12, 14; 2:25; 3:1; Col 1:1, 2; 1 Thess 1:4; 2:1; 2 Thess 1:3; 2:1; 1 Tim 4:6; 5:1; 6:2; 2 Tim 4:21; Phlm 1, 7, 16,

---

139. "ἅγιος," BDAG, 10-11.
140. "ἀδελφός," BDAG, 18.

20);¹⁴¹; (iv) ἀμέμπτως—used especially in the Greco-Roman world of people of extraordinary civic consciousness, *blamelessly* (1 Thess 2:10; 3:13 v.l.¹⁴²; 5:23);¹⁴³ (v) ἄμωμος—being without fault and therefore morally blameless, *blameless* (i.e., "of the Christian community," Eph 1:4; 5:27; Phil 2:15; Col 1:22);¹⁴⁴ (vi) ἀξίως—worthily, in a manner worthy of, suitably (i.e., "of God, the saints, the gospel, [holy] calling," Rom 16:2; Eph 4:1; Phil 1:27; Col 1:10; 1 Thess 2:12);¹⁴⁵ (vii) ἀπόστολος—of messengers without extraordinary status, *delegate, envoy, messenger* (i.e., "of messengers of the churches," 2 Cor 8:23; Phil 2:25); of messengers with extraordinary status (i.e., "of prophets" [Eph 3:5]; "of a group of highly honored believers with a special function as God's envoys" [e.g., Rom 1:1; 11:13; 1 Cor 1:1; 4:9; 9:1; 2 Cor 1:1; 11:5; Gal 1:1, 17, 19; Eph 1:1; 2:20; 4:11; Col 1:1; 1 Thess 2:6; 1 Tim 1:1; 2:7; 2 Tim 1:1, 11; Titus 1:1]);¹⁴⁶ (viii) ἀρνέομαι—disclaim association with a person or event ("repudiate Christ" [2 Tim 2:12a; cf. Matt 10:33a; 26:70, 72]; "repudiate God" [Titus 1:16]; "of Christ's repudiation" [2 Tim 2:12b]; "repudiate the Christian faith" [1 Tim 5:8]; "repudiate oneself" [2 Tim 2:13]); refuse to pay attention to, *disregard, renounce* (i.e., "the function of piety" [3 Tim 3:5]; "impiety" [Titus 2:12]);¹⁴⁷ (ix) ἄτακτος—pertaining to being out of step and going one's own way, *disorderly, insubordinate* (1 Thess 5:14);¹⁴⁸ (x) διάκονος—reference to "one who serves as an intermediary in a transaction—i.e., as a servant/agent of God [in various capacities]" (e.g., Rom 15:8; 16:1; 1 Cor 3:5; 2 Cor 3:6; 6:4; Eph 3:7; 6:21; Col 1:7, 23, 25; 4:7) and "one who gets something done at the behest of a superior—i.e., *assistant, deacon*" (Phil 1:1; 1 Tim 3:8, 12; 4:6);¹⁴⁹ (xi) δικαίως—pertaining to quality of character, thought, or behavior, *correctly, justly, uprightly* (1 Cor 15:34; 1 Thess 2:10; Titus 2:12);¹⁵⁰ (xii) δοκιμή—the experience of going through

---

141. "ἀδελφός," BDAG, 18–19.

142. For a description of this textual variant, see Nestle and Nestle, *NTG Apparatus Criticus*, 626.

143. "ἀμέμπτως," BDAG, 53.

144. "ἄμωμος," BDAG, 56.

145. "ἀξίως," BDAG, 94.

146. "ἀπόστολος," BDAG, 122. Of the thirty-four occurrences of this term in Pauline writings, seventeen of them relate to the author himself.

147. "ἀρνέομαι," BDAG, 132–33.

148. "ἄτακτος," BDAG, 148.

149. "διάκονος," BDAG, 241.

150. "δικαίως," BDAG, 250.

a test with special reference to the result, *standing a test, character* (Rom 5:4ab; 2 Cor 2:9; 9:13; 13:3; Phil 2:22); a testing process, *test, ordeal* (2 Cor 8:2);[151] (xiii) δοῦλος—one who is solely committed to another ("in a pejorative sense," Rom 6:16, 17, 19, 20; 1 Cor 7:23); one who is solely committed to another ("slave of God/Christ," Rom 1:1; 1 Cor 7:22b; 2 Cor 4:5; Gal 1:10; Eph 6:6; Phil 1:1; Col 4:12; 2 Tim 2:24; Titus 1:1);[152] (xiv) ἐκκλησία—people with shared belief, *community, congregation* (i.e., "of a specific Christian group *assembly, gathering*"; e.g., Rom 16:4, 5; 1 Cor 11:18; 14:4; Col 4:15; 1 Tim 5:16; Phlm 2); "*congregation* or *church* as the totality of Christians living and meeting in a particular locality or larger geographical area" (e.g., Rom 16:1, 16; 1 Cor 1:2; 4:17; 2 Cor 1:1; 8:1; Gal 1:2, 22; Phil 4:15; 1 Thess 1:1; 2:14; 2 Thess 1:1; 1 Tim 5:16); "the global community of Christians, *(universal) church*" (e.g., Rom 16:16; 1 Cor 6:4; 10:32; Gal 1:13; Eph 1:22; 3:10, 21; Phil 3:6; Col 1:18; 1 Thess 1:1; 2:14; 2 Thess 1:4; 1 Tim 3:5, 15);[153] (xv) ἐπακολουθέω—happen as result or appropriate event in connection with something, *follow* (i.e., "pertaining to sins going after vis-à-vis before someone," 1 Tim 5:24); apply oneself to something with eager dedication, *follow after* (i.e., "devote oneself," 1 Tim 5:10);[154] (xvi) μανθάνω—gain knowledge or skill by instruction (i.e., "learn" [Rom 16:17; 1 Cor 14:31; 1 Tim 2:11; 2 Tim 3:7]; "learn from someone as a teacher" [2 Tim 3:14b; Phil 4:9]; "learn from someone" [Col 1:7; cf. Matt 11:29]; "learn something" [1 Cor 14:35]; "learn Christian teaching" [Eph 4:20; 2 Tim 3:14a]; "learn from someone's example" [1 Cor 4:6]); come to a realization, with implication of taking place less through instruction than through experience or practice, *learn, appropriate to oneself* (i.e., "practicing piety/good deeds" [1 Tim 5:4; Titus 3:14]; "contentment" [Phil 4:11]; "idleness" [1 Tim 5:13]);[155] (xvii) μιμέομαι—use as a model, *imitate, emulate, follow* (i.e., "of behavior," 2 Thess 3:7, 9);[156] (xviii) μιμητής—*imitator*, mostly used with εἶναι or γίνεσθαι (1 Cor 4:16; 11:1; Eph 5:1; 1 Thess 1:6; 2:14);[157] (xix) ὀπίσω—marker of position behind an entity that precedes, *after* (i.e., "come after/follow someone as

---

151. "δοκιμή," BDAG, 256.

152. "δοῦλος," BDAG, 259-60.

153. "ἐκκλησία," BDAG, 303-4.

154. "ἐπακολουθέω," BDAG, 358; see also Greek-English Index (ἐπακολουθέω) in Louw and Nida, *Greek-English Lexicon*, 2:94.

155. "μανθάνω," BDAG, 615.

156. "μιμέομαι," BDAG, 651.

157. "μιμητής," BDAG, 652.

a disciple"; e.g., in a negative way re following Satan, 1 Tim 5:15; cf. Matt 4:19; 10:38; 16:24);[158] (xx) πείθω—be won over as the result of persuasion (i.e., "obey, follow," Rom 2:8; Gal 3:1 v.l.;[159] 5:7); be so convinced that one puts confidence in something (i.e., "depend on, trust in." 2 Cor 1:9; 2:3; Gal 5:10; 2 Thess 3:4; Phil 1:14; 2:24; 3:3, 4; Phlm 21); "be convinced, sure, certain" (Rom 2:19; 2 Cor 10:7; Phil 1:6)]; to attain certainty in reference to something, *be convinced, certain* (i.e., "be sure of a thing," Rom 8:38; 14:14; 15:14; 2 Tim 1:5, 12);[160] (xxi) περιπατέω—conduct one's life, *comport oneself, behave, live* as habit of conduct (i.e., "of 'walk of life', *go about*" [e.g., Rom 6:4; 8:4; 1 Cor 3:3; 7:17; 2 Cor 4:2; 10:2; 12:18; Gal 5:16; Eph 2:2, 10; 4:1, 17; Phil 3:17, 18; Col 1:10; 2:6; 3:7; 4:5; 1 Thess 2:12; 4:1ab, 12; 2 Thess 3:6, 11]; "rarely of physical life generally" [2 Cor 5:7; 10:3]);[161] (xxii) συμμιμητής—one who joins others as an imitator, *fellow imitator* (Phil 3:17);[162] (xxiii) σύνδουλος—a subordinate in total obedience to a ruler ("a fellow slave of the heavenly Lord," Col 1:7; 4:7);[163] (xxiv) συνεργός—"a helper or fellow worker" (Rom 16:3, 9, 21; 1 Cor 3:9; 2 Cor 1:24; 8:23; Phil 2:25; 4:3; Col 4:11; 1 Thess 3:2; Phlm 1, 24);[164] (xxv) συστρατιώτης—figurative reference to one who devotes himself to the service of the gospel as "a fellow soldier" (Phil 2:25; Phlm 2);[165] (xxvi) τεκνίον—"little child," a diminutive of τέκνον, which refers to those who comprise the churches of Galatia as his "spiritual children" (Gal 4:19 v.l.);[166] (xxvii) τέκνον—one who is dear to another but without genetic relationship and without distinction in age, *child* (i.e., "of a spiritual child in relation to master, apostle, or teacher" [1 Cor 4:14, 17; 2 Cor 6:13; Gal 4:19; 1 Tim 1:2, 18; 2 Tim 1:2; 2:1; Titus 1:4; Phlm 10]; "of the members of a congregation" [Gal 4:31]); one who has the characteristics of another being, *child* (i.e., "children of God," Rom 8:16, 17, 21; 9:7, 8b; Eph 5:1;

---

158. "ὀπίσω," BDAG, 716.

159. For comments regarding this textual variant, see Comfort, *Text and Translation Commentary*, 564.

160. "πείθω," BDAG, 791–92; see also Greek-English Index (πείθω) in Louw and Nida, *Greek-English Lexicon*, 2:191.

161. "περιπατέω," BDAG, 803.

162. "συμμιμητής," BDAG, 958.

163. "σύνδουλος," BDAG, 996–97.

164. "συνεργός," BDAG, 969.

165. "συστρατιώτης," BDAG, 969.

166. For comments regarding this textual variant, see Comfort, *Text and Translation Commentary*, 569.

Phil 2:15); class of persons with a specific characteristic, *children of* (i.e., "used with abstract terms," Eph 2:3; 5:8; cf. Matt 11:19 v.l.[167]);[168] (xxviii) τύπος—kind, class, or thing that suggests a model or pattern, *form, figure, pattern* (i.e., "pattern of teaching," Rom 6:17); archetype serving as a model, *type, pattern, model* (i.e., "in the moral life *example, pattern*" [Phil 3:17; 1 Thess 1:17; 2 Thess 3:9; 1 Tim 4:12; Titus 2:7]; "of the *types* given by God" [1 Cor 10:6, 11 v.l.[169]]);[170] (xxix) υἱός—person related or closely associated as if by ties of sonship, *son* (i.e., "of one whose identity is defined in terms of a relationship with a person or thing"; e.g., sons of God, Rom 8:14, 19; 9:26; 2 Cor 6:18; Eph 2:2; 5:6; Gal 3:7, 26; 4:6, 7ab; Col 3:6; 1 Thess 5:5; 2 Thess 2:3; cf. Matt 5:9, 45; 8:12; 13:38b);[171] (xxx) φιλαδελφία—*love of brother or sister* (Rom 12:10; 1 Thess 4:9).[172]

Pattern of Discipleship in the Pauline Epistles

ROMANS: BECOMING LIKE GOD THROUGH CHRIST

L. Ann Jervis reckons that Paul does not speak of discipleship either in the Gospels' sense or in sense of philosophical schools in his Letter to the Romans;[173] rather, she examines discipleship in that NT book using the

---

167. For comments regarding this textual variant, see Comfort, *Text and Translation Commentary*, 33; and Omanson and Metzger, *Textual Guide to the Greek New Testament*, 16.

168. "τέκνον," BDAG, 994–95.

169. For comments regarding this textual variant, see Comfort, *Text and Translation Commentary*, 507.

170. "τύπος," BDAG, 1019–20.

171. "υἱός," BDAG, 1024–27.

172. "φιλαδελφία," BDAG, 1055.

173. "Paul never refers to believers in Jesus Christ as either disciples or followers of Jesus—and his primary characterization of them is as those who have faith! In Romans Paul refers to believers in Christ not as disciples but as 'holy,' 'beloved,' 'called,' 'elect,' 'justified,' 'belonging to Jesus Christ,' 'those who have been baptized into Christ's death,' 'those who are under grace,' 'slaves of God,' 'those free from sin and death,' 'sons and daughters of God,' 'children of God,' 'brothers and sisters of Christ,' 'heirs of God,' 'heirs with Christ,' 'in Christ,' 'in the Spirit,' 'those who are saved,' etc. Furthermore, he does not speak of believers as learners, nor are his churches directly analogous to the ancient philosophical schools" (Meeks, *First Urban Christians*, 84); see also Jervis, "Discipleship in Romans," 143.

paradigm that fits the book's and ancient world's understanding of the goal of discipleship—i.e., to achieve likeness to God.[174]

According to Jervis, Paul focuses the believers' attention on Christ's death and resurrection without making reference to following the pattern of Jesus' earthly life. At times, Paul talks about Jesus' death and resurrection as facts to which the faithful agree (e.g., Rom 1:4; 4:24); at other times, he alludes to it as the basis for ethical behavior (14:15). Paul's focus is "Jesus as 'the Son of God' and 'the Christ,' whose death and resurrection have defeated sin and death and so provide salvation," and he interprets Jesus' death and resurrection as the means by which a person becomes like God, which happens by: (i) conformity to Christ (e.g., 3:24–35; 5:19; 6:3, 4, 5, 6, 8–11, 14; 8:1–4, 10–11; 12:5, 6–8; 13:14; 15:5; 16:2, 8, 11, 12, 13), which means that "believers are privileged to share in Jesus' death and to hope for participation in his resurrection, and so a godlike (eternal) life";[175] and by (ii) the manifestation of God's righteousness received by faith (1:17; 3:21–26; 5:9, 17; 6:19; 10:3, 4), which is not attained through human endeavor, but it is possible only through God by submitting to the "righteousness of God" (10:3).[176]

1–2 Corinthians: "Imitate Me, Just as I Imitate Christ"

Linda L. Belleville agrees that the traditional discipleship language of μαθητής and μαθητεύω is scarce in the Pauline Letters. Yet, she recognizes that the theme of discipleship is present in virtually every letter of Paul as he presents Jesus, himself, and his colleagues as models of discipleship. This theme comes to the fore in the Corinthian correspondence in Paul's calls to imitate himself and Christ in 1 Corinthians and in examples of discipleship throughout 2 Corinthians.[177]

---

174. Jervis, "Discipleship in Romans," 144 argues that "the ancient world . . . considered that the purpose of discipleship was to achieve likeness to God," and that "Paul's presentation of the significance of faith in the death and resurrection of Jesus Christ reflects an awareness of and response to just such an understanding, which pervaded the world of his day."

175. Jervis, "Discipleship in Romans," 151–55.

176. Jervis, "Discipleship in Romans," 155–61; see also Wild, "Discipleship in the Letter to the Ephesians," 127–43, esp. 133–36, who explores the theme of discipleship in Paul's letter to the Ephesians in terms of putting on "the new humanity" created after the likeness of God in true righteousness and holiness (Eph 4:24). This new humanity is characterized by justice and holiness, which is proper first and foremost to God.

177. Belleville, "Imitate Me," 120–42. On discipleship in 2 Corinthians, see

Paul exhorts his converts, "Be *imitators* [μιμητής] of me" (1 Cor 4:16; cf. 11:1),[178] the approach to which might include: (i) the cultivation of personal virtues; (ii) the relational qualities of peace, harmony, and unity; and (iii) a life of suffering.[179] Belleville suggests that "the Pauline exemplar is to be found in a common core of ethical teachings and norms of Christian practice that were routinely passed along to new congregations."[180] Paul's appeal "Be imitators of me, just as I also am of Christ" (11:1) suggests that: (i) for Paul, discipleship is part and parcel of evangelization; (ii) he shares not only the gospel with his converts, but his very self (1 Thess 2:8); and (iii) he views his life as being so bound up with the gospel that to question his conduct is to question the very gospel that he preaches. In summary, according to Belleville, imitating Christ means setting aside personal rights and privileges for the good of others (cf. Rom 15:2-3).[181]

Belleville notes three models of discipleship in 2 Corinthians. First, she observes Jesus' example of discipleship: (i) his grace (2 Cor 8:9);[182] (ii) his love (5:14); (iii) his gentleness and forbearance (10:1); (iv) his ministerial hardships (e.g., 1:5; 4:10; 13:4).[183] Second, Belleville recognizes Paul's example of discipleship: (i) his leadership style as a "coworker" (συνεργός, 1:24); (ii) his humility (4:5);[184] (iii) his self-denial (4:2; 10:1, 10; 11:7-9,

---

Thompson, "Authentic Discipleship," 1-6 who contends that Paul's second letter to the Corinthians is devoted to the question: Who is an authentic disciple of Jesus Christ? For Paul, Christian discipleship is a transformation process into Christ's likeness, the test of which is the test of the cross (1 Cor 1:18-25).

178. Fitzmyer, *First Corinthians*, 222-23 writes, "[Paul] is giving paternal advice as he urges the Corinthians to regard him as a model for their Christian mode of life"; other scholars recognize the "father-child" imitation imagery in Paul's writing, including Robertson and Plummer, *First Corinthians*, 90; Fee, *First Corinthians*, 186-88; Schnabel, *Der erste Brief des Paulus an die Korinther*, 261-63.

179. See also Fernando, "To Serve Is to Suffer," 30-33 on the NT definition of working for Christ being closely related to suffering because of that work; and Tanner, "The Cost of Discipleship: Losing One's Life for Jesus' Sake," *JETS* 56.1 (2013): 43-61 on Jesus' definition of the terms of discipleship.

180. Belleville, "Imitate Me" 121-24; see Katos, "Holy Imitation," 30-33 on Paul's statement that Corinthian Christians take him as their model (1 Cor 4:16) not creating unease in his audience's mind, despite being uncomfortable to modern ears.

181. Belleville, "Imitate Me," 124-26.

182. See Plummer, *Second Corinthians.*, 240-41 on Christ's supreme example of benevolence—i.e., being willing to give up a much to help others.

183. Belleville, "Imitate Me," 127-37.

184. Others flaunt their credentials (3:1-3), heritage (11:21-22), eloquence

28–29; 12:15).¹⁸⁵ Finally, there is the Macedonian churches' example of discipleship (8:1–5)—i.e., their generosity (8:2–3), willingness (8:4), and commitment to God (8:5).¹⁸⁶

Philippians: The Imitation of Christ

Gerald F. Hawthorne summarizes that the pattern of discipleship in Philippians has to do with imitating Christ, who is the model and pattern of authentic living. Christian disciples are to carry out their lives in conformity to the attitude and actions of Christ that are depicted in the Christ hymn (Phil 2:6–11). The whole of Christ's life, including his death, was life and death spent for benefit of others.¹⁸⁷

According to Hawthorne, the concept of discipleship has had to be reinterpreted over the course of time, and Christian vocabulary replaced with more appropriate terminology. Paul, for example, alerts his readers that to be Jesus' disciple in the post-resurrection era does not necessarily mean: (i) leaving home and employment and going to a distant land with the gospel, (ii) rigid adherence to an established set of rules and regulations, and (iii) complying unquestioningly to a certain codified belief system. "Discipleship in Philippians is, in fact, imitating the model of life exemplified by Jesus himself."¹⁸⁸

Paul refers to his Philippian readers as "saints in Christ" (Phil 1:1), and he urges them to become disciples of Christ by imitating Christ's thoughts and actions (2:5). This is consistent with the idea that ancient moral teachers urged students to pattern their lives after extraordinary people who modeled virtue and goodness. And for this reason, the apostle Paul makes Christ the supreme model for one's attitude towards life

---

(10:10), knowledge (11:6), and spirituality (12:1, 12).

185. Belleville, "Imitate Me," 137–39. Paul never abandons the model of servant (cf. 2 Cor 4:5), unlike the newly arrived ministers (11:20); rather, his relationship with them is graciously paternal (6:13; 11:2; 12:14–15) (Barnett, *Second Corinthians*, 115–16).

186. Belleville, "Imitate Me," 139; Paul's reference to the Macedonian churches as an example of giving might suggest that the Corinthians are negligent in following through on their commitment. Later, Paul mentions first the contributions from Macedonia, and only secondly those from Achaia (including Corinth, Rom 15:26) (Furnish, *Second Corinthians*, 413–14).

187. Hawthorne, "Imitation of Christ," 163–79.

188. Hawthorne, "Imitation of Christ," 165–66.

and conduct in day-to-day living, 2:5–11 being his strongest appeal to his readers to imitate Christ.[189]

Hawthorne believes that Paul's Letter to the Philippians illustrates the meaning of imitating Christ by employing several examples. First, Paul presents his own life to the Philippians as one copied from life of Jesus. He refers to himself as a "slave [δοῦλος] of Christ Jesus" (1:1; cf. 2:6–7),[190] paralleling the Christ hymn (2:5–11) with his former life of privilege and achievements (3:5–6), considering them as nothing, having given them up (3:7–8). In antiquity, the lifestyles of great teachers were as important as what they taught.[191] Second, Paul illustrates the idea of imitating Christ by utilizing the examples of Timothy (2:19–24)[192] and Epaphroditus (2:25–30).[193] Third, there is the case of Euodia and Syntyche, who, despite their imitation of Christ being less than ideal, had "struggled beside" him as his "coworkers" (συνεργός).[194] Finally, Paul exhorts the Philippians to imitate "us"—i.e., Paul, Timothy, and Epaphroditus (3:17; cf. 2 Thess 3:9; 1 Tim 4:12; Titus 2:7). He knows that he and his coworkers had been continually patterning their own lives after Christ (cf. 1 Cor 11:1; 1 Thess 1:6; 2 Thess 3:7).[195]

189. Hawthorne, "Imitation of Christ," 166–67.

190. Fee, *Philippians*, 62–63 explains that the phrase, "slaves [*douloi*] of Christ Jesus," anticipates a significant motif of the letter. In light of Paul and Timothy being "slaves of Christ Jesus," everything concerning them is "in, of, by, and for" Christ Jesus.

191. Hawthorne, "Imitation of Christ," 172–74.

192. The Philippians know of Timothy's "proven worth" (δοκιμήν, Phil 2:22); this noun is used exclusively by Paul and it embraces the ideas of "a testing process" and "the experience of going through a test with special reference to the result" (Rom 5:4ab; 2 Cor 2:9; 8:2; 9:13; 13:3) (Hawthorne, *Philippians*, 155–56); see "δοκιμή," BDAG, 256.

193. Paul uses ἀδελφόν ("brother"), συνεργόν ("fellow worker"), συστρατιώτην ("fellow soldier") to describe Epaphroditus (Phil 2:25). Together they show the intensity of Paul's feeling for his coworker (Hawthorne, *Philippians*, 162–63).

194. Hawthorne, "Imitation of Christ," 175–76.

195. Paul is aware of his potential to fail (1 Cor 9:27), lack of "perfection," and struggle to attain it (Phil 3:12–14). However, confident that his manner of life (e.g., self-renunciation, humility, and service to others) and that his presuppositions about God are correct, he is unafraid to present himself as a model for others to follow (Hawthorne, *Philippians*, 219).

Colossians: "Christ in You, the Hope of Glory"

Michael P. Knowles contends that discipleship in Paul's letter to the Colossians demands a choice between competing visions of reality, and that Paul argues for a christocentric vision of the entire created order, wherein Christ is the focus of all human thought and experience—i.e., the foundation of reality itself.[196]

The opening thanksgiving section of the letter (Col 1:3–14) sets out the relational dimensions of Christian discipleship: (i) personal interest in lives of the addressees (1:3–6); (ii) a sense of responsibility for their growth in faith, obedience, and good works (1:7–10); and (iii) a common allegiance between the apostle and the believers to "our Lord." Additionally, Paul identifies certain basic features of Christian discipleship—e.g., faith in Christ Jesus and the believer's connection to a corporate body (1:4). He prays they will "walk in a manner worthy of the Lord" (1:10b–12), and he sees himself as playing a critical role in the ongoing discipling of the addressees (1:28).[197]

Paul explores the christological foundations of discipleship in the confessional section of the letter (1:15–20): (i) God has been made fully known through Jesus; (ii) through him God reconciled to himself all things (1:20); (iii) redemption in Christ orients believers to the true nature and purpose of universe; (iv) the church represents God's intensions for the entire created order; and (v) followers of Jesus become conformed to Christ and to God whom Christ reveals.[198]

The apostle addresses two competing visions of discipleship in 2:8–19: one based on philosophy and empty deception, according to the tradition of men and the elementary principles of the world; the other that is according to Christ (2:8). Paul strives to reestablish a vision of discipleship that is rooted in the transcendent identity, authority, and power of the risen Christ.[199] He emphasizes the completeness of salvation in Christ (2:9–10), and he provides the examples of circumcision, baptism, legal victory, and triumphal procession to explain how conformation to

---

196. Knowles, "Discipleship in Colossians," 180–202.
197. Knowles, "Discipleship in Colossians," 181–84.
198. Knowles, "Discipleship in Colossians," 185–87.
199. Bruce, *Colossians, Philemon, and Ephesians*, 100 comments that "the form of teaching which was gaining currency at Colossae was something which belonged to a pre-Christian stage of experience; therefore, whatever its precise nature might be, to accept it now would be a mark of spiritual retrogression."

Christ takes place (2:11–15). For Paul, the true foundation of discipleship is not based on strict observance and pious endeavor but on identification with what Christ has accomplished.[200]

Paul proceeds to explain discipleship as death and rebirth with Christ (2:20–3:17),[201] and he concludes his letter with a household code and greetings that showcase discipleship in the Christian community (3:18–4:18): (i) not advocating social revolution (4:5–6) but recommending the transformation of societal structures from within, and (ii) advocating that believers' conduct be shaped by the conduct and character of their Lord (cf. 3:17).[202] Finally, Paul's greetings provide a glimpse into the character of the community of Christian disciples—e.g., encouraging (4:8); comforting (4:11); affirming (4:9, 13); exhorting (4:17); burden sharing (4:18; cf. 1:24); and praying for (4:2, 3, 12) one another.[203]

1 Thessalonians: "How You Must Walk to Please God"

Jeffrey A. D. Weima observes that in 1 Thessalonians Paul emphasizes holiness when he speaks about how someone ought to live as a disciple of Christ, employing such terms as: ἁγιωσύνη ("holiness," 1 Thess 3:13), ἅγιος ("holy," (3:13), ἁγιάζω ("make holy/sanctify," 5:23), δικαίως ("upright," 2:10), ἀμέμπτως ("blameless," 2:10; 5:23), and ἀξίως ("worthily," 2:12).[204] Paul's concern for holiness is most evident in 4:1–12 as he deals with specific problems that threaten the Thessalonian church, including sexual immorality and idleness (4:1–12).[205]

Paul's theme of holiness is apparent in the letter as a whole: (i) he appeals to the holy, righteous, and blameless lives of himself and his

---

200. Knowles, "Discipleship in Colossians," 187–89.

201. Knowles, "Discipleship in Colossians," 190–98; see also Thompson, *Colossians and Philemon*, 82 on the Colossians' identification as "chosen of God, holy and beloved" (Col 3:12) granting them a place within the people of God and obligating them also to live in a way "worthy of the Lord" (1:10). Because they follow Christ (2:6), they must identify with his teaching and by the pattern of his life, death, and resurrection.

202. See Thompson, *Colossians and Philemon*, 87–89 concerning the household code in Paul's letter to the Colossians being heard within multiple contexts.

203. Knowles, "Discipleship in Colossians," 198–200.

204. See "ἁγιάζω," BDAG, 9–10; "ἅγιος," BDAG, 10–11; "ἁγιωσύνη," BDAG, 11; "ἀμέμπτως," BDAG, 53; "ἀξίως," BDAG, 94; "δικαίως," BDAG, 250.

205. Weima, "Holiness and Discipleship in 1 Thessalonians," 98–119.

coworkers (2:10; cf. 1:5);²⁰⁶ (ii) he challenges the Thessalonians to walk worthy of God (2:12) and to walk honorably before non-Christians (4:1–12); (iii) he contrasts the "sons of light and sons of day" (5:5); (iv) he urges them to let holiness characterize all aspects of their lives (5:12–22); and (v) he urges God to sanctify them entirely and preserve them without blame (5:23–24).²⁰⁷

Regarding holiness in sexual conduct (4:3–8), Weima explains the historical and social context of sexual conduct and morality in the Greco-Roman world of the first century CE.²⁰⁸ Knowing the temptations faced by the young converts at Thessalonica, Paul sets out a tripartite structure in his exhortations of 4:3–8,²⁰⁹ stating that: (i) God's will for their lives is about holiness (4:3a); (ii) holiness ought to control their sexual behavior (4:3b, 4, 6a); and (iii) God has not called them for the purpose of impurity, but to holiness (4:7), and to reject holiness is to reject God (4:8).²¹⁰

Paul continues by addressing holiness in their work (4:9–12). Some of them are ἄτακτος ("disorderly, insubordinate," 5:14).²¹¹ Weima acknowledges that some scholars interpret the "disorderliness" of some in the community to be associated with "idleness" that is rooted in the "eschatological excitement" over imminent return of Christ—i.e., "since the end is near, work is a waste of time."²¹² In light of such attitudes, Paul exhorts them to exercise mutual love within the church (4:9–10a) and to

---

206. See Fee, *1–2 Thessalonians*, 78–79 on the nature of Paul's appeal in 1 Thess 2:10–12 indicating that Paul is in a "life and death" situation regarding the Thessalonians, the urgency of which is in 2:10 by Paul's use of three adverbs that emphasizes his observable behavior: (i) ὁσίως emphasizes a God-pleasing life; (ii) δικαίως emphasizes an upright life; and (iii) ἀμέμπτως accentuates observably blameless behavior.

207. Weima, "Holiness and Discipleship in 1 Thessalonians," 99–103.

208. For a detailed discussion of the historical and social context of sexual conduct and morality in the Greco-Roman world of the first century CE, see Weima, "Holiness and Discipleship in 1 Thessalonians," 104–6.

209. Fee, *1–2 Thessalonians*, 144–45 correctly observes that the opening clause in 4:3, "For this is the will of God" (4:3a), which is followed by a series of appositives (4:3b–8), serves as the "heading" for the entire paragraph.

210. Weima, "Holiness and Discipleship in 1 Thessalonians," 106–12.

211. "ἄτακτος," BDAG, 148.

212. Weima, "Holiness and Discipleship in 1 Thessalonians," 115–18; Bruce, *1–2 Thessalonians*, 89–91 comments that the missionaries (Paul, Silvanus, and Timothy) themselves had set a good example in the matter of working to earn their own living (cf. 1 Thess 4:9). "Brotherly love" (φιλαδελφία, 4:9) demands such thoughtful and industrious habits (cf. 2 Thess 3:7–10); cf. "φιλαδελφία," BDAG, 1055.

interact with each other in love, in the hope of addressing the problem of idlers (4:10b–12).

Pauline vis-à-vis Matthean Discipleship

Paul's discipleship terminology is different from Matthew's; however, they both speak to similar themes while using different language, for example: (i) leading by serving (1 Cor 10:4; cf. Matt 23:3, 11–12); (ii) not following an evil master/leader (1 Tim 5:15; cf. Matt 7:15; 24:11, 24); (iii) learning from a teacher's example (2 Tim 3:14b; Phil 4:9; 1 Cor 4:6; cf. Matt 11:29); (iv) the repercussions of *repudiating* Christ (2 Tim 2:12a; cf. Matt 10:32–33) and the avoidance of persons who *deny* godliness (2 Tim 3:5; cf. Matt 16:6, 11, 12); (v) believers in Christ being God's "children" (Rom 8:16, 17, 21; 9:7, 8b; Eph 5:1; Phil 2:15; cf. Matt 5:9); (vi) membership in the Christian community (Rom 1:13; 1 Cor 1:1; 2 Cor 13:11; cf. Matt 12:50); (vii) laboring as "fellow workers" (e.g., Rom 16:3, 9, 21) and "soldiers" (Phil 2:25; Phlm 2);[213] (viii) believers in Christ being "saints" (e.g., 1 Cor 1:2; Eph 1:1, 15, 18; 2 Thess 1:10; Phlm 5);[214] and (ix) Christians being God's "servants" (Rom 15:8; 1 Cor 7:22b; Col 1:7; 4:7; cf. Matt 10:24; 20:28).

Paul sees himself as playing a critical role in the ongoing discipling of his addressees, wanting to present them "complete in Christ" (Col 1:28). He emphasizes, *inter alia*, that Christians ought to *imitate* their disciple-maker (e.g., 1 Cor 4:16; Phil 3:17; 1 Thess 1:6–7). He describes his audience as having already begun to imitate him and his colleagues (1 Thess 1:6) and the churches of God (1 Thess 2:14), and he describes himself and his fellow workers as models whose examples his audiences are to follow (2 Thess 3:9). Matthew picks up this theme using different language. The Matthean Jesus says to his disciples, "Follow me!" (Matt 4:19; 8:22; 9:9; 19:21), and his Father says to them, "Listen to him!" (17:5). These are

---

213. The Matthean Jesus addresses this theme in his claim that his disciples are "coequals" (Matt 20:28; 23:8, 11–12) in undertaking their task of "discipling the nations" (Matt 28:19–20). The Johannine Jesus washes their feet and commands them to do the same to each other (John 13:14–15, 34–35). See also Bauer, *Gospel of the Son of God*, 204–5.

214. Paul's reference to Christians as "saints" is consistent with the Matthean Jesus' sayings that seek to hold his disciples to a standard of "exceeding righteousness" (e.g., 5:21–48; 16:6; 23:2–3). In so doing, he emphasizes that his disciples are set apart for God.

commands that imply more than Jesus' disciples simply walking behind or accompanying him and hearing his words. They embody the idea of obeying and accepting Jesus as their model.[215] The Matthean Jesus is the one in whom the Father is well pleased (3:17); therefore, since Jesus' disciples want to please the Father, they must do as Jesus does. Therefore, it is apparent that the objectives of the Matthean and Pauline modes of discipleship are very largely congruent.[216]

Other Epistles

Discipleship Terminology in the Other Epistles

The authors of the Other Epistles do not use traditional Matthean discipleship terminology; however, the following is an analysis of discipleship terms in this corpus, which includes some that are common to Matthew: (i) ἅγιος—used as a pure substantive the holy (thing, person) (i.e., "that which is holy"; e.g., the holy ones, *believers, loyal followers, saints*, Heb 6:10; 13:24; Jude 3);[217] (ii) ἀδελφή—person or thing viewed as a sister in relation to another entity, *sister* (i.e., "of a female who shares beliefs of the reference person or of others in a community of faith," Jas 2:15; cf. Matt 12:50);[218] (iii) ἀδελφός—person viewed as a brother in terms of a close affinity, *brother, fellow member, member, associate* (i.e., "one who shares beliefs"; e.g., Heb 2:11, 12, 17; 3:1; Jas 1:2, 9, 16, 19; 2:1, 5, 14, 15; 1 Pet 5:12; 2 Pet 1:10; 3:15; cf. Matt 12:50; 25:40; 28:10);[219] (iv) ἀδελφότης—group of fellow believers, *a fellowship* (1 Pet 2:17; 5:9);[220] (v) ἄμωμος—being without fault and therefore morally blameless, *blameless* (i.e., "of the

---

215. Bunch, "On Being 'just' a Follower," 64–71, esp. 65–66, describes Jesus' call to his disciples as a "calling to followership": changing their lives, helping them develop new skills, and mentoring them to become teachers.

216. I agree with Bird, "Not by Paul Alone," 98–112, esp. 112, that "Paul was not interested in creating his own party or manufacturing his own personality cult, but in serving his Lord, the Lord who saved him, the chief of sinners"; therefore, one does not have to be wary of Paul's command to imitate him because he is well aware the disciple must imitate the disciple-maker only to the extent that the disciple-maker imitates Christ (cf. 1 Cor 11:1).

217. "ἅγιος," BDAG, 10–11.

218. "ἀδελφός," BDAG, 18.

219. "ἀδελφός," BDAG, 18–19.

220. "ἀδελφότης," BDAG, 19.

Christian community," Jude 24);²²¹ (vi) ἀπόστολος—of messengers with extraordinary status, esp. of God's *messenger, envoy* (i.e., "of Christ," Heb 3:1); "of a group of highly honored believers with a special function as God's envoys" (1 Pet 1:1; 2 Pet 1:1; 3:2; Jude 17; cf. Matt 10:2)];²²² (vii) ἀρνέομαι—disclaim association with a person or event, *deny, repudiate, disown* (i.e., "of repudiating Christ," 2 Pet 2:1; Jude 4; cf. Matt 10:33a; 26:70, 72);²²³ (viii) δικαίως—pertaining to being just or right in a juridical sense, *justly, in an upright manner* (i.e., "of a judge's hearing of a case (judge) uprightly, fairly," 1 Pet 2:23);²²⁴ (ix) δοῦλος—one who is solely committed to another, *slave, subject* (i.e., "in a positive sense" [e.g., of the relationship of humans to God; Jas 1:1; 1 Pet 2:16; 2 Pet 1:1; Jude 1; cf. Matt 18:23, 26-28; 20:27; 22:3f., 6, 8, 10]; "in a pejorative sense" [2 Pet 2:19]);²²⁵ (x) ἐκκλησία—people with shared belief, *community, congregation* (i.e., "of OT Israelites *assembly, congregation*" [Heb 2:12; 12:23]; "of Christians in a specific place or area" [Jas 5:14]);²²⁶ (xi) ἐξακολουθέω—accept as authoritative determiner of thought or action, *obey, follow* (i.e., "myths," [2 Pet 1:16]; "immorality of false prophets" [2 Pet 2:2]); "imitate behavior, *follow, pursue* (i.e., "way of Balaam," 2 Pet 2:15);²²⁷ (xii) ἐπακολουθέω—use someone as a model for doing something, *follow* (i.e., "Christ's footsteps," 1 Pet 2:21);²²⁸ (xiii) μανθάνω—come to a realization, with implication of taking place less through instruction than through experience or practice, *learn, appropriate to oneself* (i.e., "through suffering," Heb 5:8);²²⁹ (xiv) μιμέομαι—use as a model, *imitate, emulate, follow* (Heb 13:7);²³⁰ (xv) μιμητής—imitator (Heb 6:12; 1 Pet 3:13 v.l.²³¹);²³² (xvi) ὀπίσω—marker of position behind an entity that precedes, *after* (someone as a disciple) (i.e., "following after the flesh," 2 Pet 2:10; Jude 7; cf.

---

221. "ἄμωμος," BDAG, 56.
222. "ἀπόστολος," BDAG, 122.
223. "ἀρνέομαι," BDAG, 132-33.
224. "δικαίως," BDAG, 250.
225. "δοῦλος," BDAG, 259-60.
226. "ἐκκλησία," BDAG, 303-4.
227. "ἐξακολουθέω," BDAG, 344.
228. "ἐπακολουθέω," BDAG, 358.
229. "μανθάνω," BDAG, 615.
230. "μιμέομαι," BDAG, 651.
231. For a description of this textual variant, see Nestle and Nestle, *NTG Apparatus Criticus*, 702.
232. "μιμητής," BDAG, 652.

Matt 4:19; 10:38; 16:24);²³³ (xvii) πείθω—be so convinced that one puts confidence in something, *depend on, trust in* (i.e., "God," Heb 2:13; cf. Matt 27:43 v.l.²³⁴); "be convinced, sue, certain" (Heb 13:18); be won over as a result of persuasion, *obey, follow* (i.e., "spiritual leaders," Heb 13:17); "re personal will," Jas 3:3); attain certainty in reference to something, *be convinced, certain* (i.e., "be convinced of something concerning someone," Heb 6:9); ²³⁵ (xviii) περιπατέω—go here and there in walking, *go about, walk around* (i.e., "generally walk, go"; e.g., re the devil, 1 Pet 5:8); conduct one's life, *comport oneself, behave, live* (i.e., "of walk of life, *go about*"; e.g., pertaining to the sphere in which one lives or ought to live, so as to be characterized by that sphere, Heb 13:9); ²³⁶ (xix) τέκνον—one who has the characteristics of another being, *child* (i.e., "of those who exhibit virtues of ancient luminaries," 1 Pet 3:6; cf. Matt 3:9); a class of persons with a specific characteristic, *children of* (i.e., "obedience" [1 Pet 1:14]; "curse" [2 Pet 2:14]);²³⁷ (xx) τύπος—an archetype serving as a model, *type, pattern, model* (i.e., "in the moral life *example, pattern*," 1 Pet 5:3);²³⁸ (xxi) υἱός—person related or closely associated as if by ties of sonship, *son* (i.e., "of a pupil or follower, or spiritual son" [Heb 12:5ab, 6, 7a, 8; 1 Pet 5:13; cf. Matt 12:27; 13:38ab]; "of one whose identity is defined in terms of a relationship with a person or thing" [e.g., *son(s) of*, Heb 2:10]);²³⁹ (xxii) Φιλαδελφία—*love of brother/sister* (Heb 13:1; 1 Pet 1:22; 2 Pet 1:7ab);²⁴⁰ and (xxiii) Χριστιανός—one who is associated with Christ, *Christ-partisan, Christian* (1 Pet 4:16).²⁴¹

---

233. "ὀπίσω," BDAG, 716.

234. For a description of this textual variant, see Nestle and Nestle, *NTG Apparatus Criticus*, 97.

235. "πείθω," BDAG, 791-92.

236. "περιπατέω," BDAG, 803.

237. "τέκνον," BDAG, 994-95.

238. "τύπος," BDAG, 1019-20.

239. "υἱός," BDAG, 1024-27.

240. "φιλαδελφία," BDAG, 1055.

241. "Χριστιανός," BDAG, 1090.

Pattern of Discipleship in the Other Epistles

HEBREWS: STANDING BEFORE THE MORAL CLAIM OF GOD

William L. Lane characterizes the Letter to the Hebrews as "a sermon on the cost of discipleship." It confronts the ultimate questions about life and death with ultimate realities. It is intended to strengthen a group of persons who live in an insecure society that provokes anxiety. In response to the culture and situation of its day, the letter addresses patterns of Christian discipleship that call for an unwavering commitment to God.[242]

The letter's addressees may have drifted from the moorings of the Christian message they have received (2:1–4); however, in reflecting on the appropriateness of the incarnation and death of Jesus Christ in 2:10–18, it becomes apparent that allegiance to Jesus is costly, for it has exposed the community to testing (2:18). They are unable to function properly because of the fear of death (2:15).[243] Jesus is portrayed as "conqueror" (2:10) and "high priest" (2:17). He identified himself with his people in order to die for them (2:9), which has opened up the way for deliverance from being in bondage to the devil and from the fear of death (2:10–16).[244]

Christians are presented in Hebrews as the people of God who, like the Israelites before them in the desert, experience the stresses of an interim existence between redemption and rest, promise, and fulfillment. They must not respond to God's voice in the same way as the desert generation (3:7—4:13), who failed to believe that God was actually present among them, directing them. The writer of Hebrews calls them to persevering discipleship (3:7–11).[245]

The writer's warning against apostasy (10:26–31) is followed by strong encouragement (10:32–35). Their past experience of responsible discipleship during times of sufferings (10:32–35) is to be the paradigm for their present situation and should strengthen their resolve. They must wait patiently with boldness and endurance for the consummation of God's redemptive plan: God will keep his promise; the eschatological

---

242. Lane, "Discipleship in Hebrews," 203–24.

243. The addressees are in danger of slipping into apostasy, of giving up their faith on account of the hardships it involves. Οἱ πειραζόμενοι are people tempted to flinch and falter under the pressure of suffering. Life is hard for them, and faith as hard if not harder; so Moffatt, *Hebrews*, 39.

244. Lane, "Discipleship in Hebrews," 204–6.

245. Lane, "Discipleship in Hebrews," 207–8.

coming of Christ is certain; however, they must be faithful amidst hardships and suffering (10:37–38; cf. Hab 2:3–4).[246]

Christians are those who have faith and preserve their souls (10:39). This necessitates a clarification of the nature of such faith, which is depicted as a quality of response to God (11:1–40). This demonstration of faith under the old covenant confirms the possibilities of faith for the Christian community, whose appropriate response of faith must be seen against the backdrop of the struggle and triumph of Christ, the "author and perfecter of faith"; therefore, they must not "grow weary and lose heart" (12:1–3).[247]

They must remember their former leaders, who spoke the word of God to them, and they are to *imitate* (μιμέομαι) their faith (13:7).[248] Finally, they must emulate Jesus himself. Just as Jesus "suffered outside the gate" (13:12), he calls them to "go out to him outside the camp, bearing his reproach" (13:13). For Lane, this appeal is an adaptation of the call to discipleship in terms of cross-bearing in the Synoptic Gospels (cf. Matt 10:38; 16:24; cf. Mark 8:34; Luke 14:27).[249] The course and goal of Jesus' life provides "the pattern for breaking loose from the grip of fear and lethargy in which every second-generation group of believers tends to live."[250]

James: Controlling the Tongue and the Wallet

For Peter H. Davids, the Letter of James has much to say about discipleship—i.e., "the shape of Christian experience"—despite its nonuse of the terms "disciple" and "discipleship."[251]

Davids makes five observations about discipleship in James. First, belief in Jesus as Lord is an important part of letter's context (1:1; 2:1; cf. 5:14–15). The letter comprises at least thirty-six parallels with Jesus'

---

246. Lane, "Discipleship in Hebrews," 208–13.

247. Lane, "Discipleship in Hebrews," 213–17.

248. For Lane, "Discipleship in Hebrews," 217–18, the reference to imitate introduces a discipleship motif despite the noun 'disciple' or the verb 'follow' not being present; Koester, *Hebrews*, 317–18 argues that "imitation" in Hebrews means not only heeding what is said by someone, but also following the pattern of that person's life.

249. See Koester, *Hebrews*, 570–71 on the options for interpreting "let us go to him outside the camp" (13:13).

250. Lane, "Discipleship in Hebrews," 218–20.

251. Davids, "Discipleship in James," 225–47.

teachings, especially those of the Sermon on the Mount. The letter appears therefore to be largely an application of the teaching of Jesus to a Jewish Christian church situation. Additionally, the letter sets out a polar contrast between the "world" and God (4:4),[252] to whom the believer is called to be committed rather than being double-minded (1:8; 4:8).[253] Second, James is not an apocalyptic writing, but the author shows apocalyptic belief in his awareness of otherworldly regions (2:9; 5:4, 6), future events (1:12; 2:5; 5:1-5, 7-8), the end of age being near (5:9), and the certainty of the reward of those who remain faithful.[254] Third, two of the letter's themes parallel important themes and concerns of the wisdom tradition—i.e., wealth and poverty, and ethics of speech. Fourth, discipleship in James is rooted in the Christian community (e.g., "my brothers" [1:2]; "conflicts within the assembly" [2:1-3; 4:1-10]). Fifth, external opposition comes from "the rich."[255]

On the discipleship of money, James does not reject material wealth outright, but he sees it as a source of danger (e.g., "illusion of permanence" [1:9-11]; "potential to cause divisions" [2:1-4]; corrupting influence [4:1-3]; causes some to forget God [4:13-17]; and blinds to the eschatological hour [5:1-6]).[256] James never refers to the rich positively, but he honors the poor (1:9; 2:5; 5:4, 6) and he explains that proper attitudes towards wealth and the poor are to shape the response of the community (e.g., "endurance amidst trials" [1:2-4; 5:7-11], "prayer" [5:13], and "sharing" [1:27; 2:14-26; 4:17]). For James, Christians ought to minimize the danger of wealth by giving it away.[257]

Concerning the "discipleship of the tongue,"[258] James perceives this member of the human body to be a potential danger (1:19-20; 3:9-12;

---

252. For additional discussion on the opposing friendships with "the world" and with God, see Johnson, "Discipleship in James," 41-61; *James*, 278-80; and Mußner, *Jakobusbrief*, 180-81 on the behaviors outlined in 4:1-3 being "adulterous," which is a form of courtship with the world.

253. Davids, "Discipleship in James," 226-27.

254. Davids, "Discipleship in James," 228-29.

255. Davids, "Discipleship in James," 226-33.

256. Davids, "Discipleship in James," 233-35.

257. Davids, "Discipleship in James," 233-36; see Johnson, *James*, 185-86, who observes that in the sayings of Jesus, "the rich" are uniformly treated harshly (e.g., Matt 19:23-24; Mark 10:25; 12:41; Luke 6:24; 12:16; 14:12; 16:19; 18:25). James continues that tradition (Jas 2:5-6; 5:1-6).

258. Davids, "Discipleship in James," 226-33.

4:11–12; 5:9)²⁵⁹ that can also be a blessing (e.g., recovering sinners [5:19–20];²⁶⁰ blessing God [3:9]; repentance [4:9]; praise [5:13]; and asking God for wisdom [1:5]). James emphasizes prayer for which the tongue is necessary (1:5–8; 4:2–3; 5:13a, 14–16). The caveat is that they are to trust God when praying to him (5:17–18).²⁶¹

1 Peter: Going to Heaven with Jesus

J. Ramsey Michaels argues that, in the NT, the journey to heaven begins when person is called to discipleship, and that 1 Peter emphasizes Christian discipleship as a journey.²⁶²

For Michaels, a believer's progress towards heaven is found in 1 Peter 1:3–9, which speaks of God giving believers new birth by raising Jesus from the dead (1:3). They look toward a salvation that is ready to be revealed at the last day (1:5), a future goal or outcome of their faith (1:9). However, they must grow up to salvation now, having "tasted the kindness of the Lord" (2:2–3). God calls them "out of darkness into his marvelous light" (2:9), and they are to see themselves as "aliens and strangers" (2:11; cf. 1:1).²⁶³

Peter's words on discipleship in 2:21–25 are at the center of his teaching. He embeds them in his advice to household servants (2:18–25), links them explicitly to life of Jesus (2:21–23), and through them he commands his audience to follow in Jesus' footsteps (2:21).²⁶⁴ Discipleship in 1 Peter involves following Jesus' example of undeserved or unjust suffering (2:22–23; cf. 3:9). The addressees of 1 Peter are probably subjected to verbal abuse (2:12; 3:16; 4:14) because of their Christian faith. As Jesus of

---

259. See Adamson, *James*, 1976), 77–78 on malicious slander (4:11), which the rabbis called "the third tongue" because it destroys "the speaker, the spoken to, and the spoken of."

260. Maier, *Brief des Jakobus*, 237–41 correctly sees an allusion to Matt 18:15–17 in James's exhortation to use the tongue to bring an erring brother back.

261. Davids, "Discipleship in James," 237–40.

262. Michaels, "Going to Heaven with Jesus," 248–68.

263. Michaels, "Going to Heaven with Jesus," 250–52.

264. See Elliott, "In His Steps," 184–209 on the exhortation in 1 Peter to follow in the steps of Jesus (2:21) demonstrating that this letter is closer to the theme of discipleship than a superficial reading of it might suggest; and Davids, 1 *Peter*, 108–10 on Christ's example implying Christian suffering.

the Gospels refuses to be drawn into a war of words with his tormentors, Peter wants Jesus' disciples to follow the example of their master.[265]

In exhorting his readers to follow Jesus' footsteps, Peter presupposes the Lord's resurrection as he concludes with "by his wounds you were healed" (2:24; cf. Isa 53:5). Jesus' resurrection becomes explicit in 3:18–22, where Peter explains that the purpose of Jesus' suffering was to "bring us to God" (3:18), the realization of which lies in the future. Furthermore, Jesus' redemptive death was "once for all" (3:18) and is not to be reenacted in the experience of Jesus' disciples, whose triumph is assured because the risen Christ is now seated at God's right hand in heaven (3:22).[266] However, although victory is assured, Peter's readers must "be on the alert" (5:8), and resist the devil (5:9) by doing good (5:6–7).[267]

Peter makes room for community in his teaching on Christian discipleship: (i) baptism is practiced (3:21); (ii) a stable household is encouraged (2:18–3:9); (iii) there exists *a fellowship* of believers (ἀδελφότης) throughout world (5:9; cf. 2:17); and (iv) love (1:22; 2:17; 4:8), hospitality (4:9), the ministry of spiritual gifts (4:10–11), acceptance of leadership responsibility (5:1–3), and mutual humility (5:5) within the community are prioritized.[268]

Discipleship in the Other Epistles vis-à-vis Matthean Discipleship

It is apparent that discipleship in the Other Epistles stands in discontinuity with Matthean discipleship in terms of their nonuse or the limited use of traditional Matthean discipleship terms. However, the terms employed by the writers of these materials and the themes that they address are consistent with Matthean discipleship principles, including: (i) the idea of *following* Jesus Christ (e.g., 2 Pet 1:16; cf. Matt 4:19; 9:9; 16:24); (ii) not following *after* the flesh, but pursuing the righteousness of God's kingdom (e.g., 2 Pet 2:10; Jude 7; cf. Matt 5:16, 48; 6:33); (iii) trusting in God (e.g., Heb 2:13; cf. Matt 6:25–33; 7:7–11) and not in ungodly spiritual leaders (e.g., Matt 16:6–12; 23:1–7); (iv) being *sons* of the heavenly Father

---

265. Michaels, "Going to Heaven with Jesus," 252–60; see Elliott, "In His Steps," 202 on Christians being given in Christ an example to follow, "not an ideal to aspire to or an achievement to ape."

266. Michaels, "Going to Heaven with Jesus," 260–61; see also Elliott, "In His Steps," 202 on the uniqueness of Christ's suffering; and Michaels, 1 *Peter*, 201–2.

267. Michaels, "Going to Heaven with Jesus," 261–63.

268. Michaels, "Going to Heaven with Jesus," 264–67.

(e.g., Heb 2:10; 12:5ab; cf. Matt 5:9, 44–45; 13:38a); (v) being children of obedience (e.g., 1 Pet 1:14; cf. Matt 1:18–25; 3:13–17; 4:1–11; 16:21–23; 26:36–46; cf. 7:21; 12:50); (vi) not denying Christ (e.g., 2 Pet 2:1; Jude 4; cf. Matt 10:33); (vii) *learning* obedience through suffering (e.g., Heb 5:8; cf. Matt 11:29); (viii) the role of the *church* in the lives of believers (e.g., Jas 5:14; cf. Matt 16:18; 18:15–20); (ix) the foundational and exemplary ministry of the *apostles* in the Christian faith (e.g., 1 Pet 1:1; 2 Pet 1:1; 3:2; Jude 17; cf. Matt 10:1–15; cf. 28:19–20); (x) the forming of believers into a community of Christian *sisters* and *brothers* whose purpose is to do the Father's will (e.g., Heb 2:11; Jas 1:2; 2:15; 1 Pet 5:12; cf. Matt 12:50); (xi) Christian disciples being *saints* who belong to God exclusively (e.g., Heb 6:10; 13:24; Jude 3; cf. Matt 5:48; 6:24; 22:37);[269] and (xii) the meaning of discipleship being "the student becoming like his teacher and the *slave* like his master" (e.g., Jas 1:1; 1 Pet 2:16; 2 Pet 1:1; Jude 1; cf. Matt 10:24–25; cf. 23:10b). As a result, Christian disciples *imitate* good models of discipleship (Heb 6:12; 13:7; 1 Pet 2:21), *comporting themselves* (Heb 13:9) according to the *pattern* (1 Pet 5:3) established by their master.

Other discipleship themes shared between Matthew and the authors of the Other Epistles include: (i) unwavering commitment to God (e.g., Heb 3:7–4:13; 10:26–31; cf. Matt 4:10; 22:37; 28:19–20); (ii) emulating Jesus, including his suffering (e.g., Heb 13:12–13; 1 Pet 2:21–25; cf. Matt 10:16–23, 24–44, 38–39; 16:24–25); (iii) good stewardship (e.g., Jas 1:9–11; 2:1–5; 4:1–3, 13–17; 5:1–6; cf. Matt 6:2–4; 10:9; 19:16–26; 25:14–30; 26:6–13); (iv) mastery of the tongue (e.g., Jas 1:19–20; 3:9–12; 4:11–12; 5:9; cf. Matt 15:1–20); (v) Christian discipleship as a journey (e.g., 1 Pet 1:3–9; 2:2–3, 11–12; cf. Matt 13:1–52); (vi) being watchful (e.g., 1 Pet 5:8; cf. Matt 24:42–43; 25:1–13; 26:36–46); and (vii) recovering an errant brother (Jas 5:19–20; cf. Matt 18:15–17).

Summary

I reserve my overall conclusion(s) regarding the meaning of μαθητεύσατε (Matt 28:19) until the next chapter of this book. However, it might be useful to provide a brief conclusion to tie together the major findings of this chapter. The Gospels of Mark, Luke, and John utilize μαθητής in

---

269. The Matthean themes of "being fully developed (like God) in a moral sense" (Matt 5:48), "service to God exclusively" (Matt 6:24), and "loving God with all one's heart, soul, and mind" (Matt 22:37; cf. Deut 6:5) collectively get to the heart of Christian disciples as "saints," being reserved for God and God's service only.

ways that are consistent with Matthew's use of the term—i.e., primarily to describe the activities of Jesus' closest adherents who follow him as their master: going from place to place, obeying his commands, observing his actions, and learning from him. Of the NT writings, only Matthew and Acts employ μαθητεύω, and they do so in the context of making a disciple of someone (Matt 28:19; Acts 14:21; cf. 2:47). The NT Epistles address discipleship themes that are similar to Matthew, but they achieve their goal with the help of alternative terminology, exchanging Matthew's μαθητεύω, μαθητής, and ἀκολουθέω for δοῦλος, ἐπακολουθέω, μιμέομαι, and μιμητής, among others. The objectives of the modes of discipleship in the NT (outside of Matthew) are largely congruent with that of Matthew. The Gospels and Acts portray to readers the character of discipleship and the process of making disciples. Paul sees himself as playing a critical role in the ongoing discipling of his addressees; he is a disciple-maker who wants to present them "complete in Christ" (Col 1:28). He and the other writers of the Epistles exhort their readers to continue to be Jesus' disciples and to replicate themselves by *being* and *following* good examples of believers in Christ (e.g., Phil 3:17; 1 Thess 1:7; 2 Thess 3:9; 1 Tim 4:12; Titus 2:7; 1 Pet 5:3).

6

Conclusion and Implications

At the beginning of this book, I made the claim that scholars have, up to the present, looked primarily to the attendant participles of μαθητεύσατε (Matt 28:19) for its meaning and have not developed and consistently upheld a line of argument that looks at the entire Gospel of Matthew for a fuller grasp of this imperative. This is not to suggest that I am inclined to the view that the participles are irrelevant for determining the overall meaning of μαθητεύσατε. Rather, I have contended that *the participles should not be viewed as the only source of meaning for this imperative*. This situation demanded that I examine whether the Matthean Jesus seeks to establish a framework in 28:16–20 that points to a fuller meaning of μαθητεύσατε that resides in the broader context of the Gospel. I have therefore argued that Matthew intends that the reader should draw the full meaning of μαθητεύσατε from the entire Gospel and should not limit the significance of the term to the sense that is supplied by one or more of its adjacent participles.

To arrive at a fuller understanding of the meaning of μαθητεύσατε, I have utilized inductive reading methods and narrative criticism to identify and examine key narrative elements of the Matthean Commission and of selected texts from the broader Gospel of Matthew. Along the way, I have investigated relevant evidence provided by the historical background of the text that could shed light on discipleship in the ancient Mediterranean world. I undertook the following major steps in my research: (i) explore relevant secondary literature from the early centuries of the Common Era to the twenty-first century thereof in order to determine how scholars have utilized the Matthean Commission (28:16–20) in their writings, and how they have interpreted μαθητεύσατε (28:19); (ii) examine 28:16–20 inductively to determine how Matthew guides his reader's understanding of μαθητεύσατε (28:19) by pointing to passages within the broader context of Matthew that illuminate the meaning of that imperative; (iii) select passages from the broader context of Matthew (1:1–28:15) to determine how those passages have contributed to the reader's interpretation of the meaning of μαθητεύσατε (28:19); and (iv) examine the discipleship terminology and patterns in the NT canon (outside the Gospel of Matthew) for the purpose of identifying any major points of similarity, difference, and development between Matthean discipleship and that of the broader NT canon. In this final chapter, I make summary judgments about the meaning of μαθητεύσατε based on inferences drawn from my analysis, and outline the implications of my research conclusions for further studies that may be required on this topic.

In my survey of literature, I have observed that scholars have utilized the Matthean Commission to write about numerous topics for a variety of reasons. However, no discernible significant effort has been given to discovering the full meaning of μαθητεύσατε (28:19a) beyond what had already been supplied by its three adjacent participles—"going," "baptizing," and "teaching." Several scholars have correctly identified that 28:16–20 is a summary of the entire Gospel of Matthew, acknowledging that: (i) several major themes come to full realization therein; and (ii) the passage is heavily reliant on what comes before. This supports the idea that earlier passages in Matthew up to the climactic 28:19 supply readers with vital information to inform their judgment about the meaning of μαθητεύσατε. Scholars speak about the meaning of μαθητεύσατε both directly and implicitly. Some exchange "make disciples of all nations" with "preach the gospel," "preach to all nations," or "preach the kingdom"; others conflate the Matthean and Markan Commissions entirely, which suggests that the meaning behind these different commands are perceived to be readily interchangeable. The majority of scholars who directly address the meaning of μαθητεύσατε suggest that its meaning is spelled out by one, or by a combination of two or more, of its adjacent participles. At the same time, some of them appear ready to embrace the idea that the rest of Matthew's Gospel has much to offer in terms of illuminating the meaning of μαθητεύσατε, but they have not followed through to fully explore their intuitive understanding of the meaning of this imperative.

From my inductive reading of 28:16–20, I have determined that the characterization of the Commission as the *climax* and/or the *summarization* of Matthew requires the reader to make judgements about the Commission vis-à-vis the entire Gospel. This requires the reader to look beyond the Commission's boundary and incorporate the broader context of Matthew to comprehend what may not be readily apparent from within its border. More specifically, I have noted that: (i) 28:16–20 prompts the reader to recall specific events from the wider Gospel and incorporate the particulars thereof into the interpretation of the Commission and its components; (ii) the repeated use of πᾶς in 28:18–20 compels the reader to interpret the Commission in the widest possible scope; therefore, the command to teach disciples to obey *all* of Jesus' commands applies to his verbal commands as well as those implied by his actions described throughout the Gospel; (iii) Matthew uses a hortatory *causation* structure in the command, "Go therefore and make disciples of all the nations," to clarify what the Matthean Jesus means by "I will make you fishers of men" (4:19); additionally, the author's use of ideological *particularization* gives rise to the understanding that the general imperative (μαθητεύσατε) may be unpacked by its adjoining participles, though not exhaustively, which requires the reader to look toward the remainder of Matthew to discover additional meaning of that imperative; and (iv) the reader is aware that the implication of broadening the universe of the Matthean Jesus' prior commands to include both verbal and nonverbal commands is that it becomes necessary to look beyond the Commission and the five great discourses of Matthew and to allow the entire life of the Matthean Jesus to be the template for making disciples.

From examining the broader context of his Gospel, I have discovered that Matthew's reader understands that "making disciples" is a process that comprises several components that are not explicitly revealed in 28:16–20, including, *inter alia*: (i) the movement of persons by God (through Jesus) from sin to salvation, which makes God the principle actor in the disciple-making process that leads to salvation, and assigns humans to the role of facilitators of the process; (ii) the emergence of persons who emulate Jesus as the model of discipleship and demonstrate, like Jesus, the resolve to obey God's will by observing all of Jesus' commands; (iii) the molding of persons into disciples whose words and actions, like Jesus', are mutually consistent; who handle the Scriptures correctly to repel the devil's advances; who unwaveringly obey the Father's will; and who understand that such obedience is the climax of worshipping God; (iv) the need to continuously seek out new disciples in the normal course of daily living, prioritizing teaching them how to reproduce themselves, and making maximum use of (familial and other) relationships and occupational skills to bring persons into Christian discipleship; (v) the disciple-maker's comprehension not only of the fundamentals of *making* a disciple, but also of the essentials of *being* a disciple—e.g., the realization that a disciple's required response to Jesus' call to follow him is immediate and ongoing obedience to him, and the recognition that Jesus' ongoing presence and authority enables the disciple to undertake the task of discipling the world; (vi) the defense and protection of new disciples against opponents who seek to destroy them; the inculcating in disciples of the ability to accurately interpret Scripture in the face of adversity and to appropriately respond to opponents of Christ and his ministry; (vii) the allowing of opportunity for new disciples to learn from difficult situations, while the disciple-maker remains watchful over them in order to recognize when they require immediate assistance; and the provision of explicit guidance to disciples about matters regarding their growth in the Christian faith; (viii) the readiness to minister to the needs of every kind of person, including those who fall outside of one's geographic, ethnic, and cultural boundaries; and (ix) the forewarning of disciples about forthcoming dangers to safeguard them against potential spiritual demise, and encouraging in these persons whom they will disciple the recognition of human vulnerabilities and the willingness to forgive and reconcile with other disciples even before they commit an offense.

I have also examined discipleship in the broader NT canon, hoping to discover any major points of similarity, difference, and development with Matthean discipleship. My examination thereof has resulted in the following general observations: (i) the Gospels of Mark, Luke, and John utilize μαθητής in ways that are consistent with Matthew's use of the term—i.e., primarily to describe the activities of Jesus' closest adherents who follow him as their master, including going from place to place, obeying his commands, observing his actions, and learning from him; (ii) of the NT writings, only Matthew and Acts employ μαθητεύω in the context of making a disciple of someone (Matt 28:19; Acts 14:21; cf. 2:47);[1] (iii) Luke-Acts, the Johannine literature, the Pauline Epistles,

---

1. In Acts 14:21-22, Luke correlates μαθητεύω with preaching the gospel and with the strengthening and encouraging of the disciples. Matthew's use of μαθητεύω in Matt 28:19 connects the term to "going," "the nations," "baptizing," and "teaching"; but he also links it to the broader context of Matthew through his use of key narrative elements in Matt 28:16-20—e.g., events, characters, setting, and rhetoric—that unite the Commission to the rest of the Gospel. Therefore, when one considers that the Matthean Jesus proclaims the gospel (e.g., Matt 4:17; 11:1, 5), and that he strengthens

and the Other Epistles have demonstrated a general broadening of their use of discipleship terminology—e.g., traditional Matthean discipleship terms like μαθητεύω, μαθητής, and ἀκολουθέω generally give way to such terms as ἅγιος, ἀδελφός, ἀπόστολος, δοῦλος, ἐκκλησία, περιπατέω, τέκνον, and υἱός, to name just a few; and (iv) the NT Epistles address discipleship themes that are similar to those of Matthew, but they achieve their goal with the help of a different and broader range of discipleship terms and with a discipleship theology that emphasizes the idea of believers *imitating, modeling,* and *following the examples of* their spiritual leaders and ultimately Jesus Christ. In summary, I have observed that the objectives of the various modes of NT discipleship (outside of Matthew) are largely congruent with that of Matthew. The writers of the Gospels and Acts narrate stories about the character of discipleship and about the process of making disciples. In the Pauline Epistles, the apostle sees himself as playing a critical role in the ongoing discipling of his addressees; he is a disciple-maker who wants to present them "complete in Christ" (e.g., Col 1:28). Paul and the writers of the Other Epistles exhort their readers to continue to be Jesus' disciples and to replicate themselves by *being* and *following* good examples of believers in Christ (e.g., Phil 3:17; 1 Thess 1:7; 2 Thess 3:9; 1 Tim 4:12; Titus 2:7; 1 Pet 5:3).

From my findings, I have arrived at various conclusions regarding the meaning of μαθητεύσατε (28:19). First, I have correctly anticipated the need for this research, given the limitation that scholars have generally placed on their definition of μαθητεύσατε by considering its adjoining participles to be the only source of meaning for this imperative. Second, Matthew utilizes several narrative elements of the Commission to direct the reader to the broader context of the Gospel in search of the full meaning of 28:16–20, including the imperative μαθητεύσατε. Third, by examining the entire life of Jesus—the model of discipleship and master disciple-maker himself—in the wider Gospel, it is evident that Matthew intends his reader to comprehend discipleship and disciple-making in terms of a single reference point—i.e., the Matthean Jesus. Fourth, while the essentials of discipleship remain relatively stable, disciple-making language and techniques may evolve over time. It is the responsibility of the disciple-maker to tailor the disciple-making approach to suit the prevailing circumstances. Fifth, disciple-makers must be ready to embrace

---

and encourages his disciples throughout Matthew (e.g., Matt 5:3–7:27; 19:27–30) as he teaches them the art of "fishing for people" (4:23–28:20), it becomes apparent that both Matthew and Luke use μαθητεύω in contexts that are largely congruent.

Paul's "imitate/model" discipleship terminology, which is congruent with the "Follow me" language of the Matthean Jesus (Matt 4:19; 8:22; 9:9; 19:21; cf. 1 Cor 4:16; 11:1; Phil 3:17; 4:9; 2 Thess 3:7, 9; 1 Tim 4:12; Titus 2:7). Demetrios S. Katos opines that Paul's demand that Corinthian Christians take him as their model may seem brazen to modern culture, which values originality, not slavish tradition.[2] I concur with Hawthorne that Paul is fully aware of his potential to fail (1 Cor 9:27). However, he is so confident that his manner of life and his view of God and Christ are correct that he is unafraid to present himself as a model for others to follow.[3]

Evidently, the term "modeling" is not an adjoining participle of the imperative μαθητεύσατε in Matt 28:19. However, I conclude from my research that Matthew's reader is acutely aware from his reading of the entire Gospel that: (i) Matthew models Jesus, as the Son of God, after his own Father (e.g., Matt 3:17; 11:27; 14:13; 16:16; 27:54; 28:18); (ii) Matthew models Jesus' disciples after their own master, even though they do not always perfectly imitate him (e.g., Matt 4:20, 22; 10:1–5, 24–25a, 38; 16:24; 17:19–20; 20:20–23; 26:31–35); and (iii) Matthew expects the members of his community to actively "make disciples," not only by "going," "baptizing," and "teaching," but also by modeling themselves after Jesus Messiah and by presenting themselves as models of him for the people of the nations to imitate.

Several implications emerge from the conclusions that I have just outlined. Christian disciple-makers will need to rethink the way they view their responsibilities—i.e., not only in terms of "going," "baptizing," and "teaching" for the purpose of making new disciples, but they will see the need to offer themselves to the world as models of Christian discipleship. More specifically, this consideration requires disciple-makers not only to teach others about observing Christ's commands, but also to be exemplars of obedience to Christ's commands. Furthermore, they will embrace the view that Matthean discipleship requires them to consider all of Jesus' life—both his commands and his actions—as learning material for Christian disciples to follow. This is especially important, given that several influential scholars have not paid enough attention to the truth that Matthew's teaching content for new disciples goes beyond Jesus' spoken commands in the five major discourses of the Gospel. By so doing,

---

2. Katos, "Holy Imitation," 30.
3. Hawthorne, *Philippians*, 219.

scholars may have neglected to focus equally on what the Matthean Jesus does and does not do, and even on the implications of his silence.

Christian disciple-makers will also have to grasp the vital connection between *being* a disciple and *making* disciples. This important concept is grounded in the truth that disciple-makers are first and foremost disciples *of* Jesus who are also responsible for making disciples *for* Jesus. The connection of which I speak always requires consistency between the disciple-maker's speech and action (behavior). Therefore, a discipler does not become engaged in the process of making disciples without first laying the groundwork in his or her own life of being an obedient follower and wholehearted servant of Christ. Disciple-makers never cease to be disciples themselves; they make disciples for Christ by using their own lives as models of Christian discipleship.

Finally, disciple-makers will embrace the truth that God (through Jesus) is the principal actor in the disciple-making process that leads to salvation. In other words, God (through Jesus) is in charge of the entire operation: (i) *he calls* people to be *his disciples* (Matt 4:19; 8:22; 9:9; 16:24); (ii) *he saves* those who *follow him* obediently (Matt 1:21; cf. Luke 2:11; John 1:29; Acts 4:12); and (iii) *he imparts his ongoing presence* to *his disciples* for the purpose of undertaking *his mission* of making disciples of "all the nations" (Matt 28:20; cf. 1:23). This truth overrules the idea that Christians (themselves) "make disciples" of other human beings. In truth, it is God (through Jesus) who initiates and sustains the process, with assistance from Christian disciple-makers, functioning as facilitators of his will—e.g., as sowers of seed (Matt 13:3–9, 18–23, 31–32; cf. Mark 4:26–29); as finders of treasure (13:44); as merchants of pearls (13:45–46); as fishermen (13:47–50); and as "fishers of men" (4:19).

My work may have implications for supplemental lines of research, employing IBS and narrative criticism methodologies wherever possible, that focus on identifying the major influences on first-century discipleship practices, including: (i) OT discipleship methods (e.g., among OT prophetic groups) in order to determine how they functioned in ancient Israel and how their practices might have influenced first-century discipleship attitudes and practices; and (ii) how a Second Temple (539 BCE–135 CE) Jewish understanding of exile and restoration might have impacted the worldview of Jesus' disciples and shaped the way they understood their master's mission of making disciples of the nations. Other interesting lines of research might also be pursued in: (i) undertaking a thorough investigation (not a survey) of discipleship in the broader

NT canon, especially the Pauline Epistles; and (ii) determining whether any of the NT writers attempt to specify a series of concrete steps that comprise the disciple-making process. Whatever additional work is undertaken concerning ancient discipleship practices augurs well for a better understanding of the foundations of Christian discipleship—that divine-human enterprise that seeks to regenerate human lives, utilizing a methodology that has been tried, tested, and modeled by the master disciple-maker himself.

Appendix

Table of New Testament Discipleship Terms

Term		Ratio of Occurrences[1]					
Greek	English Gloss	Matthew	Mark	Luke-Acts	Johannine Literature	Pauline Epistles	Other Epistles
ἅγιος	"saint"	1:10	0:7	4:73	13:31	40:76	3:36
ἀδελφή	"sister"	1:3	1:4	0:4	0:7	3:6	1:1
ἀδελφός	"brother"	4:39	1:20	39:81	22:37	125:132	29:33
ἀδελφότης	"a fellowship"	-	-	-	-	-	2:2
ἀκολουθέω	"to follow"	13:25	8:17	11:21	10:25	0:1	-
ἀμέμπτως	"blamelessly"	-	-	-	-	2:2	-
ἄμωμος	"blameless"	-	-	-	1:1	4:4	1:3
ἀξίως	"worthily"	-	-	-	1:1	5:5	-
ἀπόστολος	"apostle"	1:1	1:1	33:34	4:4	32:34	5:5
ἀρνέομαι	"to repudiate"	3:3	2:2	5:8	6:9	7:7	2:3
ἄτακτος	"disorderly"	-	-	-	-	1:1	-
διάκονος	"servant"	2:3	2:2	-	1:3	17:21	-
δικαίως	"uprightly"	-	-	1:1	-	3:3	1:1
δοκιμή	"proven worth"	-	-	-	-	7:7	-
δοῦλος	"slave"	11:30	1:5	9:29	10:25	14:32	5:5
ἐκκλησία	"church"	2:2	-	20:23	20:23	62:62	3:6
ἐξακολουθέω	"to obey, follow"	-	-	-	-	-	3:3
ἐπακολουθέω	"to follow"	-	1:1	-	-	2:2	1:1

1. The ratio of a term's occurrences in a discipleship context to its total occurrences in the NT.

APPENDIX

Term		Ratio of Occurrences[1]					
Greek	English Gloss	Matthew	Mark	Luke-Acts	Johannine Literature	Pauline Epistles	Other Epistles
μαθητεύω	"be/make a disciple"	3:3	-	1:1	-	-	-
μαθητής	"disciple, follower"	73:73	46:46	65:65	78:78	-	-
μαθήτρια	"female disciple"	-	-	1:1	-	-	-
μανθάνω	"to learn"	3:3	1:1	0:1	3:3	11:16	1:1
μιμέομαι	"to imitate"	-	-	-	1:1	2:2	1:1
μιμητής	"imitator"	-	-	-	-	5:5	1:1
ὀπίσω	follow "after"	3:6	3:6	5:9	3:10	1:2	2:2
πείθω	"to obey, follow"	0:3	-	2:21	0:1	19:22	5:5
περιπατέω	"to behave, live"	0:7	1:9	1:13	18:32	32:32	2:2
συμμαθητής	"fellow disciple"	-	-	-	1:1	-	-
συμμιμητής	"fellow imitator"	-	-	-	-	1:1	-
σύνδουλος	"fellow slave"	0:5	-	-	3:3	2:2	-
συνεργός	"fellow worker"	-	-	-	1:1	12:12	-
συστρατιώτης	"fellow soldier"	-	-	-	-	2:2	-
τεκνίον	"(little) child"	-	-	-	8:8	-	-
τέκνον	"[spiritual] child"	0:14	1:9	1:19	13:15	20:39	3:3
τύπος	"example, pattern"	-	-	0:3	0:2	7:8	1:2
υἱός	"son, pupil"	1:90	0:34	1:99	0:86	14:41	7:27
φιλαδελφία	"brotherly love"	-	-	-	-	2:2	4:4
Χριστιανός	"Christian"	-	-	2:2	-	-	1:1

Bibliography

Abrams, M. H., and Geoffrey Harpham. *A Glossary of Literary Terms*. 10th ed. Boston: Wadsworth, 2011.
Adamson, James B. *The Epistle of James*. NICNT. Grand Rapids: Eerdmans, 1976.
Akin, Daniel L. *1, 2, 3 John*. NAC 38. Nashville: Broadman & Holman, 2001.
Allison, Dale C., Jr. "Mountain and Wilderness." In *DJG* 563–65.
Ambrose of Milan. *Seven Exegetical Works*. FC 65. Washington, DC: Catholic University of America Press, 1972.
Anderson, Janice Capel. "Double and Triple Stories, the Implied Reader, and Redundancy in Matthew." In *Semeia 31: Reader Response Approaches to Biblical and Secular Texts*, edited by Robert Detweiler, 71–89. Atlanta: Society of Biblical Literature, 1985.
———. "Matthew: Gender and Reading." In *Semeia 28: The Bible and Feminist Hermeneutics*, edited by Mary Ann Tolbert, 3–27. Atlanta: Society of Biblical Literature, 1983.
———. *Matthew's Narrative Web: Over, and Over, and Over Again*. JSNTSup 91. Sheffield: JSOT, 1994.
Andrew of Caesarea. *Commentary on the Apocalypse*. FC 123. Washington, DC: Catholic University of America Press, 2011.
Aquinas, Thomas. *Catena Aurea: Commentary on the Four Gospels, Collected out of the Works of the Fathers: St. Matthew*. Vol. 1. Oxford: John Henry Parker, 1841.
Arnold, Clinton E. "Power, NT Concept of." In *ABD* 5:444–46.
Aune, David E. "Following the Lamb: Discipleship in the Apocalypse." In *Patterns of Discipleship in the New Testament*, edited by Richard N. Longenecker, 269–84. McMaster New Testament Studies. Grand Rapids: Eerdmans, 1996.
———. *The Westminster Dictionary of New Testament and Early Christian Literature and Rhetoric*. Louisville: Westminster John Knox, 2003.
———. "Worship, Early Christian." In *ABD* 6:973–89.
Baffes, Melanie. "Christology and Discipleship in John 7:37–38." *BTB* 41.3 (2011) 144–50.
Bal, Mieke. *Narratology: Introduction to the Theory of Narrative*. 3rd ed. Toronto: University of Toronto Press, 2009.
Barnes, William H. *1–2 Kings*. CrBC 4. Carol Stream, IL: Tyndale House, 2012.
Barnett, Paul. *The Second Epistle to the Corinthians*. NICNT. Grand Rapids: Eerdmans, 1997.

Barrett, C. K. *A Critical and Exegetical Commentary on the Acts of the Apostles.* ICC. Edinburgh: T. & T. Clark, 2004.

Barsanuphius and John. *Barsanuphius and John: Letters (II).* FC 114. Washington, DC: Catholic University of America Press, 2007.

Basil of Caesarea. *Against Eunomius.* FC 122. Washington, DC: Catholic University of America Press, 2011.

———. "Concerning Baptism." In *Saint Basil: Ascetical Works,* 339–430. FC 9. Washington, DC: Catholic University of America Press, 1962.

Bauer, David R. *The Gospel of the Son of God: An Introduction to Matthew.* Downers Grove, IL: InterVarsity, 2019.

———. "The Kingship of Jesus in the Matthean Infancy Narrative: A Literary Analysis." *CBQ* 57.2 (1995) 306–23.

———. "Son of David." In *DJG* 766–69.

———. "Son of God." In *DJG* 769–75.

———. *The Structure of Matthew's Gospel: A Study in Literary Design.* JSNTSup 31. Sheffield: Almond, 1989.

———. "The Theme of Mission in Matthew's Gospel from the Perspective of the Great Commission." *AsTJ* 74.2 (2019) 240–76.

Bauer, David R., and Mark Allan Powell, eds. *Treasures New and Old: Contributions to Matthean Studies.* Atlanta: Society of Biblical Literature, 1996.

Bauer, David R., and Robert A. Traina. *Inductive Bible Study: A Comprehensive Guide to the Practice of Hermeneutics.* Grand Rapids: Baker Academic, 2011.

Bayer, Hans F. *Das Evangelium des Markus.* Edited by Gerhard Maier, Rainer Riesner, Heinz-Werner Neudorfer, and Eckhard J. Schnabel. 3rd ed. HTA. Witten: Brockhaus, 2018.

Beasley-Murray, George R. *Baptism in the New Testament.* Milton Keynes, UK: Paternoster, 1962.

Belleville, Linda L. "1 Timothy." In *1 Timothy, 2 Timothy, Titus, and Hebrews: Introduction to the Pastoral Epistles,* edited by Phillip W. Comfort, 1–123. CrBC 17A. Carol Stream, IL: Tyndale House, 2009.

———. "'Imitate Me, Just as I Imitate Christ': Discipleship in the Corinthian Correspondence." In *Patterns of Discipleship in the New Testament,* edited by Richard N. Longenecker, 120–42. McMaster New Testament Studies. Grand Rapids: Eerdmans, 1996.

Bernard, J. H. *A Critical and Exegetical Commentary on the Gospel According to St. John.* Edited by Alan Hugh McNeile. ICC 2. New York: Scribner, 1929.

Betz, Hans Dieter. "Heresy and Orthodoxy in the NT." In *ABD* 3:144–47.

Bird, Michael F. "Not by Paul Alone: The Importance of the Gospels for Reformed Theology and Discipleship." *Presb* 39.2 (2013) 98–112.

Black, D. A. "Dreams." In *DJG* 199–200.

Bland, D. S. "Endangering the Reader's Neck: Background Description in the Novel." In *The Theory of the Novel,* edited by Philip Stevick, 313–31. New York: Free Press, 1967.

Blomberg, Craig. *Matthew.* NAC 22. Nashville: Broadman & Holman, 1992.

Bonnard, Pierre. *L'Evangile Selon Saint Matthieu.* Commentaire Du Nouveau Testament 1. Neuchatel: Delachaux et Niestle, 1963.

Boomershine, Thomas E. "Mark: Forming Disciples for the Way of Peace." *CurTM* 38.6 (2011) 405–11.

Booth, Wayne C. *Critical Understanding: The Powers and Limits of Pluralism.* Chicago: University of Chicago Press, 1979.

———. *The Rhetoric of Fiction.* 2nd ed. Chicago: University of Chicago Press, 1983.

———. *A Rhetoric of Irony.* Rev. ed. Chicago: University of Chicago Press, 1975.

Borchert, Gerald L. *John 12–21.* NAC 25B. Nashville: Broadman & Holman, 2002.

Bosch, David J. *Transforming Mission: Paradigm Shifts in Theology of Mission.* American Society of Missiology 16. Maryknoll, NY: Orbis, 2011.

Brands, Michael. "The Kingdom Commission, Light for the Nations: The Expanding Mission of Matthew 28:16–20 in Its Literary Context within Matthew's Gospel." PhD diss., Luther Seminary, 2007.

Brosend, William. "Abiding Love." *ChrCent* 117.16 (2000) 565.

Brown, Colin. "Miracle." In *ISBE* 3:371–81.

Brown, Jeannine K. *The Disciples in Narrative Perspective: The Portrayal and Function of the Matthean Disciples.* Leiden: Brill, 2003.

Brown, Jeannine K., and Kyle Roberts. *Matthew.* THNT. Grand Rapids: Eerdmans, 2018.

Brown, Raymond E. *The Epistles of John: Translated, with Introduction, Notes, and Commentary.* AB 30. New Haven, CT: Yale University Press, 2008.

———. *The Gospel According to John (XIII–XXI): Introduction, Translation, and Notes.* AB 29A. New Haven, CT: Yale University Press, 2008.

Broyles, C. C. "Moses." In *DJG* 560–62.

Bruce, F. F. *The Book of the Acts.* NICNT. Grand Rapids: Eerdmans, 1988.

———. *The Epistles to the Colossians, to Philemon, and to the Ephesians.* NICNT. Grand Rapids: Eerdmans, 1984.

———. *1 and 2 Thessalonians.* WBC 45. Dallas: Word, 1982.

Bunch, Wilton H. "On Being 'Just' a Follower: Rejecting the Pejorative and Pursuing a Higher Calling." *JACL* 6.1 (2012) 64–71.

Burnett, Fred W. "Prolegomenon to Reading Matthew's Eschatological Discourse: Redundancy and the Education of the Reader in Matthew." In *Semeia 31: Reader Response Approaches to Biblical and Secular Texts,* edited by Robert Detweiler, 91–109. Atlanta: Society of Biblical Literature, 1985.

Cairns, Alan. "Consubstantiation." In *DThT* 110.

———. "Mass." In *DThT* 273–74.

Calvin, John. *Institutes of the Christian Religion.* 2 vols. Louisville: Westminster John Knox, 2011.

Carter, Charles W. "The Acts of the Apostles." In *Matthew-Acts,* edited by Charles W. Carter, 475–749. WesBC 4. Grand Rapids: Eerdmans, 1966.

Carter, Warren. "Matthew 4:18–22 and Matthean Discipleship: An Audience-Oriented Perspective." *CBQ* 59.1 (1997) 58–75.

Chambers, Ross. "Commentary in Literary Texts." *Critical Inquiry* 2 (1978) 323–37.

Chatman, Seymour. *Reading Narrative Fiction.* New York: Macmillan, 1993.

———. *Story and Discourse: Narrative Structure in Fiction and Film.* Ithaca, NY: Cornell University Press, 1980.

Clement of Alexandria. *Stromateis, Books One to Three.* FC 85. Washington, DC: Catholic University of America Press, 1991.

Coleman, Rachel L. "Boundary-Shattering Table Fellowship as a Defining Mark of Discipleship in Luke-Acts." *WesTJ* 54.1 (2019) 128–42.

Combrink, H. J. B. "The Structure of the Gospel of Matthew as Narrative." *TynBul* 34 (1983) 61–90.

Comfort, Philip W. *New Testament Text and Translation Commentary*. Carol Stream, IL: Tyndale House, 2008.

Culpepper, R. Alan. *Anatomy of the Fourth Gospel: A Study in Literary Design*. Philadelphia: Fortress, 1983.

Dau, W. H. T. "Baptism (Lutheran View)." In *ISBE* 1:423–26.

Davids, Peter H. "Controlling the Tongue and the Wallet: Discipleship in James." In *Patterns of Discipleship in the New Testament*, edited by Richard N. Longenecker, 225–47. McMaster New Testament Studies. Grand Rapids: Eerdmans, 1996.

———. *The First Epistle of Peter*. NICNT. Grand Rapids: Eerdmans, 1990.

Davies, W. D., and Dale C. Allison, Jr. *A Critical and Exegetical Commentary on the Gospel According to Saint Matthew*. 3 vols. ICC. London: T. & T. Clark, 2004.

Detwiler, D. F. "Paul's Approach to the Great Commission in Acts 14:21–23." *BSac* 152.605 (1995) 33–41.

Didymus the Blind. *Commentary on Zechariah*. Translated by Robert C. Hill. FC 111. Washington, DC: Catholic University of America Press, 2006.

Dobbeler, Axel von. "Die Restitution Israels und die Bekehrung der Heiden: Das Verhältnis von Mt 10,5b.6 und Mt 28,18–20 unter dem Aspekt der Komplementarität: Erwägungen zum Standort des Matthäusevangeliums." *ZNW* 91.1–2 (2000) 18–44.

Dockery, David S. "Baptism." In *DJG* 55–58.

Donaldson, Terence L. "Guiding Readers—Making Disciples: Discipleship in Matthew's Narrative Strategy." In *Patterns of Discipleship in the New Testament*, edited by Richard N. Longenecker, 30–49. McMaster New Testament Studies. Grand Rapids: Eerdmans, 1996.

———. *Jesus on the Mountain: A Study in Matthean Theology*. JSNTSup. Sheffield: Sheffield Academic, 1990.

Drazin, Nathan. *History of Jewish Education from 515 BCE to 220 CE: During the Periods of the Second Commonwealth and the Tannaim*. Baltimore: John Hopkins University Press, 1940.

Earle, Ralph. "The Gospel According to St. Matthew." In *Matthew-Acts*, edited by Charles W. Carter, 1–125. WesBC 4. Grand Rapids: Eerdmans, 1966.

Edwards, James R. "Parallels and Patterns between Luke and Acts." *BBR* 27.4 (2017) 485–501.

Edwards, Richard A. "Uncertain Faith: Matthew's Portrait of the Disciples." In *Discipleship in the New Testament*, edited by Fernando F. Segovia, 41–61. Philadelphia: Fortress, 1985.

Elliott, John H. "Backward and Forward 'In His Steps': Following Jesus from Rome to Raymond and Beyond. The Tradition, Redaction, and Reception of 1 Peter 2:18–25." In *Discipleship in the New Testament*, edited by Fernando F. Segovia, 184–209. Philadelphia: Fortress, 1985.

Elwell, Walter A., and Barry J. Beitzel. "Marriage, Marriage Customs." *BEB* 2:1405–10.

———. "Transfiguration." In *BEB* 2:2096–99.

Farris, S. C. "Worship." In *DJG* 891–94.

Ezeogu, Ernest Munachi. "The Purpose of the Great Commission: A Historical-Critical Exegesis of Matthew 28:16–20." PhD diss., University of St. Michael's College, 2004.

Fee, Gordon D. *Paul's Letter to the Philippians*. NICNT. Grand Rapids: Eerdmans, 1995.
———. *The First and Second Letters to the Thessalonians*. NICNT. Grand Rapids: Eerdmans, 2009.
———. *The First Epistle to the Corinthians*. NICNT. Grand Rapids: Eerdmans, 1987.
Ferdinando, Keith. "Mission: A Problem of Definition." *Them* 33.1 (2008) 46–59.
Fernando, Ajith. "To Serve Is to Suffer: If the Apostle Paul Knew Fatigue, Anger, and Anxiety in His Ministry, What Makes Us Think We Can Avoid Them in Ours?" *ChrTod* 54.8 (2010) 30–33.
Fitzmyer, Joseph A. *First Corinthians: A New Translation with Introduction and Commentary*. AB 32. New Haven, CT: Yale University Press, 2008.
———. *The Gospel According to Luke I–IX: Introduction, Translation, and Notes*. AB 28. New Haven, CT: Yale University Press, 2008.
Ford, J. Massyngberde. *Revelation: Introduction, Translation, and Commentary*. AB 38. New Haven, CT: Yale University Press, 2008.
Fowler, Robert M. "Who Is the Reader in Reader Response Criticism?" In *Semeia 31: Reader Response Approaches to Biblical and Secular Texts*, edited by Robert Detweiler, 5–23. Atlanta: Society of Biblical Literature, 1985.
France, R. T. "Jesus Christ, Life and Teaching of." In *NBD3* 563–75.
———. *The Gospel of Matthew*. NICNT. Grand Rapids: Eerdmans, 2007.
Freyne, Seán. "Galilee: Hellenistic/Roman Galilee." In *ABD* 2:895–99.
Fructuosus of Braga and Braulio of Saragossa. *Iberian Fathers (2)*. FC 63. Washington, DC: Catholic University of America Press, 1969.
Furnish, Victor Paul. *II Corinthians: Translated with Introduction, Notes, and Commentary*. AB 32A. New Haven, CT: Yale University Press, 2008.
Futato, Mark D. "The Book of Psalms." In *The Book of Psalms, The Book of Proverbs*, edited by Philip W. Comfort, 1–450. CrBC 7. Carol Stream, IL: Tyndale House, 2009.
Gibson, Jeffrey B. "The Rebuke of the Disciples in Mark 8:14–21." *JSNT* 8.27 (1986) 31–47.
Gilbert, Scott Allan. "Go Make Disciples: Sermonic Application of the Imperative of the Great Commission." PhD diss., Southern Baptist Theological Seminary, 2017.
Gilmore, David G., ed. *Honor and Shame and the Unity of the Mediterranean*. Washington, DC: American Anthropological Association, 1987.
Gnilka, Joachim. *Das Matthäusevangelium*. Edited by Joachim Gnilka and Lorenz Oberlinner. 2 vols. Sonderausgabe. HThKNT. Freiburg im Breisgau: Herder, 1988.
Gould, Ezra Palmer. *A Critical and Exegetical Commentary on the Gospel According to St. Mark*. ICC. New York: Scribner, 1922.
Green, Joel B. *The Gospel of Luke*. NICNT. Grand Rapids: Eerdmans, 1997.
———. "Narrative and New Testament Interpretation: Reflections on the State of the Art." *LTQ* 39.3 (2004) 153–66.
Gullotta, Daniel N. "Among Dogs and Disciples: An Examination of the Story of the Canaanite Woman (Matthew 15:21–28) and the Question of the Gentile Mission within the Matthean Community." *Neot* 48.2 (2014) 325–40.
Gundry, Robert H. *Matthew: A Commentary on His Handbook for a Mixed Church under Persecution*. 2nd ed. Grand Rapids: Eerdmans, 1994.
Hagner, Donald A. "Law, Righteousness, and Discipleship in Matthew." *WW* 18.4 (1998) 364–71.
———. *Matthew*. 2 vols. WBC 33A, 33B. Dallas: Word, 1998.

Halliday, M. A. K. *Language as Social Semiotic: The Social Interpretation of Language and Meaning*. Baltimore: University Park, 1978.
Hanson, K. C. "Kinship." In *The Social Sciences and New Testament Interpretation*, edited by Richard L. Rohrbaugh, 62–79. Grand Rapids: Baker Academic, 2003.
Harman, Gilbert H. "The Inference to the Best Explanation." *The Philosophical Review* 74.1 (1965) 88–95.
Hartman, Lars. "Baptism." In *ABD* 1:583–94.
Hawthorne, Gerald F. "Amen." In *DJG* 7–8.
———. "The Imitation of Christ: Discipleship in Philippians." In *Patterns of Discipleship in the New Testament*, edited by Richard N. Longenecker, 163–79. McMaster New Testament Studies. Grand Rapids: Eerdmans, 1996.
———. *Philippians*. WBC 43. Dallas: Word, 2004.
Hertig, Paul. "The Great Commission Revisited: The Role of God's Reign in Disciple Making." *Missiology* 29.3 (2001) 343–53.
Herzog, II, W. R. "Sociological Approaches to the Gospels." In *DJG* 760–66.
Hiers, Richard H., and Mark Allan Powell. "Eschatology." In *HBD* 254–56.
Hilary of Poitiers. *Commentary on Matthew*. FC 125. Washington, DC: Catholic University of America Press, 2012.
Hillmer, Melvyn R. "They Believed in Him: Discipleship in the Johannine Tradition." In *Patterns of Discipleship in the New Testament*, edited by Richard N. Longenecker, 77–97. McMaster New Testament Studies. Grand Rapids: Eerdmans, 1996.
Hogan, Karina Martin, Matthew Goff, and Emma Wasserman, eds. *Pedagogy in Ancient Judaism and Early Christianity*. Atlanta: Society of Biblical Literature, 2017.
Holmes, Michael W., ed. *The Apostolic Fathers: Greek Texts and English Translations*. 3rd ed. Grand Rapids: Baker Academic, 2007.
Howard, George. "Matthew, Hebrew Version Of." In *ABD* 4:642–43.
Howell, David B. *Matthew's Inclusive Story: A Study in the Narrative Rhetoric of the First Gospel*. Sheffield: Sheffield Academic, 1990.
Hur, Unsok. "The Disciples' Lack of Comprehension in the Gospel of Mark." *BTB* 49.1 (2019) 41–48.
Hurtado, Larry W. "Following Jesus in the Gospel of Mark and Beyond." In *Patterns of Discipleship in the New Testament*, edited by Richard N. Longenecker, 9–29. McMaster New Testament Studies. Grand Rapids: Eerdmans, 1996.
Hutcheson, R. "Reformed Presbyterian Church." In *CBTEL* 8:1013–15.
Iser, Wolfgang. *The Act of Reading: A Theory of Aesthetic Response*. Baltimore: Johns Hopkins University Press, 1978.
———. *The Implied Reader: Patterns of Communication in Prose Fiction from Bunyan to Beckett*. Baltimore: Johns Hopkins University Press, 1978.
Jacob, E. M. "Discipleship and Mission: A Perspective on the Gospel of Matthew." *IRM* 91.360 (2002) 102–10.
Jaeger, Werner. *Early Christianity and Greek Paidea*. Cambridge, MA: Belknap, 1961.
James, Sujaya. *Salvation and Discipleship Continuum in Johannine Literature: Toward an Evaluation of the Faith Alone Doctrine*. Lewiston, NY: Mellen, 2014.
Jerome. *Commentary on Matthew*. FC 117. Washington, DC: Catholic University of America Press, 2008.
Jervis, L. Ann. "Becoming Like God through Christ: Discipleship in Romans." In *Patterns of Discipleship in the New Testament*, edited by Richard N. Longenecker, 143–62. McMaster New Testament Studies. Grand Rapids: Eerdmans, 1996.

Johnson, Luke Timothy. "Friendship with the World/Friendship with God: A Study of Discipleship in James." In *Discipleship in the New Testament*, edited by Fernando F. Segovia, 41–61. Philadelphia: Fortress, 1985.

———. *The Letter of James: A New Translation with Introduction and Commentary*. AB 37A. New Haven, CT: Yale University Press, 2008.

Just, Arthur A., ed. *Luke*. ACCS. Downers Grove, IL: InterVarsity, 2005.

Katos, Demetrios S. "Holy Imitation: A Manual for Disciples." *ChrCent* 128.13 (2011) 30–33.

Keener, Craig S. *Acts: An Exegetical Commentary: 3:1—14:28*. Vol. 2. Grand Rapids: Baker Academic, 2013.

———. *The Gospel of Matthew: A Socio-Rhetorical Commentary*. Grand Rapids: Eerdmans, 2009.

Kennedy, George A. *New Testament Interpretation through Rhetorical Criticism*. Chapel Hill: University of North Carolina Press, 1984.

Kingsbury, Jack Dean. "The Figure of Jesus in Matthew's Story: A Literary-Critical Probe." *JSNT* 21 (1984) 3–36.

———. "The Figure of Peter in Matthew's Gospel as a Theological Problem." *JBL* 98.1 (1979) 67–83.

———. *Matthew: Structure, Christology, Kingdom*. Minneapolis: Augsburg, 1991.

———. *Matthew as Story*. 2nd ed. Philadelphia: Fortress, 1988.

Kingsbury, Jack Dean, and Mark Allan Powell. "Lord's Prayer." In *HBD* 566–67.

Kittel, Gerhard, and Gerhard Friedrich, eds. *Theological Dictionary of the New Testament*. Translated by Geoffrey W. Bromiley. 10 vols. Grand Rapids: Eerdmans, 1964–1976.

Knowles, Michael P. "'Christ in You, the Hope of Glory': Discipleship in Colossians." In *Patterns of Discipleship in the New Testament*, edited by Richard N. Longenecker, 180–202. McMaster New Testament Studies. Grand Rapids: Eerdmans, 1996.

Koester, Craig R. *Hebrews: A New Translation with Introduction and Commentary*. AB 36. New Haven, CT: Yale University Press, 2008.

Krentz, E. "Missionary Matthew: Matthew 28:16–20 as Summary of the Gospel." *CurTM* 31.1 (2004) 24–31.

Kvalbein, H. "Go Therefore and Make Disciples . . . The Concept of Discipleship in the New Testament." *Them* 13.2 (1988) 48–53.

Lake, Kirsopp, ed. *Apostolic Fathers in Greek*. LCL 2. Cambridge, MA: Harvard University Press, 1912.

Lane, William L. *The Gospel of Mark*. NICNT. Grand Rapids: Eerdmans, 1974.

———. "Standing before the Moral Claim of God: Discipleship in Hebrews." In *Patterns of Discipleship in the New Testament*, edited by Richard N. Longenecker, 203–24. McMaster New Testament Studies. Grand Rapids: Eerdmans, 1996.

Lange, John Peter. *A Commentary on the Holy Scriptures: Mark*. Edited by Philip Schaff. Translated by William G. T. Shedd. Bellingham, WA: Logos Bible Software, 2008.

Lanser, Susan Sniader. *The Narrative Act: Point of View in Prose Fiction*. Princeton, NJ: Princeton University Press, 1981.

Larkin, William J., Jr. "Acts." In *The Gospel of Luke and Acts*, edited by Philip W. Comfort, 349–668. CrBC 12B. Carol Stream, IL: Tyndale House, 2006.

Lategan, Bernard C. "Reader Response Theory." In *ABD* 5:625–28.

Lea, Thomas D. "1 Timothy." In *1, 2 Timothy, Titus*, edited by David S. Dockery, 61–178. NAC 34. Nashville: Broadman & Holman, 1992.

Lee, Sug-Ho, and Jan Gabriël Van der Watt. "The Portrayal of the Hardening of the Disciples' Hearts in Mark 8:14–21." *HvTSt* 65.1 (2009) 145–49.
Leo the Great. *Sermons of Leo the Great*. FC 93. Washington, DC: Catholic University of America Press, 1996.
Levine, Amy-Jill. "'To All the Gentiles': A Jewish Perspective on the Great Commission." *RevExp* 103.1 (2006) 139–58.
Levinsohn, Stephen H. *Discourse Features of New Testament Greek: A Coursebook on the Information Structure of New Testament Greek*. 2nd ed. Dallas: SIL International, 2000.
Levy, Ian Christopher, Philip D. W. Krey, Thomas Ryan, and H. Lawrence Bond, eds. *The Letter to the Romans*. The Bible in Medieval Tradition. Grand Rapids: Eerdmans, 2013.
Liddell, Henry George, Robert Scott, and Roderick McKenzie. *A Greek-English Lexicon*. Edited by Henry Stuart Jones. 9th ed. Oxford: Oxford University Press, 1996.
Lightfoot, John. *A Commentary on the New Testament from the Talmud and Hebraica, Matthew–1 Corinthians: Acts–1 Corinthians*. Vol. 4. Bellingham, WA: Logos, 2010.
———. *A Commentary on the New Testament from the Talmud and Hebraica, Matthew–1 Corinthians: Luke–John*. Vol. 3. Bellingham, WA: Logos, 2010.
Lipton, Peter. *Inference to the Best Explanation*. 2nd ed. London: Routledge, 2004.
Long, Fredrick J. *Koine Greek Grammar: A Beginning-Intermediate Exegetical and Pragmatic Handbook*. Accessible Greek Resources and Online Studies. Wilmore, KY: GlossaHouse, 2015.
———. "The Pragmatics of Circumstantial Participles: Rethinking the Locations, Uses, and Semantics of 'Adverbial' Participles." Presented at the Biblical Greek Language and Linguistics section at the SBL Annual Meeting, San Antonio, Texas, November 19, 2016.
Longenecker, Richard N. "Taking Up the Cross Daily: Discipleship in Luke-Acts." In *Patterns of Discipleship in the New Testament*, edited by Richard N. Longenecker, 50–76. McMaster New Testament Studies. Grand Rapids: Eerdmans, 1996.
Luter, Jr., A. Boyd. "Great Commission, The." In *ABD* 2:1090–91.
———. "Women Disciples and the Great Commission." *TJ* 16.2 (1995) 171–85.
Luther, Martin. *Luther's Works*. 55 vols. Philadelphia: Fortress, 1999.
Luz, Ulrich. *Matthew*. 3 vols. Hermeneia. Minneapolis: Augsburg Fortress, 2001–2007.
Maier, Gerhard. *Der Brief des Jakobus*. Edited by Gerhard Maier, Heinz-Werner Neudorfer, Rainer Riesner, and Eckhard J. Schnabel. 3rd ed. HTA. Witten: Brockhaus, 2014.
———. *Das Evangelium des Matthäus*. Edited by Gerhard Maier, Rainer Riesner, Heinz-Werner Neudorfer, and Eckhard J. Schnabel. 2 vols. HTA. Witten: Brockhaus, 2015–2017.
Mailloux, Steven. *Interpretive Conventions: The Reader in the Study of American Fiction*. Ithaca, NY: Cornell University Press, 1984.
———. "Learning to Read: Interpretation and Reader-Response Criticism." *Studies in the Literary Imagination* 12.1 (1979) 93–108.
Malbon, E. S. "Disciples/Crowds/Whoever: Markan Characters and Readers." *NovT* 28.2 (1986) 104–30.
Malina, Bruce J. "The Literary Structure and Form of Matt. Xxviii.16–20." *NTS* 17.1 (1970) 87–103.

Malina, Bruce J., and Jerome Neyrey. *Calling Jesus Names: The Social Value of Labels in Matthew*. Sonoma, CA: Polebridge, 1988.
Malina, Bruce J., and Richard L. Rohrbaugh. *Social-Science Commentary on the Synoptic Gospels*. 2nd ed. Minneapolis: Augsburg, 2002.
Marcus, Joel. *Mark 8–16: A New Translation with Introduction and Commentary*. AB 27A. New Haven, CT: Yale University Press, 2009.
Margaret Beirne. *Women and Men in the Fourth Gospel: A Discipleship of Equals*. JSNTSup. London: Sheffield Academic, 2003.
Marrou, H. I. *A History of Education in Antiquity*. Translated by George Lamb. Madison: University of Wisconsin Press, 1982.
Marshall, I. Howard. *The Epistles of John*. NICNT. Grand Rapids: Eerdmans, 1978.
Martin, James Perry. "The Church in Matthew." *Int* 29.1 (1975) 41–56.
Matera, Frank J. "The Incomprehension of the Disciples and Peter's Confession (Mark 6:14—8:30)." *Bib* 70.2 (1989) 153–72.
McKnight, Scot. "Matthew, Gospel of." In *DJG* 526–41.
M'Clintock, John, and James Strong. "Arianism." In *CBTEL* 1:388–93.
———. "Church." In *CBTEL* 2:322–29.
———. "Indefectibility of the Church." In *CBTEL* 4:542–43.
Meeks, Wayne A. *First Urban Christians: The Social World of the Apostle Paul*. New Haven, CT: Yale University Press, 1983.
Meier, John P. "Antioch." In *HBD* 34–35.
———. "Matthew, Gospel of." In *ABD* 4:622–41.
Michaels, J. Ramsey. *1 Peter*. WBC 49. Dallas: Word, 1988.
———. "Going to Heaven with Jesus: From 1 Peter to Pilgrim's Progress." In *Patterns of Discipleship in the New Testament*, edited by Richard N. Longenecker, 248–68. McMaster New Testament Studies. Grand Rapids: Eerdmans, 1996.
Moffatt, James. *A Critical and Exegetical Commentary on the Epistle to the Hebrews*. ICC. Edinburgh: T. & T. Clark, 1924.
Morris, Leon. *The Gospel According to John*. NICNT. Grand Rapids: Eerdmans, 1995.
Motyer, J. T. "Name." In *NBD3* 799–802.
Mounce, Robert H. *Romans*. NAC 27. Nashville: Broadman & Holman, 1995.
Muderhwa, B. Vincent. "The Blind Man of John 9 as a Paradigmatic Figure of the Disciple in the Fourth Gospel." *HvTSt* 68.1 (2012) 1–10.
Muecke, D. C. *Compass of Irony*. London: Methuen, 1969.
Mußner, Franz. *Der Jakobusbrief*. Edited by Joachim Gnilka and Lorenz Oberlinner. HThKNT. Freiburg im Breisgau: Herder, 1975.
Nestle, Eberhard, and Erwin Nestle. *Nestle-Aland: NTG Apparatus Criticus*. Edited by Barbara Aland, Kurt Aland, Johannes Karavidopoulos, Carlo M. Martini, and Bruce M. Metzger. 28th ed. Stuttgart: Deutsche Bibelgesellschaft, 2012.
Neyrey, Jerome H. *Honor and Shame in the Gospel of Matthew*. Louisville: Westminster John Knox, 1998.
Nicetas of Remesiana, Sulpicius Severus, Vincent of Lerins, and Prosper of Acquitaine. *Writings; Commonitories; Grace and Free Will*. FC 7. Washington, DC: Catholic University of America Press, 1949.
Nickelsburg, George W. E. "Resurrection (Early Judaism and Christianity)." In *ABD* 5:684–91.
Nolan, Patrick, and Gerhard Lenski. *Human Societies: An Introduction to Macrosociology*. 11th ed. Boulder: Paradigm, 2008.

Nolland, John. *The Gospel of Matthew: A Commentary on the Greek Text*. NIGTC. Grand Rapids: Eerdmans, 2005.
Novatian. *The Trinity, The Spectacles, Jewish Foods, In Praise of Purity, Letters*. Translated by Russell J. DeSimone. FC 67. Washington, DC: Catholic University of America Press, 1974.
O'Day, Gail R. "Narrative Mode and Theological Claim: A Study in the Fourth Gospel." *JBL* 105.4 (1986) 657–68.
Omanson, Roger L., and Bruce Manning Metzger. *A Textual Guide to the Greek New Testament: An Adaptation of Bruce M. Metzger's Textual Commentary for the Needs of Translators*. Stuttgart: Deutsche Bibelgesellschaft, 2006.
Origen. *Commentary on the Gospel According to John Books 13–32*. FC 89. Washington, DC: Catholic University of America Press, 1993.
———. *Homilies on Genesis and Exodus*. FC 71. Washington, DC: Catholic University of America Press, 1982.
———. *Homilies on Jeremiah and Homily on 1 Kings 28*. FC 97. Washington, DC: Catholic University of America Press, 1998.
———. *Homilies on Joshua*. FC 105. Washington, DC: Catholic University of America Press, 2002.
———. *Homilies on Leviticus 1–16*. FC 83. Washington, DC: Catholic University of America Press, 1990.
Orosius of Braga and Pacian of Barcelona. *Iberian Fathers*. FC 3. Washington, DC: Catholic University of America Press, 1999.
Osborne, Grant R. "Resurrection." In *DJG* 673–88.
Patte, Daniel. *The Gospel According to Matthew: A Structural Commentary on Matthew's Faith*. Philadelphia: Fortress, 1986.
Penner, J. A. "Revelation and Discipleship in Matthew's Transfiguration Account." *BSac* 152.606 (1995) 201–10.
Perrine, Laurence, and Thomas R. Arp. *Story and Structure*. 8th ed. New York: Harcourt Brace Jovanovich, 1992.
Perry, Menakhem. "Literary Dynamics: How the Order of a Text Creates Its Meanings." *Poetics Today* 1.1/2 (1979) 35–115.
Petersen, Norman R. "Point of View in Mark's Narrative." In *Semeia 12: The Poetics of Faith, Part 1: Rhetoric, Eschatology, and Ethics in the New Testament*, edited by William A. Beardslee, 97–121. Atlanta: Society of Biblical Literature, 1978.
Phillips, Gary A. "History and Text: The Reader in the Context of Matthew's Parables Discourse." In *Semeia 31: Reader Response Approaches to Biblical and Secular Texts*, edited by Robert Detweiler, 111–38. Atlanta: Society of Biblical Literature, 1985.
Plummer, Alfred. *A Critical and Exegetical Commentary on the Second Epistle of St. Paul to the Corinthians*. ICC. New York: T. & T. Clark, 1915.
Porter, Stanley E. *Idioms of the Greek New Testament*. Sheffield: JSOT, 1999.
Powell, Mark Allan. "Sermon on the Mount." In *HBD* 936–38.
———. *What Is Narrative Criticism?* Edited by Dan O. Via Jr. Guides to Biblical Scholarship: New Testament Series. Minneapolis: Augsburg Fortress, 1991.
———. "Worship, New Testament." In *EDB* 1391–92.
Prince, Gerald. "Introduction to the Study of the Narratee." In *Reader-Response Criticism: From Formalism to Post-Structuralism*, edited by Jane P. Tompkins, 7–25. Baltimore: Johns Hopkins University Press, 1980.
Reid, Daniel G. "Sacrifice and Temple Service." In *DNTB* 1036–50.

Remus, Harold E. "Miracle (New Testament)." In *ABD* 4:856–69.
Resseguie, James L. *Narrative Criticism of the New Testament: An Introduction.* Grand Rapids: Baker Academic, 2005.
Reventlow, Henning Graf. *History of Biblical Interpretation.* 4 vols. Atlanta: Society of Biblical Literature, 2009–2010.
Rhoads, David M. "Narrative Criticism and the Gospel of Mark." *JAAR* 50.3 (1982) 411–34.
Rhoads, David M., and Donald Michie. *Mark As Story: An Introduction to the Narrative of a Gospel.* Philadelphia: Fortress, 1982.
Riesner, Rainer D. "Archeology and Geography." In *DJG* 34–46.
———. "Galilee." In *DJG* 252–53.
Robbins, Vernon K. "Social-Scientific Criticism and Literary Studies." In *Modelling Early Christianity: Social-Scientific Studies of the New Testament in Its Context,* edited by Philip Esler, 263–77. London: Routledge, 1995.
Roberts, Alexander, James Donaldson, Philip Schaff, and Henry Wace, eds. *The Ante-Nicene Fathers.* 10 vols. 1885–1887. Reprint, Peabody, MA: Hendrickson, 1996.
———, eds. *Nicene and Post-Nicene Fathers: First Series.* 2nd ed. Peabody, MA: Hendrickson, 1996.
———, eds. *Nicene and Post-Nicene Fathers: Second Series.* Peabody, MA: Hendrickson, 1996.
Robertson, Archibald T. *A Grammar of the Greek New Testament in the Light of Historical Research.* New York: Hodder & Stoughton, 1914.
Robertson, Archibald T., and Alfred Plummer. *A Critical and Exegetical Commentary on the First Epistle of St. Paul to the Corinthians.* ICC. New York: T. & T. Clark, 1911.
Rogers, T. "The Great Commission as the Climax of Matthew's Mountain Scenes." *BBR* 22.3 (2012) 383–98.
Romein, J. M. "The Common Human Pattern: Origin and Scope of Historical Theories." *JWH* 4 (1958) 449–63.
Saunders, Stanley P. "Matthew, Gospel of." In *EDB* 871–73.
Schnabel, Eckhard J. *Der erste Brief des Paulus an die Korinther.* Edited by Gerhard Maier, Heinz-Werner Neudorfer, Rainer Riesner, and Eckhard J. Schnabel. 4th ed. HTA. Witten: Brockhaus, 2018.
———. *Early Christian Mission.* 2 vols. Downers Grove, IL: InterVarsity, 2004.
———. "Mission, Early Non-Pauline." In *DLNT* 752–75.
Schnackenburg, Rudolf. *Das Johannesevangelium.* Edited by Joachim Gnilka and Lorenz Oberlinner. Sonderausgabe. HThKNT 1. Freiburg im Breisgau: Herder, 1984.
Schneider, Gerhard. *Die Apostelgeschichte.* Edited by Joachim Gnilka and Lorenz Oberlinner. Ungekürzte Sonderausgabe. HThKNT 3. Freiburg im Breisgau: Herder, 2002.
Schüssler Fiorenza, Elisabeth. "The Followers of the Lamb: Visionary Rhetoric and Social-Political Situation." In *Discipleship in the New Testament,* edited by Fernando F. Segovia, 144–65. Philadelphia: Fortress, 1985.
Scott, Bernard Brandon. "The King's Accounting: Matthew 18:23–34." *JBL* 104.3 (1985) 429–42.
Segovia, Fernando F. "'Peace I Leave with You; My Peace I Give to You': Discipleship in the Fourth Gospel." In *Discipleship in the New Testament,* edited by Fernando F. Segovia, 76–102. Philadelphia: Fortress, 1985.

Senior, Donald. *The Passion of Jesus in the Gospel of Matthew*. Wilmington, DE: Glazier, 1990.
Shogren, Gary S. "Authority and Power." In *DJG* 50–54.
Sim, David C. "Is Matthew 28:16–20 the Summary of the Gospel?" *HvTSt* 70.1 (2014) 1–7.
Simonetti, Manlio, ed. *Matthew 14–28*. ACCS 1B. Downers Grove, IL: InterVarsity, 2002.
Sjoberg, Gideon. *The Preindustrial City: Past and Present*. New York: Free Press, 1965.
Smit, Peter-Ben. "A Question of Discipleship – Remarks on Matthew 8:18–23." *RB* 123.1 (2016) 79–92.
Smith, Robert H. *Matthew*. Augsburg Commentary on the New Testament. Minneapolis: Augsburg, 1989.
Stein, Robert H. *Luke*. NAC 24. Nashville: Broadman & Holman, 1992.
Stock, Augustine. *Call to Discipleship: A Literary Study of Mark's Gospel*. Good News Studies. Wilmington, DE: Michael Glazier, 1982.
Suleiman, Susan R. "Redundancy and the 'Readable' Text." *Poetics Today* 1.3 (1980) 119–42.
Talbert, Charles H. "Discipleship in Luke-Acts." In *Discipleship in the New Testament*, edited by Fernando F. Segovia, 62–75. Philadelphia: Fortress, 1985.
Tannehill, Robert C. "Disciples in Mark: The Function of a Narrative Role." *JR* 57.4 (1977) 386–405.
Tanner, Paul A. "The Cost of Discipleship: Losing One's Life for Jesus' Sake." *JETS* 56.1 (2013) 43–61.
Taylor, C. *The Witness of Hermas to the Four Gospels*. Cambridge: Cambridge University Press, 1892.
Tennent, Timothy. *Invitation to World Missions: A Trinitarian Missiology for the Twenty-First Century*. Grand Rapids: Kregel, 2010.
Tertullian. *Disciplinary, Moral, and Ascetical Works*. FC 40. Washington, DC: Catholic University of America Press, 1959.
Theodoret. *Commentary on the Psalms 1–72*. FC 101. Washington, DC: Catholic University of America Press, 2000.
Thomas, R. L. "The Great Commission: What to Teach." *MSJ* 21.1 (2010) 5–20.
———. "Historical Criticism and the Great Commission." *MSJ* 11.1 (2000) 39–52.
Thompson, James. "Authentic Discipleship: An Introduction to 2 Corinthians." *ResQ* 19.1 (1976) 1–6.
Thompson, Marianne Meye. *Colossians and Philemon*. THNT. Grand Rapids: Eerdmans, 2005.
Traina, Robert A. *Methodical Bible Study*. Grand Rapids: Zondervan, 2002.
Trites, Allison A. "The Gospel of Luke." In *The Gospel of Luke and Acts*, edited by Philip W. Comfort, 1–347. CrBC 12A. Carol Stream, IL: Tyndale House, 2006.
Turner, David L. "The Gospel of Matthew." In *Matthew and Mark*, edited by Philip W. Comfort, 1–389. CrBC 11A. Carol Stream, IL: Tyndale House, 2005.
———. *Matthew*. BECNT. Grand Rapids: Baker Academic, 2008.
Twelftree, Graham H. "Temptation of Jesus." In *DJG* 821–27.
Tyson, Joseph B. "Blindness of the Disciples in Mark." *JBL* 80.3 (1961) 261–68.
Uspensky, Boris. *A Poetics of Composition: The Structure of the Artistic Text and Typology of a Compositional Form*. Translated by Valentina Zavarin and Susan Wittig. Berkeley: University of California Press, 1973.

Vanhoozer, Kevin J. *Is There a Meaning in This Text?: The Bible, the Reader, and the Morality of Literary Knowledge*. Grand Rapids: Zondervan, 2009.

———. "The Reader in New Testament Interpretation." In *Hearing the New Testament: Strategies for Interpretation*, edited by Joel B. Green, 259-88. 2nd ed. Grand Rapids: Eerdmans, 2010.

Wainwright, Elaine Mary. "Feminist Criticism and the Gospel of Matthew." In *Methods for Matthew*, edited by Mark Allan Powell, 83-117. Cambridge: Cambridge University Press, 2009.

Walker, Larry L. "Isaiah." In *Isaiah, Jeremiah, & Lamentations*, edited by Philip W. Comfort, 1-291. CrBC 8A. Carol Stream, IL: Tyndale House, 2005.

Wallace, Daniel B. *Greek Grammar beyond the Basics: An Exegetical Syntax of the New Testament*. Grand Rapids: Zondervan, 1996.

Warfield, Benjamin B. *The Lord of Glory: A Study of the Designations of Our Lord in the New Testament with Especial Reference to His Deity*. New York: American Tract Society, 1907.

Watson, Duane F. "People, Crowd." In *DJG* 605-9.

Weima, Jeffrey A. D. "'How You Must Walk to Please God': Holiness and Discipleship in 1 Thessalonians." In *Patterns of Discipleship in the New Testament*, edited by Richard N. Longenecker, 98-119. McMaster New Testament Studies. Grand Rapids: Eerdmans, 1996.

Weren, Wilhelmus Johannes Cornelis. "The Five Women in Matthew's Genealogy." *CBQ* 59.2 (1997) 288-305.

Wesley, John. *Explanatory Notes upon the New Testament*. 4th ed. New York: J. Soule and T. Mason, 1818.

———. *The Works of John Wesley*. 3rd ed. 14 vols. London: Wesleyan Methodist, 1872.

Westerholm, S. "Pharisees." In *DJG* 609-14.

———. "Sabbath." In *DJG* 716-19.

White, L. Michael. "Christianity (Early Social Life and Organization)." In *ABD* 1:927-35.

Wild, Robert A. "'Be Imitators of God': Discipleship in the Letter to the Ephesians." In *Discipleship in the New Testament*, edited by Fernando F. Segovia, 127-43. Philadelphia: Fortress, 1985.

Wilken, Robert Louis, Angela Russell Christman, and Michael J. Hollerich, eds. *Isaiah: Interpreted by Early Christian and Medieval Commentators*. The Church's Bible. Grand Rapids: Eerdmans, 2007.

Wilkins, Michael J. "Disciples." In *DJG* 176-81.

———. "Discipleship." In *DJG* 182-88.

———. *Discipleship in the Ancient World and Matthew's Gospel*. 2nd ed. Grand Rapids: Baker, 1995.

———. "Pastoral Theology." In *DLNT* 876-82.

Witherington III, Ben. "Birth of Jesus." In *DJG* 60-74.

———. *The Gospel of Mark: A Socio-Rhetorical Commentary*. Grand Rapids: Eerdmans, 2001.

Wogaman, J. P. "Homiletical Resources from the Gospel of Matthew: Faith and Discipleship." *QR* 13.2 (1993) 93-111.

Wright, J. Robert, ed. *Proverbs, Ecclesiastes, Song of Solomon*. ACCS. Downers Grove, IL: InterVarsity, 2005.

Wycliffe, John. *Select English Works of John Wyclif.* Edited by Thomas Arnold. Vol. 2. Oxford: Clarendon, 1871.

Yang, Seung Ai. "Miracles." In *EDB* 903-4.

Yarbrough, Robert W. *1-3 John.* BECNT. Grand Rapids: Baker Academic, 2008.

Zhakevich, Mark. "The Compensatory Benefits of Discipleship in the Gospel of John." PhD diss., University of Edinburgh, 2017.

Index

Abrams, M. H., 7, 10, 15, 213
Adamson, James B., 199, 213
Akin, Daniel L., 177, 178, 213
Aland, Barbara and Kurt, 167, 221
Allison, Dale C., Jr., 21, 27, 29, 30, 33, 36, 43, 54, 66, 77, 78, 79, 80, 87, 88, 94, 106, 108, 109, 111, 112, 119, 122, 124, 126, 127, 131, 132, 133, 137, 138, 140, 143, 145, 151, 213, 216
Ambrose of Milan, 33, 213
Anderson, Janice Capel, 10, 11, 12, 13, 15, 17, 18, 19, 213
Andrew of Caesarea, 62, 213
angel, 44, 54, 83, 112, 119, 120, 121, 123, 127, 158, 174
Antioch, 31, 56, 58, 164, 221
Aphrahat, 33
Apocalypse, apocalyptic, 45, 54, 62, 178, 179, 198, 213
apostle, 42, 46, 59, 61, 70, 82, 130, 148, 156, 160, 164, 165, 167, 169, 170, 174, 175, 176, 183, 189, 201, 207, 211
Aquinas, Thomas, 37, 61, 70, 71, 213
Arias, Mortimer, 25
Arius, Arians, 61, 71
Arnold, Clinton E., 95, 213
Arp, Thomas R., 7, 222
ascension, 30, 32, 64, 79, 155, 170
Athanasius, 33, 47, 61, 62
Augustine, 33, 37, 61, 70
Aune, David E., 6, 20, 90, 178, 179, 213

authority, 1, 12, 16, 22, 28, 29, 34, 39, 40, 41, 42, 43, 44, 45, 46, 47, 48, 52, 55, 58, 60, 65, 66, 70, 74, 75, 79, 81, 83, 88, 92, 93, 94, 95, 96, 98, 99, 104, 105, 123, 124, 125, 127, 128, 135, 136, 137, 138, 142, 151, 169, 189, 206
  power, 4, 24, 31, 38, 39, 41, 44, 45, 46, 47, 52, 58, 65, 68, 88, 94, 95, 103, 104, 114, 128, 138, 139, 141, 146, 189

Baffes, Melanie, 177, 213
Bal, Mieke, 7, 213
baptize, baptizing, 2, 4, 22, 23, 33, 34, 37, 40, 48, 49, 50, 51, 52, 55, 60, 61, 70, 75, 85, 96, 100, 101, 102, 103, 104, 122, 123, 124, 126, 150, 154, 164, 171, 172, 184, 204, 206, 208
  baptism, 4, 11, 22, 25, 31, 34, 49, 51, 52, 54, 55, 58, 59, 60, 61, 75, 77, 102, 103, 104, 118, 122, 123, 124, 125, 156, 168, 169, 189, 200
  infant, 22, 60
  baptismal, 24, 29, 40, 52, 53, 55
  Baptist, John the, 32, 51, 52, 55, 75, 82, 83, 103, 104, 110, 118, 122, 123, 124, 125, 158, 164, 171, 175
Barnabas (Joseph), 156, 163, 170
Barnes, William H., 39, 213
Barnett, Paul, 187, 213
Barsanuphius and John, 39, 214
Basil of Caesarea, 61, 70, 214
Basil the Great, 33

Bauer, David R., 3, 4, 5, 6, 7, 9, 10, 15, 18, 21, 26, 27, 28, 29, 32, 34, 35, 37, 38, 39, 40, 43, 45, 48, 49, 50, 51, 52, 53, 62, 63, 64, 72, 73, 75, 76, 77, 78, 79, 81, 83, 85, 86, 90, 91, 92, 94, 95, 97, 99, 100, 101, 102, 103, 104, 105, 106, 107, 108, 109, 113, 117, 118, 119, 121, 123, 124, 125, 126, 127, 128, 129, 131, 132, 134, 136, 137, 138, 139, 140, 141, 142, 145, 146, 147, 149, 151, 192, 214
Bayer, Hans F., 160, 161, 214
Beasley-Murray, George R., 124, 214
Beirne, Margaret, 176, 221
Beitzel, Barry J., 37, 119, 216
believer, 22, 24, 35, 58, 60, 63, 65, 107, 117, 140, 148, 156, 159, 165, 169, 170, 171, 172, 173, 175, 176, 180, 181, 184, 185, 189, 190, 192, 193, 194, 197, 198, 199, 200, 201, 202, 207
Belleville, Linda L., 67, 185, 186, 187, 214
Bernard, J. H., 175, 214
betray, betrayal, 34, 45, 74, 85, 86, 148, 149, 151, 161, 172, 174, 179
betroth(al), 118, 119, 120
Betz, Hans Dieter, 26, 214
Bird, Michael F., 193, 214
birth, 12, 67, 69, 112, 118, 119, 120, 199, 225
Black, D. A., 120, 214
Bland, D. S., 7, 214
bless, blessing, 49, 55, 58, 71, 99, 147, 158, 199
Blomberg, Craig L., 21, 33, 44, 50, 54, 94, 101, 214
Bonaventure, 33
Bond, H. Lawrence, 220
Bonnard, Pierre L., 121, 130, 214
Boomershine, Thomas E., 162, 214
Booth, Wayne C., 7, 10, 19, 215
Borchert, Gerald L., 176, 215
Bornkamm, Günther, 77
Bosch, David J., 26, 117, 215
boundaries, 50, 86, 102, 115, 147, 148, 168, 206

cultural, 50, 56, 102, 115, 147, 148
ethnic, 50, 102, 115, 147, 148, 206
geographical, 35, 50, 59, 102, 115, 147, 148, 173, 182, 206
religious, 50, 102, 147
Brands, Michael, 25, 26, 48, 215
Braulio of Saragossa, 39, 217
Brosend, William, 177, 215
Brown, Colin, 32, 33, 215
Brown, Jeanine K., 21, 27, 28, 35, 38, 39, 40, 41, 50, 51, 52, 53, 64, 65, 77, 94, 101, 105, 107, 108, 117, 119, 120, 124, 128, 130, 137, 139, 141, 143, 145, 162, 215
Brown, Raymond E., 175, 177, 215
Brown, Schuhler, 143
Broyles, C. C., 87, 215
Bruce, F. F., 164, 169, 189, 191, 215
Bultmann, Rudolf, 143
Bunch, William H., 193, 215
Bunyan, John, 33, 218
Burnett, Fred W., 19, 215

Cairns, Alan, 68, 215
Calvin, John, 33, 60, 68, 151, 215
Canaan, Canaanite, 18, 89, 126, 144, 145, 146, 217
  Syrophoenician, 144, 145
Carson, D. A., 25
Carter, Charles W., 50, 60, 61, 69, 215, 216
Carter, Warren, 134, 215
Chambers, Ross, 12, 215
Chatman, Seymour, 7, 10, 12, 215
Christian, 4, 18, 22, 24, 26, 28, 29, 30, 34, 41, 51, 52, 53, 55, 56, 58, 59, 60, 64, 66, 67, 68, 69, 70, 71, 74, 75, 84, 85, 87, 90, 92, 102, 103, 104, 105, 107, 110, 114, 115, 123, 130, 135, 138, 141, 142, 143, 144, 148, 152, 154, 155, 156, 157, 160, 164, 165, 166, 167, 168, 169, 170, 171, 172, 173, 174, 175, 178, 179, 180, 181, 182, 184, 186, 187, 189, 190, 191, 192, 194, 195, 196, 197, 198, 199, 200, 201, 206, 208, 209, 210, 212, 213, 215, 221, 223, 225

Christianity, 31, 161, 218, 221, 223, 225
Christman, Angella Russell, 47, 61, 70, 225
Chrysologus, Peter, 33
church, 4, 10, 16, 17, 22, 23, 24, 26, 29, 30, 31, 32, 34, 35, 38, 39, 42, 43, 45, 46, 48, 50, 52, 53, 54, 55, 56, 57, 58, 59, 60, 61, 62, 63, 64, 68, 69, 70, 71, 78, 83, 86, 90, 91, 103, 106, 107, 109, 123, 130, 143, 147, 150, 156, 166, 167, 170, 171, 173, 182,189, 190, 191, 198, 201, 211
- assembly, 166, 171, 173, 182, 194, 198
- community, 16, 17, 19, 31, 35, 42, 46, 51, 52, 54, 55, 56, 57, 58, 64, 65, 66, 69, 73, 79, 84, 103, 145, 159, 166, 169, 173, 177, 180, 181, 182, 190, 191, 192, 193, 194, 196, 197, 198, 200, 201, 208
- congregation, 32, 48, 64, 166, 171, 173, 175, 182, 183, 186, 194
- ecclesiology, ecclesiological, 29
circumcision, 31, 45, 189
Clement of Alexandria, 71, 215
Coleman, Rachel L., 164, 215
Combrink, H. J. B., 11, 216
Comfort, Philip W., 70, 166, 183, 184, 214, 216, 217, 219, 224, 225
command, 2, 4, 17, 23, 25, 26, 27, 29, 30, 32, 36, 40, 41, 45, 49, 50, 52, 55, 59, 61, 62, 63, 64, 65, 66, 67, 69, 70, 74, 75, 76, 77, 79, 83, 92, 93, 95, 96, 97, 98, 99, 100, 102, 103, 104, 106, 107, 108, 109, 110, 111, 113, 114, 116, 117, 119, 122, 125, 126, 127, 129, 130, 131, 132, 134, 136, 138, 140, 142, 143, 147, 151, 152, 153, 154, 155, 157, 159, 162, 163, 165, 172, 173, 177, 178, 179, 192, 193, 199, 202, 204, 205, 206, 208
- commandment, 30, 31, 33, 45, 46, 56, 63, 65, 66, 107, 108, 109, 160, 172, 177, 179

ἐνετειλάμην, 1, 17, 23, 25, 26, 63, 108, 109, 111, 112
ἐντέλλω, 25, 63, 65, 107, 108, 109
ἐντολή, 25, 63, 107, 109
confess, confession, 51, 54, 55, 80, 85, 103, 124, 146, 172, 175
crowds, 9, 11, 16, 32, 46, 54, 82, 86, 90, 94, 107, 129, 136, 158, 164, 165, 220
crucify, crucifixion, 14, 42, 47, 86, 90, 149, 158, 162, 172
Cross, 14, 47, 95, 120, 125, 128, 136, 162, 168, 169, 186, 197, 220
Culpepper, R. Alan, 7, 216

Damian, Peter, 33
Dau, W. H. T., 55, 60, 216
Davids, Peter H., 197, 198, 199, 216
Davies, W. D., 21, 27, 29, 30, 33, 36, 43, 50, 54, 66, 77, 78, 79, 80, 94, 106, 108, 109, 111, 112, 119, 122, 124, 126, 127, 131, 132, 133, 137, 138, 140, 143, 145, 151, 216
death, 11, 12, 13, 28, 41, 45, 55, 94, 149, 151, 160, 172, 178, 179, 184, 185, 187, 190, 191, 196, 200
deeds, 30, 46, 109, 112, 135, 182
- works, 71, 103, 189
demon (possessed), 14, 89, 91, 141, 144, 146, 161
deny, denial, 26, 34, 74, 85, 149, 150, 151, 159, 161, 166, 172, 173, 174, 179, 186, 192, 194
Detweiler, Robert, 213, 215, 217, 222
Detwiler, D. F., 164, 216
Didymus the Blind, 62, 216
disciple, 9, 11, 12, 13, 14, 16, 17, 18, 22, 23, 24, 25, 27, 28, 29, 30, 31, 32, 33, 34, 35, 36, 37, 38, 39, 40, 41, 42, 43, 45, 46, 48, 49, 51, 52, 53, 54, 56, 59, 60, 61, 62, 63, 64, 65, 66, 67, 68, 69, 74, 75, 76, 77, 79, 80, 81, 82, 83, 84, 85, 86, 87, 88, 89,90, 91, 92, 93, 94, 95, 96, 97, 98, 99, 100, 101, 102, 103, 104, 105, 106, 107, 108, 109, 110, 111, 113, 114, 115, 116, 117, 118, 121, 122, 123, 125, 126, 128, 129,

INDEX

(disciple continued)
130, 131, 132, 133, 134, 135, 136, 138, 139, 140, 141, 142, 143, 144, 145, 146, 147, 148, 149, 150, 151, 152, 153, 154, 155, 156, 157, 158, 159, 160, 161, 162, 163, 164, 165, 166, 167, 168, 169, 170, 171, 172, 173, 174, 175, 176, 177, 178, 179, 180, 183, 186, 187, 190, 192, 193, 194, 197, 198, 202, 205, 206, 207, 208, 209, 210, 212

adherent, 44, 74, 82, 84, 129, 155, 162, 172, 202, 206

Andrew, 130, 131, 133

apprentice, 82

discipleship, 9, 15, 16, 17, 18, 20, 23, 24, 25, 26, 31, 32, 35, 36, 37, 39, 41, 42, 48, 49, 52, 57, 58, 59, 60, 62, 67, 68, 69, 74, 82, 84, 86, 91, 96, 99, 104, 113, 114, 116, 121, 125, 129, 130, 133, 134, 135, 152, 153, 154, 155, 156, 157, 158, 160, 161, 162, 163, 164, 165, 167, 168, 169, 170, 171, 172, 175, 176, 177, 178, 179, 180, 184, 185, 186, 187, 189, 190, 191, 192, 193, 196, 197, 198, 199, 200, 201, 202, 203, 204, 205, 206, 207, 208, 209, 210, 211, 213, 214, 215, 216, 217, 218, 219, 220, 221, 222, 223, 224, 225, 226

discipline, 48, 54, 82, 122

fall away, 34, 85, 86, 148, 149, 150, 151, 152, 179

fishermen, 130, 131, 133, 134, 209

fishers of men, 27, 57, 75, 96, 97, 98, 129, 130, 131, 132, 133, 134, 162, 205, 209

follower, 24, 25, 26, 27, 31, 39, 41, 43, 54, 55, 63, 68, 78, 83, 84, 128, 148, 156, 160, 164, 165, 166, 167, 168, 169, 170, 171, 172, 174, 175, 176, 177, 180, 184, 189, 193, 195, 209, 212

follow, 18, 36, 41, 52, 57, 74, 76, 82, 83, 84, 85, 86, 89, 96, 97, 98, 110, 111, 114, 115, 121, 122, 125, 127, 129, 130, 131, 132, 133, 134, 135, 150, 155, 156, 157, 158, 159, 161, 162, 165, 166, 170, 172, 173, 174, 177, 178, 179, 182, 183, 187, 188, 190, 192, 194, 195, 197, 199, 200, 202, 206, 208, 209, 211, 212

imperative (make disciples), 2, 3, 8, 22, 24, 26, 34, 50, 72, 73, 75, 96, 98, 101, 108, 112, 114, 121, 127, 133, 154, 203, 204, 205, 207, 208

James, 130, 131, 133

John, 130, 131, 133, 169

Judas, 19, 34, 74, 85, 148, 149, 150, 151, 161, 169, 172, 174, 179

leader, 157, 192

learner, 84, 129, 134, 180, 184

learn, learning, 25, 64, 82, 86, 115, 141, 142, 152, 153, 155, 157, 159, 162, 168, 173, 180, 182, 192, 194, 201, 202, 206, 208, 212

make disciples, 1, 2, 22, 23, 24, 25, 26, 29, 32, 33, 34, 40, 48, 49, 50, 51, 52, 53, 54, 57, 58, 59, 60, 63, 69, 74, 75, 76, 84, 92, 96, 97, 98, 99, 100, 101, 102, 104, 105, 107, 109, 111, 114, 115, 116, 117, 121, 122, 125, 128, 129, 132, 133, 134, 135, 139, 142, 143, 147, 148, 152, 153, 154, 157, 163, 189, 192, 202, 204, 205, 206, 207, 208, 209, 210

master, 25, 84, 89, 157, 160, 175, 183, 192, 201

pupil, 82, 84, 96, 110, 129, 134, 164, 167, 174, 195, 212

Simon-Peter, 14, 34, 38, 39, 42, 54, 58, 74, 85, 90, 91, 125, 130, 131, 133, 139, 140, 141, 149, 150, 151, 155, 156, 161, 167, 169, 172, 174, 176, 179, 199, 200, 216, 219, 221

skills, 114, 134, 135, 182, 193, 206

student, 24, 65, 157, 187, 201

the Eleven, 1, 24, 30, 32, 34, 48, 69, 79, 81, 84, 85

the Twelve, 23, 34, 41, 46, 57, 64, 83, 96, 97, 114, 132, 133, 143,

148, 154, 155, 156, 160, 161, 162, 167, 168, 169, 172, 175, 176, 180
Thomas, 172, 175
μαθητεύσατε, 1, 2, 3, 8, 9, 21, 22, 23, 25, 26, 28, 34, 48, 50, 51, 59, 72, 73, 75, 80, 100, 101, 102, 106, 112, 113, 114, 115, 116, 117, 118, 121, 122, 125, 126, 128, 129, 133, 136, 138, 139, 141, 144, 147, 149, 151, 154, 201, 203, 204, 205, 207, 208
Dobbeler, Axel von, 40, 49, 99, 142, 143, 216
Dockery, David S., 103, 216, 219
Donaldson, James, 70, 223
Donaldson, Terence L., 87, 88, 116, 216
doubt, 1, 22, 37, 38, 39, 74, 89, 90, 91, 92, 93, 139, 140, 141, 142, 151, 154
Drazin, Nathan, 107, 216
dream, 89, 118, 119, 120, 121

Earle, Ralph, 66, 216
earth, 1, 35, 42, 43, 44, 45, 46, 47, 49, 50, 53, 58, 62, 86, 88, 93, 94, 95, 96, 99, 125, 128, 147, 171, 173, 179
Easter, post-Easter, 17, 27, 30, 34, 35, 37, 45, 49, 63, 68, 70, 143, 147
Edwards, James R., 167, 216
Edwards, Richard A., 116, 133, 216
Elijah, 41
Elliott, John H., 199, 200, 216
Elwell, Walter A., 37, 119, 216
end of the age, 2, 29, 50, 65, 66, 68, 69, 71, 78, 79, 99, 104, 105, 106, 118, 122, 142
enthrone, enthronement, 30, 39, 40, 44
eschatology, eschatological, 17, 26, 30, 31, 35, 58, 64, 66, 78, 86, 88, 106, 124, 161, 191, 196, 198
Eunomius, 62, 71, 214
Eusebius, 33
evangelize, evangelism, 22, 24, 33, 50, 59, 62, 77, 186
 evangelistic, 24, 26, 60

Evans, Craig, 33
exalt, exaltation, 30, 40, 42, 46, 47, 54, 93, 94, 98, 142, 178
Ezeogu, Ernest Munachi, 24, 49, 216

faith, 4, 18, 22, 28, 33, 34, 36, 37, 38, 39, 49, 51, 56, 58, 64, 67, 68, 74, 80, 82, 87, 91, 92, 103, 115, 116, 128, 133, 134, 140, 141, 142, 144, 145, 146, 147, 148, 151, 159, 161, 163, 164, 168, 170, 172, 175, 179, 180, 181, 184, 185, 189, 193, 196, 197, 199, 201, 206, 216, 218, 222, 225
 little faith, 22, 39, 41, 68, 91, 92, 139, 140, 141, 142, 148, 155, 162, 163
family, 58, 68, 74, 82, 84, 85, 96, 114, 129, 130, 134, 135, 160, 162, 168, 170, 177, 206
 fictive kin, 84
 household, 84, 135, 144, 190, 199, 200
 surrogate, 74, 84, 85, 148, 162, 170
Farris, S. C., 90, 216
Father, 2, 22, 28, 39, 40, 42, 43, 45, 46, 47, 51, 52, 58, 61, 68, 71, 79, 88, 98, 99, 102, 103, 104, 114, 121, 122, 124, 125, 128, 138, 147, 152, 161, 173, 177, 192, 193, 200, 201, 205, 208
Feast of Unleavened Bread, 35
Fee, Gordon D., 186, 188, 191, 217
Ferdinando, Keith, 26, 33, 217
Fernando, Ajith, 186, 217
Fitzmyer, Joseph A., 168, 171, 186, 217
five major discourses in Matthew, 11, 12, 16, 17, 23, 27, 63, 64, 76, 107, 108, 110, 111, 113, 117, 205, 208
Ford, J. Massyngberde, 178, 179, 217
forewarn, forewarning, 85, 86, 115, 138, 149, 151, 158
forgive, forgiveness, 17, 46, 48, 51, 89, 94, 95, 103, 115, 121, 135, 149, 150, 151, 152, 206
 unforgiveness, 17
Fowler, Robert M., 115, 217

France, R. T., 21, 25, 36, 41, 42, 43, 44, 50, 63, 66, 67, 93, 94, 99, 101, 109, 119, 121, 122, 123, 124, 126, 130, 131, 136, 138, 140, 146, 150, 217
Freyne, Seán, 86, 217
Friedrich, Gerhard, 219
Fructuosus of Braga, 39, 217
fulfill, fulfillment, 7, 10, 11, 12, 13, 14, 16, 19, 26, 40, 42, 43, 49, 50, 54, 58, 59, 61, 62, 64, 86, 87, 88, 97, 98, 110, 119, 120, 121, 123, 124, 125, 131, 133, 137, 196
Furnish, Victor Paul, 187, 217
Futato, Mark D., 58, 59, 217

Galilee, 1, 12, 27, 31, 34, 35, 36, 37, 41, 56, 74, 81, 82, 83, 85, 86, 87, 88, 97, 107, 118, 119, 123, 129, 130, 132, 133, 139, 140, 141, 144, 147, 150, 151, 158, 159, 161, 162, 168, 171, 217, 223
gender, 10, 15, 17, 18, 120, 213
genealogy, 12, 14, 80, 99, 105, 118
George, Henry, 220
Gibson, Jeffrey B., 162, 217
Gilbert, Scott Allan, 24, 25, 217
Gilmore, David G., 217
glory, glorious, 42, 53, 93, 126, 127, 189, 219, 225
Gnilka, Joachim, 119, 123, 130, 141, 144, 145, 150, 217, 221, 223
Goff, Matthew, 107, 218
Gould, Ezra Palmer, 163, 217
Green, Joel B., 20, 165, 168, 169, 217, 225
guide, guidance, 4, 8, 10, 72, 81, 116, 123, 126, 133, 138, 204, 216, 222
Gullotta, Daniel N., 145, 217
Gundry, Robert H., 123, 146, 217

Hagner, Donald A., 21, 36, 37, 38, 48, 62, 67, 87, 121, 124, 126, 132, 137, 146, 150, 217
Hahn, Ferdinand, 143
Halliday, M. A. K., 218
Hanson, K. C., 84, 218
Harman, Gilbert H., 218

Harper, William Rainey, 4
Harpham, Geoffrey, 7, 10, 15, 213
Hartman, Lars, 103, 218
Hawthorne, Gerald F., 70, 187, 188, 208, 218
healing, 12, 41, 48, 82, 87, 88, 89, 98, 129, 143, 144, 146, 148, 158, 164, 172
heal, 46, 47, 82, 91, 94, 95, 135, 141, 146, 161
heaven, 1, 18, 32, 40, 42, 43, 45, 46, 55, 66, 68, 69, 80, 93, 95, 96, 99, 107, 123, 125, 128, 130, 199, 200
Hellenistic, 31, 44, 84, 86, 110, 134, 170, 217
Hertig, Paul, 32, 218
Herzog, II, W. R., 218
Hiary of Poitiers, 33, 47, 218
Hiers, Richard H., 58, 218
Hillmer, Melvyn, 175, 176, 177, 218
Hogan, Karina Martin, 107, 218
Hollerich, Michael J., 47, 61, 70, 225
Holmes, Michael W., 62, 218
Holy Spirit, the Spirit (of God), 2, 29, 39, 51, 52, 55, 60, 61, 65, 66, 68, 95, 102, 103, 104, 110, 112, 118, 119, 120, 121, 122, 123, 124, 126, 138, 150, 169, 177, 184
gifts, spiritual, 60, 61, 200
Howard, George, 29, 218
Howell, David B, 10, 11, 12, 13, 14, 15, 16, 17, 18, 19, 20, 218
Hur, Unsok, 161, 218
Hurtado, Larry, 160, 161, 162, 218
Hutcheson, R., 53, 218

imitate, imitation, 25, 157, 162, 182, 185, 186, 188, 192, 193, 194, 197, 201, 208, 212
emulate, 114, 152, 174, 182, 194, 197, 205
example, 18, 24, 59, 63, 148, 153, 157, 160, 182, 184, 185, 186, 187, 188, 191, 192, 195, 199, 200, 202, 207, 212
model, 23, 25, 32, 48, 51, 60, 76, 84, 98, 101, 102, 110, 111, 114, 115, 122, 125, 129, 152, 154, 162, 170,

174, 182, 184, 185, 186, 187, 188, 192, 193, 194, 195, 201, 205, 207, 208, 209
  pattern, 27, 52, 162, 184, 187, 190, 195, 197, 201, 212
  type, 84, 184, 195
inductive Bible study (IBS), 4, 5, 6, 8, 20, 76, 117, 209
Iser, Wolfgang, 15, 19, 113, 115, 116, 218
Israel, 14, 17, 19, 27, 28, 32, 34, 40, 43, 49, 50, 56, 57, 59, 61, 63, 64, 68, 75, 82, 87, 88, 95, 98, 99, 110, 120, 121, 127, 129, 134, 136, 139, 141, 142, 143, 144, 145, 146, 147, 168, 209

Jacob, E. M., 153, 218
Jaeger, Werner, 107, 218
James, Sujaya, 177, 218
Jerome, 33, 39, 70, 71, 218
Jerusalem, 12, 16, 33, 35, 41, 63, 78, 83, 86, 88, 90, 109, 125, 129, 138, 149, 150, 158, 165, 168, 170, 171
Jervis, L. Ann, 184, 185, 218
Jesus, 1, 3, 4, 9, 10, 11, 12, 13, 14, 15, 16, 17, 18, 19, 20, 22, 23, 24, 25, 26, 27, 28, 29, 30, 31, 32, 33, 34, 35, 36, 37, 38, 39, 40, 41, 42, 43, 44, 45, 46, 47, 48, 49, 50, 51, 52, 53, 54, 55, 56, 57, 59, 61, 62, 63, 64, 65, 66, 67, 68, 69, 70, 71, 73, 74, 75, 76, 77, 78, 79, 80, 81, 82, 83, 84, 85, 86, 87, 88, 89, 90, 91, 92, 93, 94, 95, 96, 97, 98, 99, 100, 101, 102, 103, 104, 105, 106, 107, 108, 109, 110, 111, 112, 113, 114, 115, 116, 117, 118, 119, 120, 121, 122, 123, 124, 125, 126, 127, 128, 129, 130, 131, 132, 133, 134, 135, 136, 137, 138, 139, 140, 141, 142, 143, 144, 145, 146, 147, 148, 149, 150, 151, 152, 153, 154, 155, 156, 158, 159, 160, 161, 162, 163, 164, 165, 166, 167, 168, 169, 170, 171, 172, 173, 174, 175, 176, 177, 178, 179, 180, 184, 185, 186, 187, 188, 189, 192, 193, 196, 197, 198, 199, 200, 201, 202, 203, 205, 206, 207, 208, 209, 214, 216, 217, 218, 219, 221, 224, 225
  Beloved, 14, 122
  Christ, 14, 24, 29, 30, 36, 37, 42, 44, 45, 47, 48, 51, 52, 53, 55, 58, 59, 60, 61, 66, 67, 68, 69, 70, 71, 74, 78, 84, 90, 95, 96, 103, 104, 114, 118, 119, 122, 126, 136, 139, 149, 157, 159, 166, 167, 168, 170, 173, 175, 177, 178, 179, 180, 181, 182, 184, 185, 186, 187, 188, 189, 190, 191, 192, 193, 194, 195, 196, 197, 199, 200, 201, 202, 206, 207, 208, 209, 214, 217, 218, 219
  christocentric, 39, 189
  christological, 28, 29, 30, 42, 45, 69, 138, 168, 189
  Christology, 38, 39, 42, 46, 47, 55, 65, 160, 162, 165, 177, 213, 219
  high priest, 196
  Immanuel ("God with us"), 14, 30, 42, 45, 47, 64, 65, 68, 69, 105, 118, 119, 120, 121
  infant, 80, 89, 112
  King, 14, 17, 19, 42, 75, 89, 93, 95, 99, 146, 214, 223
  leader, 111, 114, 154
  Lion of the tribe of Judah, 178
  Lord, 19, 28, 30, 31, 33, 37, 39, 43, 44, 45, 46, 47, 53, 55, 56, 58, 59, 60, 61, 66, 68, 69, 70, 74, 76, 83, 85, 87, 90, 92, 93, 96, 99, 103, 104, 105, 106, 117, 118, 120, 121, 126, 127, 134, 137, 138, 139, 140, 141, 146, 147, 149, 150, 151, 156, 158, 175, 183, 189, 190, 193, 197, 199, 200, 219, 225
  Messiah, 14, 19, 32, 43, 47, 75, 93, 95, 118, 121, 123, 130, 144, 146, 178, 208
  messianic, 10, 12, 52, 88, 146
  Nazarene, 14
  Resurrected One, 35
  Servant, 14, 42, 43
  son of Abraham, 14, 30, 49, 99, 147

(Jesus continued)
- son of David, 14, 119, 137, 146, 147, 214
- Son of God, 2, 14, 15, 19, 27, 30, 32, 34, 35, 37, 39, 40, 41, 42, 43, 44, 45, 46, 47, 49, 50, 51, 52, 54, 55, 61, 62, 63, 64, 71, 75, 80, 89, 91, 94, 95, 102, 103, 112, 113, 118, 121, 122, 123, 124, 125, 126, 127, 128, 129, 131, 134, 136, 137, 138, 139, 140, 141, 142, 145, 147, 149, 151, 178, 185, 192, 208, 214
- Son of Man, 30, 40, 42, 43, 44, 46, 47, 66, 75, 82, 93, 94, 95, 99, 137, 138, 165
- Teacher, master-teacher, 18, 30, 31, 44, 64, 82, 84, 98, 114, 149, 150, 154, 155, 158, 162, 179, 200, 202, 206, 207, 208, 209, 210
- the Lamb, 173, 178, 179, 213, 223
- the Logos, 45
- universal (authority, lordship, mission, power, rule), 17, 28, 38, 41, 43, 44, 45, 46, 47, 48, 49, 50, 53, 54, 57, 59, 60, 64, 74, 88, 92, 93, 94, 95, 98, 99, 104, 142, 166, 171, 178, 182

Jew(s), Jewish, 12, 13, 14, 16, 18, 19, 22, 24, 26, 28, 29, 31, 32, 39, 49, 53, 55, 56, 57, 58, 59, 66, 70, 71, 75, 86, 88, 89, 90, 93, 99, 100, 103, 107, 110, 119, 126, 133, 136, 142, 143, 144, 145, 146, 147, 160, 176, 198, 209, 216, 220, 222
- chief priests, 14, 57, 94, 107
- elders, 14, 57, 94, 144, 159
- Herodians, 107
- Judaism, 44, 55, 56, 62, 78, 143, 144, 176, 178, 218, 221
- leaders, 12, 16, 18, 32, 39, 42, 46, 54, 56, 62, 63, 136, 157, 197, 200
- particularism, 26, 49, 75, 99, 142
- Pharisees, 55, 56, 68, 71, 78, 83, 107, 109, 128, 136, 137, 138, 144, 164, 165, 167, 172, 225
- Sadducees, 71, 107

scribes, 14, 24, 44, 51, 56, 57, 68, 78, 94, 107, 109, 128, 144, 160, 165

synagogue, 11, 56, 57, 89, 90, 109, 126, 176

Johnson, Alan, 25
Johnson, Luke Timothy, 198, 219
Joseph (husband of Mary), 18, 112, 118, 119, 120, 121, 122
Josephus, 86
Judea, 82, 119, 171
judge, judgment, 6, 10, 12, 17, 22, 44, 45, 46, 47, 55, 57, 58, 66, 68, 78, 95, 99, 124, 135, 137, 194, 204
Just, Arthur A., 47, 219

Karavidopoulos, Johannes, 221
Katos, Demetrios S., 186, 208, 219
Keener, Craig S., 21, 29, 36, 37, 40, 48, 50, 63, 66, 77, 99, 102, 105, 107, 110, 111, 117, 120, 122, 123, 124, 130, 131, 134, 136, 146, 147, 164, 219
Kennedy, George A., 16, 219
kingdom (of God, of heaven), 18, 22, 25, 26, 32, 33, 44, 46, 48, 51, 52, 54, 56, 57, 66, 67, 68, 69, 80, 82, 89, 95, 99, 107, 129, 130, 132, 134, 136, 137, 139, 144, 145, 157, 158, 159, 160, 164, 168, 200, 204, 215, 219
Kingsbury, Jack D., 7, 10, 11, 12, 13, 15, 17, 18, 58, 69, 79, 83, 140, 219
Kittel, Gerhard, 219
Knowles, Micahel P., 189, 190, 219
Koester, Craig R., 197, 219
Krentz, E., 77, 219
Krey, Philip D. W., 220
Kvalbein, Hans, 34, 219

Lake, Kirsopp, 47, 219
Lane, William L., 162, 196, 197, 219
Lange, John Peter, 159, 160, 161, 219
Lanser, Susan Sniader, 7, 219
Larkin, William J., Jr., 30, 219
Lategan, Bernard C., 115, 219
Lea, Thomas D., 60, 219

Lee, Sung-Ho, 161, 220
Lenski, Gerhard, 221
Leo the Great, 39, 62, 220
Levine, Amy-Jill, 49, 220
Levinsohn, Stephen H., 80, 220
Levy, Ian Christopher, 61, 220
Liddell, Henry George, 220
Lightfoot, John, 37, 220
Lipton, Peter, 220
literary criticism, 6
Long, Fredrick J., 100, 220
Longenecker, Richard, 167, 168, 169, 170, 213, 214, 216, 218, 219, 220, 221, 225
Lord's Supper, 55, 68, 83, 90, 149, 151, 158, 168
  Eucharist, eucharistic, 58, 90
Lukan Commission, 33, 156, 171
Luter, Jr., A. Boyd, 28, 35, 220
Luther, Martin, 33, 60, 68, 70, 215, 220
Luz, Ulrich, 21, 27, 28, 29, 30, 34, 35, 36, 44, 45, 46, 47, 50, 55, 56, 57, 67, 68, 69, 94, 95, 96, 97, 101, 106, 108, 118, 119, 120, 122, 124, 125, 127, 132, 133, 137, 140, 141, 143, 144, 147, 149, 151, 220

M'Clintock, John, 61, 71, 221
Maier, Gerhard, 119, 123, 124, 126, 127, 130, 138, 141, 144, 150, 199, 214, 220, 223
Mailloux, Steven, 19, 115, 220
major structural relationship (MSR), 6, 113, 118
  causation, 75, 76, 96, 97, 98, 105, 117, 130, 132, 205
  climax, 22, 23, 27, 28, 30, 31, 38, 40, 43, 57, 73, 74, 76, 77, 78, 93, 105, 106, 113, 114, 115, 117, 123, 125, 127, 128, 140, 141, 147, 148, 175, 176, 204, 205
  summa, 29
  contrast, 18, 39, 40, 41, 54, 57, 73, 80, 81, 85, 89, 90, 91, 95, 103, 106, 118, 124, 127, 134, 135, 136, 137, 141, 144, 145, 146, 148, 149, 150, 151, 155, 163, 168, 176, 178, 191, 198
  cruciality, 75, 98, 124, 142
  pivot, 75, 98, 99, 124, 142, 143
  inclusio, 28, 57, 64, 65, 76, 105, 106, 117, 118
  instrumentation, 100, 120
  interchange, 127, 130, 140, 145, 150
  interrogation, 82, 136, 138, 139
  particularization, 75, 97, 100, 102, 132, 154, 205
  preparation-realization, introduction, 73, 74, 81, 93, 98, 118, 119, 120, 126, 130, 133, 140, 145
  recurrence, repetition, 18, 19, 28, 34, 74, 81, 92, 120, 124, 127, 130, 131, 136, 145
  substantiation, 76, 104, 138
  summarization, 73, 76, 77, 78, 205
Malbon, E. S., 16, 220
Malina, Bruce, 14, 50, 84, 220, 221
Marcus, Joel, 163, 221
Markan Commission, 22, 33, 163, 204
Marrou, H. I., 107, 221
Marshall, I. Howard, 177, 221
Martin, James Perry, 17, 221
Martini, Carlo M., 221
Mary (wife of Joseph, mother of Jesus), 67, 118, 119, 120, 121
  virgin, 105, 117, 119, 120
Matera, Frank J., 161, 221
Matthean Commission, Great Commission, the Commission, 3, 4, 8, 21, 22, 23, 24, 25, 26, 27, 28, 29, 30, 31, 32, 33, 34, 35, 36, 40, 48, 49, 50, 52, 53, 54, 57, 58, 59, 60, 62, 65, 66, 67, 69, 70, 72, 73, 74, 75, 76, 77, 78, 79, 80, 81, 87, 88, 92, 95, 96, 99, 101, 102, 104, 105, 106, 108, 111, 113, 116, 117, 118, 132, 133, 135, 142, 147, 148, 154, 156, 163, 164, 171, 203, 204, 205, 206, 207, 214, 215, 216, 217, 218, 220, 223, 224
  commissioning, 24, 27, 29, 30, 35, 41, 74, 77, 80, 92, 93, 94, 103, 149
McKenzie, Roderick, 220

236

INDEX

McKnight, Scot, 32, 221
Meeks, Wayne A., 184, 221
Meier, John P., 21, 30, 31, 50, 57, 58, 69, 93, 221
Metzger, Bruce M., 166, 169, 184, 221, 222
Michaels, J. Ramsey, 199, 200, 221
Michie, Donald, 7, 15, 223
ministry, 4, 12, 17, 27, 28, 30, 32, 35, 37, 40, 42, 43, 44, 48, 52, 56, 64, 65, 74, 75, 82, 85, 86, 88, 95, 97, 98, 99, 100, 101, 105, 108, 110, 112, 113, 114, 118, 123, 125, 128, 132, 133, 134, 135, 136, 139, 141, 142, 147, 150, 156, 158, 161, 162, 164, 167, 172, 175, 179, 200, 201, 206, 217
miracle, 32, 33, 39, 68, 82, 146, 158, 164, 172
mission, 10, 13, 16, 17, 21, 22, 23, 24, 25, 26, 27, 28, 29, 30, 31, 33, 34, 35, 37, 38, 39, 40, 41, 42, 43, 46, 48, 49, 50, 51, 52, 53, 54, 56, 57, 59, 60, 61, 62, 63, 64, 65, 66, 67, 69, 73, 75, 77, 78, 79, 81, 83, 85, 86, 90, 91, 92, 94, 95, 96, 99, 100, 101, 102, 103, 104, 105, 106, 107, 109, 110, 114, 117, 118, 121, 122, 125, 132, 133, 137, 142, 143, 144, 146, 147, 149, 153, 155, 156, 163, 167, 171, 209, 214, 215, 217, 218, 223, 224
    commission (appoint[ment], mandate), 9, 26, 33, 35, 36, 38, 39, 54, 58, 60, 64, 96, 98, 108, 117, 148, 158
Mitsein, 28, 64, 76, 106, 121
mock, mocking, 42, 54, 93, 125
Moffatt, James, 196, 221
Morris, Leon, 176, 221
Moses, Mosaic, 22, 25, 29, 30, 35, 41, 63, 65, 78, 83, 87, 108, 109, 134, 172, 215
Motyer, J. T., 55, 221
Mounce, Robert H., 70, 221
mountain, 1, 27, 29, 33, 34, 35, 36, 37, 74, 81, 83, 87, 88, 90, 91, 128, 139, 140, 141
    Gerizim, 87
    Olives, 87, 88
    Sinai, 87, 88
    Zion, 87, 88
Muderhwa, B. Vincent, 172, 221
Muecke, D. C., 19, 221
Mußner, Franz, 198, 221

name, 2, 4, 13, 14, 31, 33, 51, 52, 55, 61, 70, 80, 82, 86, 102, 103, 104, 105, 118, 119, 120, 121, 122, 145, 160, 178, 207
    triadic, 31, 55
narrative criticism, 3, 5, 6, 7, 8, 20, 24, 76, 203, 209
    audience, 10, 11, 12, 13, 15, 16, 17, 18, 37, 106, 147, 163, 186, 192, 199
    character, 6, 7, 8, 9, 10, 11, 12, 13, 14, 15, 16, 17, 18, 19, 20, 28, 34, 35, 42, 49, 52, 72, 74, 76, 81, 84, 92, 94, 97, 106, 109, 110, 111, 119, 128, 130, 131, 132, 143, 145, 150, 153, 154, 164, 181, 182, 190, 202, 206, 207
    conflict, 6, 20, 43, 56, 68, 78, 94, 149
    discourse, 7, 8, 10, 11, 12, 13, 17, 19, 24, 27, 49, 56, 72, 80, 88, 100, 108, 117, 142, 160, 215, 220, 222
    event, 6, 7, 8, 10, 11, 12, 13, 14, 16, 17, 19, 20, 21, 29, 32, 36, 37, 38, 41, 58, 62, 72, 73, 74, 76, 78, 79, 81, 83, 87, 88, 90, 91, 93, 95, 97, 118, 119, 120, 124, 126, 130, 131, 132, 136, 139, 144, 145, 149, 150, 159, 164, 166, 167, 169, 173, 181, 182, 194, 198, 205, 206
    gap, 6, 116, 163
    ideal reader, 6
    implied author, 2, 3, 6, 7, 8, 9, 10, 11, 12, 13, 14, 15, 16, 17, 18, 19, 20, 26, 31, 53, 73, 74, 75, 77, 78, 79, 80, 81, 91, 93, 94, 95, 96, 104, 105, 109, 119, 121, 122, 124, 126, 129, 130, 132, 138, 139, 140, 145, 154, 160, 170, 177, 181, 198, 205

INDEX

implied reader, 2, 3, 6, 7, 8, 9, 10, 11, 12, 13, 14, 15, 16, 17, 18, 19, 27, 35, 38, 51, 53, 69, 72, 73, 74, 75, 76, 77, 78, 79, 80, 81, 83, 85, 86, 88, 90, 92, 93, 95, 96, 97, 98, 99, 100, 101, 102, 103, 104, 106, 107, 109, 110, 111, 112, 113, 114, 115, 116, 117, 118, 119, 120, 121, 122, 123, 125, 126, 127, 128, 129, 130, 131, 132, 133, 135, 136, 137, 138, 139, 141, 142, 144, 145, 147, 148, 149, 150, 151, 152, 154, 160, 161, 162, 171, 203, 204, 205, 207, 213, 218

irony, 8, 14, 19, 42, 74, 93, 95, 215, 221

narratee, 15, 16, 222

narrator, 6, 9, 10, 11, 12, 13, 15, 16, 17, 18, 19, 20, 79, 93, 105, 106, 117, 119, 121, 131, 133

plot, 6, 14, 20, 28, 38, 76, 77, 80, 107, 138

point of view, 6, 7, 8, 10, 11, 12, 13, 14, 15, 17, 18, 20, 44, 73, 79, 80, 83, 89, 115, 127, 219, 222
  evaluative, 10, 13, 14, 73, 79, 80, 89

redundancy, 19

rhetoric, rhetorical, 6, 7, 8, 16, 19, 24, 105, 164, 206, 213, 215, 218, 219, 222, 223, 225

setting, 3, 6, 7, 8, 20, 29, 65, 72, 73, 74, 78, 79, 81, 84, 88, 106, 140, 156, 158, 162, 164, 171, 186, 206
  cultural, 16, 20, 49, 78, 152
  political, 78, 85, 86, 136
  social, 3, 15, 20, 26, 33, 49, 53, 60, 78, 84, 86, 145, 152, 190, 191
  spatial, 11, 13, 28, 78, 127
  temporal, 10, 11, 12, 13, 17, 19, 28, 49, 73, 78, 79, 100, 102, 106
  timeless, 73, 78, 79, 106, 118

story, 2, 3, 6, 7, 10, 11, 12, 13, 14, 15, 16, 17, 18, 19, 20, 29, 30, 32, 33, 36, 39, 42, 56, 68, 76, 77, 78, 79, 80, 81, 83, 84, 87, 88, 91, 94, 105, 106, 113, 116, 120, 131, 136, 144, 145, 207, 215, 217, 218, 219, 222, 223

symbolism, 8, 87

worldview, 7, 79, 209

nations, 2, 4, 10, 17, 22, 23, 26, 28, 29, 31, 32, 33, 34, 35, 40, 41, 43, 48, 49, 50, 54, 57, 58, 59, 62, 64, 66, 68, 69, 71, 73, 75, 76, 77, 80, 84, 86, 92, 96, 98, 99, 103, 104, 105, 108, 109, 116, 118, 129, 132, 133, 135, 142, 143, 147, 156, 163, 164, 192, 204, 205, 206, 208, 209
  Gentile(s), 22, 24, 26, 28, 29, 31, 32, 35, 41, 43, 49, 55, 56, 57, 58, 62, 65, 68, 71, 75, 80, 86, 99, 100, 142, 143, 144, 145, 146, 147, 155, 163, 170, 171, 217, 220
  inclusion, 49, 75, 99, 100, 142, 147
  universalism, 26

Nazareth, 85, 86, 87, 125, 169

Nestle, Eberhard and Erwin, 167, 181, 194, 195, 221

Neudorfer, Heinz-Werner, 214, 220, 223

Neyrey, Jerome H., 14, 84, 104, 221

Nicetas of Remesiana, 70, 221

Nickelsburg, George W. E., 33, 221

Nolan, Patrick, 221

Nolland, John, 21, 36, 37, 38, 41, 42, 53, 54, 65, 66, 87, 93, 94, 108, 117, 222

Novatian, 33, 47, 61, 222

NT (New Testament), 7, 9, 35, 36, 40, 51, 53, 58, 60, 66, 75, 84, 103, 110, 120, 150, 153, 154, 155, 163, 171, 184, 186, 199, 202, 204, 206, 207, 210, 211, 213, 214

NT Greek Discipleship Terms
  ἅγιος (saint), 165, 172, 180, 190, 193, 207, 211
  ἀδελφή (sister), 158, 159, 180, 193, 211
  ἀδελφός (brother), 156, 159, 165, 170, 171, 172, 173, 178, 180, 181, 193, 207, 211
  ἀδελφότης (a fellowship), 193, 200, 211

(NT Greek Discipleship Terms continued)
ἀκολουθέω (follow), 84, 129, 156, 159, 165, 166, 173, 177, 178, 202, 207, 211
ἀμέμπτως (blamelessly), 181, 190, 191, 211
ἄμωμος (blameless), 173, 178, 181, 193, 194, 211
ἀξίως (worthily), 173, 181, 190, 211
ἀπόστολος (apostle), 82, 156, 159, 165, 166, 170, 173, 181, 194, 207, 211
ἀρνέομαι (repudiate), 159, 166, 173, 181, 194, 211
ἄτακτος (disorderly), 181, 191, 211
διάκονος (servant), 159, 173, 181, 211
δικαίως (uprightly), 166, 181, 190, 191, 194, 211
δοκιμή (proven worth), 181, 182, 188, 211
δοῦλος (slave), 159, 166, 173, 182, 188, 194, 202, 207, 211
ἐκκλησία (church), 156, 166, 170, 171, 173, 182, 194, 207, 211
ἐξακολουθέω (obey, follow), 194, 211
ἐπακολουθέω (follow), 159, 182, 194, 202, 211
μαθητεύω (be/make a disciple), 24, 25, 33, 34, 48, 50, 82, 96, 97, 129, 156, 158, 163, 164, 166, 171, 180, 185, 202, 206, 207, 212
μαθητής (disciple, follower), 25, 48, 82, 97, 129, 155, 156, 158, 162, 164, 165, 167, 169, 170, 171, 172, 178, 180, 185, 201, 202, 206, 207, 212
μαθήτρια (female disciple), 35, 166, 212
μανθάνω (learn), 48, 82, 156, 159, 173, 174, 180, 182, 194, 212
μιμέομαι (imitate), 174, 182, 194, 197, 202, 212
μιμητής (imitator), 182, 186, 194, 202, 212
ὀπίσω (follow), 96, 129, 159, 166, 174, 182, 183, 194, 195, 212

πείθω (obey), 166, 183, 195, 212
περιπατέω (behave, live), 159, 166, 174, 183, 195, 207, 212
συμμαθητής (fellow disciple), 174, 212
συμμιμητής (fellow imitator), 183, 212
σύνδουλος (fellow slave), 174, 183, 212
συνεργός (fellow worker), 174, 183, 186, 188, 212
συστρατιώτης (fellow soldier), 183, 212
τεκνίον (little child), 156, 174, 175, 177, 180, 183, 212
τέκνον ([spiritual] child), 156, 160, 166, 167, 175, 177, 180, 183, 184, 195, 207, 212
τύπος (example), 184, 195, 212
υἱός (son, pupil), 167, 184, 195, 207, 212
φιλαδελφία (brotherly love), 184, 191, 195, 212
Χριστιανός (Christian), 155, 167, 170, 171, 195, 212

O'Day, Gail R., 19, 222
Oberlinner, Lorenz, 217, 221, 223
obey, obedience, 14, 17, 18, 19, 33, 35, 42, 45, 52, 54, 56, 58, 59, 62, 64, 65, 66, 69, 70, 74, 76, 83, 84, 88, 92, 95, 110, 111, 114, 120, 122, 124, 125, 127, 128, 130, 134, 135, 153, 157, 167, 168, 174, 176, 177, 179, 183, 189, 194, 195, 201, 205, 206, 208, 209, 211, 212
observe (keep) commands, 2, 25, 28, 30, 33, 34, 50, 62, 63, 64, 65, 67, 70, 78, 92, 106, 107, 108, 109, 110, 117, 122, 153, 177, 179, 190
τηρεῖν, 1, 23, 25, 26, 63, 109
τηρέω, 25, 63, 67, 107, 109, 177, 179
Omanson, Roger L., 166, 169, 184, 222
opponent, opposition, 18, 27, 73, 80, 92, 114, 123, 135, 136, 139, 140, 143, 158, 161, 164, 206
Origen, 47, 61, 62, 71, 222

Orosius of Braga, 222
Osborne, Grant R., 80, 222
OT (Old Testament), 10, 11, 12, 13, 14, 16, 30, 40, 42, 45, 54, 63, 66, 99, 106, 110, 120, 123, 127, 137, 138, 140, 144, 145, 166, 194, 209
  commissioning, 30, 66
Owen, John, 33, 60

Pacian of Barcelona, 222
parable, 12, 13, 16, 17, 27, 56, 57, 66, 82, 96, 108, 132, 133, 146, 158, 164, 174, 179
Park, Eung Chun, 143
Parousia, 10, 12, 16, 17, 22, 29, 46, 69, 79, 88, 92, 93, 106
participle, 2, 3, 15, 16, 22, 23, 25, 26, 48, 50, 51, 100, 101, 102, 106, 154, 203, 204, 205, 207, 208
  βαπτίζοντες, 1, 2, 48, 50, 75, 100, 101, 154, 164
  διδάσκοντες, 1, 2, 23, 25, 26, 48, 50, 63, 75, 100, 101, 106, 107, 109, 154, 164
  πορευθέντες, 1, 2, 24, 48, 50, 75, 100, 101, 102, 154, 164
passion, 12, 14, 18, 27, 32, 35, 41, 62, 74, 83, 87, 93, 125, 149, 160, 165, 168, 169, 224
Passover, 35, 140, 158, 165, 169
Patte, Daniel, 17, 18, 123, 124, 222
Paul (Saul, apostle), 155, 156, 157, 163, 165, 167, 170, 180, 184, 185, 186, 187, 188, 189, 190, 191, 192, 193, 202, 207, 208, 214, 216, 217, 221, 222, 223
Penner, J. A., 41, 222
Pentecost, 60, 150
Perrine, Laurence, 7, 222
Perry, Menakhem, 15, 19, 222
persecute, persecution, 16, 66, 86, 92, 136, 138, 164
Petersen, Norman R., 14, 222
Phillips, Gary A., 14, 222
Plummer, Alfred, 186, 222, 223
poor, poverty, 57, 158, 198
Porter, Stanley E., 50, 80, 222

Powell, Mark Allan, 6, 7, 8, 58, 76, 78, 79, 87, 99, 106, 118, 214, 218, 219, 222, 225
pray, prayer, 44, 55, 58, 60, 68, 82, 87, 90, 139, 140, 141, 165, 168, 169, 198, 199, 219
preach, preaching, 4, 18, 22, 24, 33, 36, 48, 50, 51, 56, 58, 62, 67, 80, 82, 98, 101, 102, 103, 118, 123, 129, 147, 163, 164, 170, 172, 186, 204, 206
Prince, Gerald, 16, 222
promise, 16, 17, 27, 28, 29, 32, 34, 40, 41, 43, 45, 63, 64, 66, 69, 71, 76, 78, 79, 81, 92, 93, 94, 97, 98, 104, 105, 106, 113, 117, 121, 122, 132, 133, 134, 138, 147, 162, 170, 196
prophesy, prophecy, 11, 13, 54, 66, 87, 88, 108, 110, 119, 120, 123, 150, 158
prophet, 16, 19, 57, 61, 86, 99, 105, 110, 112, 117, 119, 121, 138, 150, 165, 173, 181, 194
prophetic, 56, 110, 130, 209
Prosper of Acquitaine, 221

Quirinus, Romulus, 30

read, reading, 3, 5, 7, 11, 12, 15, 17, 18, 19, 24, 27, 36, 37, 45, 68, 81, 93, 98, 115, 116, 133, 136, 166, 167, 199, 203, 204, 208, 213, 215, 218, 220
reader-response criticism, 115, 220, 222
redaction criticism, 20, 67
redeem, redemption, redemptive, 27, 48, 60, 167, 169, 189, 196, 200
Reid, Daniel G., 90, 222
remorse, remorseful, 34, 85, 148
Remus, Harold E., 33, 223
repent, repentance, 34, 51, 62, 85, 103, 121, 124, 149, 168, 199
Resseguie, James L., 6, 7, 76, 78, 115, 223
resurrect, resurrection, 10, 12, 16, 17, 19, 27, 28, 29, 30, 31, 32, 33, 35, 37, 38, 39, 40, 41, 42, 43, 44, 45,

(resurrect, resurrection continued)
47, 62, 64, 66, 69, 74, 75, 76, 79, 80, 81, 83, 84, 85, 86, 87, 88, 90, 91, 92, 93, 94, 98, 99, 100, 106, 107, 109, 125, 135, 143, 149, 150, 151, 156, 158, 172, 185, 187, 190, 200
  raising, 81, 164, 172, 199
  risen, 28, 29, 39, 45, 46, 52, 54, 55, 56, 65, 66, 69, 74, 76, 78, 79, 83, 87, 88, 90, 91, 92, 93, 95, 104, 105, 107, 116, 117, 118, 125, 126, 128, 138, 139, 147, 189, 200
reveal, revelation, 12, 17, 30, 32, 34, 35, 41, 46, 59, 73, 74, 80, 84, 87, 88, 95, 108, 110, 111, 113, 114, 115, 120, 121, 125, 135, 141, 145, 148, 151, 152, 155, 174, 176, 178, 179, 189, 199, 205, 217, 222
Reventlow, Henning Graf, 62, 223
Rhoads, David M., 6, 7, 15, 223
rich, riches, 134, 174, 198
  money, 82, 198
  wealth, 160, 198
Ridderbos, H. N., 33
Riesner, Rainer D., 85, 87, 140, 144, 214, 220, 223
righteous, righteousness, 40, 62, 67, 110, 112, 122, 123, 124, 157, 175, 185, 190, 192, 200, 217
Robbins, Vernon K., 3, 223
Roberts, Alexander, 70, 223
Roberts, Kyle, 21, 27, 28, 35, 38, 39, 40, 41, 50, 51, 52, 53, 64, 65, 77, 94, 101, 105, 107, 108, 117, 119, 120, 124, 128, 130, 137, 139, 141, 143, 145, 215
Robertson, Archibald T., 102, 186, 223
Rogers, T., 35, 223
Rohrbaugh, Richard, 84, 218, 221
Romein, J. M., 223
Ryan, Thomas, 220

Sabbath, sabbatical, 70, 90, 136, 137, 138, 139, 225
sacrament, 22, 55, 60, 61
saint, 35, 42, 165, 172, 180, 181, 187, 192, 193, 201, 211
salvation, 28, 30, 32, 42, 49, 55, 56, 57, 58, 62, 63, 99, 105, 113, 114, 120, 121, 122, 125, 126, 138, 140, 141, 143, 144, 145, 146, 147, 150, 152, 154, 184, 185, 189, 193, 199, 205, 209
Samaria, 86, 171
sanctify, 60, 137, 190, 191
Satan, the devil, 14, 45, 88, 89, 95, 111, 114, 118, 125, 126, 127, 128, 129, 168, 179, 183, 195, 196, 200, 205
  tempter (the), 127
Saunders, Stanley P., 28, 223
Schaff, Philip, 219, 223
Schlatter, Adolf, 143
Schnabel, Eckhard J., 28, 29, 30, 33, 59, 69, 186, 214, 220, 223
Schnackenburg, Rudolf, 175, 223
Schneider, Gerhard, 164, 223
Schüssler Fiorenza, Elisabeth, 223
Scott, Bernard Brandon, 17, 223
Scott, Robert, 220
Scripture, 4, 5, 12, 13, 19, 59, 70, 71, 86, 89, 95, 110, 114, 128, 139, 150, 151, 205, 206, 219
Segovia, Fernando F., 176, 216, 219, 223, 224, 225
Senior, Donald, 14, 18, 224
Sermon on the Mount, 17, 36, 65, 68, 85, 87, 108, 109, 117, 198, 222
Shogren, Gary S., 33, 95, 224
Sim, David C., 47, 77, 78, 224
Simon, Menno, 33, 60
Simonetti, Manlio, 71, 224
sin, 42, 46, 51, 60, 63, 94, 95, 99, 103, 113, 120, 121, 122, 124, 135, 152, 182, 184, 185, 205
Sjoberg, Gideon, 224
Smit, Peter-Ben, 163, 224
Smith, Robert H., 21, 26, 31, 44, 50, 77, 87, 95, 101, 224
soldier, 14, 54, 157, 183, 188, 192, 212
  centurion, 14, 18, 68, 80, 99
Stein, Robert H., 33, 224
Stock, Augustine, 18, 224

Strong, James, 61, 71, 221
suffer, suffering, 63, 109, 127, 128, 129, 140, 149, 158, 169, 178, 186, 194, 196, 197, 199, 200, 201
   hardship, 16, 186, 196
Suleiman, Susan R., 19, 224
Sulpicius Severus, 221
Synoptic (Gospels), 4, 9, 20, 58, 148, 161, 197, 221
Syria, 31

Talbert, Charles H., 167, 224
Tannehill, Robert C., 18, 224
Tanner, Paul A., 186, 224
Taylor, C., 61, 224
teach, teaching, 2, 3, 11, 12, 16, 17, 18, 22, 23, 24, 25, 28, 30, 31, 33, 34, 36, 39, 40, 42, 45, 48, 50, 51, 52, 53, 59, 62, 63, 64, 65, 66, 67, 69, 70, 71, 74, 75, 76, 78, 82, 84, 85, 87, 88, 92, 94, 95, 96, 98, 100, 101, 102, 104, 106, 107, 108, 109, 111, 113, 114, 117, 128, 129, 134, 135, 137, 143, 153, 154, 158, 160, 163, 164, 165, 168, 172, 182, 184, 186, 189, 190, 198, 199, 200, 204, 205, 206, 207, 208
   instruct, instruction, 9, 24, 25, 62, 63, 67, 70, 82, 84, 90, 91, 99, 101, 106, 108, 109, 120, 143, 152, 159, 163, 173, 182, 194
   teacher, 24, 44, 64, 67, 82, 84, 107, 111, 126, 129, 134, 136, 146, 154, 157, 160, 164, 174, 175, 182, 183, 187, 188, 192, 193, 201
temple, 19, 33, 44, 64, 75, 78, 83, 88, 90, 95, 107, 109, 111, 126, 136, 137, 138, 158, 209, 222
   priest, 44, 136, 172
temptation, 33, 36, 88, 89, 111, 125, 126, 127, 128, 129, 169, 191
Tennent, Timothy, 26, 50, 171, 224
Tertullian, 33, 224
testify, testimony, 56, 124, 179
   witness, 55, 60, 80, 123, 125, 129, 156, 158, 164, 172, 179
Theodoret, 62, 224
Thomas, R. L., 4, 65, 224

Thompson, James, 186, 224
Thompson, Marianne Meye, 190, 224
tongue, 197, 198, 199, 201, 216
Torah (Law), 31, 44, 45, 55, 57, 62, 64, 71, 78, 88, 107, 109, 132, 136, 137, 138, 160, 167, 179, 217
train, training, 24, 51, 98, 134, 148
Traina, Robert A., 3, 4, 5, 6, 9, 10, 15, 72, 73, 75, 76, 77, 81, 92, 97, 127, 132, 136, 214, 224
transfiguration, 36, 37, 41, 82, 87, 88, 93, 110, 158
Trinity, trinitarian, 4, 22, 29, 39, 45, 47, 52, 53, 55, 61, 77, 123, 138, 222, 224
Trites, Allison A., 33, 224
Turner, David L., 21, 35, 42, 43, 50, 54, 64, 80, 94, 224
Twelftree, Graham H., 33, 127, 224
Tyson, Joseph B., 162, 224

Uspensky, Boris, 7, 13, 14, 17, 224

Van der Watt, Jan Gabriël, 161, 220
Vanhoozer, Kevin J., 15, 225
Vincent of Lerins, 221
vindicate, vindication, 30, 39, 41, 42, 43, 44, 75, 94

Wace, Henry, 223
Wainwright, Elaine Mary, 35, 225
Walker, Larry L., 44, 225
Walker, Nach, 143
Wallace, Daniel B., 40, 50, 80, 93, 100, 101, 102, 130, 145, 225
Warfield, Benjamin B., 53, 225
Wasserman, Emma, 107, 218
watch, watchful, 92, 107, 115, 161, 201, 206
Watson, Duane F., 32, 225
Weima, Jeffrey A. D., 190, 191, 225
Weren, Wilhelmus Johannes Cornelis, 99, 225
Wesley, John, 33, 34, 87, 225
Westerholm, S., 136, 137, 225
White, L. Michael, 31, 225
White, William Webster, 4
Wild, Robert A., 185, 225

Wilken, Robert Louis, 47, 61, 70, 225
Wilkins, Michael J., 21, 31, 32, 59, 60, 69, 84, 96, 131, 134, 148, 162, 163, 170, 225
Witherington III, Ben, 120, 161, 225
Wogaman, J. P., 58, 225
world, 3, 6, 10, 12, 16, 28, 31, 33, 42, 43, 45, 46, 47, 50, 53, 54, 58, 59, 63, 68, 70, 89, 95, 99, 102, 103, 106, 109, 114, 121, 122, 126, 127, 128, 144, 145, 147, 176, 181, 185, 189, 191, 198, 200, 203, 206, 208
worship, 1, 35, 37, 38, 39, 54, 55, 58, 63, 65, 74, 89, 90, 91, 92, 93, 107, 111, 126, 127, 128, 139, 140, 144, 146
Wright, Christopher, 26
Wright, J. Robert, 39, 225
Wycliffe, John, 39, 226

Yang, Seung Ai, 33, 226
Yarbrough, Robert W., 177, 226

Zahn, Theodor, 143
Zhakevich, Mark, 177, 226

www.ingramcontent.com/pod-product-compliance
Lightning Source LLC
Chambersburg PA
CBHW050850230426
43667CB00012B/2227